the series on school reform

Patricia A. Wasley
Coalition of
Essential Schools

Ann Lieberman
NCREST

Joseph P. McDonald
Annenberg Institute
for School Reform

SERIES EDITORS

WITHDRAWN

This series also incorporates earlier titles in the
Professional Development and Practice Series

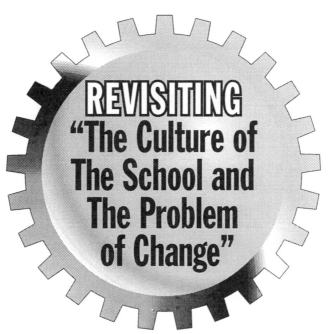

REVISITING "The Culture of The School and The Problem of Change"

WITHDRAWN

Seymour B. Sarason

TEACHERS
COLLEGE
PRESS

Teachers College • Columbia University
New York and London

Published by Teachers College Press, 1234 Amsterdam Avenue, New York, N.Y. 10027

Library of Congress Cataloging-in-Publication Data
Sarason, Seymour Bernard, 1919–
  Revisiting "The culture of the school and the problem of change" /
Seymour B. Sarason.
    p. cm. — (The series on school reform)
  Includes bibliographical references and index.
  ISBN 0-8077-3544-2 (cloth : alk. paper). — ISBN 0-8077-3543-4
(pbk. : alk. paper)
  1. Sarason, Seymour Bernard, 1919– Culture of the school and the
problem of change. 2. Educational innovations—United States.
3. Educational change—United States. 4. School environment—United
States. 5. Education and state—United States. 6. Special
Education—Law and legislation—United States. I. Sarason, Seymour
Bernard, 1919– Culture of the school and the problem of change
(2nd ed.) II. Title. III. Series.
LA210.S34 1996
370. 19'3'0973—dc20   96-2143

ISBN 0-8077-3543-4 (paper)
ISBN 0-8077-3544-2 (cloth)

Printed on acid-free paper
Manufactured in the United States of America
09 08 07 06 05   8 7 6 5 4

Part I
To my late wife, Esther, and dear friends Murray Levine and
Anita Miller for their help and support, particularly during the first
two years of the Psycho-Educational Clinic when it was not at all
clear whether we would make it.

Part II
This is for Irma Miller
With Love

Contents

PART I

The Culture of the School and the Problem of Change

PART II
Revisiting: 25 Years Later

Foreword

First published in 1971, *The Culture of the School and the Problem of Change* raised complicated and critical ideas in terms that were both insightful and accessible. Describing the importance of "behavioral and programmatic regularities" to defining a school culture, Seymour Sarason related these concepts to understanding the organization of a school and the attachments that school people have to their ways of working. His compelling argument—that both of these complex realities must be changed if real improvement is to take place—was radical at the time, and still is. Since then, as innovations of all kinds have been constantly pressed on schools, Sarason's book has helped us to understand some essentials: that schools are complicated places; that principals are isolated and often lonely in their positions; that teachers responsible for student learning often have little time to learn new ideas; and that innovative ideas must be worked on through the whole system of relationships and ways of working if they are to be effective in changing teacher and student practice. An immediate classic, the book taught a generation of educators that changing a school culture is tough work and must be done in a comprehensive way if it is to happen and be of any lasting significance.

Sarason has now written a sequel to the original landmark book which is incorporated in this edition as Part II. Describing the contemporary context for school change—where there is literally a struggle to maintain public education as we know it—Sarason deepens his work by attending to several new insights. He uses a 3-year study of school change by Pat Wasley and her colleagues that deals with the struggles of five high schools deeply committed to change, all of them members of the Coalition of Essential Schools, a large national network. In all of these schools, teachers and principals try to make real the educational values of "personalization" and solid academic work. But, as Sarason reminds us, they must still figure out how to support the learning of adults so that they in turn can facilitate active learning for their students. This school change study is carefully dissected under Sarason's analytic eye, and we learn once again that the "culture"—its regularities, values, practices, and people—is at the core of the problem and the process of change.

The power relationships that exist between principal and teacher and teacher and student—absent from most books about change and improvement—are an important part of this discussion. To change the way their students learn, teachers have to change the way they teach. By relinquishing their total control over students' opportunities to learn, teachers allow students to take more responsibility for their own learning. Easy to say, difficult to do—but necessary if we are to change the culture of the school and classroom.

Placing education within a broader context, Sarason involves us in a discussion of Kenneth Wilson's view that, in the final analysis, systems must create the mechanisms for improving themselves. This discussion provides theoretical support for the current attempts to create self-correcting and self-renewing schools. It expands our thinking and helps us understand what a system is, how it must think about change, and how the system itself must become its own best critic.

The difficulty of understanding schools and the process of improving them makes both a "Visit" and a "Revisit" to *The Culture of the School and the Problem of Change* an important part of our learning, and an indispensable part of thinking about this most vexing and vital institution.

Ann Lieberman, co-editor
the series on school reform

Preface to the Revisit

The payoff for a writer is when what he or she wrote has staying power. Frankly, the staying power of my book is of a degree that surprises as much as gratifies me. Consequently, when Teachers College Press offered me the opportunity to "revisit" the issues contained in the book, I jumped at it. There were several reasons, but at this point I wish only to mention one of them.

When we use the word *crisis* we ordinarily mean a point in time when a dangerous situation contains conflicting forces of an intensity or seriousness that in near term will be dramatically altered depending on which forces win out. If one force wins out, the other will view it as a disaster. The one that "wins," of course, will feel otherwise. Social crises are a kind of turning point and only future historians will tell us whether the turn was for good or for bad.

When I wrote the book a quarter of a century ago, I did not regard our schools as in crisis. They were in trouble, deep trouble, but there was no reason to believe that their basic characteristics, let alone their existence, would be changed. The fact is that the thrust of the book *implied* that if the reform movement proceeded as it was, there would be a crisis sometime in the future. What I did not say in the book was that my intuition, my very personal opinion, was that a crisis would come sooner rather than later. It has, in my opinion, come.

Why did I feel that way? The brief answer is that for many reasons I had concluded that what happens in our cities and their schools will determine the fate of our society. Today I am convinced of that. There is a crisis. The competing forces in the reform arena are gaining strength, especially those who for diverse reasons would not be sorry to see the dismantling of the public school system. With the best of intentions those who seek to preserve the nation's schools do not, with a few exceptions, focus on what I consider to be the root problems. And by root I mean those few issues or problems which, if they do not become recognized, accepted, and a goal for action, rule out hope for improving our schools.

It is that sense of urgency that made it easy for me to seize the opportunity to revisit the arena of educational change. And it was that sense of urgency that, after thinking that I had finished the revisiting, caused me to write a postscript. I do not want to be seen as a total pessimist, a prophet of doom and gloom. As I shall indicate, there are some signs that the root problems are being recognized. I cannot judge whether those signs will gain the kind of currency that is necessary for a general impact to occur. In any event, I have said it the way I think it. This is no time to be reticent or circumspect or indirect. The stakes are too high. If anything has changed since I wrote the book 25 years ago, it is the degree of disappointment and disillusionment in regard to reform experienced by the public at large as well as in the educational community where public statements are at variance with private opinion.

ACKNOWLEDGMENTS

I am grateful to a dear friend, Ann Lieberman, for encouraging me to revisit, and to Carole Saltz who is as good a person as she is a chief editor. As usual, Lisa Pagliaro graciously suffered my handwriting and other peculiarities.

Preface to the Second Edition

I was, of course, extremely grateful for the very positive reception of the first edition of this book. I am not indulging undue modesty when I say that the reception was more positive than my own judgment of the book. As I point out later, the culture of the school is too differentiated and complex, available knowledge and viewpoints too variegated, to be encompassed by one person. And when, in addition, one sets out to see that culture from the standpoint of efforts to change it, the difficulty of the task can overwhelm you to the point where you give up and look for more manageable problems to study and understand. But I have been directly involved with schools since 1942 and my interest in and concern for our schools were too strong to permit me to ignore what I came to see I had to do, however incomplete my effort would have to be. My experience forced on me the fact that there are no better ways to comprehend the culture of the school than either by looking at how it responds to pressures for change or how it responds to someone who is trying to be helpful to people within it. I have been in both roles and that undoubtedly influenced much that is this book. Those who have been in different roles inevitably will see things somewhat differently, but, as the published and personal response to the first edition indicates, there is an encouraging degree of overlap or agreement between their conclusions and mine.

I was quite aware when I completed the first edition that a set of problems with which I have long been associated, problems that later became crucially important in the educational setting, were deliberately excluded by me. I refer to mental retardation in particular, and handicapped children in general. I excluded these problems for two related reasons. For one thing, I was very sensitive to the possibility that the book would be read as an un-sympathetic criticism of schools, a reading that was quite the opposite of what I intended. But it was obvious that there was little in the book that could serve as a basis for an optimistic view of schools' future. Now, in regard to mental retardation I have always had strong feelings, i.e., I was a partisan for retarded people and their teachers, both of whom were segregated, second- to third-class citizens in the school culture. If I in-cluded this set of problems in the first edition, I was not sure that I could be dispassionate because I had long felt that these aspects of the school culture contained morally reprehensible features. Besides, when the book was written in 1969–1970, I would have talked about special classes (which were on the rise) and their encapsulated, alien status in most schools. Then I would have gone into the legal-moral basis for special classes because I predicted then that the 1954 desegregation decision would some day serve as the basis for challenging special classes. But, I asked myself, would the reader understand? Would it appear as if I was critical and perhaps even nihilistic? Would the space I would have to devote to these problems ap-pear as unexplainably disproportionate to their significance? So, I said lit-tle or nothing. A decade later it is a different ballgame and that is reflected in this second edition. Needless to say, I regret that early judgment because if that first edition had spoken to the issues of handicapped children, it might have been more edifying than it was.

There was one other set of problems that suffered the same fate in the first edition and which occupies many pages in this edition. I refer to the in-creasing role of the federal government in seeking to improve and change the public schools. When I was writing the first edition, no one within the schools, and few from without, questioned the federal government's role, style, impact, and ultimate success. I saw the governmental effort as well intentioned and, to put it mildly, misguided. My perception did not stem from a matter of principle, but from my observations of government sup-ported programs and from my experience as a consultant to government agencies. Here, too, if I included my conclusions I feared I would be seen as a gloomy pessimist. This was before the evaluations of these programs were initiated or published and so it was my personal experience versus scant empirical evidence. I take no satisfaction in having predicted the ma-jor conclusions of those evaluations.

At the time this book was finished the winds of policy change seemed to be changing directions, shifting from Washington to the state capitals. I say "seemed" because it is by no means clear the extent to which the federal role will become a minor factor in American education. But even if that were to happen, every issue that has cropped up in relation to federal efforts at educational change will reappear if and when state departments of education become powerful in matters of policy. On the stage and behind the scenes mammoth struggles are going on that have more to do with power than with substantive educational issues. This is not to say that these power struggles are unimportant and will have no influence on how substantive issues will be posed and implemented, but rather that we tend to confuse changes in power with changes in substance. It would be more correct to say that we have the tendency to *hope* that changes in power automatically lead to meaningful changes in the substance and understanding of issues. There is one other factor that makes predictions about the pace and direction of change a risky affair. I refer to the fact that court decisions have been the most potent factors in bringing about changes in educational policy, and that fact may well continue to be true in coming decades.

Perhaps the wisest thing I ever said was that two major problems in life are parking and secretaries and that if we could not deal effectively with them, we should not be optimistic about the outcomes of our efforts with other problems that beset us, e.g., poverty, loneliness, war, discrimination. Fortunately, this second edition was started when Marlene Twarowski became my secretary and it would not have been completed without her. The truth is that when I saw what a sterling human being she was I knew the second edition had better be written while she was on the scene. That was one of my wiser decisions because the book was finished only days before she left on maternity leave.

I am also grateful to Carl Milofsky (sociologist), Richard Murnane (economist), and Edward Pauly (political scientist) who, housed with me in Yale's Institute for Social and Policy Studies, shared with me, and allowed me to share with them, our deep interest and involvement in public education. I have indeed been fortunate in being able to experience meaningful interdisciplinary collegiality. I am grateful to Yale's Institute for Social and Policy Studies for making this possible.

PART I

THE CULTURE OF THE SCHOOL AND THE PROBLEM OF CHANGE

Chapter 1

The Plan of the Book

In the 1976 presidential campaign the candidate that won promised to create a separate cabinet Department of Education. That department was given legislative sanction toward the end of President Carter's tenure in office. In the presidential campaign of 1980 the candidate that won promised to eliminate the Department. At the time this book was completed, several months after President Reagan's inauguration, it was too early to say if and when the Department of Education would be abolished. The significance of these facts lies in the unprecedented degree to which education has become a focus of *national* public policy. However one defines or labels a social-historical era or period, it has always been the case that the purposes and accomplishments of the public schools were significant issues bearing that era's distinctive stamp. But it has only been in the post-World War II era that the public schools became a major and controversial concern of the federal government. Before World War II public education was a local and state affair. Even so, in each era some controversial aspect of the public schools occupied the attention of the larger society. We are used to hearing that we have always been a nation of immigrants, and we respond, justifiably, with feelings of pride. But what we are not told with any clarity is that the ambivalence with which the waves of immigrants were (and are) greeted insured that the content and goals of schooling would be seen very differently by different groups and classes in the society. Parents, business and industry, and colleges and universities have never been indifferent to what goes on in schools. And, of course, elected public officials have been far from indifferent if only because they must make economic decisions that affect schools.

Persistent myths to the contrary notwithstanding, the public schools have always had a transactional relationship with their communities: affected by them and in turn affecting them. It is understandable that when we think of a school or a school system the image of buildings comes to mind, buildings that have a distinctive internal physical structure and populated by distinctive groups having distinctively different functions. And when we think of a school system the image of many such buildings related to a central administrative site gets conjured up. But if those images are understandable they nevertheless tend to have the unfortunate practical consequence of overlooking the myriad important ways that those bounded buildings are integrally a part of a larger picture. As a result, when we try to understand what goes on in a classroom or school we seek explanations in terms of *that* classroom in *that* school in *that* school system. That kind of approach to understanding is legitimate and can lead to productive knowledge as long as its limitations are explicitly recognized. The major limitation is that such an approach obscures the implicit and explicit transactions between school and community. *That limitation goes unrecognized until, either from within or without, an attempt is made to effect a significant change in the schools.* Then it becomes glaringly apparent that what goes on is not explainable only by riveting on what goes on *in* schools. We tend to be unaware that we use the concept of the encapsulated school system in ways that blind us to the daily realities of the school-society relationship.

This is a major theme that I take up in Chapter 2, but it is one that I come back to many times in subsequent chapters because one cannot understand the failure of efforts to change and improve schools unless one deals with school-community relationships and their largely implicit character—implicit, that is, until their legal-traditional-cultural features are pushed into the forefront by conflict and controversy. So, for example, up until the mid-fifties teachers stood in a certain relationship to the community: in matters of salary, seniority, promotion, and transfer, *each* teacher negotiated with representatives of the community. From the standpoint of community and teachers that relationship was "right, natural, and proper." That is the way it was, the way it is, and the way it should be. It may have been unsatisfactory to the individual teacher, it certainly was a relationship of unequal power, but there seemed to be no acceptable alternative. Twenty-five years later teacher unions have a size and strength few people would have predicted. That dramatic change has no simple explanation, but certainly one part of a complex explanation would be that teachers took and exercised power that was *always* potentially available to them, i.e., the means had long existed whereby teachers could demonstrate something that was obvious to everybody: schooling cannot take place if teachers are not in the classroom. What teacher unions demonstrated was that the relationship between teacher and community was always characterized by power. What the unions sought was to alter the distribution of power. What requires explanation is not that there are power struggles between teacher unions and the community, but why those struggles erupted when they did and led so quickly to alterations in power relationships. Suffice it to say here, only in small part can those questions be answered by pointing to what was happening inside of schools. And I cannot refrain from noting that as the unions gained in strength and militancy they exploded once and for all time the myth that schools and school systems were enclaves walled off from the baleful influences of "politics." Where the public political arena ends and the educational arena begins is a boundary that never existed, but it took teacher strikes and collective bargaining to underline the realities. Schools are physically bounded structures. In all other respects their boundaries are porous to a degree their physical appearance and the traditional concept of a school system obscure.

What are the special problems a person faces when he or she enters schools for the purpose of understanding and changing them in some way? As I have already suggested, one of the major "industries" (a peculiar blend of the public, private, and nonprofit sectors) in the post-World War II period could be given the awkward title, "changing and improving schools." And most of the people engaged in such efforts were not indigenous to the schools. Many of the acknowledged leaders came from the university. To what extent, and with what clarity, did these people confront the obstacles of the "outsider-insider" dichotomy? Unfortunately, as I indicate in Chapter 3, these spearheaders of the change effort seemed massively insensitive to the culture of schools. Their efforts resulted largely in failure and that was in part due, and sometimes it was totally due, to ignorance about the distinctive, tradition-based axioms, values, and outlook of school personnel. As Chapter 3 emphasizes, faced with failure these well-intentioned proponents for change could only understand school personnel in terms of personality traits, e.g., rigid, paranoid, unmotivated. They were applying an individual psychology in a most egregiously inappropriate fashion. It might seem that I am arguing that if one was indigenous to the schools, one would be far more effective in changing them. But, as I attempt to demonstrate in Chapter 3, that is not the case at all. To take distance from the setting in which one is an integral part is a ubiquitous problem in dealing with the culture of the school and the problem of change.

Chapter 4 describes two efforts at educational change. I call them "modal" because I believe that from the standpoint of their initial conception, tactics, process, and outcome they contain most of the major features of the change process. These two efforts had disheartening results. It is not because of any intention on my part to accentuate the negative and to deemphasize the positive that I use these instances. The main intent of Chapter 4 is to give some feel for what that process means in practice.

Chapter 4 is prologue to Chapter 5 in which I present the evidence, unfortunately compelling, for the conclusion that the federal effort to change and improve schools has largely been a failure.[1] The notion that schools will change if only the federal government will make a commitment to the public schools, and commitment is measured by increasing budgets, receives no support from the available evidence. If I devote special attention in Chapter 5 to the federal Experimental Schools Program, it is for several reasons: it was announced with much fanfare, for all practical purposes money was not a problem, selected school systems were to be given wide latitude in "coordinating" programs ("putting it all together"), and there was to be different levels of evaluation. Why was it such a dismal failure? That is the question that Cowden and Cohen's (unpublished) recent evaluation of the program helps to clarify.

In Chapters 6 and 7 I take up the problem of how one ascertains the overt behavior and programmatic regularities in the school. An overt behavioral regularity, for example, would be the rate at which teachers ask questions or the rate at which children ask questions. An example of a programmatic regularity is the fact that for every school day from first grade through high school a child is expected to do something with, or learn something about, numbers. Once these kinds of regularities have been discerned, one can ask two questions: How is the regularity justified? From what universe of alternatives of action was this particular regularity chosen?

What then emerges from this discussion is a point I consider of utmost importance: *any attempt to introduce a change into the school involves some existing regularity, behavioral or programmatic.* These regularities are in the nature of intended outcomes. It is a characteristic of the modal process of change in the school culture that the intended outcome (the change in the regularity) is rarely stated clearly, and if it is stated clearly, by the end of the change process it has managed to get lost. It certainly was not an intended outcome of the introduction of the new math that it should be taught precisely the way the old math was taught. But that has been the outcome, and it would be surprising if it were otherwise.

Discerning overt behavioral or programmatic regularities requires that one look at the school culture from a nonjudgmental, noninterpretive stance, a requirement that is not natural to us. We are so used to thinking about what other people are thinking that we pay little attention to what

1. After this book was put into the publication process, I read, thanks to Professor Michael Fullan of the Ontario Institute for Studies in Education, a draft of his forthcoming book *The Meaning of Educational Change* (Teachers College Press). Fullan has written a most thoughtful and important book that, given its focus, is more comprehensive than mine in its analysis of discrete studies of efforts at change. The two books are both overlapping and complementary in substance and conclusions.

there is to see. I hope readers will find helpful in these chapters my use of the man from outer space who is parked on his space platform above a school, incapable of comprehending written or oral language, capable of seeing everything that goes on, and (of course) possessed of the most advanced computers, which allow him to discern any and all kinds of behavioral and programmatic regularities. The regularities he discerns permit us to ask why they exist and what alternative ways of thinking would give rise to different regularities. The man from outer space has taught me much about the school culture.

If the evidence on outcomes of federal intervention is so discouraging, if the efforts this intervention supported paid lip service to the systematic use of behavioral and programmatic regularities as criteria for evaluation, that same evidence did not disconfirm the belief that the school principal was crucial in determining the fate of the change process. In the bulk of instances where the effort failed, and in the small number of instances where it succeeded, the principal was a key actor. I take this matter up in Chapters 8 and 9 where several themes are central. First, there is the increasing complexity and built-in dilemmas of the role: on the one hand, the bewildering array of pressures from the community with which the principal must deal and, on the other hand, the pressures on the principal from within the school to preserve and protect strongly held attitudes and practices. Second, the ways in which most principals deal with these dilemmas cannot be understood by only studying principals in school, but one must also look to the substance of university training programs that prepare principals for the realities of the school culture. Third, we are living in a time when the issue "who owns the schools?" has been forcefully posed, an issue for which the training of the principal ill prepares him or her. As I discuss in these chapters, many principals have come to feel that they should have been lawyers before they became principals. But how do we understand why some principals seem to transcend the boundaries of their training and are able imaginatively and courageously to walk that fine line on one side of which is passive resignation and the other side of which is what someone termed "creative unresponsiveness"? If as a group the behavior of principals lowers one's expectation about the outcome of efforts at educational change, that is no excuse for not appreciating that under the best of circumstances (however defined) with the best people (however defined) the principal's role is an inordinately demanding one—demanding, that is, if the principal confronts and does not avoid conflict, controversy, and change.

Much that I have to say about principals holds for teachers (Chapters 10 and 11). The evidence is rather clear that although it is true that the principal is the gatekeeper in regard to the change effort, the ultimate outcome depends on when and how teachers become part of the decision to initiate change. As I emphasize in these chapters, teachers tend to be viewed and "managed" by their administrative superiors in much the same way that teachers view and manage their pupils in the classroom. Through their unions teachers and boards of education have forged new "constitutions," i.e., coming to agreement about the rules by which they will live together. However, as I stress in Chapter 11, in the classroom the constitution is not a mutual affair. It is written by the teacher.

There is a place for criticism, but uncontrolled by a conscious effort to understand (to see the world the way the other person sees it), it too often results in polarization between the "good guys and the bad guys." This type of polarization may be permissible at football games where personal expression and victory are the ends sought. However, I have too frequently witnessed the *consequences* of such polarizations in the school culture, so I am not really able to distinguish the good from the bad guys. Some will conclude that I am one of the bad guys because I do not describe the thinking and actions of the modal teacher and principal as adequate either to the possibilities of their roles or to the problems that those in the roles inevitably face. I can only say that much of what I say represents not only what I have observed and thought about, but, more important, what teachers and principals have told me after we had come to know each other. One of the definite advantages of a sustained helping relationship (primarily the kind of relationship I have had with school personnel) is that once one gets past the initial stages of a mutual "casing the joint," the barriers of role are lessened and straight talk begins (with the inevitable ups and downs, of course). It is certainly not a peculiarity of school personnel that what they will say in public will not always square with what they think privately, particularly if they know what that particular public expects them to say—a lesson, incidentally, that anthropologists learned the hard way. It is difficult to learn from the experiences of others.

There have been two revolutions in American education. The first was the introduction of compulsory education. The second was a consequence of the 1954 desegregation decision. We are currently at the beginning of a third revolution: federal legislation mandating the integration of handicapped children (*all* handicapped children) into the regular classroom. This legislation is Public Law 94-142. It is popularly known as the "mainstreaming" law, but, as I point out in Chapter 12, the absence of that word from the legislation was not fortuitous. The significance of 94-142 is in several factors. First, it is the most explicit and ambitious federal effort to effect changes in *all* schools. Second, its emphasis on "due process" further underlines the significance of the influence of legal thinking and procedures on the school culture, a point I discuss at some length in the chapters on the principal. Third, the explicit power the legislation gives to parents of handicapped pupils raises in a restricted but nevertheless powerful way the question posed in earlier chapters: who owns the school? P.L. 94-142 not only presents a challenge to the behavioral and programmatic regularities in the school culture, but to those seeking to understand that culture the consequences of that legislation will provide the basis for determining how well we truly understand that culture.

From my standpoint the overriding significance of 94–142 is that it forces onto the public agenda the question: what are schools for? In some form or other that question is raised and discussed on a daily basis within the school culture, but with such a restricted focus that for all practical purposes the discussion obscures more than it illuminates. If it illuminates anything, it is that socialization into a culture is a massive obstacle to taking distance from it. Chapter 13 represents a beginning effort on my part to examine the question.

The final chapter contains an attempt to pinpoint what I have come to believe are the crucial features of a change effort that stands a chance of achieving some of its objectives. Given all that has preceded that chapter it will come as no surprise that the concept of constituency, the fact of limited (and shrinking) resources, and the questions "who owns the school?" and "what are schools for?" loom large in that chapter.

What I have tried to do in this book is to describe and to understand certain aspects of the culture of the school from a certain perspective and on the basis of my experience with and in schools. I have not dealt with all aspects of the problem, but I believe that what I have dealt with is important and has significances for these other aspects.

This book could have been planned and organized differently. I am told that one of the characteristics of authors is that they dearly believe that their books could only be written in a certain way, that is, the way they did it. Whatever the validity of that assertion may be, it contains an assumption that is central to this particular book: there is no one way of looking at and understanding the school culture. There is a universe of alternative approaches or ways of thinking. What I present in the following chapters is one of the ways one can think about the culture of the school.

Chapter 2

The Encapsulated School System

No major social institution has been more subject to pressure for change than the public school system. The 1954 Supreme Court desegregation decision, and the recent Education For All Handicapped Childrens' Act (Public Law 94–142, popularly known as the "mainstreaming" law), are but two instances of major efforts in the post-World War II era to alter features of school systems. Those two instances, although separated by almost a quarter of a century, are by no means unrelated because the philosophical and legal justifications for Public Law 94–142 derive from the 1954 decision. The significance of that relationship is threefold. First, the most potent source for change has come not from within the school system, or from state and federal policy makers, but from the courts. Second, precisely because major educational policies and legislation are rather direct derivatives of court decisions, schools have had little option about assimilating and accommodating to change. For all practical purposes, change is mandated. Third, there is the sense that there is something "wrong" in our schools that the legislation will rectify, i.e., if schools had been doing what they should, if they were not structured in such traditional ways, if school personnel thought and acted differently, there would be no need for remedial legislation. Put in another way, schools had been making errors of omission and commission. It is true that in regard to any of these efforts there have always been school personnel who welcomed and even fought for these changes. But the fact remains that the strongest pressures for change have come from outside the school system.

I did not start with these remarks in order to suggest that the relationship between schools and outside forces has some adversarial features.

Those features are clear enough and we shall be discussing them throughout this book. The point of my opening remarks is the basis they provide for the question: Does it make sense to talk about schools as if they are part of a closed system that does not include groups and agencies outside that system? Why is it that when we use the phrase "school system" we think in terms of pupils, teachers, principals, school buildings, boards of education, superintendents, etc., and we automatically relegate other groups and agencies (e.g., parents, finance board, politicians, schools of education, state and federal departments of education) to an "outside" role? We are, of course, begging the question: What do we mean by a system? At this point we shall not attempt to answer that question except to suggest that it is more confusing than clarifying to talk about a school system as if it were a closed rather than an open one, as if the system is comprehensible only in terms of those who have roles to play within school buildings. For example, shall we regard departments and colleges of education as a part of a school system, or rather as another system that interacts with school systems?[1] Take another example: by tradition, law, and rhetoric school systems are supposed to be independent of the political system (local, state, and federal), but is there anyone knowledgeable about either system who would deny that their independence is a myth, that it was a myth long before the rise of militant teacher unions and equally militant ethnic and racial groups in the community?

For certain purposes, by no means unimportant ones, it may be fruitful to consider these systems as independent but interacting, but if your aim is to understand why schools do or do not change, the usual concept of a school system can be an effective barrier because it restricts the scope of what you will look at and consider. Let me illustrate the point with three anecdotes.

The first anecdote derives from a once-a-week inservice workshop I was conducting for teachers in a suburban school system. One of the major foci of the first five meetings led me at the sixth one to say, "If you had to choose between a thousand dollar raise and a written guarantee that you would never again have to talk to a parent, I think I know what your choice would be." My statement was greeted with that kind of nervous laughter indicating that the choice would be a difficult one. My comment of course reflected the frustration and dissatisfaction these teachers had described in

---

1. Green's (1980) recent book, *Predicting the Behavior of the Educational System*, is a major contribution toward a more productive and comprehensive conception of the educational *system*. His conception, which is tightly and logically reasoned, is not like the one most of us use but rather deals with interrelated variables, impersonal and abstract, that have dynamic and predictable consequences. These consequences are in large part what we ordinarily mean by the educational system, unaware of their derivation from the prior, unrecognized, and interrelated variables that Green so well illuminates. In Green's use of the concept system, universities are integral parts of that concept.

their encounters with parents. Needless to say, that is precisely what many parents experience in their interactions with teachers. (As someone once said, the original cold war was between parents and school personnel.) How shall we understand this? The answer has many parts, but there is one ingredient that will never be identified if you rivet attention only on the characteristics and roles of teachers and parents. That ingredient is in the fact that I know of no college or university teacher training program that exposes teachers to the issues surrounding and the skill required for talking with (not to) parents. That omission could be justified only if one assumed that talking productively with parents was a God-given gift that training could neither improve or interfere with. In focusing on this omission I did not intend criticism of teachers, parents, or teacher training programs, but rather wished to emphasize that if your aim is to understand parent-teacher interactions, you have to look at how people are trained "outside" the school system to adopt roles within it.[2] But if you hold a traditional view of a school system—circumscribed as that view is by such factors as who is in school buildings, how they relate to each other administratively and functionally, and how goals are stated and measured—it is most unlikely that you will look "outside" the system to understand what goes on within it. Since the need to understand is frequently associated with the desire to change a particular state of affairs, this circumscribed view is of very practical import because if you are overlooking factors not discernible in the school setting but nonetheless important for what is happening there that you want to change, you lower the chances that your efforts will have the desired consequences. This does not mean that if you are not a prisoner of the traditional concept of the encapsulated school system, which means that you have a more realistically complicated picture of the formal and informal networks in which schools and school systems are embedded, that your efforts at change will necessarily be more successful. On the contrary. The more sensitive you become to this complicated embeddedness, the more you realize how many different "systems" have to change if the change you seek in the schools can be successfully introduced and maintained. Nothing has been more characteristic of efforts to change schools

---

2. When I say I do not intend criticism, I mean that I am not explaining what people do in terms of deficits or inadequacies in their motivation, sophistication, or knowledge. That is to say, the problem does not inhere in them as individuals but rather has to be seen as an outgrowth of processes that, for purposes of brevity, I shall call socialization and acculturation. Each of us experiences these processes, the consequence of which is to provide us with a picture of what reality is and should be. It is precisely when the relationships between groups, or between individuals representing these groups, is conflictful over time that we must look beyond the characteristics of individuals and their personalities to fathom the social-cultural forces and contexts that are, so to speak, the stage that give form and direction to the relationship among the actors in the drama. If there is any central theme in this book it is that efforts to change any aspect of a school or school system will misfire to the extent that the problem is defined in terms of characteristics of individuals and their personalities.

than oversimple conceptions of the change process, an oversimplicity matched only by (indeed, deriving from) a very narrow conception of what a school system is.

The second anecdote comes from my participation on a task force, appointed by a local citizen-educator committee, on preservice and inservice programs for school administrators. As in the first anecdote, the creation of the task force reflected in part dissatisfaction with the style, quality, and the apparently fruitless and endless character of discussions between different community groups and school administrators. Administrators felt beleaguered, if not persecuted. Community groups saw themselves as victims of administrator insensitivity, if not of outright deception. At the initial meeting of the task force I asked the following question: "If each of us spent a day following school administrators around, what would that day look like?" School administrators and teachers were represented on the task force, and those who were not formally part of the school "system" were knowledgeable about schools. As anyone familiar with schools would have predicted, school administrators spend a large fraction of their time participating in, or planning for, or chairing *meetings* (e.g., with community groups, school faculties). To what extent and in what ways do training programs in colleges and universities prepare administrators for how to think about, plan, and run meetings? Again the answer is that such preparation does not occur. And, again, that omission is comprehensible only if one assumes that meetings are unimportant or that the knowledge and skills necessary for having productive meetings are possessed by everyone. Here, too, I note this omission not in the spirit of criticism, but only to emphasize that the effort to understand and to change something in and about schools should not be constricted by a narrow conception of a school system. It is all too easy to pinpoint a problem *in* schools and to propose changes *within* schools, unaware that the problem did not arise only in the context of schools. This is true if the aim of change is remedial; it is even more true if the aim is to prevent the frequency with which the problem occurs.

The third anecdote is in the form of a question I have put to small groups of educational policy makers, educational researchers, and school personnel. The question is put when two conditions exist: there is consensus that the degree and direction of change in our schools have not been proportional to the amount of money spent for these efforts, and there is agreement that we seem to lack an effective theory of institutional change. The question is: "Assume that you can make one and only one change in schools. Obviously (I think), you will make your choice in terms of what will produce the greatest 'ripple effect', i.e., the change will over time have percolating and spreading effects consistent with the purposes of the change. The only restriction on your choice is that it will require little or no extra funds. What is your proposed change?" The most frequent reaction to the question is one of silence and obvious puzzlement. The puzzlement does not stem from incomprehension, but rather from unfamiliarity with how to think about what one participant called the "whole shebang." The second reaction, once the participants are able to let their minds roam, was a variety of proposals of which the following are examples:

1. Eliminate the role of the school principal and place responsibility for the school in the hands of teachers and parents.
2. Drastically deemphasize the teaching of reading and arithmetic in the early grades.
3. Eliminate boards of education as they are currently constituted. Have a board for each school which will then send a representative to a district or central board.
4. Change the curriculum and organization of the high school so that students spend at least half of the day in a community activity that is educationally and intellectually justifiable. (These participants came up with this proposal recognizing that it derives from *Youth: Transition to Adulthood* by Coleman et al. (1974).)
5. Change the substance of teacher preparation programs in the direction of much more emphasis on child and adolescent development.
6. Make it illegal for schools to mount any "human service" program that diverts attention and time away from the teaching of fundamentals.
7. Require teacher preparation programs to provide their students with a better understanding of cultural and racial diversity as it relates to the school setting.

The proposals did not come easily and at least half of the participants felt too uncomfortable or simply were unable to come up with a response. The third reaction, and here almost everyone participated, consisted of vigorous critiques of each proposal. Each proposal was found wanting in several respects: either it would have no effect, or it would not benefit students, or the cure was worse than the disease. Given the nature of these meetings, discussion could not go on very long, but it lasted long enough for most of the participants to agree that they rarely thought about what they meant by *the* system as a whole or that they had anything like a clear idea or set of criteria by which to judge proposals for change. As one participant said, "If we take seriously the proposals on the blackboard, it is obvious that when we talk about a school system we in practice refer to more than school buildings and the people inside of them." I had to reluctantly disagree with this participant because *in practice* when we talk about a school system we see it more as an encapsulated, geographically located entity sharply bounded from an "outside." This view, of course, contains a kernel of truth, but only in the sense that it is part of our psychological reality and, therefore, governs our actions. Once we see and accept other kernels of truth we are redefining what we mean by our reality and transforming our reactions to it.

CULTURE AND THE OBSERVER

If, as I have suggested, our conception of a school system is narrow and self-defeating, how do we explain the pervasive strength of that conception? Before anyone devotes one's energies to understanding and changing schools, does not one first have to try to understand where one's conceptions about schools come from? As observers of schools we do not come to the task with blank minds. We come with images, expectations, and implicit and explicit attitudes. We come to the task after a long process of socialization and acculturation from which in countless ways, witting and unwitting, we have absorbed conceptions of and attitudes toward school settings. Far from being a random process, acculturation is directed to shaping a person's definition of reality, *not only what it is but what it should be.* To a very large extent we are passive participants in the process, beginning as the process does from the day of birth. The carriers of culture (e.g., parents, teachers) ordinarily do a very effective job of inculcating in children their view of what is and what should be, what one should do and not do depending on where and with whom one is—so effective, in fact, that it takes very special, upsetting conditions to force one to ask why one has thought and acted the way one has. The women's liberation movement, the civil rights-racial-ethnic movements, and the sexual "revolution" are only some of the more familiar examples of societal dynamics reflecting, among other things, how certain groups have questioned and from their standpoint overcome their acculturation experience and, as a consequence, the pressures that exerts on other segments of society to reexamine what their acculturation taught them to be right, natural, and proper.

The observer of any part of the educational scene has a task that is prior to observing, and that is to confront the fact that he or she was born into this society with its distinctive culture; that before entering any kind of school the observer had already developed conceptions of and attitudes toward being in school; that he or she had spent a dozen years in public schools during which pictures and conceptions of what schools are were crystallizing, if not being locked into conceptual and attitudinal concrete; and that in the course of undergraduate and graduate education that same observer was hearing and reading about schools in the mass media and was being taught what schools are by college professors. It would be no small research task to study not only the sources from which we learn about schools but what these sources are telling us. From the different things such a study might reveal, I have no doubt that several things would stand out. First, there is something "wrong" in our schools, i.e., they are not doing what they should do as well as "outsiders" expect. Second, ways have to be devised to change what goes on *within* schools so that they can do a better job. Put in another way: it is the very rare observer who will not come to his or her task with a critical stance, who will not unreflectively define and literally place problems (defined by the observer or others) *within* schools, and whose recommendations for change will not focus exclusively on internal practices and structures.

When an anthropologist decides to study a foreign culture, one just does not take off and go. Built into the training of the anthropologist is the dictum that his or her acculturation into this society presents problems for understanding people in another culture. The anthropologist will read what others have said about the foreign culture, as much to learn about the culture-bound mistakes others have made as to acquire a variety of facts and perspectives. The history of anthropology (as well as that of exploration, missionary work, and foreign aid) is the history of how difficult it has been to prevent your own acculturation from unduly distorting what you observe about, and how you interpret, the behavior of people in another culture. There is another fateful problem that the anthropologist confronts and about which one makes a decision and then prays: he or she must choose an informant in the foreign culture, a kind of cultural guide, but how can one be sure that this informant is not an unwitting distorter of the culture? Because someone is a product of a culture in no way guarantees that what you are being told is the truth. You may be given facts but not the truth without which the facts can be quite misleading.

The observer of schools has kinship with the anthropologist. On the one hand, he or she is observing a setting that has inevitably over the years influenced how the observer will view it. But when we say observer we refer to more than the act of looking or seeing. The observer talks to people who, like the observer, have experienced a similar acculturation process. Precisely because the school observer and informants have shared that process the thinking of both may reflect the same sources of distortion or narrowness.

I am not raising a problem that has a solution in the sense that "four divided by two is two" is a solution. One never can fully flush out and control the precipitants of the culture that is in us. If we can at best only enjoy a partial success in this regard, if we are inherently imperfect observers (which does not mean we are poor or inadequate observers), if there are no methodological gimmicks that "solve" the problem (although there are some that can be helpful), that is no cause for pessimism or inaction. What is distressing is that the problem has hardly been taken seriously. As a consequence, and despite the recognition that past efforts to change schools have been disappointing, we are unable to entertain the possibility that much of the difficulty is in the narrow perspective from which we view schools, a narrowness that is cultural in origin.

As I was writing these pages the following article appeared in the *New Haven Register* on October 12, 1980. It was the lead article on an inside section, and spread across the top of the entire page was the headline: "More time on math said needed for 9th grade teachers, class."

AN INTERIM REPORT FROM A STATE PANEL PROBING LOW SCORES ON LAST year's ninth grade proficiency test in math suggests more classroom time on that subject for students and their teachers.

Scheduling pressures now frequently encourage rote memorization "without the essential underlying conceptual understanding" of math, said the group.

In many classrooms, math instruction is limited to a daily average of 30 minutes in grades one through three and 45 minutes in remaining school years, the panel found.

"These time allocations are insufficient to effectively develop satisfactory levels of achievement in all students," it said, proposing instead a minimum of 45 minutes daily for the first three grades and an hour in the other nine.

The amount of time the majority of students today spend on math study "does not correlate with the importance of mathematical understanding to their lives," counseled the 14 experts chosen from schools and colleges around the state to come up with remedies.

"Just as a full interaction with our society demands an ability to read, so does it demand an ability to compute, understand basic numerical concepts, and solve basic math problems," the unit said.

But there is ample evidence that the "average level of math understanding in the nation, as well as Connecticut, is distressingly low." Last year's test revealed that one of every five students then in ninth grade could need more help in math.

The panel made similar recommendations on the teacher training process.

While many elementary teachers take courses on how to teach reading, relatively few take the equivalent in math instruction, the group said.

"Further, many secondary school teachers have not had specific training in techniques for working with low achieving students," the panel reported.

"Some teachers are uncomfortable departing from the structure of a textbook and some administrators give little attention to math instruction."

The role of calculators or computers in class, as well as new research on math instruction, suggest "the need for updating instructional skills, techniques and activities among the professional staff," it said.

The fact that metric instruction or revised algebra programs are "in the book" or in the curriculum "does not guarantee they will be taught or learned," the group warned.

An effective math program "recognizes this and provides opportunities for teachers and administrators to further develop their skills and acquire new ones," it said.

Workshops to update skills should be planned with teachers and address their specific needs. These workshops should be provided as part of the implementation on new classroom programs or other curricular changes which teachers are expected to undertake, the panel advised.

Moreover, these sessions should be of practical value to teachers and focus on specific instruction techniques rather than theory.

Beyond more time on math for students and their teachers, the panel recommended "record cards" on math skills to monitor individual performance, allowing teachers to spot students needing remedial help as well as those with talent.

"It is extremely important to monitor student progress on a skill by skill basis, and provide a means for this information to be passed from teacher to teacher and school to school," said the state group.

Support personnel should also be part of the school package. "In most schools, when a student is having difficulty with reading, the classroom teacher can turn for assistance to a reading consultant or specialist," it found.

But that option is rarely available in math.

"Without such specialized assistance, the problem is left unresolved or dealt with at the expense of the remainder of the class," said the group.

While the departmentalized nature of secondary schools allows for math supervisors, the same is not true at elementary or middle schools.

Additional personnel need not necessarily be full-time. These positions could be filled by using expertise of existing staff through time-release arrangements, team leaders or other dual positions, the unit said.

Assignments of more staff "is certainly not a panacea for overcoming all of the problems with mathematics," the panel said, but commitment to better math programs "strongly suggests the need for specialized math personnel."

The panel's report is expected to go before the state Board of Education in final form next month. ∎

We shall have occasion to refer to this article in later pages. The article is relevant at this point in several respects:

1. The reinforcement it gives to the view held by many readers that schools are not doing their job as well as they should.
2. The observers-experts locate a good deal of the problem in the way schools are organized, the priorities they adopt, and the deficiencies of teachers and administrators.
3. What teachers need is technical help, not "how to think about it" but "how to do it."
4. Teachers need additional math courses.
5. If the recommendations are implemented, math scores will discernibly improve.

Almost all of these points (the exception being "how to think it") were made with much national fanfare two decades ago when the (then) new math was introduced, and they have been reiterated countless times since, following which there has been a decline in math scores. Why should one now expect that by putting old wine in old bottles the results will be different? Is it possible that by defining the problem as one that arises in or is exacerbated by features of schools and school personnel we are blinding ourselves to equally important features outside of our schools? That our traditional conception of a school and a school system is simply inadequate to grasp the changing interconnections between schools and the communities in which they are embedded? And precisely because we are products of the system that we seek to change that we are attributing an importance to math that it simply does not have in the lives of young children outside of school?

I do not ask these questions because I think that the decline in math scores is independent of features of schools and teachers. That the teaching of math has become very problematic for teachers and students, that as a group teachers are aware that what and how they are teaching are far from effective, that teachers want to do a better job, are glimpses of the obvious. What is equally obvious, but hardly dealt with, is that school personnel (almost without exception, in my experience) believe that the decline in academic performance has its roots within and without the schools. At this point in our discussion the validity of that belief is not important. What is important is that school personnel have a definite explanation: by virtue of changes in the larger society, changes that have drastically altered the climate, structure, and practices of schools, the effectiveness of teaching has suffered and will continue to suffer. If the society had not changed the way it has, schools could do the job they are supposed to do. No explanation could be more illustrative of how effectively school personnel have absorbed culturally determined pictures and conceptions of what schools should be: oases of learning shielded from its social surround, a "system" minimally related to other systems. As I said earlier, these pictures and conceptions (and the values they imply) were not learned by school personnel the way one learns the dictionary definition of a word or concept, but rather over the course of a lifetime during which in myriad ways the picture and conception of what a school is or should be evolved. They, like the rest of us, cannot remember how they learned this just as they cannot remember how they learned to walk.

Basically there is little difference in the picture of what schools should be between that of school personnel and of those who seek to change or improve schooling. When you examine proposals to improve the teaching of math, for example, they in no fundamental way suggest alterations in teacher-pupil roles, in what a classroom should look like, in teacher-teacher, teacher-administrator, teacher-parent relationships, that conflict with the conceptions of school personnel. The conception conjured up by these proposals is the encapsulated classroom in an encapsulated school in an encapsulated school system. The rest of the world is "out there" and should stay out there, at the same time that those who hold such a conception are poignantly aware that it has become inadequate and maladaptive.

One of the major consequences of the acculturation process is not only in how it influences our view of the present and future, but in how both are related to a past. So, for example, school personnel tend to see the present (and the future) as representing a sharp break with the past. This is no less true for most observers of the school scene. That is to say, what is now happening between schools and society supposedly reflects new societal dynamics impinging on schools and forcing them to change their character. Assume for the moment that this view of the relationship between present and past is factually wrong, that our view of the past in regard to these issues is grossly misleading. What difference would or should that make in the way we think? If the break between present and past that informs the current view is only one of many such perceived breaks in the history of our schools, does not that require us to redefine our present view? Does that not suggest that we ask why we are so set to see discontinuities rather than continuities with the past? If the continuities are far greater than we have believed, does that not suggest the possibility that there is something about our society and culture that not only has made for tensions and conflicts between schools and the communities they serve, but has also been a source of strong and relatively constant pressure on schools to change? If the "good old days" were not all that good, if they bear striking similarities to the present, should not that fact in some way alter our attitudes, strategies, time perspective, and orientation to the future? Should it not suggest to those who seek to change schools that theories and actions based implicitly on the premise that our society was born yesterday or the week before will have mischievous consequences? And should it not suggest to school personnel that their view of what schools are or should be may be seriously flawed and is and has been an unwitting contributor to a long history of school-society conflicts? Let us turn to that history, not to recite facts or to draw lessons, but simply as a way of challenging the beliefs we treasure and protect. And if we avoid that kind of challenge it is because a part of us knows that if our beliefs do not stand up to that challenge, we will have to change. Like individuals, institutions are amazingly resourceful in avoiding and resisting change, and in saying that I refer not only to the target of change, but to those who regard themselves as the agents of change.

A BRIEF LOOK INTO THE PAST

Sharp conflicts between school and community have been frequent in our history. For example, Troen's account of the attendance of black children at the segregated schools of St. Louis indicates how quickly attendance increased once the school board decided to replace the white teachers with black. "From 1876 the year before black teachers were hired, through 1880, enrollment had more than doubled, from about 1,500 to more than 3,600 pupils, even though the city's black population had remained constant" (Troen, 1975, p. 92). William Torrey Harris, then superintendent of the St. Louis system, directly attributed the increase to the changeover to black teachers, and Troen indicates that what had taken place prior to the changeover was in effect a boycott of the public schools unaccompanied by the public demonstrations and legal protests that occurred in later decades in other cities.

Ravitch (1974) has described "The Great School Wars" of New York City, beginning before the middle of the last century and involving the Public School Society and the Catholic Church. Catholic objections to Bible reading in the schools was one of the major issues leading to the Philadelphia riots of 1844, and in subsequent years there were scattered instances of Catholic children subjected to physical punishment and expulsion for refusing to participate in the reading of the Protestant Bible within the public schools (Billington, 1938).

In 1920, the Scottish Rite Masons, Southern Jurisdication of the United States, publicly proclaimed their belief that the only sure foundation of our free institutions was the education of all children in public primary schools in which instruction should be restricted to the English language (Tyack, 1968). With Scottish Rite support, a proposed amendment to the Michigan constitution requiring public school attendance for all students was advanced in the same year, but soundly defeated in referendum (Holsinger, 1968). The scene of activity in this campaign to destroy the parochial schools then shifted to the Northwest where, with Masonic support and vigorous backing by the Ku Klux Klan, Oregon voters exercised that favorite democratic device of the progressive era, the initiative, to pass a law in 1922 essentially requiring all children between the ages of eight and sixteen to attend public schools. Penalties of fines and imprisonment were to be imposed on parents who failed to comply. Sponsors of the law had aimed it specifically at the Catholic school system, but with populist and patriotic fervor they extended their rhetoric to the snobbish private schools of the bluebloods and those private schools which were designated to further the cause of Bolshevism (Holsinger, 1968; Tyack, 1968).

Prior to the projected date of implementation of the law, the Society of Sisters of the Holy Names of Jesus and Mary which operated a parochial school and the Hill Military Academy sought a court injunction. Before the U.S. District Court, counsel for the Sisters argued that the law would, among other things, deprive the society of property without due process of law and deprive the parents of the right to control the education of their children. The state argued that increased attendance at nonpublic schools had been accompanied by an increase in juvenile delinquency and that compulsory attendance at public schools was necessary as a "precautionary measure against the moral pestilence of paupers, vagabonds, and possibly convicts," and "bolshevists, syndicalists, and communists" (Jorgenson, 1968, p. 462). Further, if any one denomination were permitted to conduct schools, others would do so and that would lead to the destruction of the public school system. The state therefore freely admitted that the intent of the law was to destroy nonpublic schools. "The necessity for any other kind of school than that provided by the State has ceased to exist" (Jorgenson, 1968, p. 462).

The District Court issued an injunction restraining the state from putting the law into effect. The state appealed to the Supreme Court. Meanwhile, the excesses of nativism and nationalism of World War I began to subside; immigration was well below the pre-War levels and the Ku Klux Klan mentality was beginning to recede. On the whole, the national press was vigorous in its denunciation of the Oregon law, and the court challenges of the Sisters were vigorously supported by Protestant and Jewish groups.

In its decision of June 1, 1925, to uphold the lower court's decision, the Supreme Court indicated that:

NO QUESTION IS RAISED CONCERNING THE POWER OF THE STATE REASONably to regulate all schools, to inspect, supervise, and examine them, their teachers and pupils; to require that all children of proper age attend some school, that teachers shall be of good moral character and patriotic disposition, that certain studies plainly essential to good citizenship must be taught, and that nothing be taught which is manifestly inimical to the public welfare (Jorgensen 1968, p. 463). ■

But the court denied the state's right to exercise arbitrary, unreasonable, and unlawful interference with the property rights of the appellees, and with wider scope and implication the Court stated:

. . . WE THINK IT ENTIRELY PLAIN THAT THE ACT OF 1922 UNREASONABLY interferes with the liberty of parents and guardians to direct the upbringing and education of children under their control. As often heretofore pointed out, rights guaranteed by the Constitution may not be abridged by legislation which has no reasonable relation to some purpose within the competency of the state. The fundamental theory of liberty upon which all governments in this Union repose excludes any general power of the state to standardize its children by forcing them to accept instruction from public teachers only. The child is not the mere creature of the state; those who nurture him and direct his destiny have the right, coupled with the high duty, to recognize and prepare him for additional obligations (Stokes 1950, vol. 2, p. 740). ■

A final example has to do with the attempt in the second decade of this century to introduce the Gary Plan into the New York City schools. Let us listen to Adeline and Murray Levine's (1970a) description of what happened:

Resistance to the Gary Plan in New York

AT FIRST IT SEEMED THERE WOULD BE SOMETHING SATISFACTORY FOR everyone: a school curriculum attuned to an urban, industrial community, taught in the modern, progressive style, while utilizing existing resources. The Mitchel administration was so committed to the Gary Plan that by 1916 approval of the Board of Education budget was made contingent upon an agreement to "Garyize" the entire school system.

However, there was immediate resistance to the Gary Plan. Professional jealousy, resentment aroused by the interference of society ladies and politicians, the attempt to guard professional prerogatives, and the undesirable features of the New York version all influenced the school administrators who opposed and sabotaged the implementation of the plan. The professional administrators were also motivated by a desire to eliminate Wirt from consideration as a candidate for the superintendency when the aging incumbent retired. City teachers opposed the system, partly from an instinctive aversion to change and partly as a reaction to administration criticism of the efficiency of teachers. With good reason they feared that the installation of the Gary system in New York would be at their expense, for the administration had been hostile to their concerns about pensions and salaries. In the fall and winter of 1915 there was a brief but heated controversy about provisions for released time for religious education. Anticlerical feelings and arguments for the separation of church and state met head on with the usual pieties about providing for religious education for youth.

In the 1917 mayoralty election, Tammany ran an undistinguished, obscure judge, John F. Hylan, against Mitchel. A strong socialist candidate and a regular Republican completed the field. Hylan in particular hit the school issue hard. Labor unions drew effectively on stored-up anger against the capitalists, for the name of Elbert Gary was associated with the plan. Two Rockefeller employees, Abraham Flexner and Raymond Fosdick, were Gary Plan supporters on the New York Board of Education, a fact enabling its opponents to persuade immigrant parents that the plan's intent was to prepare their children for the factories. The presence of society ladies on the speaking platform in favor of the Plan did not help.

There were many sources of resentment against Mitchel and his administration. He seemed to favor the very wealthy; he had fought against raises for teachers and other city employees; inflation struck in 1917, sending food prices soaring, and his administration's response was unsympathetic and ineffectual. Mitchel campaigned on a preparedness ticket at a time when there was much antiwar sentiment.

The smoldering resentments flared up during the latter part of October 1917 in week-long riots centered in the schools of upper Manhattan, the Bronx, and Brooklyn. Primarily they were protests against the attempt at "Garyizing." Throughout the week children formed into mobs, going from school to school, trying to disrupt activities. Armed with sticks, stones, and bottles, they smashed windows, fought the police, and regrouped every time they were dispersed. Some of the worst of the disorders occurred in the Williamsburg and Brownsville sections of Brooklyn, where at the height of the trouble 10,000 children and their parents marched and demonstrated.

The disorders occurred in Jewish neighborhoods, and most of those arrested, as reported in the newspapers, bore Jewish names. Parental aspirations for children had been threatened by the Gary Plan, and deepseated resentment was elicited. The concept of community control was invoked. One newspaper reporter's account of an uproarious mass meeting during the strike included a paragraph that seems to sum up a great deal!

> One mother cried out from the platform against the Gary system, shouting: "We want our kinder to learn mit der book, der paper und der pensil (*sic*) und not mit der sewing and der shop!" Another aroused the parents with a vehement denunciation of what "they are doing mit unserer kinder. Dey are unserer kinder, not theirs." The law compelled them to send their children to school and when they had asked that this Garyizing not be done they were not listened to; but it was done (*The Globe and Commercial Advertiser,* October 18, 1917).[3] ■

3. Reprinted with permission.

Throughout our national history, conflicts produced by differences in religion, race, and ethnicity have been frequent and intense. It was inevitable that one of the sites of these battles would be the schools. It is a cliche to say that we are a nation of immigrants, but it is not a cliche to say that few people realize how the pluralism of our society has made schools frequent scenes of ideological battle. The 1954 desegregation decision, the fights in the sixties about "community control of schools," the acrimony that suffuses discussion of how to handle bilingualism, similar acrimony in regard to bias (racial, ethnic, religious, and sexual) in textbooks, and the ever recurring controversy about "prayer in schools"—these are the more recent versions of an old story, the central themes of which have been and still are: What are schools for? Who owns the schools? How do we change schools? The good old days were no better than the bad new days! There have been, of course, interludes of quiet between school and community, between school personnel and students. But they were interludes always broken by the eruption of some combination of religious, ethnic, and racial factors interacting either with large-scale immigration or with large-scale movement of groups from one part of the country to another. The culture of the school is not understandable apart from the social-history of the nation.

A lack of social-historical perspective is one of the major obstacles to a balanced understanding of the culture of the school and the problem of change. Another obstacle, almost the polar opposite of the social-historical perspective, is the tendency to explain phenomena in the school scene primarily in terms of the characteristics of individuals. As we shall see in the next section, explanations that are based on the characteristics of individuals may contain a kind of truth, but that truth is obtained at the expense of discerning regularities that persist despite individual variations in behavior and the passage of time.

THE LIMITATIONS OF A PSYCHOLOGY
OF THE INDIVIDUAL

What perspective should we adopt in trying to understand why schools are pressured to change in certain ways? Why is there so much dissatisfaction with the consequences of these efforts at change? Why are we at such a loss to explain this unhappy state of affairs? Why do we seem to have learned little from these experiences? I have suggested, in a very preliminary way, several interrelated ingredients that a comprehensive answer will have to take into account. The first was that we have not directly confronted the fact that our conception of what a school and school system are or should be is a derivative of our socialization into the society and its culture. The second ingredient, stemming directly from the first, was that "insiders" and "outsiders," however much they may differ about the goals and need for change, paradoxically (only on the surface) share the same picture and conception of what a school and school system are and should be. The third ingredient was social-historical: our conception of what schools and school systems are in the present has to be realistically judged and related to what they were in the past. The import of these ingredients is that we cannot understand where our conceptions come from by relying on a psychology of individuals, a focus that has been a major feature of American psychology. To illustrate what I mean let me describe a familiar situation.

NUMEROUS PEOPLE FROM A VARIETY OF FIELDS, PREVIOUSLY UNCONNECTED with schools, have approached a school or school system to do a study requiring the cooperation of children, teachers or both. Far fewer people have approached the schools with the specific aim of rendering some kind of service within the schools, requiring that in some way they become part of the school. In either case, one of the most frequent reactions they come away with is that the school is a "closed" place that views with marked suspicion any outsider who "wants in" in some way. The outsider feels he is viewed as some kind of intelligence agent whose aims, if not nefarious, are other than what he states. The adjectives that the puzzled outsider applies most frequently to school personnel are *insecure, uncooperative, paranoid,* and *rigid.* The adjectives vary, depending on how far beyond the principal's or superintendent's office the outsider gets. ■

Now let us ask this question: What permits the outsider to apply these characterizations? One factor is his or her inability to consider the possibility that the response of the school, far from being explainable in terms of the individual personality characteristics of the school person, *may* be based on a realistic and statistical appraisal of past experience. In the past the school (particularly the urban one) has "learned" that if a stranger comes into the school the odds are very high that when or after the stranger leaves, he or she will have some very unkind things to say. If this is the case, one could argue that the response of the school, rather than being pathological in any sense, indicates some good reality testing.

A second factor, related to the first, is the unquestioned assumption that the response of the school person is understandable only or primarily in terms of *that* individual's personality—the pejorative adjectives reflect an individual psychology. It rarely occurs to the outsider that the response of the school person reflects in some measure the fact that he or she is in a role that is characterized by duties and responsibilities and is defined by a complicated set of personal and professional relationships with many other people in the setting. The school principal, for example, no less than the outsider, is part of a social-professional structure that places constraints upon him or her independent of personality.[4] In short, the outsider responds as if his or her own knowledge about one's self and one's role in his or her own complicated setting has no bearing on how one understands and approaches the school.

There is a third factor that permits the outsider to respond in the way I have indicated, a factor that, when recognized, would make for a less personal response at the same time that it would facilitate an appreciation of the complexity with which one is dealing. I refer here to the fact that the response of the school person to the outsider is a frequent one to others *within the school culture.* The response of the school person to the outsider is not unique, but occurs frequently to those who represent other parts of the school system and who wish in some way to introduce a change of some sort into particular schools. Many school supervisory and administrative personnel talk about their experiences the way outsiders do about their experiences. The icing on this cake of vexation is that principals talk similarly about some of their teachers into whose classroom they may try to introduce some change.

Finally, of course, teachers frequently talk about their principals, supervisors, and administrators as uncomprehending, rigid, and uncooperative in matters of change. The outsider is unaware of the degree of kinship to those within the schools!

But why is the outsider unaware of this state of affairs? In my opinion the primary reason is that so many of us are intellectually reared on a psychology of the individual; that is, we learn, formally or informally, to think and act in terms of what goes on inside the heads of individuals.[5] In the process it becomes increasingly difficult to become aware that individuals operate in various social settings that have a structure not comprehensible by our existing theories of individual personality. In fact, in many situations it is likely that one can predict an individual's behavior far better on the basis of knowledge of the social structure and position in it than one can on the basis of his or her personal dynamics.

All that I am saying at this point is that when we say a setting is "organized," or that cultures differ from each other, we mean, among other things, that there is a distinct structure or pattern that, so to speak, governs roles and interrelationships within that setting. *What is implied, in*

---

4. A situation illustrating the identical principle is one in which the beginning undergraduate or graduate student blithely assumes that a full professor is a law unto himself or herself, operating under no constraints and perfectly capable, if he or she but willed to do so, to accede to any student request.

5. American psychology has been, from its formal beginnings a century ago, quintessentially a psychology of the individual organism. The consequences of this narrowness is the focus of my book *Psychology Misdirected* (1981).

addition, is that structure antedates any one individual and will continue in the absence of the individual. It may well be that it is precisely because one cannot see structure in the same way that one sees an individual that we have trouble grasping and acting in terms of its existence.

One aspect of structure will loom large in later discussion. What I have suggested up to now is that existing structure of a setting or culture defines the permissible ways in which goals and problems will be approached. Not so obvious, particularly to those who comprise the structure, is that existing structure is but one of many alternative structures possible in that setting and that the existing one is a barrier to recognition and experimentation with alternative ones. In fact, as Garner (1966) has so well shown and discussed in relation to visual and auditory patterns or structures, the response to any one pattern cannot be understood without considering the matrix of possible patterns from which the particular one was taken. Analogously, the significance of the structure of a setting has to be viewed in light of alternative structure. The ability to generate alternative structures, and the capacity to evaluate each alternative dispassionately in terms of the stated purposes of the setting, pose an extraordinarily difficult theoretical problem. For practical purposes it is a near-impossible one for most people because it confronts them with the necessity of changing their thinking, then changing their actions, and, finally, changing the overall structure of the setting. If the theoretician, in the quiet of his or her thoughts and office, finds this a complex task, one should be tolerant of those within the school setting who struggle successfully against change.

Let me briefly illustrate this point here because it is so central to what comes later in this book. On numerous occasions I have said the following to a variety of educators:

BEGINNING IN THE FIRST GRADE AND CONTINUING THROUGHOUT THE elementary and secondary school years, every child on every school day receives instruction and drill in the use of numbers. This is an amazing regularity within the school culture. I confess to not understanding why this is so. Why *must* first grade children be exposed to such instruction and drill? Why *must* arithmetic and mathematics be taught every year? For the child, teacher, and arithmetic supervisor (among others) arithmetic is a part of a highly structured day. I am tempted to say that it is an involuntary activity of each day but that would be quite wrong, because to everyone concerned that is the way it is and that is the way it should be. But are there no alternative ways of looking at arithmetic in terms of when or how often it should be taught? ■

The most frequent and prepotent response to these comments is to justify the existing regularity and to avoid anything resembling a dispassionate consideration of possible alternatives. In fact, my comments are not viewed as an intellectual task, but as criticism of the existing school culture and its formal workings. The way things are is the way things should be because alternative ways of structuring school life are seen, clearly or dimly, as requiring changes within individuals and within the structure.

A number of educators asked, "If I didn't teach arithmetic for a whole year, what would I teach instead?" That is an extremely important question because it implies that there is an existing "order" and alternatives to that order, but that the existing order is not explicitly understood or justified in light of the universe of alternatives in which the existing regularity characterizing the teaching of arithmetic is but one possibility.

In different ways in this chapter I have endeavored to illuminate one major theme: our conception of schools in terms of their purposes, structure, and functions has many sources among the most important of which is our own socialization into our society. Our conception is not only a matter of formal thinking, rigorous observation, and rational investigation, but largely a derivative of countless experiences that define for us what is right, natural, and proper. This is no source of concern, or of untoward consequences, as long as schools are perceived as congruent with our conceptions. Yet, not only has such congruence hardly ever been a characteristic of our schools during the last century, they have been under continual pressure to change. Under these conditions of pressure for change, the failure or inability to fathom the cultural sources of our conceptions have led to actions that have had disappointing outcomes. As a consequence of our disappointments, we remain imprisoned in conceptions that are based on assumptions that never get verbalized and, therefore, challenged. Today we may support this effort at educational change, tomorrow that one, or we may do both at the same time, but when we see that the more things seem to change the more they seem to remain the same, we direct blame outward because we cannot entertain the possibility that we, and those we blame, have basically the same conception of what schools are and should be. Precisely because they are such culturally determined conceptions it is extraordinarily difficult to see how they drastically restrict the universe of alternatives we permit ourselves to think about.

If our conceptions of what schools are and should be are culturally determined, that is not the only source of difficulty in comprehending the culture of schools for the purpose of changing them. In the next chapter we turn to other (related) difficulties that complicate the task of observing the school scene. And if we concentrate on the observer-critic from the university, it is because the university has never lacked for critics of our schools, and because these observer-critics have been very influential in spearheading efforts at educational change.

Chapter **3**

University and School Cultures

The attempt to gain perspective on the structural characteristics of the school culture, particularly as they have bearing on the processes and problems of change, runs headlong into the problem that the observer is not neutral. By virtue of the fact that the observer is personally part of a structure—be it in the school culture or in one outside of it—his or her perception and thinking are in various ways incomplete, selective, and distorted. In the normal course of living we do not deliberately adopt a stance that permits us to see clearly how our thinking and behavior are determined by the characteristics of the structure of which we are a part; that is, we do not see the characteristics of the structure independent of our particular place in it. Variants of this problem were the basis of some of the enduring contributions of Darwin, Marx, Freud, and Einstein. The position of an observer in relation to events is a problem that any theory or interpretation of those events must deal with explicitly. But as we shall now see, this is not something of which observers of the school culture have been willing or able to be aware.

THE OBSERVER FROM THE UNIVERSITY

Over the years some of the most vocal critics of the school culture have been found in our universities, particularly in the arts and sciences departments. It is unlikely that any aspect of what goes on in schools has escaped criticism. A partial list of such criticisms follows:

1. Textbooks and curricula tend to be dull and out of date.
2. Teachers are not well grounded in their subject matter.
3. Teachers do not make the learning experience stimulating and exciting.
4. Teaching is primarily a "pouring in" of knowledge rather than a "getting out" of interests, curiosity, and motivations. Put in another way, children learn for extrinsic rather than intrinsic reasons and rewards.
5. Teachers are too conforming, intellectually and personally, and resist new ideas and the need to change.
6. There are selective factors at work determining who goes into teaching. One of the consequences is that those who go into teaching tend, on the average, not to be as bright as those who go into many other professions.
7. Schools are over-organized settings, top-heavy with supervisors and administrators who are barriers to the individual teacher's initiative and creativity and not responsive to the needs of individual children.

What this list does not convey, what words can only inadequately reflect, are the disdain, heat, and emotion with which these criticisms are offered and surrounded—characteristics that, in other contexts, the university critic would say do not suggest the neutral observer or the quest for understanding. (It should, of course, be recognized that although strong emotion may be conducive to "weak" thinking, it does not necessarily invalidate the content of criticism.) There is one characteristic of these criticisms that is a more secure basis than emotion for suggesting that they may not be the consequences of dispassionate observation. I refer to the *shoulds* and *oughts* that are contained or implied in these criticisms. There is nothing inherently wrong in making value judgments. Difficulty arises when, as is usually the case, there is no explicit, objective statement of criteria by which to decide whether things are the way they ought to be, or whether the consequences of actions are consistent with the values to which they are supposed to be related. In the absence of such objective criteria the university critic, like those he or she criticizes, remains in a realm of discourse conducive to passion rather than to clarification, to the defense of values rather than to what constitutes their manifestation in behavior.

But we cannot get to the heart of the matter—in fact, we effectively obscure its recognition—by looking at the university critic as *an* individual who happens to hold to certain values and to think in certain ways. To look at the critic in this way—in terms of a psychology of the individual—would be identical to the way the critic looks at a school person like a teacher, principal, or supervisor; that is, as if the individual's behavior could be comprehended without considering that person's place in a structure of a particular subculture. Let us approach this problem by presenting a partial list of frequently expressed criticisms of the university culture:

1. College teachers have no training for teaching and are not very much interested in teaching (as compared with research). Their hiring and promotion have little or nothing to do with the quality of their teaching or the opinions of their students.
2. Most courses are dull rather than exciting affairs in which the student, usually in large classes, "takes in and down" what the instructor says and gives it back to him or her on examinations.
3. The needs, interests, and curiosities of individual students seem not to be the primary concern of the university, in part reflected in small amount of contact between student and faculty member.
4. College life is unrelated to "real life" and is an inadequate preparation for it. In addition, universities are unresponsive to the needs of the surrounding community.
5. The university has been amazingly successful in resisting change that might represent a break, small or large, with its traditions and accustomed style of functioning.
6. Universities are hierarchically and elaborately organized within both the faculty and the administration, so that several consequences are frequent: change is slow and diluted, bureaucratic struggle is ever present and exhausting, and "deviant" proposals and individuals tend to be screened out.

Those readers who are *not* members of a university faculty, will have noted some marked similarity between this and the previous list. Those who are, however, may maintain that the similarities are only superficial and divert one from the obvious differences between the university and the public school culture, by which is meant the superiority of the university as an educational institution. What is so noteworthy is that for many university people it is difficult, if not impossible, even to think seriously about possible similarities. As one colleague remarked, "You are comparing apples and oranges." *My colleague seemed unaware that from certain ways of looking at nature, apples and oranges are indeed comparable.* But to see them as comparable requires that one go beyond one's concrete or subjective or personal relation to apples and oranges.

Because of an inability to face the issue, and a subsequent resistance to the possibility of some marked similarities, the university critic unwittingly concedes the argument that his or her particular setting is organized and has a tradition, a structure, and vehicles for the attainment of goals. The critic assumes that his or her setting is not comprehensible in individual terms. When, however, the possibility of similarities is rejected between his or her and the school culture, the individual is, of course, confusing opinion, on the one hand, with the world of reality, on the other hand. As he or she so well knows, hypotheses should require validation, particularly when the hypothesis is, or will be, the basis for social action and change.

I wish to make three rather simple points. First, the university critic is part of a very complicated social system that, in diverse ways, determines his or her view of self and that system. Second, how a person views or observes the school culture will in large part be influenced by implicit and explicit conceptions of his or her own setting and one's place in it. Third, the university critic, like the rest of humanity, has extraordinary difficulty in viewing his or her culture independent of one's place in it (it is hard to "see" one's mother or father independent of the fact that one is their child). As a consequence of these points, when the university critic goes to the school culture he or she is very much like the traveller to foreign lands who begins by taking for granted that life elsewhere is truly different than in his or her own country and ends up proving it. That the "proofs" may in part be valid allows one's selectivity to go unchallenged and unnoticed.

One other factor has to be mentioned. It has to do with the critic's desire to change the school culture. On the basis of whatever observations are made he or she ends up with *shoulds* and *oughts*. The important problem here is that any suggestion for change implies two related considerations: first, that one has an explicit theory of institutional change, and second, that this theory is appropriately formulated for the setting in which the desired change will be effected. As I have already suggested, we have no firm basis for enthusiasm about the university critic's knowledge of the school culture or his or her own. I would maintain that the same is true about theories of change, which may be why a number of people feel that in the university and school cultures the more things change the more they remain the same. To illustrate the point:

ELSEWHERE (SARASON AND SARASON, 1969) WE HAVE DISCUSSED IN DETAIL some observations on the teaching of new math. As the reader may know, for some time before the first Russian Sputnik in 1957 there was a good deal of dissatisfaction with the teaching of mathematics in the public schools. The leadership of this dissatisfaction was primarily in the universities, and the content of the criticism took different forms. But on at least one point there was complete agreement—the way children were being taught math was an unmitigated bore and disaster that very few children could survive either in the sense that they experienced the joy of the world of numbers or pursued mathematics as a career. The Russian Sputnik catalyzed the effort to change the teaching of math, and various new maths were developed in university centers and introduced into the schools. After several years of the new math we observed the teaching of the new math in a number of classrooms in several school systems. As we pointed out, joy is the last word in the English language that one could apply to the children in those classrooms. We have also been told that the hoped for increase in math majors, proportional to the increase in the college population, has not occurred. ■

The new math was introduced into those schools without taking into account their structural and cultural characteristics, and without any discernible theory of how change was to be effected and the criteria by which its effects were to be evaluated—and we shall not dignify change by reason of faith, good intentions, and administrative fiat as constituting a theory of change.

THE CRITIC FROM THE SCHOOLS

It is not necessary to emphasize that whatever makes it difficult for the university critic to be a dispassionate observer of the school settings operates in identical fashion with school personnel. What is ordinarily not recognized by the university critic, however, is that the schools are, and have been in the past, far from devoid of critics from their own ranks, that the contents of some of their criticisms are very similar to those of the university critics, and that these school critics often have been in position of leadership and power. Why, then, have so many of their efforts been unsuccessful? And why has their morale been so poor? Why do so many of their efforts appear to others within the system to be as effective as shadow-boxing? In my experience the critic from the schools does not have an understanding of the school culture adequate to his or her efforts to change some aspect of it. That is to say, by virtue of immersion in, and relation to, the school culture he or she is ordinarily prevented from perceiving those characteristics fateful for the processes of change. Although I would agree with this, I am stressing another and more general point: the theory or problem of change is not in the focus of their thinking and *they would think and go about the change process as they did regardless of whether they were in the school or some other culture.* It is not that these people are antitheoretical or untheoretical, because many of them are quite sophisticated as to the theoretical bases for what should or ought to be. What their theories fail to do is to face the problem of how one gets to one's goals, i.e., to direct one to the kinds of actions one must consider, to alert one to the kinds of actions one must avoid, and to provide a basis for a realistic time perspective by which one's actions and goals can be judged. For a theory to be practical it has to have been formulated as a consequence of systematic efforts to understand and change the setting. That is to say, the theory emerges from and continues to reflect practice in the setting. That reality has so frequently and stubbornly refused to conform to our theories and categories of thought says more about the theorist's relation to practice (i.e., the lack of it) than it does about anything else. This is a point that John Dewey made abundantly clear in 1899 in his presidential address to the American Psychological Association. That address was titled "Psychology and Social Practice" and it was about education and schools. Dewey understood then, as few understand now, that theorists who are unconnected to practitioners, that theories that do not derive from practice, and that theories that do not change with practice are sources of confusion and disillusionment.

It is interesting that within the school culture there is at least one group that agrees with what I have been saying about the critic from the schools who is in a position to effect change. The classroom teacher, who so often is viewed as if he or she is a mechanical transmitter of change, can frequently be heard to say that the critic has "good" ideas but "bad" or impractical methods of implementation. Basically, the complaint of the teacher is that the critic really does not know the system to the degree that he or she is aware of obstacles and can adopt the means to deal with them. To the teacher, the school critic is impractical—he or she does not "know" enough in the sense of sheer knowledge or information. But in voicing this complaint the teacher unwittingly is underlining the significance of what is behind this impracticality: a theory that was incompletely or invalidly related to practice.

In focusing in the way I have on the critic from the schools I may well have diverted attention from what I consider to be a major barrier to our understanding of the school culture: the lack of systematic, comprehensive, and objective description of the natural history of the change process in the school. We have loads of anecdotes, and even more opinions, about the change process, but nothing resembling adequate description. What is troublesome is that what we do have is frequently misleading. For example, Lauter (1968) begins his description of his view of the Adams-Morgan Community School Project in this way:

ON MAY 18, 1967, THE DISTRICT OF COLUMBIA BOARD OF EDUCATION approved a memorandum prepared by the then Superintendent, Carl Hansen, which turned effective control of the Morgan Elementary School over to Antioch College. The memorandum provided that Antioch, with the advice of a "Parents' Advisory Board," would be able to select staff, determine curriculum, and allocate resources within normal budget allotments; a final staffing pattern and budget were to be worked out and approved at a later meeting. The memorandum did not accurately reflect the real agreement that had been made, neither in terms of its history nor the intentions of the parties to it. Another memorandum, prepared by the Vice-President of Antioch, Morris Keeton, and representatives of the Adams-Morgan Community Council, but never finally ratified by any body, spelled out somewhat more of the project's character. This document made clear that there were three parties to the agreement: schools, College, *and* Community Council; that decision-making power—within the general framework established by the law and the District of Columbia Board—was to be exercised by College and community somehow working "within a policy of consensus"; and that all parties contemplated launching a whole set of quite radical experiments over and above that of community participation.

The rather different pictures these documents convey reflect one of the fundamental problems of the Adams-Morgan Project: people with very disparate views and interests agreed to certain words on a page without revealing, or perhaps recognizing, that they assigned various meanings to the words. The general feeling seemed to be, "Let's get started, and we'll find out just what we're doing as we go along." The submerged differences and the haste were rooted in the history of the project and the structure of the neighborhood, but, I would suggest, the history of Adams-Morgan is indicative of the currents in urban education generally.[1] ■

Lauter then proceeds, in a refreshingly candid manner, to detail some of the problems encountered in a never-ending obstacle course. Lauter's description does more than demonstrate that his description and those of others are far from identical. For example,

. . . THE IMPETUS FOR OBTAINING A "COMMUNITY-CONTROLLED" SCHOOL lay with the whites from the first meeting on. Subsequent planning hardly involved the population "served" by Morgan school. Negro people in the neighborhood were told they might have a chance to run their school; but what, exactly that might mean beyond, presumably, an end to overcrowding and abuse of the children, no one could be very clear. No real program of community discussion or education was conducted; there were, to be sure, large general meetings and a campaign for petition signatures. But there was no sustained opportunity for people to discuss and compare their educational ideas and aspirations, to look at new programs, to talk about how children learn and what they might want from a school. Thus, people from different backgrounds proceeded with very different expectations, linked only by an overwhelming urgency to put the project into operation immediately or sooner. Suggestions for a year of planning or even for beginning with a small experimental unit were quickly rejected. People would lose interest, it was said, and would be disappointed in the promises of the Council. Begin

---

1. P. Lauter, "The Short, Happy Life of the Adams-Morgan Community School Project," *Harvard Educational Review* XXXVIII (1968): 236.

now at Morgan, some people whose children went to Adams said, and if things work out, expand to Adams next year. It was, unfortunately, such personal and political motives that established the context in which the school project was to operate.

It was not only the parents of most of the Morgan children who were excluded from the development of the program; so was most of the school administration. Negotiations were carried on, for the most part, with the Superintendent and one or two Board members in a semi-private fashion, but backed by the threat of the community's general anger at the schools. Plans were not considered by the Elementary and Research offices. (Indeed, the Superintendent called in his assistants only when the agreement had been reached.) This procedure might have been necessary to avoid bogging down in the school bureaucracy. On the other hand, it meant that many of the school officials felt absolutely no stake in the project; in fact, they harbored a good deal of resentment for it, at worst, and were very confused by its status, at best. Their tendency was not to bother the project if it didn't bother them, which provided a large degree of freedom, but also a great let-down of normal services.[2] ■

Let us assume that Lauter is correct, that at its inception there was not a meeting of minds as to the details of what was to be done or what was agreed upon. And now let us ask the following questions of his description: Were the disagreements explicit at the inception? If so, what were the contents of the disagreements? What was done to deal with the disagreements? What consideration was given, and by whom, to alternative ways of dealing with disagreements? What were the explicit ground rules for dealing with disagreements, or was the problem of ground rules never discussed and formulated? These questions are not answerable by Lauter's description. Without data relevant to these questions one is left with the strong impression that this was an ill-fated project that from the beginning was doomed to failure. One of the major values of an adequate description of what was done is that it might provide us with a basis for deciding what could have been done, and until one faces the fact that there are many alternatives the significance of what was done for future action is drastically reduced.

The problems involved in obtaining adequate descriptions in the natural setting are enormous, and we should disabuse ourselves of the notion that all that is involved is looking, recording, and reporting. I shall have more to say about this in later chapters. The point I would stress here is that until we have more comprehensive and dispassionate descriptions of the processes of change in the school culture—which, of course, would be

---

2. Ibid., p. 238.

revealing of the formal and informal structure of the school—any effort to introduce change maximizes the role of ignorance with its all too familiar consequences. In this respect my experience has not permitted me to distinguish between the critic from the university and the critic from the school.

THE UNTESTABLE ABSTRACTION

Thus far I have discussed three major barriers to our observing and understanding the school culture: (1) We put undue reliance on a psychology of individuals that, as C. Wright Mills (1959) has so clearly pointed out, is no adequate basis for studying structural characteristics of a society or one of its important parts. (2) Observers are not neutral, and what they observe about their own or someone else's setting is to an undetermined extent biased by the structure, traditions, and ideology of their own setting. (3) Particularly in relation to the school culture, our ignorance about how change occurs is vast.[3] Another barrier to which we now must come is what I shall call the well-intentioned but untestable abstraction. These are the "should be" and "ought to be" types of statements that refer to virtue and sin without any specification to the listener about criteria he can use to determine if actions based on these statements are consistent with them or not.

> The classroom should not be a dull and uninteresting place but one which brings out the *creativity* in children.

> The *potential* of children is not being *realized*. The classroom should be a place where self-actualization is constantly occurring.

> School systems in general, and classrooms in particular, are authoritarian settings. The *democratic spirit* must become more pervasive.

> Schools have become encapsulated settings within our society and unresponsive to it. They must become more *open*.

---

3. We have, of course, learned a great deal about schools in the past decade from formal evaluations of efforts at change (see Chapter 5). However, what we have learned is how *not* to go about trying to change schools. I do not underestimate the significance of learning what not to do or of what past failures tell us about the school culture. But neither do I want to overestimate how much that we have learned has significantly altered the substance and direction of educational change. It is, I believe, fair to say that we have learned a lot about why schools have not changed. We have learned much less about how they assimilate and sustain change.

Teachers are inadequately prepared for understanding ghetto children and culture. *Their training must be broadened if they are to become knowledgeable about and sensitive to these disadvantaged children.*

These types of statements can be multiplied interminably without exhausting the supply. Most people would probably nod assent upon reading or hearing them. What such ready assent obscures is that these types of statements are rarely elaborated in a way that tells one what observable consequences (in behavior, practices, or relationships) must be obtained in order to decide whether intent and action are consistent with each other. The problem, of course, is a very general one, by no means restricted to statements about the school culture. Sidney Hook (1966) has discussed the problem incisively in his essay "Abstractions in Social Inquiry."

WHAT THEN IS THE DIFFERENCE BETWEEN ANALYZABLE AND unanalyzable abstractions? To begin with we must observe that all meaningful terms are employed in sentences or propositions or statements. Indeed, it is only when a sentence or a proposition or a statement (I shall use these terms interchangeably) taken as a whole is meaningful, that its terms can be said to have meaning. When are sentences meaningful? Briefly, a sentence is meaningful if we know how to go about testing it, and what would constitute evidence tending to confirm it or refute it. If we know what would be evidence one way or another for our proposition, then we know what kind of situation to look for or construct (as the case may be). We then would know whether our proposition is probably true or probably false, or, when judgment has to be suspended, what kind of possible situation would be relevant to our inquiry. Every statement, then, which purports to be a true account of what is so or isn't, enables us by the use of certain rules or inference to derive other statements that direct us to do certain things and to make certain observations.

How, then, do we recognize that a sentence contains abstractions that are unanalyzable? Not by any special terms employed but, roughly speaking, by the inability of the speaker or writer to state at some point the conditions or situations in which certain observations can be carried out to test it. Let us consider a few illustrations:

(1) We often hear such expressions as "The will of the people is sovereign in the United States." This seems to have a meaning, for it is often affirmed or denied with some heat. Now as soon as we inquire what evidence can be advanced for this statement, perhaps someone will point to the fact that at certain periodic intervals municipal, state and national elections are held; that the results are more or less carefully tabulated; and that depending upon their outcome, one group of men or another is invested with certain powers of office. But now we observe an

interesting and characteristic thing. If this were the state of affairs which we would be prepared to accept as indicating that the sentence "the will of the people is sovereign" is true, there could hardly be any dispute about it for any protracted period of time. But the dispute continues even when there is no question about the existence of elections. It turns out that those who assert this proposition maintain that they mean something *other* than this or *more* than this. What is this other or additional meaning? Is it something of the same kind as election procedures, i.e., something about which by making experiments and observations we can come to a decision? Or is it something concerning which no statement of an empirical kind will be accepted as adequately expressing its meaning? In the first case, we are dealing with a legitimate abstraction, i.e., one which promotes intelligent discourse and makes possible the acquisition of knowledge. In the second, we are dealing with an unanalyzable abstraction, with nothing except a sound that has certain causes and effects.[4] ■

And now let us look at some "recommendations requiring action" from Conant's *The Education of Teachers* (1963).

PUBLIC SCHOOL SYSTEMS THAT ENTER CONTRACTS WITH A COLLEGE OR university for practice teaching should designate, as classroom teachers working with practice teaching, only those persons in whose competence as teachers, leaders, and evaluators they have the highest confidence, and should give such persons encouragement by reducing their work loads and raising their salaries.[5] ■

Some of the consequences of this "should be" type of statement are quite clear: there should be a contract between two agencies, the school system will designate the practice teacher, work loads will be reduced, and salaries will be raised. Quite clear. But what about the statement that the teachers to be designated ought to be "only those persons in whose competence as teachers, leaders, and evaluators they have the highest confidence?" How are we to decide if those chosen are those of whom Conant would approve? Would he be satisfied, as the statement requires him to be, with choices meeting the sole criterion that "they" (who are they?) say they have the highest confidence in the competence of the person designated? Are we to assume that Conant and those who will make the choices agree on a definition of competence?

---

4. Sidney Hook, *Reason, Social Myths and Democracy* (New Jersey: Humanities Press, Inc., 1966), pp. 14–16. Reprinted by permission of the publisher.

5. J. B. Conant, *The Education of American Teachers*, pp. 212, 213, 214. Copyright 1963 by McGraw-Hill Book Company, New York. Reprinted by permission of the publisher.

Let us take another of Conant's recommendations:

IF THE INSTITUTION IS ENGAGED IN EDUCATING TEACHERS, THE LAY BOARD
of trustees should ask the faculty or faculties whether in fact there is a
continuing and effective all-university (or interdepartmental) approach to
the education of teachers; and if not, why not?[6] ■

What is indisputably clear is that one group will ask a question of
another group—a point that is quite testable; that is, one group asks or
does not ask a question of another group. But what does Conant
mean—what does he want a lay board of trustees to mean—by an *effective*
all-university approach? I do not know of anyone who would oppose an effective approach, just as I know of nobody who is in favor of starvation.
One must know what Conant believes are the defining characteristics of an
"effective" approach, so that one can decide whether or not one agrees
with the characteristics so that, *regardless of agreement,* one knows how to
test for the presence or absence of these characteristics. It is the case with
many of Conant's recommendations that he is most clear about unimportant matters and most vague about the important ones. One more example:

TO INSURE THAT THE TEACHERS ARE UP TO DATE, PARTICULARLY IN A
period of rapid change (as in mathematics and physics), a school board
should contract with an educational institution to provide short term
seminars (often called workshops) during the school year so that *all* the
teachers, without cost to them, may benefit from the instruction. Such
seminars or workshops might also study the particular educational problems of a given school or school district. (No credit toward salary increases would be given.)[7] ■

With one exception this is a clear statement of what Conant thinks
should happen. The one exception is the phrase "may benefit from instruction." How are we to decide when and in what ways teachers benefit from
the instruction? How are we to determine that teachers may not be
benefiting at all? How are we to know when they are being adversely affected? Conant would probably be the last person to defend the statement
that the mere presence of a child in a classroom benefits that child. Are the
issues any different when the pupil is a classroom teacher in a seminar
taught by a member of a college faculty? As long as "benefit" remains
undefined, or defined in a way which defies testability, we indulge our
good intentions at the expense of clarity.

---

6. Ibid., p. 214.
7. Ibid., p. 213.

THE GREAT DEBATE AND A CHANGING SOCIETY

Conant—formerly president of Harvard, a respectable scientist, a statesman on the politics of science—was, unfortunately, victim of almost every source of error to which the observer and judge of the school culture is subject. In that respect, he was not alone two decades ago in "The Great Debate" about how schools should change and how teachers should be educated. Koerner (1959) and Rickover (1959, 1960) were among those others who were sharply critical of schools and teachers. Rickover, certainly not the most caustic or clamorous, was very clear about why he thought schools had the weaknesses they had:

1. The preparation of teachers in this country is notoriously inadequate as compared with programs for European teachers that provide liberal education for its teachers equal to that of our lawyers and other professionals.
2. Comprehensive multipurpose high schools with a variety of curricula from precollege preparation to vocational training impair the development of the talented.
3. Talented youth are not being identified and, therefore, few adequate provisions are made for them in the schools.
4. Although Dewey improved what was once too autocratic a relationship between teacher and child, he did great harm to our traditional curriculum through his great influence in establishing the "Progressive Education" movement.
5. We need national standards for children as well as for teachers. Local control impedes progress in education. "Everywhere in Europe there are uniform standards for educational goals, while the running and financing of schools is generally left to local initiative" (Rickover, 1960, p. 5).
6. The business of allowing children to choose elective subjects to be studied in high school is disturbing, permitting them to decide on programs that may negatively affect their futures.

To remedy the preceding weaknesses, Rickover suggested that the following changes are needed in our educational system: (1) homogeneous classes, (2) a return to rugged intellectual discipline in the curriculum, (3) attention to standards of excellence, and (4) an overhauling of teacher preparation programs with particular consideration given to a study of present certification laws in the various states.

To such criticism some educators countered charges of anti-intellectualism with the reiteration of what they saw as the philosophy of the modern school (Kelley, 1947):

1. Knowledge is not something that can be handed down on
    authority.
2. Subject matter taken on authority is not necessarily educative.
3. The best way to teach is not through the setting out of subject
    matter in unassociated fragments.
4. Education is not preparatory to life; it is life itself.
5. Working out purposeless tasks will not necessarily produce
    good discipline.
6. The answer to a particular academic problem is less important
    than the process.

At the same time this debate was picking up steam, the gathering storm that
we call the turbulent sixties was also picking up steam and would later give
an antique quality to the debate. The fact is that the so-called silent fifties
were not all that silent and it was already obvious to some people and agencies that changes were taking place in our urban settings that were already
impacting on schools, but with which schools seemed unable to cope (e.g.,
Marris and Rein, 1969; Sarason, 1978). It was, in fact, during the fifties
that Sarason, Davidson, and Blatt (1962) became sensitive to the obvious:
schools and communities were on a collision course with each other. They
open their book, *The Preparation of Teachers. An Unstudied Problem in
Education* (1962), with an appraisal of what was happening:

IT WOULD TAKE A BOOK OF FORMIDABLE SIZE TO PRESENT A COMPREHEN-
sive picture of what has taken place in and around our educational
system over the last decade or so. We say "in and around our educational system," because it has become clearer than ever before (perhaps
because it is truer now than before) that events and conditions outside
physical boundaries of the school profoundly affect the processes, goals,
and quality of education. We refer here to more than just the influences
of sputniks and the space age on education—profound influences, to be
sure, but far from being the only ones. Unprecedented population shifts
(south to north, east to west, etc.), predicted but still startling population increases, the influx of various emigre groups (Puerto Rican,
Cuban, Mexican), the eruption of the civil rights issue into the national
consciousness—these and other developments have had no less an effect
than sputniks and astronauts on what takes place in our schools. ∎

The participants, pro and con, in the debate were for all practical purposes
insensitive to what was happening, unable as they were to free themselves
from traditional conceptions of what a school and school system are and
should be, unaware that where they were in the social order was influencing
what they looked at and proposed, and oblivious to the need to inquire into
how *any* teacher preparation program related to the changing realities of

classrooms, schools, and school system. The point of the Sarason, Davidson, and Blatt book was that until we understood better the ways in which
school personnel were defining and experiencing problems in their daily
work—*not* the way the combatants in the debate were defining the problem
or how as outsiders they were experiencing schools, if they were
experiencing them at all—efforts to change and improve schools would
fail. It was not fortuitous that that book emphasized the practical
significances of the discomfort that school personnel experience in their interactions with parents or other community representatives. I do not want
to convey the impression that my colleagues and I saw clearly at that time
that the frequency, substance, and quality of school-community contacts
would change drastically, so drastically that the issues characterizing The
Great Debate would fade into the background and into the foreground
would come such questions as: Who "owned" the schools? What role
should the community have in educational decision making? How does one
exorcise racism from the curriculum and how does one introduce ethnic-
racial content with which students can identify? Should there not be an
alliance between neglected community groups and teacher unions seeking
more income and influence for their members? If our vision about the consequences of what we saw happening was vague and superficial, we never
were in doubt that the poor quality of interaction between school personnel
and "outsiders" would become an even more effective obstacle to many of
the efforts to change and improve schools.

In this and the previous chapter I have in different ways tried to illustrate some of the major culturally determined obstacles (not individual
or personality ones) we have to overcome if our view of schools and proposals for change are not to be unduly in error. More than that, the general
failure to recognize and confront these obstacles, and to overcome them if
only in part, is due to the fact that behind the diversity of views one finds in
educational controversies is a surprising similarity in the picture and conception of what a school and school system are and should be. Precisely
because of this shared but unverbalized similarity, people with apparently
very different views tend to be equally insensitive to changes in school-
community relationships until, so to speak, those changes hit them in the
face, i.e., the pictures and conceptions with which they started led to views
and conclusions that misled them and others. Finally, and fatefully, the
shared similarity in picture and conception of what a school and school
system are or should be, together with the faulty and incomplete information they provide about the problematic ways society impacts on schools,
and vice versa, give rise to conceptions of the change process that almost
always are self-defeating.

To make the major themes of this and previous chapters more concrete, I shall in the next one describe two efforts at educational change. As
we shall see, the issues surrounding the change process in schools are by no

means peculiar to those settings. In fact, I would argue, to the degree that we view the change process primarily in terms of the school setting, we set definite limits to our understanding of the ubiquitous nature of the process and its outcomes in our society. *Far from being peculiar to schools, the problem of change is the problem of every major institution in our society, and that fact alone suggests that our conceptions of institutional change have deep roots in the nature of our society.*

Chapter **4**

The Modal Process of Change

This chapter has two major purposes. The first is to describe two efforts at educational change: one in elementary schools and one in a university. It is all too easy to discuss and judge efforts to change schools without recognizing the possibility that one's conclusions may not be peculiar to schools, i.e., the characteristics of the change process, their implicit and explicit rationales, *may* be modal for *any* effort to change *any* institution. The object of the change may be a church, a business, a social agency, a governmental bureau, or any other tradition-rooted, socially complicated setting. What if efforts to change these settings are strikingly similar in process and outcomes to those that have schools as their objects? The fact is that if one only perused the vast literature on organizational change, one would be struck by many similarities in the way the problem of change is posed, the strategies employed, and disappointment expressed in the amount, quality, and viability of outcomes. But, above all, one would be struck by the simple fact that ours has long been a society in which *all* of its major institutions have been under pressure to change. That fact alone has very sobering implications, not the least of which is the possibility that one can never understand efforts at educational change independent of changes in other major social institutions. And it alerts us to the possibility that if we, as a society, are on balance dissatisfied with the outcomes of our efforts at institutional change, we must turn our attention to the cultural determinants of our theories of institutional change, those assumptions that seem so obviously correct that we are unable to take distance from them in order critically to examine them. In previous chapters I have identified one such assumption: that the boundaries implied in our picture and concept of a school and school system are realistic guides for efforts at educational change. That assumption is not only invalid for changing educational settings, but it has been an invalid assumption underlying theories of institutional change devoted to other major social institutions. We are now used to hearing that "everything is related to everything else," and there is a part of each of us that knows (with a lot of ambivalence) that that maxim contains a large kernel of truth. But our theories of institutional change have hardly taken that maxim seriously, and nowhere is that more true than in the rationales that have undergirded strategies for educational change.

It is beyond the scope of this book to compare theories of changing schools with theories of changing other major social institutions. Such a comparison would require another book. In this chapter I have a more restricted focus: to describe change efforts in two settings that in practice are far more fatefully intertwined than our strategies have recognized.

A second purpose in making this comparison is to indicate how institutional traditions transmit attitudes and concepts that facilitate all of the dynamics of the self-fulfilling prophecy; more specifically, how the elitist traditions of the university in blatant and subtle ways inculcate attitudes and conceptions in educators that render them vulnerable to disillusionment and resistant to change.[1]

It may be helpful if, before turning to the major foci of this chapter, I illustrate the point I have just made. The illustration does not concern an educational change, but it does concern a training practice that deserves far more critical scrutiny from those intent on educational change.

Over the years I have asked numerous students who have just finished their practice teaching to review that experience with the following questions in mind:

---

1. One must constantly keep in mind that, historically, colleges and universities would have no part of the field of education because it was generally assumed that teaching was an occupation that required no professional knowledge (Sarason, Davidson, and Blatt, 1962). The first "normal schools" for teachers in the nineteenth century were largely adaptations of the existing secondary school. The fact that normal schools developed outside the universities (resulting in an ever-widening intellectual and philosophical gulf between the two) is largely responsible for the heat accompanying educational debates then and now. As we shall see later in this chapter, the incorporation into the modern university of training programs for educators has hardly altered the second-class citizenship of the field of education in the university. In my experience, the degree to which faculty in university departments and schools of education identify with the scholarly and research traditions of the university, with the values by which worthiness is determined in the university, they regard the educational practitioner if not as unworthy then as inferior in status and accomplishment. This is not a matter of personality or morality, but of how one absorbs the culture of a setting, how the structure and dynamics of a setting have the intended effect of socializing its members to regard themselves and others in specified ways.

1. How much time did you spend in the classrooms adjoining the one you were in?
2. Did you meet and talk with the school principal? If so, how many times and for what purposes?
3. Did you meet the school psychologist? The school social worker? Other specialists in the department of pupil personnel services?
4. Did you meet the superintendent of schools? Supervisors?
5. Did you attend meetings of the board of education?

The results were unequivocal: the student teacher obtains an extraordinarily narrow view of what a school and school system are. But I do not use this illustration only to labor the obvious implications of the results for what they mean to teachers when they become full-time participants in the school culture, or what they might mean for people who seek changes in schools. I use this illustration because of what it suggests about the conceptions university faculty have of the role and institutional realities of teachers. It is a "picture" that is more in keeping with the role of the narrow technician than it is of the professional practitioner who has a broad conceptual *and* institutional framework within which his or her activities take on meaning and justify actions. It is a picture spatially and conceptually circumscribed, stemming from and reinforcing the view that the teacher is a kind of engineer who has a variety of methods to apply to a spatially restricted set of tasks. Finally, it is a picture that when accepted by the teacher (maladaptive as that picture is to the realities of being part of a very complicated social organization) tends to produce self- and role-derogatory attitudes. Those attitudes are implicit in the rationale of teacher training programs. We will meet this issue again as we turn to a description of two efforts at educational change.

THE NEW MATH

To anyone who was not an adult in 1957 it will be difficult to convey what a "narcissistic wound" the American pride experienced when Russia successfully launched its first Sputnik. The reactions were diverse and pervasive. One of these reactions was the opinion that our educational system was not training enough scientists and, perhaps more important, that its teaching techniques and curricula were effectively extinguishing students' interest in science and scientific careers. Even before the first Sputnik, a number of individuals and groups had voiced dissatisfaction with the teaching of mathematics in the public schools, and some had been working to develop new curricula, the contents and goals of which would prevent the student from being bored by numbers.

The most vocal critics, as well as those who were developing new curricula, were not indigenous to the school culture; they were mostly university people. The significance of this fact can be put in the form of two statements and one question:

1. One of the most important groups calling for change was part of the university culture.
2. There was nothing like a clamor for change from those within the school culture.
3. How did those in the university group understand this lack of clamor? Put more generally, to what extent was there explicit awareness that people in one subculture in our society wanted to introduce a change in another subculture?

The question, obviously, suggests that we are dealing with a problem that in principle has nothing to do with mathematics. As best as I can determine there was no realization on the part of the "change agents" that changing the content and techniques of teaching math may have involved them in the problem of institutional change. I may be guilty of slight oversimplification when I say that far from such a realization was the "engineering" way of thinking that seemed to characterize the formulation of the problem: a curriculum is developed, tried out, and revised; teacher's manuals undergo a similar process; and training and retraining institutes for teachers and other school personnel are developed. There is nothing wrong with this "delivery of curriculum" approach as long as one can assume that there are no characteristic features of the school culture that can interfere with stated objectives. Let me be concrete at this point by asking the readers to perform a *tentative* act of faith and assume that the following statements are correct:

1. The relation between teacher and pupil is characteristically one in which the pupil asks very few questions.
2. The relation between teacher and pupil is characteristically one in which teachers ask questions and the pupil gives an answer.
3. It is extremely difficult for a child in school to state that he does not know something without such a statement being viewed by him and others as stupidity.
4. It is extremely difficult for a teacher to state to the principal, other teachers, or supervisors that she does not understand something or that in certain respects her teaching is not getting over to the pupils.
5. The contact between teacher and supervisor (e.g., supervisor of math, or of social studies) is infrequent, rarely involves any sustained and direct observation of the teacher, and is usually unsatisfactory.
6. One of the most frequent complaints of teachers is that the school

culture forces them to adhere to a curriculum from which they do not feel free to deviate, and, as a result, they do not feel they can, as one teacher said, "use [their] own heads."
7. One of the most frequent complaints of supervisors or principals is that too many teachers are not creative or innovative, but adhere slavishly to the curriculum despite pleas emphasizing freedom.

If one assumes that these are some characteristics of the school culture, it becomes clear that introducing a new curriculum should involve one in more than its development and delivery. It should confront one with problems that stem from the fact that the school is, in a social and professional sense, highly structured and differentiated—a fact that is related to attitudes, conceptions, and regularities of *all* who are in the setting. Teaching *any* subject matter, from this viewpoint, is in part determined by structural or system characteristics having no intrinsic relationship to the particular subject matter. If this assertion is even partly correct, any attempt to change a curriculum independent of changing some characteristic institutional features runs the risk of partial or complete failure.[2]

But we are running ahead by talking of outcome. At this point one should bear three things in mind about the beginning context: (1) the stimulus for change came primarily from outside the school culture; (2) there was little or no attention to the characteristic regularities of the institutional culture and their possible social and psychological correlates; and (3) there seemed to be the unverbalized assumption that the goals of change could be achieved independent of any change in these regularities.

THE BEGINNING CONTEXT: THE SMALLER SOCIETY

Within the school system the impetus for change came from personnel with supervisory responsibilities for the mathematics curriculum and from those members of the board of education who had university affiliations. There are no grounds for assuming that any aspect of the impetus for change came from teachers, parents, or children. The teachers were not "hurting" because of the existing curriculum. In addition, at the point at which a decision to change was made there had been no formal attempt to inform or otherwise involve teachers. But the teachers did know two things: that a change was being discussed and contemplated, and that they, the teachers, were in on nothing.

---

2. The issue here is identical to one that has been raised in relation to the so-called "war-on-poverty"; that is, that certain aspects of the problem were a consequence of how certain institutions (e.g., the welfare system) viewed and serviced poverty groups, and that the expectation that these institutions could do a better job without some fundamental changes in their structure and culture doomed their "new" efforts to failure.

To a number of teachers this situation caused no particular upset or concern, not only because "that is the way things are," but also because "that is the way it ought to be." It did not occur to those teachers to question the process—to question the relation between the process and its possible consequences—and only a few of them raised an issue in terms of "courtesy." In a fundamental sense the teachers were not questioning their relationship to the process. Both the administrative personnel and the teachers seemed to agree on where decision-making should and did reside. They also agreed that bringing the teachers into the process would be a (desirable) matter of form rather than of substance.

Another group of teachers, albeit not clearly, questioned the wisdom of a process in which the knowledge and opinions of the classroom teacher were not utilized or solicited. Here, too, one did not get the feeling that the validity of the process was being questioned, but rather that the judgment of their administrative superiors was not held in high regard. I had the impression that if these teachers could have put different people into the decision-making role they would have been content, because those people would possess better judgment. The teachers were questioning the judgment of individuals and their relationship to the process. By and large, they accepted the nature of the system and its decision-making processes.

Needless to say, the mathematics supervisors also accepted the nature of the system and its decision-making processes. What is not clear is why they were so eager for a change. The teachers were not dissatisfied or clamoring for a change. Nor was there pressure from above to change the curriculum. Several factors seemed to be at work: the supervisors had various kinds of contacts with university settings where new curricula were being developed or the inadequacies of the old curriculum were under discussion; they were dissatisfied with the attitudes of children to math and their difficulties with the subject matter; and they very much wanted "to do good."

What I think deserves emphasis is that the supervisors, far more than teachers, knew more about and identified with the activities and values of the university culture. When one remembers that supervisors were once classroom teachers, that they sought to "rise above" that position, that in order to do so they had to return to the college or university for advanced graduate work, and that, in effect, promotion was determined by performance outside the school setting, then it is reasonable to assume that supervisors may identify with the activities, attitudes, and values of the university culture.

If this is true, as my experience indicates, it further suggests that supervisors will tend to view teachers as so many university people do: teachers as a group tend to be mediocre intellects, uninspired and unimaginative, and more often than not obstacles to, rather than facilitators of, progress. This hypothesis goes a fair way to understanding the lack of relationship of teachers to the decision-making processes. It is not only that supervisors have more decision-making power than teachers, or that they are higher up in the organizational chart, but that they tend to have values that, as they see it, come from sources different from those from which the values of teachers come. It is these values, as much as conflict arising from differing roles, that are frequently (and silently) at work.[3]

THE NATURE OF THE DIAGNOSIS

I am not aware that anyone at any time viewed the problem in terms of the following: a diagnostic process requiring a description of "symptoms"; the differing significances that could be attached to any one symptom or combination of symptoms; possible alternative explanations (differential diagnosis); the relationship of any explanation to remedial tactics; and the investigative procedures to gain new information that would support the diagnostic formulation on which one will act. Diagnosis is problem-locating, problem-solving, decision-making, and action-producing based on processes subsumed under such terms as calculation, reflection, and conceptualization. But what is often taken for granted and, therefore, left unsaid is that diagnosis requires the awareness that one is engaged in processes that are intellectually demanding precisely because of people's capacity to think and do foolish things. And, it should be emphasized, diagnosis as a process requires sensitivity to alternative explanations, a sensitivity that acts as a control against narrow, oversimple thinking.

The decision to change the curriculum did not reflect this awareness of these processes. The diagnosis went something like this:

THE PRESENT CURRICULUM IS ANTIQUATED AND DOES NOT REFLECT NEWER or different ways of thinking about or using numbers. It erroneously assumes that young children are not capable of learning important

---

3. My observations in a variety of school systems suggest the hypothesis that the greater the discrepancy between the values of the teachers and those of the supervisors, the greater the conflict between them, or the less likely they are to talk to each other, or the poorer the morale of teachers. I have seen instances when the supervisors, far from sharing the values of the university, had an anti-university stance and experienced little or no conflict with teachers. I am quite aware that the issue is far more complicated than I have stated, and, of course, I am not suggesting that the presence or absence of conflict is inherently good or bad. My comments are intended not for the purposes of convincing the readers or proving a hypothesis but rather to suggest that in the school culture the change process and its outcomes cannot be understood only in terms of differing roles and responsibilities, but in terms of values and attitudes and their sources. I also want to emphasize that values are not intrinsically related to roles, but they frequently have their source in roles characteristic of settings other than the school. In regard to the problematic nature of the teacher-supervisor relationships in the school culture and an approach to improve it, I strongly recommend Goldhammer's (1969) *Clinical Supervision*.

mathematical concepts. It works against understanding by virtue of its emphasis on drill and rote memory. It tends not only to extinguish interest in mathematics but also to produce negative attitudes toward the subject matter. Because mathematics is so basic to understanding of, and performance in, all the sciences, and is increasingly important in vocational adaptation in the modern world of science and technology, the negative aspects of the present curriculum have consequences beyond a particular subject matter. ∎

I should emphasize that we are not concerned here with the validity of the diagnostic formulation. The significance of the formulation resides in two interchangeable words: *it* and *curriculum*. It is not a diagnostic formulation that says something about teachers or the teaching process. In no explicit way does it say teachers are related to the condition requiring change. What the formulation states is that "it" must be changed; "it" is the etiological agent without which the condition would not exist; and if "it" changes, the condition would be ameliorated, if not cured. My point is a simple one: there is nothing in the formulation that would *require* involving teachers for the purposes either of getting new or more information before a decision is made, or of discussing the contribution of teachers to the presenting symptoms.

As I indicated in the previous chapter, what I am describing could not be more antithetical to the position of John Dewey in regard to theory-practice, theoretician-practitioner dichotomies. I discuss Dewey's position in greater detail in my recent book *Psychology Misdirected* (1981). (Indeed, that book is dedicated to Dewey because he saw so clearly and alone that the social sciences generally, and psychology and education in particular, were creating dichotomies that not only would contribute to failure but to harm as well.)

As I indicated earlier, teachers could have been involved on the basis of *courtesy,* a word reflecting considerations of tact, style, ethics, and morality. That basis for involvement is quite different from one that demands involvement by virture of the way the problem is formulated. The point I am making is identical to a problem of which researchers in recent years have become aware. If, in *thinking* about a psychological experiment with humans, one never realizes that the attitudes of the subjects to the experiment and the experimenter will in some way be related to the results, one cannot take steps that will protect one against overinterpretation of results or simply getting results that are not explainable. If one is aware of the problem—if it is part of one's way of conceptualizing problems—one takes certain actions because the way the problem is formulated *demands* them. This is quite a different basis for action than if one thinks in terms of courtesy toward the human subject, the obligations of the experimenter, or the rights of the subject.

However, in the particular case I am attempting to describe, the diagnosis that was made public did not contain a factor that was contained in the private diagnosis of some of those pushing for change, and we now turn to a discussion of that factor. As so frequently happens in the communication of clinical diagnoses to patients and their families, there was much that deliberately was not said aloud.

THE NONPUBLIC ASPECT OF THE PROBLEM

At least some of those pushing for change were of the opinion that not all of the inadequacies of the old math resided in the old math *as such,* but also reflected inadequacies of many teachers.[4] The least insulting opinion was that the inadequacies were consequences of teacher training—they were not given the appropriate attitudes toward, and conceptualizations of, productive learning and the goals of the educative process. The more insulting opinion was that selective factors work against the "best" people going into public school teaching. I use the word *insulting* because those who held either or both of these views knew that if they were expressed, teachers would understandably feel insulted. *The important point is that this nonpublic aspect of the formulation of the problem put into different perspective what could be expected to be accomplished by substituting one curriculum for another.*

There were, of course, those who seemed to believe that the problem was the curriculum and that changing it would have all kinds of desirable consequences. But even these people recognized that going from an old to a new curriculum—involving in this case subject matter that would be new to teachers—would require some retraining of teachers. One can change the curriculum in American history drastically, but the teacher is still dealing with familiar facts and concepts (e.g., Civil War, Constitutional Convention, etc.). The proposed change in the math curriculum was qualitatively of a somewhat different order because for many teachers what they had to learn and then teach was truly new.

All were agreed that teachers would for a time become pupils again and learn the new math. No one formulated the problem as one requiring teachers to *unlearn and learn*—to give up highly overlearned ways of thinking at the same time that they were required to learn new procedures and new ways of conceptualizing. To state the problem in this way would require, at the very least, the acute awareness that one must make explicit and examine the degree to which one's theory of change takes account of the

---

4. This view was not peculiar to the individuals in this particular system. It was also the view of many university people, who viewed the general and specific training programs for teachers as an unmitigated disaster (Sarason, Davidson, and Blatt, 1962).

important social and psychological dimensions that characterize the setting. Such awareness was clearly not present.

THE CURRICULUM AND THE TRAINING WORKSHOPS

Once the decision to change the curriculum was made, a series of meetings was held to decide which of several curricula should be adopted, and to determine the time and length of the training workshops for teachers. At this point some classroom teachers became part of the working groups. I do not know how those teachers were chosen. But in formal and informal ways all teachers came to know that the curriculum was to be changed beginning the following September, approximately seven calendar months from the time the decision was made.

Teachers seemed to react in one of two ways, sometimes in both ways. On the one hand, they were caught up in the enthusiasm surrounding the change and looked forward to the stimulation expected from what was intellectually novel and prestigeful; on the other hand, they became increasingly anxious as it became increasingly clear that the new math was indeed new (to most of them), that learning it to a criterion of security was not going to be easy, and that summer workshops of five weeks duration might expose their insecurity and, in the case of some, their inadequacy.

The summer workshop took place in an atmosphere of tension and pressure. One might characterize what went on by saying that the teachers were taught (by supervisors and outside experts) in precisely the same ways that teachers had been criticized for in their teaching of children. There was little sensitivity to the plight of the teachers—they were being asked to learn procedures, vocabulary, and concepts that were not only new but likely to conflict with highly overlearned attitudes and ways of thinking. Many of the teachers were unable to voice their uncertainties and lack of understanding. *The pressure and tension stemmed not only from being in a group-learning situation with peers, but also from the scary knowledge that in several weeks they would have to teach the new math to their pupils.*

The energy output of the teachers, at the workshop meetings and at home, was somewhat awesome. The more anxious they became, the harder they worked to try to master the material, all the time asking themselves that if *they* were having difficulty what would their pupils experience?

But the content and depth of feelings could only indirectly reach the surface in workshop activities for two major reasons: (1) the teachers perceived themselves as pupils whose job it was to learn what the teacher was presenting, and (2) the workshop teachers perceived themselves as imparters of knowledge and overseers of skill training. In short, both teachers and pupils in the workshop implicitly agreed that personal attitudes and feelings, as well as the nature of the relationship between pupil and teacher, was not an inevitable part of the educative process and, therefore, had little or no claim to workshop time—despite the fact that these factors were impeding productive learning. What was going on in the workshop also characterized the relation between these people outside the classroom, as well as the relation between the classroom teacher and her children.

At this point I am not suggesting anything concrete about the workshop—what might have been done, how it might have been conducted, etc. The sole point I am making is that within the workshop or the classroom, or in other types of relationships within the school culture, there is a conception of learning that makes it next to impossible to take account of factors *that are always present.* One might wish that they were not present or would go away, or hope that they were not important, or hope that they had facilitating effects (as they sometimes do). Hopes and wishes aside, they are inevitably there, and to fail to take them into account is to avoid reality, which many of us in education apparently do rather well.

THE SCHOOL YEAR AND THE PROBLEM
OF SUPERVISION

It had been expected that teachers would need help and support once the school year began, and these were to be provided through individual meetings with the math supervisors, as well as group meetings. Two things became clear to the supervisors after the close of the workshops. First, the number of supervisors was inadequate to meet the individual needs and problems of the teachers. Second, the supervisors had seriously underestimated the difficulty teachers would have learning the new material to a degree of mastery comparable to that they had attained with the old curriculum.

Even with the old curriculum, individual help to, or observation of, the classroom was virtually impossible. As in most suburban school systems there was one supervisor and perhaps one or two persons part of whose duties was to assist the supervisor. When one remembers that in the case we are describing there were eleven elementary schools, it is clear that individual supervision was and would be a rare occurrence.

It is worth emphasis that in the school culture supervision rarely means observing and working with the classroom teacher. But, one may ask, is not this type of supervision the responsibility of the principal of the school? We shall take up this question later. At this point in our discussion I wish to point out that even if one assumes that individual supervision was primarily the responsibility of the principal, he or she was not, in the case of the new math curriculum, competent to perform the task; that is, the principals of the schools were no more knowledgeable about the new curriculum than were their teachers. If, as we have discussed elsewhere (Sarason et al., 1966), teaching is a lonely profession, it became even more so with the introduction of the new math curriculum.

For the purposes of this chapter it is not necessary to describe in detail what happened during the year. Teachers generally were anxious, angry, and frustrated; many children were confused and many parents began to raise questions about what was going on and about their own inability to be of help to their children; parent workshops were organized. It was an unsettling year for practically everyone involved.

It was inevitable that all of those who participated in, or were affected by, the unfolding social drama would, at some point, "explain" what happened or was happening, a polite way of saying that blame assignment would be an important issue and topic of conversation. Of all the participants (administrators, supervisors, principals, children, parents, and teachers) the teachers were in the center of the stage. In a real sense, they were the actors and the rest were audience. It is not surprising, therefore, that the teachers were the chief recipients of blame. No one viewed the situation as the consequence of processes taking place in and characterizing a particular social organization, or as reflecting conceptions (implicit or explicit) about the nature and structure of the settings that determine how the change process will be effected.[5] Some teachers were dimly aware of what had happened and was happening, but even among them one sensed that they were interpreting the situation as reflecting some inadequacy on their part. Put in another way: *many teachers agreed with the diagnosis that indeed they were largely to blame.* It is not surprising that teachers should have tended to view themselves as they thought other people viewed them.

SOME OUTCOMES

Approximately ten years after the new math was introduced into American schools, and by virtue of our rather intimate involvement in classrooms in a variety of school systems during that period, an informal observational study of the teaching of the new math was done (Sarason and Sarason, 1969).

---

5. An analogous situation would be one in which one would go about trying to understand strange behavior in a child as if it existed in the child independent of the most important settings (e.g., home, school) in which he or she lives. In other words, one would view the child as if he or she was not part of highly structured settings that in different ways are related to the child's behavior, both in the past and present. In addition, if one held such a view and one wished to change this behavior, one's actions would be quite different than if one viewed the behavior as reflecting something about the child *and* the structured settings of which he or she is part.

OVER A PERIOD OF SIX WEEKS WE OBSERVED SIX CLASSROOMS, TWO IN EACH of three school systems, during those hours in which math was taught. Only sixth grade classrooms were chosen. In each of the three schools there were two sixth grade classrooms. Each classroom was observed at least three times a week. Principals and teachers rearranged schedules so that the two classrooms in each school could be observed on the same day. In two schools the School Mathematics Study Group (SMSG) program was used while in the third school they were using the Addison-Wesley program. In all schools the SMSG program had been used in the previous grades. ■

All three school systems were suburban and the intelligence level of the pupils was well above national norms.

It will be recalled from an earlier section of this chapter that one of the bothersome features of the old curriculum was that children did not *enjoy* the world of numbers; they found it dull, unstimulating, and a chore. To use more modern parlance: rather than being turned on to, the children were turned off from, mathematics. We now turn to the most dominant impression of the observers of the new curriculum:

. . . THE TWO OBSERVERS CAME AWAY WITH THE IMPRESSION THAT ENJOY-ment was one of the last words they would use to characterize their impressions of the feelings of the children. Struggle was certainly one way of characterizing what was going on but it was not that kind of intellectual struggle which generates its own sources of internal reinforcement or elicits such reinforcements from others—in this case the teacher. At no time in our discussions did any of the six teachers say anything which disconfirmed our opinion that neither children nor teachers enjoyed what they were doing in the sense of feeling intellectual excitement, a desire to persist, and a joy of learning. One had the overwhelming impression of a task having to be done not because children desired to do it but because that is the way life is. Using the "joy of learning" as a criterion there appears to be no difference between new and old math.[6] ■

In light of the observations made in this study the authors conclude that the goal of attracting more students to mathematics as a career would not likely be achieved:

6. E. K. Sarason and S. B. Sarason, "Some Observations on the Teaching of the New Math," in *The Yale Psycho-Educational Clinic: Collected Papers and Studies,* ed. S. B. Sarason and F. Kaplan, Monograph Series (Boston: Massachusetts State Department of Mental Health, 1969), p. 99.

IT IS FAIR, WE THINK, TO SAY THAT ONE OF THE MAJOR AIMS OF THE NEW
math concerned not only schools and children but our entire society in
the sense that the new math was viewed as one important way of helping
to produce more and better mathematicians and scientists because that is
what our society was viewed as needing. If our observations and those
of others have validity and generality, one would have to predict that
the goal of more and better mathematicians and scientists (relative to the
total population)—or the number of college students majoring in math
and physics—will not be met. If so, we will have another sad example of
how the more things change the more they remain the same.[7] ∎

It is perhaps too charitable to conclude that "the more things change
the more they remain the same," if only because so many people continue
to be unaware that basically nothing has changed; in addition, and perhaps
more to the point, many of those who are aware that intended outcomes
have not been achieved have no clear understanding of the factors contributing to failure. It is unlikely that in the future we will be spared the
development of newer curricula, that is, new programs, attractively bound,
surrounded by evangelism and the spirit of reform, and unrelated to the
realities of the school culture.[8]

Alfred North Whitehead (1929), in his 1916 presidential address to the
Mathematical Association of England, said of curriculum change:

THIS QUESTION OF THE DEGENERATION OF ALGEBRA INTO GIBBERISH, BOTH
in word and in fact, affords a pathetic instance of the uselessness of
reforming educational schedules without a clear conception of the attributes which you wish to evoke in the living minds of the children. A few
years ago there was an outcry that school algebra was in need of reform,
but there was a general agreement that graphs would put everything
right. So all sorts of things were extruded, and graphs were introduced.
So far as I can see, with no sort of idea behind them, but just graphs.
Now every examination paper has one or two questions on graphs. But I
wonder whether as yet we have gained very much. You cannot put life
into any schedule of general education unless you succeed in exhibiting
its relation to some essential characteristic of all intelligent or emotional
perception. It is a hard saying, but it is true; and I do not see how to
make it any easier.[9] ∎

---

7. Ibid., p. 107.

8. There have been some rather scathing criticisms of new curricula in the different subject
matters, in terms of both their underlying conceptions and their outcomes (e.g., Fehr, 1966;
Ausubel, 1967; Weinberg, 1965; and Greenberg, 1967, pages 38–39). My own position is very
similar to that expressed by Epstein (1964).

9. Alfred North Whitehead, *The Aims of Education* (New York: Mentor, 1929), p. 19.

I have endeavored to describe and discuss the modal way in which changes are introduced into the school culture. In characterizing the process as "modal" I am quite aware that I am expressing an opinion; that is, the characterization is not derived from a number of descriptions (mine and others) that are compellingly similar. I would also not argue with the criticism that the description I have presented is neither complete nor systematic. As I indicated earlier, I am less concerned with the absence of relevant description than I am with the failure to recognize and state the problem.

Obviously, we cannot have relevant descriptions and studies until we recognize that the description of the change process involves, or is based on, the most fundamental (and unchallenged, if not unverbalized) assumptions determining three general types of social relationships: those among the professionals within the school setting, those among the professionals and pupils, and those among the professionals and the different parts of the larger society. Any proposed change—be it the new math, the new physics, busing, decentralization, etc.—affects and will be affected by all of these types of social relationships, and that is precisely what is neither stated nor faced in the modal process of change in the school culture.

The goals of change, the outcomes sought, surely are not to see if it is possible to substitute one set of books for another, change the racial composition of a class or a school, or have children read or listen to black or Mexican history. Those possibilities are relatively easy to realize, and I have seen them realized in precisely the same way as in the case of new math, with precisely the same outcome: the more things change the more they remain the same.[10]

Realizing these types of possibilities simply begs the question of their *intended consequences,* and in these as well as in other instances the intended consequences—the basic goals and outcomes—always intended a change in the relationships among those who are in or related to the school setting. But these intended consequences are rarely stated clearly, if at all, and as a result, a means to a goal becomes the goal itself, or it becomes the misleading criterion for judging change. Thus, we have the new math, but we do not have those changes in how teachers and children relate to each other that are necessary if both are to enjoy, persist in, and productively utilize intellectual and interpersonal experience. If these are not among the

---

10. My colleague, Richard Murnane, has made the observation that in occasional reports of school changes that were successful there is the tendency to focus on "mechanical" factors such as curricula and staffing ratios, and to neglect to report that the participants did respond to issues of institutional change. That is to say, in writing up what happened the power struggles always associated with institutional change are either forgotten or slighted. "Success stories" are written up long after the change was initiated and, although it is understandable that early struggles and issues can lose their intensity and salience, it nevertheless can give an incomplete and distorted explanation of the outcomes.

intended consequences, then we must conclude that the curriculum reformers have been quite successful in achieving their goal of substituting one set of books for another.

THE MODAL PROCESS OF CHANGE: AN EXAMPLE
FROM THE UNIVERSITY

Why has it been so easy for intended consequences to be stated, when they are stated at all, in vague and untestable language? Why do so many efforts at change unknowingly proclaim abysmal ignorance of the social structure within classrooms and schools? Is it possible to effect a significant educational change in a classroom or school without changing regularities therein? To what extent do the most vociferous and powerful-prestigeful critics of our schools (and I include our curriculum reformers here) differ fundamentally from those they criticize? Is it an oversimplification to say that efforts at educational change have been based on an asocial theory of human behavior, just as American human psychology was based, for years, on rigorous, ingenious, systematic, "objective," sterile, and irrelevant studies of the Norway rat (Beach, 1950)?

The purpose of these questions is to focus attention on the thought content of those who view themselves (or find themselves) as agents of change, that is, their planning, anticipating, decision-making, problem-solving, and tactical behavior. But it would be unduly confining, and even misleading, if we were to focus on the agent of change only in relation to the public school setting because, as I pointed out earlier, it may very well be that the individual's conception of the change process is to an important extent independent of one's knowledge of the school setting. "They would think and go about the change process as they did regardless of whether they were in the school or some other culture."

If this is true, then one's knowledge and understanding of a particular setting or subculture (e.g., the public school), however important that is (and it *is* important), becomes somewhat less crucial than one's generalized conception of the change process. What then becomes more understandable is the frequency with which we find persons who possess a good deal of knowledge and understanding of the culture of a particular setting but who, when they try to change it in some important way, fail disastrously.

In previous chapters I stressed the importance of the degree of one's understanding of a particular culture for how one goes about introducing change. In this chapter, however, I stress a somewhat different, and more significant, point: depth of understanding or familiarity with a setting may have no intrinsic relationship to one's conception of the change process. One may know a good deal about schools, and much of it may be both factual and truthful, but it does not follow that such knowledge confers any validity on one's conception of how to change schools. (We know, for example, that individuals may have understanding of why they are what they are without being able to use this understanding for purposes of change.) If only because the change process arouses different reactions in different people (and between and among groups), has different meanings for different people, brings to the fore infrequently expressed reactions, and arouses all kinds of protective and defensive attitudes, one cannot assume that the usual knowledge one has of schools is a sufficient basis for conceptualizing what the change process will create and encounter. *By its very nature the change process creates and encounters obstacles not ordinarily observed in the prechange period.*

I shall try to illustrate my point by a concrete example in which the outside critics of the school culture attempted an educational innovation *in their own bailiwick:* the university culture, with which they had great familiarity.

AN EDUCATIONAL INNOVATION IN A UNIVERSITY

Shortly after the first Russian Sputnik—in the context of much national breast-beating, wounded pride, and fantasies of national decline—a major university (Yale) initiated a new program for the training of secondary school teachers. The major force behind this move was the president of the university, who had achieved attention on the national scene because of his criticisms of the usual teachers' college programs. His major criticisms were familiar ones: there was an excessive emphasis on so-called technique or "how to do it" courses; teachers did not have a deep enough grasp of the subject matter they had to teach; and the training of teachers tended not to take place in the context of the traditions of the liberal arts (i.e., the arts that "liberated" the mind of humanity from the shackles of old ideas, dogma, and static practices). It should be obvious that the specific criticisms of the old math discussed in the previous chapter were variants of these more general statements.

One criticism was never made as explicit as the degree of importance attached to it by the local and national university critics; namely, that the usual teacher training programs were stifling and technique-oriented and did not attract the best students. On the contrary, it was maintained, the best students were driven away from any consideration of a teaching career. A major goal of the proposed program at this university was to attract the best students from the best liberal arts colleges and universities, deepen their knowledge and intellectual horizons in the subject matter they wanted to teach, give them a bare minimum of the usual "how-to-teach-it-courses," and provide them with practice-teaching experiences under supervision.

As in the case of the new math, the faculty in no way clamored for this new program. *In fact, not too long before the new program was proposed the faculty had warmly approved the president's decision to eliminate the department of education because it was considered alien to the scholarly and research traditions of the university.*

There were two major reactions among the faculty to the proposed program when it was presented to them for discussion and vote. Some could not care less what happened as long as the university did not give education anything resembling an important status. Among those voicing this reaction, a significant number would have preferred that the university do nothing, but if a token gesture would keep the president happy (and it was recognized that he was strongly interested in education) they felt that their approval of the program was not a high price to pay. The second major reaction was more positive because people in that group saw the program as fulfilling an obligation of a university to the larger society in a manner consistent with its traditions (*including that of noblesse oblige*); that is, the students would be of high quality, they would take the regular courses in the area of their special interests, and they would be treated and evaluated like any other student in the university.

As in the case of the new math those few people who took responsibility for the program concerned themselves almost exclusively with "organizational" issues. Unlike the new math there was not going to be a new curriculum; very little new was going to be taught or changed because the existing courses were considered to be precisely what prospective teachers needed. What existed, unlike the old math, was in principle what was to be protected. One might say that the content of these courses and the quality of relationship between student and instructor were the kinds of criteria the proponents of the new math would have liked to have seen met in the public school classroom.

Readers will recall that in the case of the new math no one anticipated that a process was being started that could engender hostility and resentment; that is, the conception of the process did not permit awareness that when people are asked or required to change, a part of them will resist changing, and if such resistance is then reacted to as incomprehensible human perversity, the level of hostility increases. In the case of the university, the situation was different in that one had to be deaf, dumb, and blind (and in a fatal coma) not to know that the new program was being initiated in a setting very hostile to anything resembling the field of education, particularly the training of teachers. What conception of the change process did the proponents of the new program have, and how did that conception help them anticipate problems and take steps to prevent or minimize their occurrence and consequences?

Let us first note that they did nothing to handle the problem of a hostile atmosphere. I really cannot say what conception of change was in the minds of these people, but I have no evidence to contradict the statement that they neither faced the problem nor deliberately took steps to ameliorate it.

There is no reason to believe that their conception of change *required* that they develop vehicles for dealing with the problem. Similarly, there is no evidence that they thought through the subtle and not so subtle ways in which the purposes of the program could be subverted. For example, since the students in the new program would be enrolled in existing courses, and since some of the instructors were likely to be among those who looked with disdain on education and educators, could this have untoward effects on the students? Would they be regarded as second-class citizens? Would they be differently evaluated? Would they be given similar opportunities to participate in courses? Prejudice, be it in relation to race, status, or occupation, does not operate differently in college teachers than among any other group.

Theory of the change process is helpful to the extent that it says not only what would happen but also what could happen under certain conditions. Theories are practical, particularly in relation to the change process, because they tell what one has to think and do, and not what one would like to think and do. A theory of the change process is a form of control against the tendency for personal style, motivation, and denial of reality to define the problem and its possible solutions along lines requiring the least amount of personal conflict.

When we were describing the introduction of the new math we emphasized the inordinate significance attached to substituting one set of books for another. It would, perhaps, be more correct and fair to say that as the change process started, more and more hope and faith had to be placed in the new curriculum (a book with hard covers) as the major agent bringing about desired outcomes. In the case of the new university program there never seemed to be much doubt that the curriculum (a collection of courses) would have the desired outcomes: intellectual stimulation for the students, deeper grasp of subject matter, a greater feeling of confidence in the teaching situation, and, as a final consequence, models of what secondary school teachers should be. Put more briefly, the emphasis on subject matter courses would have a very positive transfer of training effect in the classroom situation.

I should warn that, as in the case of the description of the introduction of the new math, my description of the new teacher training program is undoubtedly far from complete as a description of a process. In the case of the new math my justification for attempting a description stemmed from the obvious failure of the change to achieve its intended outcomes—the simple idea that failure must have a history and in some ways reflect what people thought or did not (could not) think, what people did or did not do. And so the question: Is it possible that failure was in large part contained in the statement of the problem and conceptions about the processes of solution? Let us now turn to some data which are the justification for discussing the new university program.

SOME SERENDIPITOUS DATA ON OUTCOMES

In 1968 a study was done at Yale by A. G. Levine (1968) with the title "Marital and Occupational Plans of Women in Professional Schools: Law, Medicine, Nursing, Teaching." It was not a study conceived of or directed toward the issues and problems in this book. The study was sociological and its focus can be gleaned from the first paragraph of the report:

THE MARITAL AND OCCUPATIONAL AMBITIONS OF WOMEN IN FOUR PROFESsional schools is the subject of this dissertation. The main body of the study will describe the women's plans and the way the social class, mother's education and employment, and facets of the professional education are related to those of well-educated women's work careers. First, like other working women, their careers are complicated by marital and familial responsibilities. Second, the majority of well-educated women enter but a few of the occupations requiring long years of educational preparation, despite widespread shortages of personnel. ■

The women in the study were all enrolled in the four professional programs at Yale and, as one might expect, the bulk of them came from the highest socioeconomic classes (I and II). Each subject in the study was interviewed and filled out a variety of questionnaires. To the investigator's surprise the response of the women in the teaching program sharply differed from those in the other programs, particularly from those in medicine and law.

THE LAW AND MEDICAL STUDENTS ARE PREPARING FOR PROFESSIONS WHICH have very high prestige in our society. At Yale, they are in professional schools respected both within the professions and within the university. The students, when they had complaints, expressed "gripes" which were focused around certain conditions whose correction could improve the educational process for everyone. However, they feel fully integrated into the professional training programs, they have the same access to the intellectual and material resources of the school that the men do, and they feel prepared to enter their professions, as neophytes to be sure, by the end of their programs. ■

In the case of the nursing group Dr. Levine points out: "While their schools are accorded respect within the professions, their prestige within the university is not high relative to the other departments and schools." And now to the teachers in Yale's Master of Arts in Training (MAT) program, the object of our interest and discussion:

WHEN THE TEACHING STUDENTS WERE ASKED, "HOW HAS IT BEEN HERE for you? Has it been the way you thought it would be?" 14 of the 22 interviewed burst out vehemently that "it" had been "terrible," "bland and confusing," "a terrible disappointment," and the like. The reasons for their bitter discontent touched every phase of their program.

First, most of the students said that they found the core of education courses to be dull, almost completely irrelevant to classroom needs. They categorized these courses as appropriate to educational settings not as prestigious as those to which they had become accustomed. One Class I young woman pointed out, "I thought these courses would be different from a state teacher's college."

Second, they attend classes in their major areas in the appropriate departments of the University. This feature of the program attracted many of the women who want to teach but had dreaded the "intellectual insult of being undergraduate education majors."

However, as one student summed it up, "As good as it sounded in the catalog, that's how bad it is." For when they attend classes in the other departments, many of them are faced with unanticipated difficulties.[11] The courses are shaped to the needs of graduate students who will be scholars in their fields, and whose interests are best served by exploring in depth the details of the subject matter.

" . . . their idea of higher scholarships in this area [a language] cuts out all the lyricism, and concentrates on things that I don't like and cannot use . . . things like textual criticism. A little formalism is fine and helpful, but not when it is the whole thing."

The MAT students feel that they need broad coverage, and some question why some of the course requirements cannot be shaped for them to some extent. The few professors who take the MAT students' professional problems into consideration (and there were some of these professors) were spoken of with warm gratitude.

These young women are made keenly aware in a variety of ways that in a social setting whose value hierarchy is based upon advanced scholarship, people who are going to be high school teachers command

---

11. We are not discussing the student's being able to keep up in the courses as far as required performance goes. They were all passing the courses, and no one complained of the intellectual difficulty of the work.

little respect. For example, analogous to the "last hired, first fired" phenomenon, they say that sometimes they must get special permission to enter courses, and if the section becomes crowded, they may be asked to leave. They spoke bitterly of being treated with scorn by graduate students and condescension by many professors.

> The professors are so condescending to the MAT students. The students are worse. I am planning to enter the doctoral program next year, in the _____ department, so I can tell the difference. As an MAT I was talked down to. As doctoral candidate, my intelligence has improved. The amusing thing about the _____ department is that they use a special jargon, and the women are most prone to use it for they are so afraid of being mistaken for MAT students. It is maddening, because the MAT girls are just as bright and twice as lively.

The third part of the learning process for the MATs is their practice teaching, which for most of the group has been concurrent with their course work. For a few the experience has been a good one, for they have had "good" classrooms, have found they like to teach, and enjoy their pupils. But most of the students complain that practice teaching is the discouraging counterpart to their own classroom experiences. The irrelevance of their education courses is brought home to them with dismal regularity.

> I'll tell you what I could use. I could use some sort of psychology of tough adolescents. I learned all about toilet training and weaning in my psych. course, and I am faced with a bunch of tough boys a few years younger than myself, and believe me, what they don't know about sex, drugs, gambling, and everything else isn't worth knowing. But the most elementary reading is beyond them.

Many students say that they lack supervision, and they feel that they have no one to turn to with their day by day practical problems. Many of them, like the young woman quoted above, have been assigned to difficult classes in urban schools. Such assignments compound the problems they face as neophytes. For women who come from protected, Class I–II surroundings, such confrontations are quite upsetting.

The effect of all these experiences is to make them doubt their own feeling of being capable *people* and of being able to perform as teachers.

> I feel dissatisfied with myself. I truly feel that if I had some guidance of a meaningful sort that I could feel more certain about what I'm doing and more interested in staying in teaching. As it is, I am hoping that I will stay in, but I have such self-doubts about achieving the standards that I have set for myself, that I don't know. . . . After all, a good teacher should be able to work in any situation by adapting her methods.

One girl summed up the feeling expressed by many:

It is just so awful to see the girls lose heart and decide not to teach—to quit entirely, or to teach in some nice, quiet private school or suburban school, because they aren't getting anything from the program.

Indeed many of the students said that they had originally felt very strongly that they should teach in city schools. The need is great, they point out. Many of them, aware of the good schools they had themselves attended, interested in "doing good," said that they had eagerly anticipated their first encounters with the real problems of the world. Now they feel that they simply do not have the ability to tackle such overwhelming tasks. These students have had few mentors to tell them which of their "failures" were inherent in the situation, and have had almost no one to turn to, to help them over the many rough places in the road.

Fully thirty percent expressed a "great deal of regret" about their choice of profession, and they plan to leave the field after graduating. Their responses were in marked contrast to the women in the other three school groups. We have noted before that in the process of randomly selecting MAT subjects for this study, we found that 5 of the students had already left the program. The reason they left is unknown, but of the other three school groups in this study, only 1 other (unmarried) young woman had quit the program since registering in the fall semester prior to this study.[12] ■

Dr. Levine's formal study coincides in all details with my own informal observations from afar. Further comment in this instance about the relationship between intended outcomes, the processes of change, and actual outcomes would seem to be superfluous.

It is obvious that I regard the outcomes of efforts to change schools as disappointing and disillusioning. Such outcomes, I have contended, were retrospectively and prospectively predictable. Lest you gain the impression that my assessment is unduly pessimistic or a reflection of a too personal and parochial set of experiences, I shall in the next chapter marshall some of the evidence that contradicts such an impression. That evidence was for all practical purposes not available when the first edition of this book was written. But in the decade that followed that evidence steadily mounted to a degree and with a thoroughness that is forcing people to reexamine the culture of schools and the problem of change. That such a reexamination is taking place is encouraging. That it will be illuminating and productive for future efforts for change should not be taken for granted. There are too many booby-traps.

---

12. A. G. Levine, "Marital and Occupational Plans of Women."

Chapter 5

The Evaluation of
Educational Change

What is the evidence that efforts at educational change have largely been failures? In previous chapters I have presented "cases," but they should not be dignified by calling them evidence. It is true that I would not have used such cases if discussions with other people did not compellingly suggest that these descriptions and disappointing outcomes were consistent with their own experiences and observations. And if further support was necessary, it came from scores of people who read these cases and wrote to tell me how similar their experiences were to what I had described. But again, that is hardly evidence that would stand up in the courts of science. Initially, it was my own experiences and observations, together with the absence of published adequate descriptions of educational change efforts, that emboldened me not to seek more systematic evidence but rather to make sense of the failures I observed, assuming that when systematic evidence became available it would not conflict in any important way either with my observations or interpretations. Some of the consequences of that decision are contained in the previous chapters in which I raise issues that unless directly confronted by the proponents of change maximize the chances of failure, partial or complete. I emphasize that the character of those issues stem directly from the assumption that when efforts at change *repeatedly* end up with disappointing outcomes (and sometimes harmful ones) that is warning enough that a major source of the difficulty is a cultural one in that we are not able to take distance from ideas and conceptions that were highly overlearned by us in the course of our socialization.

It is only in the past few years that serious attempts to study change efforts have been made. In this chapter we shall focus on studies that aimed to assess federal programs each of which supported educational change in many schools differing widely in region, size, and demography.[1] In short, these studies are not single case reports (although they contain some) but analyses of extensive samples and intensive surveys of schools funded by the federal government to accomplish a particular innovative educational change.

THE RAND STUDIES

Without question the most ambitious (even heroic) attempt to assess outcomes of efforts at educational change was the several-year study by Berman and McLaughlin for the United States Office of Education. That study appeared in eight volumes. In what follows I shall draw from the final one because it contains a clear and fair summary of the findings. Precisely because the study was sponsored by the U.S. Office of Education there was the possibility, which should never be given short schrift, that it would be unduly favorable to the sponsor who, after all, had spent huge sums of public money to foster educational change. Anyone, like myself, who has spent a lot of time reading evaluation reports submitted by school systems and other agencies to federal bureaus gains a healthy respect for the capacity of program directors to write what agencies want to hear, especially if continued funding depends on "success." Generally speaking, these evaluation reports are among the most uncritical documents one will ever read. This is not because program directors are as a group more immoral than the rest of us (they probably are not), but that commitment to an effort at change frequently is so passionate that it colors and distorts its proponents' description of reality. And if passion is not strong, one can count on intra-institutional politics to forge an identity between program and individual survival. The school culture, like that of any other major social institution, is political in the narrow and general sense of that word, i.e., the behavior of people (students, teachers, administrators, parents) and the stability *and* transformations in classroom, school, and school system structures have to be seen in terms of the seeking, allocation, and

---

1. In earlier pages I cautioned the reader to avoid the oversimple, indeed invalid, conclusion that only schools have been under severe pressure to change and that the characteristics of the change process and its outcomes are peculiar to the educational setting. Here I would add another caution: efforts at educational change and bewilderment about disappointing outcomes are not unique to our society. I have had occasion to meet with researchers and educators from several western European countries and I have been struck by the similarities between their efforts and ours. Indeed, the people with whom I have talked were visiting this country because their efforts at educational change and innovation were so frustratingly disappointing. I shall have more to say about this in later pages because it suggests that the basic problem is not educational in the narrow sense but in the underlying, unverbalized assumptions on which traditional conceptions of institutional change rests.

uses of power. Introducing, sustaining, and assessing an educational change are political processes because they inevitably alter or threaten to alter existing power relationships, especially if that process implies, as it almost always does, a reallocation of resources. Few myths have been as resistant to change as that which assumes that the culture of the school is a nonpolitical one, and few myths have contributed as much to failure of the change effort.

Berman and McLaughlin are refreshingly exempt from the criticism that they sought, wittingly or unwittingly, to write about what the U.S. Office of Education may have wanted to hear. It is neither a "hatchet" job or an uncritically positive interpretation of findings. Nor do they claim that the studies were ideally designed, or that the findings are definitive in some ultimate sense and that their implications are unambiguous. What they can legitimately claim is that the scope and intensiveness of their studies *and* the consistency of the findings have to be given the most serious attention and respect. They can also claim that their formal findings confirm what other people had predicted or adumbrated. And, as we shall see later in this chapter, their findings are very similar to other studies that have not yet appeared in published form.

Berman and McLaughlin begin their summary with this statement about background:

FEDERAL FINANCIAL AID NOW MAKES UP AN IMPORTANT FRACTION OF MANY local school district budgets, but its effectiveness in improving local educational practices is uncertain. Federally sponsored evaluations reveal inconsistent and generally disappointing results, and, despite considerable innovative activity on the part of local school districts, the evidence suggests that:

No class of existing educational treatments has been found that consistently leads to improved student outcomes (when variations in the institutional setting and nonschool factors are taken into account).

"Successful" projects have difficulty sustaining their success over a number of years.

"Successful" projects are not disseminated automatically or easily, and their "replication" in new sites usually falls short of their performance in the original sites.

Consequently, although federal support for local school services has become well established, the "decade of reform" that began with ESEA (Elementary and Secondary Education Act) has not fulfilled its expectations, and questions continue to be raised about what might be the most appropriate and effective federal role in improving the public schools.

To aid in reexamining federal education policies, the U.S. Office of Education awarded a contract to the Rand Corporation to study a national sample of educational innovations funded by federal programs. The study aimed to help improve federal change agent policies by describing how the process of innovation works in its local setting, and by trying to discern what factors affect the innovative process and its outcomes. This report reviews the findings of Rand's research (p. v).[2] ■

The above statement is one with which almost everyone would agree. However, the statement describes a relationship between schools and the federal government that should not be quickly passed over. The significance of that relationship is in the support it gives to my earlier argument about the inadequacy and invalidity of conceptualizing a school system as if it were a closed one, i.e., as if it were explainable in terms internal to the "system." That kind of thinking, as I emphasized, has never mirrored the realities of schools and what Berman and McLaughlin describe is only the latest transformation in the porous boundaries between school and society. Whereas before the 1950s one could talk about schools without talking about the federal government, that is no longer possible. It is not only that schools have become financially dependent on federal funds, or that schools have become very vigilant about the kinds of programs the federal government seeks to promote and fund, or that schools find themselves required to accede to federal regulations, or that schools seek in turn to influence and change federal policies as well as the level and mode of funding—it is the combination of all of these that makes it impossible to talk about the culture of a school as if it were explainable in narrow spatial terms. Just as it makes no sense to study a school as if it were unrelated to other schools and to a central administration ("downtown"), it makes no sense to try to understand school systems as if they were unrelated to another "downtown": federal bureaus. But if schools and federal agencies are dynamically interrelated, does it make sense to talk about how *schools* innovate or seek to change, as if the federal bureaus are not integral to the process, as if failures are failures of schools and not of federal agencies *and* schools? There are times when Berman and McLaughlin seem to recognize the significance of the distinction, e.g., when they ask: "What might be the most appropriate and effective federal role in improving the public schools?" They go on to say that "their studies aimed to help improve federal change agent policies by describing how the process of innovation works in the local setting." But if only to be consistent about the role of federal agencies in innovation and change are we also not required to ask: *How does the process of innovation work in the federal agency?* Why ask

2. P. Berman and M. W. McLaughlin, *Federal Programs Supporting Educational Change, Vol. VIII: Implementing and Sustaining Innovations* (Santa Monica, Calif.: Rand Corporation, 1978).

the question only of the local setting?[3] In light of the frequency with which initiatives for change emanate from governmental agencies, as well as the frequency with which educational change is mandated, should we not ask how these initiatives arise, why certain ideas are accepted and others rejected, how the form of and criteria for implementation are chosen, and the similarities and continuities between the innovative process in its federal and local aspects? What if the major factors contributing to failure in the change effort on the local level are no less present in the innovative process at the federal level? But these questions cannot be raised, let alone discussed, as long as the change process is seen as taking place *within* what we call a school or school system, and as long as the federal policy maker does not confront the possibility that what contributes to failure at the local level is a continuation of a way of thinkng that characterized the change process at the federal level.

Consider this example. Several years ago I participated in a meeting at the National Institute of Education (NIE) on educational networks. The purpose of the meeting was to discuss how a particular division of the institute could foster research that would speak to how schools could more effectively utilize concepts of social networks for purposes of more cooperative interaction within and among schools, and between schools and community individuals and groups. The discussion was both free wheeling and far ranging, but the only things about which everyone seemed to agree were that we needed to obtain more basic knowledge about how networks develop and grow, and that such knowledge could be used by school personnel to overcome isolation, social fractionation, and competition for resources among those in and around schools. Although I was part of the consensus, I objected to the implication in the discussion that our knowledge was as paltry as others thought and that schools were especially in need of network concepts. For example, I said, is there any basis for assuming that the diagnosis of what was wrong with schools, and the application of network concepts as a way of meeting these deficiencies, were no less valid for NIE generally and in particular the division that had called this meeting? I then went on to demonstrate the identity between NIE and schools in terms of the ways lack of cooperativeness, zero sum (if you win, I lose) competitiveness, duplication of resources, and insensitivity to outside constituencies characterize the two settings. In fact, I asserted, the people who called this meeting had a substantial basis for considering themselves experts on the obstacles one would encounter in developing the

---

3. See, for example, *Organizing an Anarchy* by Sproull, Weiner, and Wolf, (1978). This is the sad story of the creation of the National Institute of Education. Their book should be required reading for those who think the problems of creating and/or changing a federal bureau are different from those of schools. Murnane's review (1981, in press) of that book should also be consulted.

kinds of networks they wanted schools to develop. If the personnel in this division were apparently unable to foster appropriate networks in their own bailiwick, why should they expect school personnel to do better? Before asking schools to effect a change, should they not try to achieve the same goal in their setting? Or, at the very least, should not their knowledge of the sources of difficulty that their efforts encounter inform the direction of the research this division would support as well as the nature of the relationships between schools and this division? Needless to say, my remarks were not received with interest, let alone anything remotely resembling enthusiasm. This division wanted to study schools, it wanted ultimately to influence and change schools, but it could not recognize how the formulation of these aims, and ultimately the character of the evaluations that would be made of schools' efforts to meet these aims, would be influenced by the failure of this division to see what it had in common with schools. The division pointed itself to changing the "out there" as if the division was not an integral part of the change process. The division did not see itself as a part of the schools they wanted to see change.

We shall return to this issue many times in the course of this book. Let us now turn to Berman and McLaughlin's statement of their major findings. We can do no better than to use their summary:

Findings about the Effects of Federal Programs

WE EXAMINED TWO QUESTIONS RELEVANT TO THE EFFECTS OF THE FEDERAL programs:

> How did the "seed money" policy common to the change agent programs affect local projects?
> Were the differences in guidelines and objectives among the federal programs reflected in their projects' implementation and continuation?

We found that federal change agent policies had a major effect in stimulating local education agencies to undertake projects that were generally consistent with federal categorical guidelines. This local response resulted from the availability of federal funds and, in some programs, from guidelines that encouraged specific educational practices.

But the adoption of projects did not insure successful implementation; moreover, successful implementation did not guarantee long-run continuation. Neither those policies unique to each federal program nor those policies common to them strongly influenced the fate of adopted innovations. The net return to the federal investment was the adoption of many innovations, the successful implementation of few, and the long-run continuation of still fewer (with the exception of the special case of bilingual projects, where federal and state funding continues to be available).

All the federal programs had funded some successfully implemented projects as well as dismal failures and many projects in between. The difference between success and failure depended primarily on how school districts implemented their projects, not on the type of federal sponsorship. The guidelines and management strategies of the federal change agent programs were simply overshadowed by local concerns and characteristics.

Similarly, "more" money supplied by federal funds did not necessarily purchase those things that mattered; it did not "buy," for example, more committed teachers, more effective project directors, more concerned principals, and so on. In other words, project outcomes reflected not the amount of funds available, but the quality and behavior of the local staff.

This is not to say that "federal money doesn't matter." Federal seed money allowed some districts to undertake activities that their staff were anxious to pursue but that could not be supported out of district funds. Moreover, federal funding has bestowed legitimacy on local projects and given them the aura of "special status," which can provide some measure of "protection" for politically controversial or pedagogically untested educational practices.

Yet few districts in our sample planned for the long-term stability of projects. The end of federal funding generally resulted in a reduction of resources, particularly expensive ones. Many districts complained of insufficient resources to carry on project activities, although the financial requirements for project continuation could have been foreseen and planned for from a project's inception. Instead, budget and personnel decisions typically perpetuated the "special project" status of innovations, thereby leaving them particularly vulnerable to the financial and political fortunes of the district.

While the overall effects of federal policy may be disappointing, the positive results should not be overlooked. Some local projects worked well, and from these successes, we can identify factors that determine the fate of innovations.

Factors Affecting Implementation and Continuation

IN ADDITION TO ANALYZING THE EFFECTS OF FEDERAL POLICIES, WE EXamined how characteristics of projects and school districts affect the outcomes of innovations. We studied the projects' educational method, resource levels, scope, and implementation strategies; the district characteristics we analyzed were school climate and leadership, teacher attributes, and district management capacity and support. We found:

1. *Educational methods.* A project's methods determined its implementation, effect, and continuation to only a small and

limited extent. This is so because projects with essentially the same educational methods can be, and usually are, implemented very differently and thus with varying effectiveness. In short, what the project *was* mattered less than how it was done.

2. *Project resources.* More expensive projects were generally no more likely than less expensive ones to be effectively implemented, elicit teacher change, improve student performance, or be continued by teachers. Nor did variations in the number of project schools per district or in the funding per student strongly affect project outcomes in most cases.

3. *Scope of project.* Ambitious and demanding innovations promoted teacher change and teacher continuation of project methods without necessarily causing unmanageable implementation problems or diminishing gains in student performance. Teachers must clearly understand their project's goals and percepts; such clarity comes during implementation. We doubt whether projects aiming at significant change can be effectively implemented across a whole school system at once.

4. *Implementation strategies.* Implementation strategies are the local decisions and choices, explicit or implicit, on how to put the innovation into practice. We found that these strategies could spell the difference between success or failure, almost independently of the type of innovation or educational method involved; moreover, they could determine whether teachers would assimilate and continue using project methods or allow them to fall into disuse. The following strategies were frequently *ineffective* because they were not consonant with the conditions of school district life or with the dominant motivations and needs of teachers:

Outside consultants.
Packaged management approaches.
One-shot, preimplementation training.
Pay for training.
Formal evaluation.
Comprehensive projects.

Effective strategies promoted *mutual adaptation,* the process by which the project is adapted to the reality of its institutional setting, while at the same time teachers and school officials adapt their practices in response to the project. Effective strategies provide each teacher with necessary and timely feedback, allow project-level choices to be made to correct errors, and encourage commitment to the project. The following were effective strategies, particularly when applied in concert:

Concrete, teacher-specific, and extended training.
Classroom assistance from project or district staff.

Teacher observation of similar projects in other class-
rooms, schools, or districts.
Regular project meetings that focused on practical problems.
Teacher participation in project decisions.
Local materials development.
Principal participation in training.

5. *School organizational climate and leadership.* Three elements of
a school's organizational climate powerfully affected the project's implementation and continuation—the quality of working
relationships among teachers, the active support of principals,
and the effectiveness of project directors. The importance of
the principal to both short- and long-run effects of innovations
can hardly be overstated. The principal's unique contribution to
implementation lies not in "how to do it" advice better offered
by project directors, but in giving moral support to the staff
and in creating an organizational climate that gives the project
"legitimacy." The principal's support was also crucial for continuation. Teachers were unlikely to continue a fully array of
project methods without the sanction of their principal, even if
the methods were successful and had been assimilated.
Moreover, after the end of federal funding, many districts took
a laissez-faire attitude of letting the principals decide the fate of
the project within their schools. Unless principals actively promoted the project, particularly in regard to seeking district
financial support and replacing staff that moved elsewhere,
even "successful" projects could wither away. All told, the
principal amply merits the title of "gatekeeper of change."
6. *Characteristics of schools and attributes of teachers.* Change
was typically harder to obtain and continue at the secondary
level. Three teacher attributes—years of teaching, sense of efficacy, and verbal ability—significantly affected project outcomes. The number of years teaching had *negative* effects: the
longer a teacher had taught the less likely was the project to
achieve its goals, and the less likely was the project to improve
student performance. Furthermore, teachers with many years
on the job were less likely to change their own practices and
less likely to continue using project methods after the end of
federal funding. The teacher's sense of efficacy—a belief that
the teacher can help even the most difficult or unmotivated
students—showed strong positive effects on all outcomes,
whereas teachers' verbal ability had a positive correlation only
with improved student achievement.
7. *District management capacity and support.* Districts differ
sharply in their capacity to manage change agent projects and
in their receptivity toward them. Though we could not measure

these factors with precision, our observation and interview data leave little doubt as to the importance of constant and active support from LEA officials and specialized staff for the project's short-run outcomes and especially its long-run fate (pp. vi–ix). ■

For our present purposes I shall concentrate on three of Berman and McLaughlin's conclusions. The first, and one that I emphasized in previous chapters, is that the way in which the change process is conceptualized is far more fateful for success or failure than the educational method or content (e.g., reading, social studies) one seeks to implement. More simply, you can have the most creative, compellingly valid, educationally productive idea in the world, but whether it can become embedded and sustained in a socially complex setting will be primarily a function of how you conceptualize the implementation-change process. The significance of this conclusion is that it invalidates the commonly held view that the change process is a social engineering one that requires you to follow a step-by-step recipe that will lead to a final goal or product. Such a "how-to-do-it" view effectively obscures a complex of "how-to-think-about-it" issues. For example, it bypasses the task of coming to grips with the characteristics and traditions of the setting and the ways in which they ordinarily facilitate and frustrate change. It is a view that in ignoring history and tradition vastly oversimplifies what would be involved in implementing and sustaining change. And, as we shall see later, it is a view that does not permit its proponents to ask a central question: Given the goals of change, how does one determine what would be a realistic time perspective to adopt in regard to achieving one's goals? Two examples of what I mean: What if someone came to us and asked why we cannot teach children to read in twenty-four hours? Assuming that we knew the person to be sane and we could control the tendency to throw the individual out of our office, what would we say? It would probably take us twenty-four hours of uninterrupted talk to explain how children develop physically, mentally, and socially; the inevitable social and interpersonal context in which learning takes place; the complexity of motivation and its vicissitudes; the knowledge and cognitive skills that are necessary for the productive assimilation and use of symbols; and the problems that can be created when external pressures do not take developmental stages or readiness into account. Besides, we might ask this irritating ignoramus, "Do you mean why can't we teach *a* child to read in twenty-four hours or do you mean a *group* of children in a classroom?"

A second example: What if we asked a psychoanalyst friend to level with us and explain how he or she justifies seeing *a* patient for one hour a day, four or five days a week, perhaps for two, three, four, or more years. "Why does it take that long? Do you really believe," we may ask, "that it takes that long to be helpful to someone? Aren't there quicker ways of giving help?" "Friend(?)," the analyst replies, "there is much you do not understand." Our friend then proceeds to summarize for us what the human organism is at birth, how its cognitive and affective equipment is organized and develops, the ways in which it becomes increasingly psychologically and physically differentiated, how it develops and utilizes a variety of coping mechanisms, the sources of inevitable internal and external conflict, the nature and strength of resistances to change, the relationship of all of this to the interpersonal dynamics of the nuclear family, and on and on, depending on whether our psychoanalyst friend is summarizing Freud's *Introductory Lectures* or multivolumed collected works. (If he or she happens to be a true believer, we would also hear about parracide and the primal horde in the dawning history of mankind.) "Now," our friend would say, "you can begin to understand why psychoanalytic treatment takes so long. It is not that we desire to prolong it but rather that our understanding of an individual requires it if we are to be able to meaningfully help somebody radically change accustomed ways of thinking and acting."

In almost every study that Berman and McLaughlin evaluated there was uncritical acceptance of the assumption that the adopted time perspective was appropriate to the goals of change. In almost every instance the time perspective was determined not by people in the schools but by federal policy makers and legislators, i.e., by the assumptions underlying funding policies. That the schools willingly accommodated to such a time perspective indicates how widespread is the tendency to oversimplify what is involved in cultural and institutional change.

Let us now turn to a second major conclusion of Berman and McLaughlin, which I would put in this way: to the extent that the effort at change identifies and meaningfully involves all those who directly or indirectly will be affected by the change, to that extent the effort stands a chance to be successful. That is stating it positively. In the bulk of the studies the proponents for change proceeded in ways that by isolating the project guaranteed conflict and failure precisely because the needs and self-interests of significant people were ignored. It was less that they were ignored, because that implies a conscious decision, than it was a failure to recognize what should be obvious: an effort at institutional change, however circumscribed it may be, is observable by, has different meanings for, and will be differently judged by a variety of people in the setting in which change is being sought. As someone once said: "The name of the game is constituencies." The wisdom in that statement was absent in the thinking of a very large fraction of educators intent on change. It is important to point out that as soon as one grasps the significance of constituencies for the change effort, it forces one to appraise the basis for one's time perspective, because developing and sustaining constituencies are and should be time-consuming affairs, no less important than other aspects of the change effort.

In my experience those who seek to effect a change in schools tend to divide people into three groups. The first consists of those people who apparently need no convincing and on whose support one can count. This is usually a relatively small group that frequently turns out not to be as homogeneous in motivation and values as one fantasied. Whereas the first group may be termed "the good guys," the second group are the "bad guys": people who are seen as resistant to change or who for other reasons cannot be counted on to be supportive and, therefore, to be avoided or, if one has the power, to be run over. When the project fails, "the bad guys" are blamed in accord with the dynamics of the self-fulfilling prophecy. The third group, by far the largest, are those people who one assumes have no direct or indirect interest in the particular change and, therefore, one can safely ignore them, an assumption the invalidity of which becomes clear after the project is, so to speak, in stormy seas and about to capsize. As Berman and McLaughlin emphasize, if, in practice, constituency refers only to "the good guys," the stage for failure is being erected. It is missing, if not trivializing, the point to criticize this view as poor human relations. What makes for poor human relations, and prior to them, is the failure to comprehend the inevitable ramifications of the change effort into the different parts of the larger setting, to be sensitive to how each of these parts will react, and, therefore, to develop strategies that will give one as variegated and as large a constituency as possible. More often than not, what people mean by poor human relations are far less the cause of failure than they are the consequences of a self-defeating conception of the change process. A lot of very lovely people who ordinarily would be described as having very good human relations are otherwise described after they have taken the responsibility for implementing an educational change.

The third major finding is perhaps the most discouraging and instructive of all. Whereas a very small percentage of efforts at change were judged to have been successfully implemented, only a small percentage of them were sustained after funding ceased, a fact that forcefully underlines the importance of the development of constituencies. As we shall see later, this does not mean that if a successful project had developed a strong and differentiated constituency that its continuation after funding ceased was only a matter of course. What it does mean is that without the appropriate constituency one stands little or no chance to survive the competition for limited resources.

There is one statement in the summary by Berman and McLaughlin that requires clarification: "Implementation strategies are the local decisions and choices, explicit or implicit, on how to put the innovation into practice." In two respects that statement can be both misleading and reinforcing of some faulty conceptions. For one thing, any federally funded effort at change starts out as a local response to a federal program, which is another way of saying that the local response is an interpretation of federal descriptions and guidelines. It is unduly cynical to say that the local funding request is only an attempt to say what the "feds" want to hear, but it is not cynical to say that the local grant writers are mightily influenced by the implicit and explicit strategies suggested by federal announcements. So, although in one respect it is correct to say that implementation strategies are local choices, it is not correct in a phenomenological sense, i.e., local people see themselves as actively seeking to develop their strategies in ways that they think the federal agencies would consider conceptually appropriate. I have had sufficient experience in consulting on the formulation of federal programs to conclude that local personnel are well advised to read on and between the lines of statements of criteria for funding a particular program. Those statements are not written in a random fashion. On the contrary, they are products of painstaking efforts to convey what would be appropriate and inappropriate at the same time that they seek to avoid describing the criteria for funding in ways that would give them the appearance of being narrow and rigid. It is impossible for any individual or group of individuals to write federal guidelines without those guidelines reflecting something about what the writers consider good or bad practices. Local personnel may misinterpret or misread the guidelines, but that does not argue against the point that to regard implementation strategies as local decisions is to reinforce the view of the bounded, encapsulated school system and, therefore, to regard failure as something explainable *within* that system.

The statement by Berman and McLaughlin is about *funded* programs. What about the ones that failed to be approved and funded? The very fact that many programs were not approved has to be regarded as evidence that those who participated in funding decisions had criteria about what were good or bad implementation strategies, criteria that those who sought grant support did not meet. The point in all this is that local decisions about implementation are not unrelated to federal decisions. This is a point that Berman and McLaughlin also make and, in fact, they make the following recommendations about how federal initiatives and decision making might be changed and improved in this regard.

Implications for Federal Policy

OUR RESEARCH SUGGESTS THAT FEDERAL POLICY HAS OFTEN BEEN BASED ON misconceptions about the reality of school districts and the factors that produce change in their organizational and educational practices. Correct assumptions would not, of course, automatically improve policy effectiveness, because any policy may be poorly implemented. But faulty assumptions—indeed even *one* faulty assumption among otherwise good ones—can lead to ineffective and counterproductive programs. Federal policy to date has largely been based on a research and development point of view—that the federal government should develop new technologies, provide incentives for their adoption, and introduce these technologies into school districts by projects that were targeted, and thus accountable. In a very real sense, school districts were thought of as "black boxes." Federal "inputs" would be supplied to change and control district behavior so that a desirable educational "output" could be achieved. This R&D point of view was embodied in the following assumptions:

1. Improving educational performance requires innovative educational technologies.
2. Improving educational performance requires the provision of missing resources to school districts.
3. Improving educational performance requires a targeted project focus.

We believe that federal officials should set aside the largely ineffective R&D point of view. Instead, they might consider an approach that assumes school districts are ultimately responsible for improving their own performance but require both short- and long-run aid to achieve this end.

School districts need institutional assistance, but an institutional development strategy can work only if federal officials identify those aspects of the local change process and of district organizational characteristics where federal resources and influence can be effective. The following premises might provide building-blocks to formulate this point of view:

1. Educational performance could be improved if more attention were paid to all stages of the local change process.
2. Educational performance could be improved with adaptive implementation assistance.
3. Educational performance could be improved if the capacity of school districts to manage change were enhanced.

These premises, as well as more specific recommendations suggested in the report, direct attention to areas that federal policy has tended to neglect. For example, they suggest that local adoption of projects should not be the sole federal policy focus; that federal efforts to improve the change process within school districts should take precedence over their past concern with improving educational products; that federal evaluators should expect and encourage the adaptation of programs to suit local needs; that the federal government should promote local institutional development in addition to more targeted project approaches;

and that federal legislation should establish ways to provide more differentiated and flexible support to school districts. In short, these premises suggest a shift in the federal role toward the process of educational change, which might well imply a strengthened role for state educational agencies. We believe that policy should reflect the assumption that state education agencies are potentially better suited than federal agencies to influence and provide opportune assistance to school districts (pp. ix–x).[4] ■

Not only do Berman and McLaughlin make clear that local decision making about implementation strategies have not been unrelated to federal decision making, but what they recommend would make that relationship even more explicit and direct. More than that, their discussion recognizes that the day is long past when one can talk about educational change at the local level independent of changes at the state and federal levels. The problem of change is no longer a local one, and that fact underlines the vast change that has taken place in the culture of the school in the post-World War II era. In the daily lives of students, parents, and teachers, that vast change may be barely sensed or not recognized at all, but to administrative personnel and boards of education that vast change is mightily influential. To the observer of the school scene, the traditional concept of a school system makes less sense than ever before.

THE EXPERIMENTAL SCHOOLS PROGRAM

The Experimental Schools Program (ESP) was initiated in the early seventies with much fanfare. The program was described in glowing terms by President Nixon in a special message to Congress on "Reform and Renewal" in education. It was described as a major innovative effort in bridging the gap between educational research and practice. The program not only had presidential support, but that of the President's Science Advisory Committee and the top officialdom in the Department of Health, Education, and Welfare.

What makes the ESP so relevant for our purposes is that it reflected on the part of federal policy makers a very deliberate change of mind about how to bring about educational change. Unlike some of the programs assessed by Berman and McLaughlin, where it is really stretching things to say that these programs stemmed from a clearly articulated conception of change, the ESP program explicitly was based on a recognition of the inadequacies of past efforts. Briefly, the ESP was based on several considerations:

---

4. Berman and McLaughlin, *Federal Programs.*

1. Past federal efforts to improve and change schools were largely failures.

2. Federal programs had a buckshot quality: there was a program for this part of the school system and for that one; there was a program for this educational problem and for that one. It was as if the federal government kept reacting to whatever problem was brought to its attention. Sequence and interconnectedness were not important.

3. The federal government should provide the resources for *comprehensive* change in a school system, i.e., sufficient resources to permit a school district more meaningfully and efficiently "to put it all together" in a single direction.

4. There was merit in the complaints of local districts that federal imposition of programs, or too many intrusions by federal personnel into planning at the local level, robbed local people of initiative, creativity, and control. In the ESP local people would have more control over ESP projects. If local districts were sincerely given the opportunity to change their schools in ways they considered most appropriate, one could then count on their commitment to initiate and sustain the change process.

5. Federal efforts to evaluate past reform efforts had been inadequate and they bore no relationship either to changes in federal policy or local program management. The ESP would use innovative and rigorous social science methodology to understand and assess the change process better. Indeed, somewhat less than one-third of the 60–70 million dollars that the ESP would cost would go to an evaluation scheme no less comprehensive than the changes that local districts would bring about in their schools.

The ESP was a disaster and anyone who has any doubts on that score should read Cowden and Cohen's (unpublished) federally sponsored assessment. Their write-up is a model of pithiness, clear description, and thoughtfulness. Let us listen to how they state the promise and the outcome:

ESP APPEARED TO PROVIDE A RARE OPPORTUNITY FOR REFORM. FOR ONE thing, it was not mandated by Congress and tied to specific program or funding categories. Unlike the programs that had preceded it (Title I, Headstart, and Follow Through), ESP was funded from the discretionary monies made available to the Commissioner of Education. Thus, ESP could pick program targets and local sites without bargaining or Congressional direction and avoid the politics associated with educational legislation. Secondly, ESP was not to be another "top-down" reform effort relying on federal authority over state and local systems of governance, which, critics argue, leads to conflict and eventually frustrates federal intentions. Rather, while ESP was to be formulated by a federal executive agency, it depended upon the willingness of local agents to participate.

Yet despite its promising beginnings, ESP did not escape the fate of other federal programs. The central notion of ESP—comprehensive change—failed of achievement. Like its predecessors, the program produced only piecemeal and fragmented activities. The policy of local autonomy also failed. The federal ESP staff were committed to local control, but where the substance of their reform was being diluted, they tried to take control themselves. The more they sought to insure local implementation of comprehensive change, the more did they encroach upon local control. Similarly, the federal evaluation scheme fell on dark days. It was unable to provide new social science knowledge about the program and the local change process. Instead, it involved the federal ESP staff in political and managerial conflict, which colored what little knowledge was produced. . . .

Federal practitioners saw local central administrations as the seat of local control and tried to work with them to insure program implementation. But because school districts and school operations are so decentralized, their central administrators could not achieve the comprehensiveness dear to federal reformers. So ESP became a variety of local creations within a single school or district. Federal reformers tried to stem this tide, but that meant abrogating some local control. This, in turn, led to local cries of outrage and to conflict. . . .

Federal reformers tend to believe that local practice is bankrupt of ideas, and often seek to reform it by improving on or replacing local knowledge. Social science has been a favorite source of new knowledge. Federal educational agencies thus contract with researchers, developers, and evaluators whose specialized, professional, and ostensibly scientific knowledge is supposed to replace the ordinary and presumably deficient knowledge of local practitioners. But teaching and administration seem to entail skill and knowledge quite different from social science, and practitioners find little of interest in social science knowledge. This creates further conflict with federal officials over the need for and use of that knowledge.

This was reflected in ESP. The ESP staff devised an elaborate, well-financed evaluation scheme based on their notions about social science knowledge in the reform of local practice. But the evaluation proved of little use. Local administrators and teachers relied on their own skill and knowledge instead. They saw the evaluation as serving other federal purposes—political ones—and this contributed to tensions and management problems (pp. 2–6).[5] ■

---

5. Reprinted with permission.

Most assuredly, I gain no satisfaction from having predicted the failure of the ESP. One had to be inordinately obtuse not to have made such a prediction. Somewhere near the point when the policy makers were to decide which score or so of school districts would be part of the ESP, I was asked to come to Washington to advise on these decisions. It was a chaotic visit on several scores. For one thing, federal personnel felt under tremendous pressure to launch this well publicized program as soon as possible, preferably yesterday. I could not decide whether the pressure was more internal than external, although as the meeting wore on the former rather than the latter seemed to be the major source. That feeling of pressure seemed to be very much related to the fact that the federal personnel had vastly underestimated how much time it would take to select school districts. Granted that the local districts would have the most to say about how they would bring about comprehensive change, that kind of freedom made the task of selection very difficult. How does one choose on the basis of a written grant request (and telephone calls) except by resort to one's own conception about how comprehensive change *should* be accomplished. That issue came quickly to the fore when one perused the written documents at different stages of their submission; they were the most vague statements of virtuous intent giving one no sense of security about how "comprehensive change" was being defined. However committed federal personnel had been to the idea of local initiative and control, that commitment quickly started to dissolve as they concluded that local districts were defining comprehensive change in strange and various ways. The written documents were more like inkblots, forcing the reader to intuit what local districts meant by what they said and wrote. The point is that the local districts were as much at sea about the meaning of "comprehensive change" as the federal personnel were. This is but another instance of the point made earlier in this chapter about how unrealistic and unfair it is to view the change process only in local terms, and it underlines the concern Berman and McLaughlin expressed about the unproductive (if not frequently harmful) relationship between federal and local personnel.

My second contact with the ESP was a year later when I was asked to visit and assess the plans and resources of a private consulting firm seeking the contract for the first in a series of evaluation studies. By this time most of the local districts to be part of the ESP had been chosen and their final grant applications were made available to us. Each application was no less than four inches thick and weighed five or more pounds. Their bulk was matched only by their lack of substance. That may sound like an excessively harsh judgment, but the fact is that no one at this second meeting came to a contrary conclusion because it was so obvious to everyone that these applications presented no focus to evaluate, i.e., no conceptual or procedural foci. It was painful to observe how the staff of the consulting firm, a methodologically sophisticated group, were trying to reconcile their desire to get the contract with the inkblot character of what they were supposed to do. The federal staff wanted a rigorous evaluation, but they had maneuvered themselves into a classically tragic situation in which the beginnings already contained the seeds of eveyone's ultimate defeat. This judgment is well documented by Cowden and Cohen and will not be further discussed here.

Cowden and Cohen entitled their report "Divergent Worlds of Practice" because if anything was clear about the ESP it was that the culture of federal policy making, guideline writing, and monitoring and the culture of local districts are not only different from but incompatible with each other. Put more simply, the people in each of these cultures did not comprehend each other. As Cowden and Cohen state in their summary:

THE FEDERAL ESP STAFF'S AMBITIOUS HOPES FOR A COMPREHENSIVE PROgram of change in which school personnel worked together toward a new educational outcome never approached fulfillment. What change occurred, and the degree varied from site to site, did so in fragmented ways, and was typically modest and piecemeal. This reflected differences in practice at the federal and the local level. In the view of the federal ESP staff, past federal reform efforts had foundered through the lack of coordinated far-reaching change in each project. Comprehensive change across whole school districts thus seemed reasonable. But a school district is not a single, centrally directed, coherent system that can, upon a decision, change direction. It consists of many units and individuals with different needs, interests, and opinions. And the work of central administrators, principals, and teachers is only weakly interdependent—they by no means all pull together. Each has his or her own views of what changes should take place, and there is little incentive for concern with those of others. In this situation, comprehensive change—even had it been clearly understood—could not take place; and so the program failed (p. 21). ■

In saying that the program failed, and in describing how that came about, Cowden and Cohen are underlining the significant point that failure is not explainable only by factors internal to schools and, therefore, that any conception of the change process has to start with the modal ways in which what we call a school system ordinarily relates and responds to "outside" forces. By "modal ways" I am referring not only to those times when schools are being pressured to change but also to those times when they have appeared to be in relative harmony with their social surround. Is it possible that these modal ways derive from unverbalized, culturally determined assumptions that guarantee that when pressures for change do arise they will be assimilated in ways that confirm the adage that the more things change the more they remain the same? Is it possible that the problem is less in the conception of change and more in the social-historically determined view of what a school system is and should be? As I emphasized earlier, when efforts at educational change *repeatedly* founder, despite everyone's good intentions, it is safe to assume that we are prisoners of ways of thinking that seem so right, natural, and proper that we never critically examine them or, if we do, we fear talking about them in public. And, as we shall see below, if such fear is lacking, that is no basis for unbridled optimism that it will lead to intended consequences. For illustrative purposes, let us turn to the issues about power that are behind the question: Who owns the school? Wrapped up in that question are two others: In practice, who wields power in educational decision making? On what basis should customary practice be changed? Those are "loaded" questions because they are intended to suggest that efforts at educational change have been disappointing in their consequences in part because of the way that power is distributed in regard to educational decision making. Put in another way: the failures of school reforms require one to critically examine those who participate in or make educational policy, i.e., those who seek reform or seek to block or dilute it. And as soon as one focuses on those with power, one has to ask why they have power and others do not.

We have already met the problem of power in our discussion of the ESP. You will recall that the federal policy makers had concluded that past failures at reform initiated in Washington were in part due to the imbalance in power between federal bureaus and local districts, the former calling the tune to which the latter would dance, when they would have preferred doing something more related to their perceived needs. So, the argument went, let us give the local district more power to change what it wants to change. Let us, at least in regard to federal programs, redefine who has power to do what. *We* haven't done all that well when we exercised power, so let us transfer power to make decisions to *them*. It will be *their* program, not *ours*. Rarely has power and those wielding it been so directly criticized, and rarely has the purpose of transferring (or sharing) power been so clear. The only thing that went wrong was that once they went beyond rhetoric the federal staff found all kinds of reasons for not transferring power, i.e., they had adapted a noblesse oblige stance which got transformed rather quickly to an authoritarian one. (Those who are used to wielding power do not easily give it up and can be counted on to find reasons why they should not.) As a result, the attempt to reassert power led to a level and variety of struggle between federal staff and local district that, as Cowden and Cohen describe, was (at times) as hilarious as it was deadly. The only unequivocal outcomes of the ESP were that the federal staff saw the wisdom of having and wielding power, and the local district saw the wisdom in never underestimating the perfidy of the federal staff. The ESP was conceived in terms of power, foundered on naked power struggles, and contributed nothing to furthering our understanding of power in educational decision making. And yet, in one very important respect the saga of the ESP should sensitize us, and direct our attention to, issues of power within the local district. Is it not possible that what happened between the federal bureau and the local district is in all respects identical to what happens between the power wielders in the local schools and others in and outside the schools?

POWER AND CHANGE

What is the relevance of this brief discussion of power for the efforts to change schools? In regard to federal efforts at educational change there can be little doubt that many federal programs had as their goal an alteration in the distribution of power. More specifically, they sought to give more power to parents and other community groups. What got overlooked was that in seeking ways to alter the distribution of power, the federal government itself became a source of power. But something else got overlooked: the sources of conflict about power *within* the schools. One cannot read Berman and McLaughlin or Cowden and Cohen without gaining a lot of respect for the role of power within the culture of the school. Any non-trivial effort at institutional change that is insensitive to the issue of power courts failure.

The failure of federal efforts has many sources, but one of the most significant is their superficial understanding of (or token gestures in regard to) the role of power in schools. In this and earlier chapters I have argued that at the root of federal failures, as well as most of those that originated within schools, is an inadequate, unclear, parochial conception of what the culture of the school was and has become. I, as did Berman and McLaughlin, have argued that efforts at educational change have lacked a productive conception of the change process, i.e., of institutional change be it in the school setting or in any other complicated organization. That lack is by no means peculiar to efforts to change schools, a fact that should restrain critics from scapegoating schools, as if as societal institutions schools have cornered the market on how to defeat the efforts at change. However, in recognizing that we lack a viable conception of institutional change, we should not underestimate how incomplete our understanding of the school culture is.

Later in this book we shall return to sociological aspects of issues surrounding the culture of the school and the problem of change. But before doing so I wish to raise a point that tends to be glossed over or simply neglected in discussions of educational change. In raising questions such as who owns the schools or who should participate in what ways and to what degrees in educational decision-making, one gets answers ranging from "professionals only" to "everyone who will be affected by decisions." These are radically different answers, suggesting that they rest on different values related very differently to actions and outcomes. That is to say, if you hold one set of values, you presumably proceed in one way, and if you hold another set of values, you proceed in another way. Different answers derive from differing conceptions of how things should be and of how one gets from what is to what should be. Proponents of different answers may agree on what should be but differ on the best way to get there. In fact, it is by no means infrequent to hear groups say that they agree about ends but disagree about means. But if there is agreement about ends, why such fierce conflict about means? The answer is that each group "knows" two things: means *transform* ends, and there are *moral imperatives* that dictate how people should *structure their relationship* to each other when their fates are intertwined. In the process of disagreeing about means they are saying that whichever means are adopted will produce ends about which there will also be disagreement. What appears to be only disagreement about means is also a disagreement about ends. In regard to educational decision-making issues, the context in which they arise, get discussed, and decided is usually one that highlights disagreements and polarization. What tends to get totally ignored in that context is that regardless of the answer for which one advocates, *everyone* is faced with the same self-interest: "What do I have to do, whose support do I need to get, how do I change opponents into supporters, how do I identify and capitalize on other people's self-interests, so that I avoid winning the battle and losing the war, or losing both battle and war?" When the point is reached where proponents for each answer see themselves in a win-lose situation, they increase the chances that no one will win.

When it is said in regard to educational change in schools that the evidence indicates that the more things change the more they remain the same—that almost irrespective of moral stance and view of means-ends relationships the outcomes are disappointing, and where they are not they are very transitory—it speaks volumes about how people manage to ignore their self-interests. From the standpoint of self-interest, those holding very different conceptions about educational decision-making face the same question on the level of action: "What do I have to do to mobilize what kind of support to introduce and sustain the change?" The inability to ask that question, because it is almost always embedded in a win-lose context suffused with passion and polarizations, prevents one from recognizing how narrowly one is defining self-interest. Self-interest has nothing intrinsically to do with selfishness or manipulativeness. It has a great deal to do with how one defines, locates, and uses resources. The point I am stressing is that the history of efforts at educational change suggests the surprising conclusion that proponents for change rarely took their self-interests seriously. After all, when the outcomes monotonously suggest self-defeating thinking and action, does that not suggest that people have had an unrealistic conception of the relationship between their self-interest and action?

It is obvious from what I have just said that issues of power in the school culture are very much related to how one views professionalism. One does not become a professional to have others tell you how to do your work. Indeed, one of the goals of professional training is to instill the sense of distinctiveness, if not uniqueness, about how one renders services, and it is unprofessional to allow others who do not possess your knowledge and skills to determine your actions. Inherent in the concept of the professional is power, albeit circumscribed power.

For a long time school teachers were not regarded as professionals, i.e., whatever they were or did was not determined by a theoretical and empirical knowledge base that was always changing by virtue of new ideas, scholarship, and research. The teacher was not a professional in the sense that a physician was. That view did not change because those who held it changed their minds, but rather because of efforts within the educational community to meet the traditional criteria for professionalism. These efforts were not restricted to teachers, but to the increasing variety of educational personnel (e.g., administrators, school psychologists, school social workers, curriculum specialists) that began to populate schools.

With the advantage of hindsight it is not surprising that this striving for professional status would be fateful. It raised the problem of who within the schools should have a voice in educational decision-making. The more that schools contained a variety of educational professionals—each of whom saw himself or herself as having specialized knowledge and functions essential to the purposes of schooling—the more each of them sought a role in decision-making if only because those decisions frequently affected how each would render service or how that service would be regarded by others. Power struggles took two forms: among the professionals and between each group of professionals and those (the superintendent and the board of education) with ultimate decision-making power. Up until two decades ago neither of these power struggles reached public attention if only because there were no developments external to the schools that played into these struggles. This is not to say that these power struggles were more or less severe than what one would have found in any other large bureaucratically organized setting, but rather to emphasize that the variety of professionals in the schools guaranteed that power would be a central feature of the struggles. The more types of professionals a setting contains, the more it will be characterized by conflicts about power. (A general hospital or a medical center illustrates this point even more clearly than schools.)

Two external developments gave force and brought attention to these conflicts. The first in point of time was the fantastic growth in the school population after World War II together with the changing racial and ethnic composition of urban schools. It was not only that urban schools did not have the money to build and staff schools to keep up with the population explosion, but also that school personnel were faced with a changing school population for which traditional curricula and criteria for educational growth seemed no longer adequate or appropriate. Indeed, it was the severity of the "urban problem" that brought about change in the traditional view that education was a local and state responsibility and that the federal government had no business "meddling" into what was a parental-local-state affair.

A story is relevant here. A colleague of mine, Dr. Samuel Brownell, was the U.S. Commissioner of Education in the early years of the Eisenhower presidency. Dr. Brownell was quite sensitive to the dimensions of the urban problem and its increasing disorganizing and morale lowering impact on schools. It was obvious to him that neither the cities nor the states had the resources to deal with the problems, and that unless the federal government entered the picture the consequences of inaction would be socially disruptive. It was arranged for Dr. Brownell to present his case for a change in federal policy to President Eisenhower and his cabinet, a fact testifying to the significance attached to such a policy change. Dr. Brownell presented his case, following which the President asked each member of the cabinet to express an opinion. Without exception each member advised against the policy change, although some recognized the gravity of the situation. Finally, President Eisenhower turned to Vice-President Nixon for his opinion and he unequivocally supported Dr. Brownell's argument and recommendation. At this point President Eisenhower expressed agreement with both Nixon and Brownell and the wheels were set in motion to develop vehicles for federal intervention.

For our purposes here the significance of that policy change was the impetus it provided for increasing the number and variety of professionals in schools. Especially in our urban areas the flow of federal funds, a flow that in subsequent years seemed to be more of a torrent, led to such an increase in the size and varieties of educational personnel as to make administration a preoccupation of everyone. Neither before, then, or now has the management of quick growth been handled well. To those who lived through those days, their experience was made up of optimism about the future and frustration about the increasing and bewildering bureaucratization of schools. The growth in internal complexity brought with it an escalation of power struggles among the diverse professional groupings.

The second external development that played into these internal power dynamics was somewhat more complicated and subtle, at its beginnings at least. There are different but related ways by which one may label the decade or so after World War II. The Age of Psychology, The Age of the Child, and The Age of Mental Health are labels that reflect the heightened awareness and concern of parents about child rearing and education (Sarason, 1977). Those were the years when Spock's book on child rearing was the bible for millions of parents intent on insuring that their children

would grow and learn, i.e., take maximum advantage of educational opportunities. Those were also the days when the phrase "to develop the
child's potential to the fullest" entered common parlance. Parents became
interested in and articulate about learning and schooling as never before.
They wanted "good" schools and they fought for them. But in advocating
for and supporting increased educational budgets, parents were in no way
challenging the responsibility of educators to decide the substance of the
educational process. Generally speaking, the community and school personnel saw eye-to-eye about what needed to be done. This was a period
when schools enjoyed a rare degree of community support. People today
need to be reminded that one of the sources of the militancy of teacher
unions in those early decades after World War II was parental support.
How could you expect teachers to do a good job with such pitiful compensation? And what that question obscured was the fact that the diverse professional groups in schools each in its own way had begun to challenge the
educational decision-making process, a process that at its core deals with
the allocation of resources. *Those challenges, however, were based on the
assumption that decision-making, however the process might be altered,
was the responsibility of the professionals.* The power struggles within the
school reinforced the longstanding principle that, in practice, decision-
making was primarily the responsibility of the professional educator, legal
fictions to the contrary not withstanding. But beginning with the 1954
desegregation decision, helping to set the stage as it did for the "turbulent sixties," the questions of who owns the schools and who should
have a voice in determining the *substance* of education came to the fore.
And when it came to the fore the core issue was the role of parents and
other community groups in educational decision-making. That proposed
role presented a direct challenge to the power of the school professionals.
That power struggle, *that* polarization was far more public and violent than
the struggles and polarizations among the professionals. Far from community groups viewing school professionals as part of the solution, they
came to see them as part of the problem. The polarization continues to today, the level of conflict waxing and waning, but always there.

We have been dwelling on the change process. Let us now turn to a
different set of issues that are suggested by these questions: How can one
describe the school culture so as to provide more clear criteria by which to
judge whether an intended change in it has been achieved? Is it possible
that criteria can be developed that will reduce the role of personal opinion
in evaluating outcomes? We have suggested that inadequacies in our conception of the change process and of our understanding of the school
culture have contributed mightily to disappointing outcomes. But are we
more clear about the outcomes we seek than about the ways to obtain
them?

Chapter 6
Programmatic and Behavioral Regularities

The attempt to introduce a change into the school setting makes at least two assumptions: the change is desirable according to some set of values, and the intended outcomes are clear. In this chapter we shall be concerned with the clarity of the intended outcomes.

The new math (Chapter 4) illustrates the problem of intended outcomes clearly. Was one of its intended outcomes to demonstrate that children could learn the new math to certain criterion levels? Was another outcome to show that children would enjoy the new math more than children enjoyed learning the old math? Was it an intended outcome that exposure to the new math would have some demonstrable effect on how children thought about other subject matter in school? Was it an intended outcome that the new math would affect the thinking and activities of children outside of school, more than the old math did? Was it an intended outcome to change in any way the nature of relationships between teacher and child? Was it an intended outcome to change the quantity and quality of questions that children asked about numbers and problem solving? Was it an intended outcome that children would learn that the principle that a particular thing (e.g., a number) can have different significances, is a principle equally applicable to other kinds of events, such as those they study in history?

Undoubtedly, one can ask about other possible intended outcomes. Neither in the specific case we described nor in the general literature is it clear what outcomes were intended, whether or not there was a priority among outcomes, and what the relationship is between any outcome and the processes of change leading to it. As a colleague remarked: "In a way this is a happy state of affairs. You don't have to think about important problems, you have little or nothing to evaluate, and faith and personal opinion carry the day.'' But more than the new math is at stake, and we cannot allow ourselves to be content with studying states of illusory happiness.

THE EXISTING REGULARITIES

Let us approach the general problem of outcomes by indulging in a fantasy. Imagine a being from outer space who finds himself and his invisible space platform directly above an elementary school. Being superior to earthly beings he is able to see everything that goes on in the school. But he does operate under certain restrictions: he does not comprehend the meaning of written or spoken language, and it can never occur to him that things go on inside of what we call heads. He can see and hear everything and, being an *avant garde* outer-spacer, he, of course, possesses a kind of computer that records and categorizes events on any number of dimensions, allowing him to discern what we shall call the existing regularities. (Let me anticipate the discussion of the latter part of this chapter by advancing the hypothesis that *any attempt to introduce change into the school setting requires, among other things, changing the existing regularities in some way. The intended outcomes involve changing an existing regularity, eliminating one or more of them, or producing new ones.)*

Let us start with one of the more obvious regularities. Our outer-spacer will discern (but not understand) that for five consecutive days the school is densely populated while for two consecutive days it is devoid of humans. That puzzles him. Why this 5-2 pattern? Why not a 4-3 or some other kind of pattern like 2-1-2-1-1?

What if the outer-spacer could talk to us and demanded an explanation for this existing regularity? Many of us earthlings would quickly become aware that we have a tendency to assume that the way things are is the way things should be. But our outer-spacer persists. Is this the way it has always been? Is this the way it is in other countries? Is it demonstrably the best pattern for achieving the purposes of schooling? Does the existing regularity reflect noneducational considerations like religion, work patterns, and leisure time? Is it possible that the existing regularity has no intrinsic relationship to learning and education?

The significance of an existing regularity is that it forces, or should force, one to ask two questions: *What is the rationale for the regularity? and What is the universe of alternatives that could be considered?* Put in another way: Can the existing regularity be understood without considering its relationship to the alternatives of which it is but one possibility?[1] I would suggest that if we could peruse this issue in the case of the 5-2 pattern we would become increasingly aware not only of the universe of alternatives but also of the degree to which the existing pattern reflects considerations that have little or nothing to do with the intended objectives of schooling.

Let us take another "population" regularity. After a period of time our outer-spacer notes that at regular intervals (what earthlings call once a month) a group of people come together at a particular time in the evening. No small people are there, only big people. With few exceptions, the big people tend not to have been seen in the school during the day. The exceptions are those who are in rooms during the day with small people.

At this meeting most of the people sit in orderly rows, very quietly, and rarely say anything. When someone in these rows says something it is most frequently preceded by the raising of his or her right hand. There are a few people who do most of the talking and they sit in front at a table.

Several things puzzle the outer-spacer. For example, his computer tells him that there is no relationship between this meeting and any existing regularity during the day; that is, any existing regularity during the day is in no way affected by the occurrence of these meetings. This puzzles the outer-spacer because there are obvious similarities between the evening meeting and what goes on in the daytime. For example, both times most people sit quietly in orderly rows—in the evening big people sit quietly, while during the day it is the little people who sit quietly. At both times it is the big people "in front" who do most of the talking—in the evening there is one big person who talks the most, while during the day it is the only big person in the room who does most of the talking. What complicates matters for the outer-spacer is that he has seen that in both instances as soon as the people leave their rooms they speak much more, and they have a much greater variety of facial expression.

How do we respond to our celestial friend when he learns English and demands explanations for these regularities and similarities? What do we say to him about why there is no apparent relationship between what goes on at a PTA meeting and anything else that goes on at the school? What do

---

1. It is an interesting digression to suggest that one of the major sources of the conflict between generations is that the younger generation has the annoying ability not only to discern existing regularities but also to force the older generation to the awareness that there are alternative regularities. This, of course, the older generation finds difficult to accept because of the tendency to confuse the way things are with the way things should or could be. I remember as a child being puzzled and annoyed that no one could satisfactorily explain to me why one could not eat fried chicken for breakfast. It was obvious what the existing breakfast regularities were, but I could not understand why the alternative of chicken aroused such strong feeling.

we say when he demands that we tell him the alternative ways that were considered for organizing a PTA meeting or classroom, and the basis used for making a choice?[2]

Earlier in this chapter I said that "any attempt to introduce change into the school setting requires, among other things, changing in some way the existing regularities." At this point I would further suggest that this statement should be preceded by the statement that *the attempt to introduce a change into the school setting usually (if not always) stems from the perception of a regularity that one does not like.* We, like the outerspacer, are set to see regularities, but unlike the inhabitant of the space platform we are not set either to observe the tremendous range of existing regularities or to inquire naively about the rationale for any one of them and the nature of the universe of alternatives of which the existing regularity is but one possibility.

Let us now leave both fantasy and heavenly friend and take up several existing regularities that not only illustrate the fruitfulness of this approach for understanding the school culture but also help clarify the problem of how to state intended outcomes in ways that are testable.

THE PHYSICAL EDUCATION PROGRAM

In most schools there is a place, usually large, where physical education programs are conducted. Those who conduct these programs are expected to have special training.

WHAT HAPPENS WHEN, AS I HAVE DONE IN NUMEROUS OCCASIONS, I SAY to groups of teachers that I simply do not comprehend why there should be physical education programs in the schools? As you might imagine, the most frequent response is staring disbelief followed by a request to reformulate the statement. Without going into the details of the discussion—which is usually quite heated—I shall indicate the significances I attribute to the initial response and the ensuing discussion. First, there is the implicit recognition both by the teachers and myself that we operate

---

2. Most people are aware that a good part of the controversy surrounding large urban school systems arises precisely because some community groups are pushing for an alternative way of implementing "community control," a way that would presumably change, if not eliminate, some of the PTA and classroom regularities described above. I say "presumably" because I have neither seen, heard, nor read anything to indicate that aside from changing the curriculum (as in the case of new or old math) there is any intent to change the most significant existing regularities in the classroom, for example, the passivity of the learner or the teacher as talker and question-asker. My reservation may become more clear later in this chapter when we take up in detail some of the existing regularities in the classroom. The point I wish to emphasize here is that those who are in favor of "community control" state their intended outcomes for the classroom, when they state them at all, in terms so vague and virtuous that they would defy subsequent attempt at evaluation—quite in contrast to the specificity of intended outcomes as to the role of parents in decision-making.

in different worlds, i.e., I perceive them and they perceive me as having different backgrounds and experiences. Second, it is inconceivable to the teachers that a school could or should be without a physical education program. They have a conception of a school which, if changed or challenged, they strongly defend. Far from being indifferent to the conception they defend it to a degree which illuminates how their sense of identity is related to their conception. Third, they justify the physical education program in terms of what they think children are and need. Put in another way, their justification is psychological and philosophical (Sarason, 1969b, p. 6). ■

One of the most frequent responses to my question is that children need an opportunity "to get rid of all that energy which they have in them." This energy cannot be discharged by sitting and doing work in classrooms. It is interesting to note that in the minds of teachers this response seems to assume that at least three things are true: (1) the greater the amount of continuous time a child spends in a classroom the more restless he or she becomes; (2) much energy is discharged in gym activities, and (3) following the discharge of energy the child's restlessness in class is discernibly less than before gym.

As to the first assumption, I am not aware that anyone has demonstrated that increased restlessness is a function merely of time. I have seen classrooms where I could discern no increase in restlessness, and I have seen other classrooms where the increase was predictably related to subject matter interacting either with teacher interest or adequacy, or with style. Teachers responding to my question in a group do not say what many have said to me when I have talked with them alone while their classes were in gym: *the gym period is one during which the teacher can recoup his or her energy losses, or get some paper work done.*

As to the second assumption, I do not doubt that there is much energy discharged in gym. But I do doubt, as do many teachers, the third assumption. *Observation rather compellingly suggests that following gym there is frequently an increase in restlessness and listlessness that interferes with class work. The intended outcome does not seem to occur; in fact, the reverse of it may be the modal consequence.* In connection with outcomes, my observations suggest that the level of class restlessness before gym is highly related to level of restlessness after gym.

The rationale for the regularity of gym frequently includes intended outcomes other than the ones given above. Increasing motor skill, teaching cooperation in group or team effort, and preparing children for productive use of leisure time are some intended outcomes advanced to justify gym programs. Although these are statements about intended outcomes, they do not in any clear way tell me how existing behavioral regularities of children are changed or new ones are added.

I know of several suburban school systems in which the major gym activities of girls during the fall and spring are field hockey and a variety of kickball games. If *one* of the intended outcomes of such activities is to influence leisure time behavioral regularities (types of physical activities, their frequency, etc.), I must report the fact that I have never seen girls engage in these activities outside of school. But, one can maintain, there are other and perhaps more important outcomes for out-of-school activities. Agreed; but without knowing the out-of-school behavioral regularities one cannot determine what effects, if any, gym activities have on them.

What *would* happen if gym programs ceased? This alternative would probably arouse reactions similar to those that surrounded the withdrawal of certain universities from intercollegiate football competition. But these universities have suffered no baleful effects.

Physical education personnel are not likely to believe that I have no strong feelings for or against their programs. My purpose in discussing these programs has been to make several points: first, that they represent a programmatic regularity in the school culture; second, that any programmatic regularity, explicitly or implicitly, describes intended outcomes that involve either new behavioral regularities or the changing of old ones; third, that there are alternatives to the existing programmatic regularity; and, fourth, that any challenge to a programmatic regularity is more likely to engender feeling than reason. This last point is certainly not peculiar to the school culture.

It has not been my intention here, nor will it be in the later pages, to convey the impression that I am demanding proof or justification for the programmatic regularities that exist in the school culture. The absence of proof does not mean that the underlying rationale is invalid. Even where there is apparently disconfirming evidence we must be clear as to whether the rationale is being relevantly tested. My position in these pages is that the intended outcomes for programmatic regularities can and should be stated in terms of overt behavioral regularities that the dispassionate observer can record. To state intended outcomes in any other way increases the chances that we will be dealing with all the confusion and controversy produced by what Hook has called the unanalyzable abstraction (Chapter 3).

THE ARITHMETIC-MATHEMATICS
PROGRAMMATIC REGULARITY

We turn to the arithmetic-mathematics regularity in order to see how easy it is to assume that the way things are is the way they should be, and to help grasp how difficult it is to examine what I have called the universe of alternatives. In an earlier chapter I alluded to the following programmatic regularity: beginning in the first grade and on every school day thereafter until graduation from high school the child receives instruction and drill in the use and understanding of numbers. Like eating and sleeping regularly, one may assume that this degree of regularity reflects considerations vital to the development of children.

The naive person might ask several questions: Would academic and intellectual development be adversely affected if the exposure was for four days a week instead of five? Or three instead of five? What would happen if the exposure began in the second or third grade? What if the exposure was in alternate years? Obviously, one can generate many more questions, each of which suggests an alternative to the existing programmatic regularity. From this universe of alternatives how does one justify the existing regularity?

Before taking up this question we must first deal with the emotional reactions I have gotten when on numerous occasions I have asked different groups (e.g., educators, psychologists, and parents) questions that challenge what exists and implicitly suggest that there may be other ways of thinking and acting. I focus on the emotional reactions because they reveal the distinctive characteristics of the culture more than other ways of understanding the setting, particularly if one is or has been a member of that setting. Because we have spent so much of our own lives in schools, and watched our own children in school, we may never be aware of the process whereby we uncritically confuse what is with what might be. In fact, in diverse ways, one of the most significant effects of school on children is to get them to accept existing regularities as the best and only possible state of affairs, although frequently this is neither verbally stated nor consciously decided.

The first response to my statement of alternatives is essentially one of humor; that is, the listener assumes that I intended something akin to a funny joke.[3] Having established myself as a comic, however, I usually persist and insist that I am quite serious. To keep the discussion going I then say the following:

LET ME TELL YOU THE RESULTS OF AN INFORMAL POLL I HAVE BEEN CONducting among friends and colleagues, and I will take this opportunity to get your answers to this question: When you think back over the past

---

3. This reminds me of the suggestion that a former colleague, quite eminent, made in the course of a discussion about how a university could get rid of tenured professors who were "dead wood" (i.e., whatever contribution they made was a long time ago and there was no reason to believe that they served any function other than to stand in the way of younger teachers). His suggestion was that all beginning instructors be given tenure and as they get promoted (from assistant, to associate, to full professor) they have increasingly less tenure so that when they become full professors they have no tenure at all. The suggestion, of course, was treated as a joke and no one (including myself) considered for a moment that there *were* alternatives to the existing structure (the way things are is the only way things should be).

few months, how many times have you used numbers other than to do *simple* addition, subtraction, multiplication, and division? The results of the poll are clear: highly educated, productive people very rarely use numbers other than in the most simple ways, leaving aside, of course, those individuals whose work requires more advanced number concepts (e.g., mathematicians). On what basis is it illegitimate to suggest that these results have no significance for the fact that a large part of what children learn in twelve years of arithmetic and mathematics is content other than the simple computations? Incidentally, I have also polled many far less educated individuals and, needless to say, the results contain no exception to the use only of simple computations. ■

And now the fur begins to fly. Among the more charitable accusations is the one that I am anti-intellectual. Among the least charitable reactions (for me) is simply an unwillingness to pursue the matter further. (On one occasion some individuals left the meeting in obvious disgust.) One can always count on some individuals asserting that mathematics "trains or disciplines the mind" and the more of it the better, much like Latin used to be justified as essential to the curriculum.[4]

The fact is that whenever I have presented these thoughts I have been extremely careful to state them so that the words and sentences I employ do not contain any preference for any alternative, *simply because I have no adequate basis for choosing among the universe of alternatives*—and neither do the audiences. The intent of the thoughts is twofold: to indicate that there is always a universe of alternatives from which to choose, and to show that when any programmatic regularity is no longer viewed in terms of that universe of alternatives, rational thought and evaluation of in-

---

4. It is important for an understanding of the school culture, although it certainly is not peculiar to it, that one not assume that the *public* positions taken by groups within that culture are those held *privately* by all or most individuals comprising those groups. Many within the school culture question many aspects of programmatic regularities and are willing to consider the universe of alternatives. However, several factors keep this seeking and questioning a private affair. First, there is the untested assumption that few others think in this way. As we have said elsewhere (Sarason et al., 1966) "teaching is a lonely profession" despite the fact that the school is densely populated. Second, existing vehicles for discussion and planning within the school (faculty meetings: teacher-principal contacts, teacher-supervisor contacts, etc.) are based on the principle of avoidance of controversy. Third, at all levels (teacher, principal, administrator) there is the feeling of individual impotence. Fourth, there is acceptance of another untested assumption: that the public will oppose any meaningful or drastic change in existing regularities. In short, these and other factors seem to allow almost everyone in the culture to act in terms of perceived group norms at the expense of the expression of "deviant" individual thoughts, a situation conducive neither to change nor to job satisfaction. It was only after I had worked intensively for months in schools, and had developed a relationship of mutual trust with school personnel, that I came to see that there was a difference between public statements and private positions.

tended outcomes are no longer in the picture, overwhelmed as they are by the power of faith, tradition, and habit.

A final example. What are the rites of passage for becoming a teacher? In most instances, following graduation from high school the person selects a college that has a teacher trainee program. The first two years of college are devoted to courses in the arts and sciences, and it is usually in the third year that education courses are taken preparatory to practice teaching and more advanced seminars. What if one required that anyone graduating high school and intent on becoming a teacher would have to spend one year learning the culture of the school? That is to say, it would be a year during which the person would have duties in different places (elementary, middle, and high schools; pupil personnel department; board of education meetings, etc.) that would *begin* to expand and deepen their understanding of educational rites. This would be a carefully organized and supervised year geared to observation of and experience with problems and issues that are distinctive to the educational scene. Some college credit would be given. How do I justify this recommendation when I present it to groups of teachers, administrators, and college faculty? For one thing, I point out, the usual teacher training program gives the student very narrow experience in schools (see page 46), an informational and conceptual narrowness that in no way can be considered adaptive. For another thing, at the present time the student taking education courses has no experiential basis for determining whether the picture of schools reflects the realities of schools. Put in another way, too many college faculty no longer have a firsthand, sustained experience with schools and, therefore, they ill prepare the student for what he or she will encounter. But the most clear, empirical justification for coming up with alternatives to present practices is, as Lortie (1975) has indicated, the feeling among teachers that their professional preparation was markedly inadequate. The reaction to my proposal has never been favorable. "Do you mean," I am asked, "that you would give responsibilities to people who never had an education course?" I answer, "Why not?" "Do you mean that someone right out of high school would be allowed to spend the year as you described?" "Yes."

I did not offer my proposal because I was convinced that it would be more effective than either the existing practice or any other alternative I or someone else could come up with. The fact is that I believe my proposal has some merit, but I believe even more strongly that the present practice has not been maintained *because* of its demonstrable superiority to alternatives. In listening to the defenders of the present practice, one comes away with the feeling that any departure along the lines of my proposal would be predictably harmful. They are unaware that for decades in the last and the present century those who became teachers had somewhat less than a four-year high school education following which they became teachers very quickly. And although we like to believe that anything we do today is obviously superior to the way we did those things in earlier times, we should try to be sensitive to the possibility that we are victims of "generational chauvinism." These defenders of today's regularities are also unaware that at the height of the population explosion in the fifties and sixties, when there was a formidable teacher shortage, people were allowed to start teaching with no formal professional background whatsoever. Nobody has ever demonstrated that these people on average were more or less ineffective than teachers who had the formal preparation. The perceived universe of alternatives expands somewhat when there is an institutional crisis as there was during the population explosion. That expansion is dramatically greater when it is a societal crisis, e.g., during war. In war time there is quick and willing alteration in standards, practices, and training, and here too there is no compelling evidence of harmful consequences. The point of my proposal is that present practices are not choices rationally selected from a universe of alternatives. That we justify them as if they were so selected says far more about our capacity to delude ourselves and to resist the consequences of change than it does about the effectiveness of the present practice. This is not peculiar to people in the school culture. If I use the phrase "culture of the school," it is, of course, to suggest that there are features of that setting that differ from those of other settings. But in response to proposals for change, people in schools and other distinctive types of settings are similarly allergic to the implications of the concept of the universe of alternatives.

Thus far in this chapter we have discussed examples of regularities to which all within the school must adapt, since there is little or no element of individual choice. They are predetermined characteristics of the setting. Let us now turn to what might be termed *behavioral regularities,* which have to do with the frequency of overt behaviors. Laughing, crying, fighting, talking, concentrating, working, writing, question-asking, question-answering, test behavior and performance, stealing, cheating, unattending—these are *some* of the overt behaviors that occur with varying frequency among children in school. That they occur is important to, and expected by, school personnel. But what is equally important is that they are expected to change over time. *Behavioral regularities and their changes represent some of the most important intended outcomes of programmatic regularities. Deliberate changes in programmatic regularities are intended to change the occurrence and frequency of behavioral regularities.*

Some behavioral regularities are concerned with individual pupils while others reflect pupil-pupil interactions, such as boys with girls, older pupils with younger pupils, and black with white. As important as any of these are the behavioral regularities characterizing teacher-pupil interactions. We shall take up now a teacher-pupil behavioral regularity fateful for the intended outcome of any change in programmatic regularities.

QUESTION-ASKING:
A BEHAVIORAL REGULARITY

As in our discussion of programmatic regularities I shall not start with questions about assumptions, values, intended outcomes, or alternative patterns, but rather with the discernible regularity. It is, I think, only when one is confronted with a clear regularity that one stands a chance of clarifying the relationship between theory and practice, intention and outcome. Let us, therefore, start by asking two questions: At what rate do teachers ask questions in the classroom? At what rate do children ask questions of teachers?

From a theoretical and practical standpoint—by which I mean theories of child development, intellectual growth, educational and learning theory, techniques of teaching, presentation and discussion of subject matter—the importance of question-asking has always been emphasized. It is surprising, therefore, that there have been very few studies focusing on this type of behavior, Susskind (1969, 1979) did a comprehensive review of the literature. He expresses surprise that a type of behavior considered by everyone to be of great importance has hardly been investigated. However, he points out that although the few studies vary greatly in investigative sophistication, they present a remarkably similar state of affairs. But before we summarize the findings, the readers may wish to try to answer Susskind's (1969) question:

BEFORE EXPLORING THE RESEARCH LITERATURE WE SUGGEST THAT THE reader attempt to estimate the rates of two classroom behaviors. Imagine yourself in a fifth grade, social studies classroom in a predominantly white, middle-class school. During a half-hour lesson, in which the teacher and the class talk to each other (there is no silent work), how many questions are asked (a) by the teacher, (b) by the students? How do the two rates correlate? (p. 38). ■

The first two questions are deceptively simple because, as Susskind has made clear, there are different types of questions, and there are problems as to how questions (and which questions) are to be counted. For example, if the teacher asks the same question of five children should it be counted once or five times? Susskind developed a comprehensive, workable set of categories, and the interested reader is referred to his work. We will now summarize the answers to the above questions in light of existing studies, including the ones by Susskind, whose findings are very similar to those from older studies.

1. Across the different studies the range of rate of teacher questions per half-hour is from 45–150.

2. When asked, educators as well as other groups vastly underestimate the rate of teacher questions, the estimated range being 12–20 per half hour.
3. From 67 to 95 percent of all teacher questions require "straight recall" from the student.
4. Children ask *fewer* than two questions per half hour. That is to say, during this time period two questions by children will have been asked.
5. The greater the tendency for a teacher to ask straight recall questions, the fewer the questions initiated by children. This does not mean that children do not have time to ask questions. They do have time.
6. The more a teacher asks "personally relevant" questions, the higher the rate of questioning on the part of children.
7. The rate of questions by children does not seem to vary with IQ level or with social-class background.

These statements derive from existing studies, but, as Susskind points out, scores of people have come to similar conclusions from informal observations.

We have here a clear behavioral regularity. How should we think about this? Is this behavioral regularity an intended outcome? Put in another way, this is the way things are; is this the way things should be? I know of no psychological theory or theorist, particularly those who are or have been most influential on the educational scene, who would view this behavioral regularity as a desirable outcome, that is, as one kind of barometer indicating that an organized set of conceptions are being consistently implemented. In addition, I have never read of or spoken to curriculum specialists and reformers who would not view this behavioral regularity as evidence that their efforts were being neither understood nor implemented. Finally, the fact that teachers and other groups vastly underestimate the rate of teacher-questioning (in Susskind's study teachers were quite surprised when confronted with the rates obtained in *their* classrooms) suggests that this behavioral regularity is not an intended outcome according to some part of the thinking of teachers.[5]

We have, then, an outcome that practically nobody intends, a situation that would not be particularly upsetting were it not that practically everybody considers question-asking on the part of teachers and children one of the most crucial means of maintaining interest, supporting curiosity, acquiring knowledge, and facilitating change and growth.

In Chapter 4, where we used the new math to illustrate the modal process of introducing change into the school culture, we emphasized the point

---

5. Children are the one group who realistically estimate or know the behavioral regularity. My informal poll of scores of children leaves no doubt in my mind that they view the classroom as a place where teachers ask questions and children provide answers.

that the curriculum reformers seemed quite aware that they wanted to do more than merely change textbooks; they realized that classrooms tended to be uninviting and uninspired places in which teachers were active and children passive. Their intended outcome was to change, among other things, behavioral regularities such as the one we are discussing here. But this intended outcome was never systematically discussed (or even written about) or stated as a criterion by which the new curriculum was to be judged. Certainly the teachers who underwent retraining could not focus on this issue, if only because they were in the same passive role that characterized, and would continue to characterize, their own students.

For our purposes here, the generalization that requires emphasis is that *any change in a programmatic regularity has as one of its intended outcomes some kind of change in existing behavioral regularities, and these behavioral regularities are among the most important criteria for judging the degree to which intended outcomes are being achieved.* At this point I am not interested in whether or not one likes or agrees with the programmatic change, but rather in the fact that these changes require changes in some kind or kinds of behavorial regularities. It is almost always true that changes in the behavioral regularities will be assumed to be effected or mediated by internal emotional and cognitive processes and states, but the behavioral regularities remain as our most sccure, albeit not infallible, criterion for judging what we have achieved. In fact (and the question-asking regularity is a good example), behavioral regularities are probably our best means for inferring internal cognitive and emotional states.

It is the rare observer of classrooms who has not inferred from the overt behavior of children and teachers that the great majority of children seem "inside" to be neither strongly interested in, curious about, nor feeling satisfaction in regard to what they are doing or what is going on. They are, in short, not having a particularly good time. But, someone can say, this is an inference, and it may frequently be a wrong one, which of course, is true. To what behavioral regularities can we look that could serve as a kind of check on these inferences?

One of them, of course, requires asking children to respond to relevant questions about what they are feeling, but this will be regarded as either too obvious or naive because of the frequently held assumption that what people, particularly children, report about what they feel should not be given much weight. But what if we were to look at the behavior of children in the hall *immediately* after they leave one classroom to go to another, as in the case in junior and senior high? How does one account for the noise level, the animated talking, running, and formation of groups, and the absence of talk about the intellectual substance of what they had just experienced? *Why is it that one of the most trouble-producing (from the standpoint of school per-*

sonnel) times in the school day is when students are in the halls going from one room to another? When the behavioral regularities in the hall are ascertained, I have no doubt that they will be found to be related to regularities in the classroom in a way that confirms inferences made about the internal states of children in the classroom. ■

But we cannot understand the question-asking regularity without briefly trying to understand what aspects of the school culture contribute to a state of affairs that few, if anyone, feel is the way things should be.

1. *Teachers tend to teach the way in which they themselves were taught.* I am not only referring to the public schooling of teachers but to their college experiences as well—and I am not restricting myself to schools of education. In general, the question-asking regularity we have described does not, in my experience, differ markedly from what goes on in college classrooms. The culture of the school should be expected to reflect aspects of other types of educational cultures from which the teachers have come. As suggested in an earlier chapter, university critics of the public schools frequently are unable to see that their criticisms may well be true of their own educational culture. It would indeed be strange if teachers did not teach the way they had been taught.

2. *In their professional training (courses, practice teaching) teachers are minimally exposed to theories about question-asking and the technical problems of question-asking and question-producing behavior—the relationship between theory and practice.* To those who may be surprised at this, I would suggest consulting the most frequently used books in educational psychology, learning, or child development courses. Such readers may conclude either that it is not an important question or that the obvious is being overlooked.

3. *Whatever educational help or consultation is available to the teacher (principal, supervisors, workshops, etc.) does not concern itself directly with the question-asking regularity.* Particularly in the earliest months and years of teaching, the primary concern of everyone is "law and order," and the possibility that discipline may be related to, or can be affected by, the question-asking regularity is rarely recognized. The anxiety of the beginning teacher about maintaining discipline too frequently interferes with sensitivity to, and desire to accommodate to, the questions and interests of his or her pupils.

4. *The predetermined curriculum that suggests that teachers cover a certain amount of material within certain time intervals with the expectation that their pupils as a group will perform at certain levels at certain times is responded to by teachers in a way as to make for the fantastic discrepancy between the rate of teacher and student questions.* This factor touches on a very complicated state of affairs. From the standpoint of

the teacher, the curriculum is not a suggestion but a requirement, for if it is not met the principal and supervisors will consider the teaching inadequate. In addition, the teacher whom the pupils will have in the next year will consider them inadequately prepared. Therefore, the best and safest thing to do is to insure that the curriculum is covered, a view that reinforces the tendency to ask many "straight recall" questions.

From the administrator's standpoint the curriculum is only a guide, and the trouble arises because teachers are not "creative"; that is, the problem is not the curriculum but the teacher. As many administrative personnel have said, "We *tell* them to be creative but they still stick slavishly to the curriculum as if it were a bible." To which teachers reply, "What they want to know at the end of the year, and what I will be judged by, are the achievement test scores of my children."

Although both sides *correctly* perceive each other's behavioral regularity, the administrator feels unable to change the state of affairs—that is, he or she is of no help to the teacher—and the teacher continues to feel unfree to depart from the curriculum. In short, we are back to a familiar situation in which no one sees the universe of alternatives to current practices.

There are, of course, alternatives. For example, as Susskind's studies show, there is variation among teachers in the question-asking regularity; some teachers can utilize a curriculum without being a question-asking machine and without requiring pupils to respond primarily to "straight recall" questions. In addition, and a source of encouragement, Susskind obtained data suggesting that when a group of teachers were confronted with the question-asking regularities in their classroom, and this was discussed in terms of theory and intended outcomes, the teachers as a group were able to change the regularity. *But here one runs smack into the obstacle of another characteristic of the school culture: there are no vehicles of discussion, communication, or observation that allow for this kind of variation to be raised and productively used for purposes of help and change.* Faculty meetings, as teachers are acutely aware, are not noted for either their intellectual content or their sensitivity to issues that may be controversial or interpersonally conflictful.[6] (As our man from outer space could well have discerned, the classroom, the PTA meeting, and the faculty meeting are amazingly similar in the question-asking regularity.) We shall have more to say on these issues later.

---

6. The absence in schools of the tradition of the case conference, a vehicle whereby teachers present to and learn from each other, is discussed in a later chapter, where we take up Public Law 94–142, popularly known as the "mainstreaming" law. That law requires the spirit and procedures of the case conference. It remains to be seen whether the case conference in the school takes hold as a learning device for staff and a helping device for pupils and parents. To my knowledge, in all the research that is going on in relation to 94–142, there is not a single study on the "placement team" meetings.

For our purposes here, what is most important is not the particular behavioral regularity or the factors that may account for it, but the obvious fact that within the school culture these regularities, which are in the nature of intended outcomes, are not recognized, and it is not traditional to have means for their recognition. What is not recognized or verbalized cannot be dealt with, and if it is important and not recognized, efforts to introduce substantive change, particularly in the classroom, result in the illusion of change.

WHAT IS THE INTENDED OUTCOME?

We will now take up something that is not the usual behavioral or programmatic regularity, although it has features of both. It is a regularity that will not be found in all schools; in fact, it may be rather infrequent. The first justification for presenting it is that it illustrates well the fruitfulness of discerning regularities, using them to determine their intended outcomes, and squaring these outcomes with what actually happens. The second justification is that the data we possessed were surprising to all concerned. I should add that these data were gathered in relation to a study (Sarason, Hill, and Zimbardo, 1964; Hill and Sarason, 1966) tangential to the purposes of this book, and it was not until we experienced "surprise" at some findings that we examined the purposes of the regularities in terms of intended and actual outcomes.

In the two junior high schools of a suburban school system, when a student considered capable of good work is doing poorly in any subject, an "interim" is sent home indicating that he or she is in danger of failing the course. The student may be doing failing work or the level of performance may be significantly below expectations. If the low or failing performance is considered a true indication of the student's intellectual capacity, no interim is sent. Since the average IQ in these schools is discernibly above the national average (not surprising in light of the predominantly middle-class composition of the community), there are relatively few students who do not possess the capacity to get passing grades in their courses. In the bulk of instances, when an interim is sent home the student is in danger of getting an F or a D for that marking period.

The study we were doing involved two large samples of children. We had been following one sample since they were in Grade 1; the other since they were in Grade 2. There was no reason to believe that each sample was not representative of all children in that particular class. One question in which we were interested was what happened to these children in their first year of junior high school?

One could say that we were dealing with a behavioral regularity in which the failing or near-failing performance of certain students gave rise to a certain action on the part of school personnel resulting in a standard written message being sent to the home. What was the intended outcome of the relationship between performance and school action? Was it merely *to inform* the home? If that were the sole intended outcome, then one could expect the parents to treat the information in much the same way as they would if they had been informed about the exact height of their children; there would be no intention that the parents act on the information. It is not violating the canons of reflective thinking to say that the intended outcome was to raise the level of the student's performance by actions that parents would take on the basis of the message from school. That, of course, is what school personnel explicitly expected.

Our surprise began when our data indicated that receiving interims was by no means infrequent. Some 47 percent of the boys in one sample, and about 49 percent in the other sample, received at least one interim during the four marking periods. For girls in the same samples, the figures were 33 and 32 percent, respectively.

We then asked what happened to the student's grade in the subject in which he or she had received an interim—did the student's grade increase, decrease, or remain the same compared to the grade in the previous marking period? Since the previous grade was typically a D or F, it was obvious that for many students they had only one direction in which to go, and that was up. *What the data clearly revealed was that in half the cases the grade remained the same, in 38 percent the grade went down, and in 12 percent the grade went up.* If the intended outcome of this procedure was to raise grades it clearly was not successful. School personnel were unaware of these actual outcomes, and when they were made aware of them they were surprised at the discrepancy between intended and actual outcomes.

We then asked the following question: In the three major courses (English, social studies, mathematics) what was the frequency and pattern of interims over the four marking periods? We expected, as did the school personnel, that mathematics would have the highest frequency in each marking period. *To the surprise and consternation of everyone, social studies was far and away the subject matter in which the most interims were received in each marking period, with English and mathematics following in that order.*

Number of Interims in Relation to the Marking Period
(All Boys and All Girls from the Two Samples in the Two Schools)

	Boys Marking Period				*Girls* Marking Period			
	I	II	III	IV	I	II	III	IV
English	50	78	62	74	21	27	28	13
Social Studies	80	91	65	86	54	40	54	29
Math	40	66	72	64	23	20	20	19

One of the major advantages of viewing the school culture in terms of regularities and intended outcomes is that it requires one, at least temporarily, to suspend or control the role of opinion, values, or bias. As we shall see in later chapters, viewing the school culture in this fashion is but one way of understanding it, and I have been emphasizing and illustrating this way because so much of what is written about the school culture centers around issues of values and objectives without relating them to existing regularities or defining new regularities by which to judge the consistency between intent and outcome.

A second advantage of viewing the school culture in terms of existing regularities and intended outcomes is that one frequently comes up with unanticipated findings that further illuminate the existence of other kinds of regularities, and one's understanding of the setting deepens. For example, why should social studies have the greatest number of interims? Why is it apparently difficult for so many students in their first year of junior high school?

DISCONTINUITIES AND SOCIAL STUDIES

When so large a number of first-year junior high school students in a middle-class, suburban community receives at least one interim in major subjects, and in very few instances can intelligence level be a factor, one is forced to speculate about possible explanations. Consistent with our approach in this chapter (the outer spaceman approach) we can begin by comparing the elementary and junior high school settings on the more obvious regularities.[7] For example, in contrast to the elementary schools, the junior high schools are physically larger and contain more people. The students come from more than one neighborhood, they move more frequently from room to room, they have more teachers, and they have more freedom in that there is not one teacher who is *their* teacher and whose responsibility it is to oversee them. In light of these and other differences, there is a host of new rules and regulations that the students must observe. The students are like people who have spent their lives in a small town and suddenly find themselves in a large, unfamiliar city.

There are many discontinuities between elementary and junior high

7. We are apparently in an era when the term *junior high* is somewhat in disrepute and the more fashionable term is *the middle school.* In some communities the pupil comes to the middle school at a somewhat earlier age and remains there somewhat longer than was the case with the junior high. Typically, the building remains the same, but the label changes. This is like the elementary school whose principal prided himself on the initiation of ungraded classes. I was impressed until I strolled through the halls and saw that each door contained grade signs (e.g., Grade 1, Grade 2). Observation in the classrooms provided no good evidence that they should be viewed as other than traditionally organized units.

schools that require a good deal of unlearning and learning on the part of young people, and if one had to make any prediction it would be that many children would respond maladaptively. This expectation is reinforced by the fact that the usual orientation exercises are brief and ritualistic. I have sat through some of these exercises, and I have read the materials provided the children, and I can only conclude that the intended outcome was to impress on the new students that there was much to learn about socially navigating in this culture and most of that was what not to do.

Now let us ask some "regularities" questions. What information is provided the junior high about the new students? Who provides this information? What is done with the information? What we found out was that the elementary school record, including personality and academic evaluation by the student's last teacher, is sent ahead. We also found out that the teachers who made the evaluations were: (1) resentful of the fact that junior high personnel never spoke to them or sought their advice, particularly in relation to children with one or another kind of problem; and (2) puzzled at the number of children who had not been any kind of problem in elementary school but who had various difficulties in junior high. As best as we could determine, the information sent on to the junior high was read and filed. It was the truly rare instance when junior high personnel (e.g., guidance counselors) acted on the information before the child showed up or shortly after. *Our study revealed that the single best predictor of the occurrence of academic or personality problems in the first year of junior high school was the evaluation of the last teacher the children had in elementary school.* [8]

If the intended outcome of this record-keeping and its transmittal to the junior high was to *anticipate* problems with the aim of taking action to prevent their reoccurrence or to lessen their consequences, it clearly was not achieved. When this was discussed with junior high personnel it was pointed out to us that the size of the freshman class simply did not allow effective use of the information, a fact that concedes the argument that the major intended outcome was not achieved. Whatever the reason, the fact remains that these record-keeping regularities were not serving their intended purposes.

As I indicated earlier, discerning and examining regularities in relation to intended outcomes frequently lead one to questions, issues, or other observations that illuminate important aspects of the school culture. For example, in the process of doing this study—spending time in the elemen-

8. In this study we were given the names of all first year junior high children who were referred to any administrator because of a problem, or who had received an interim. We were then able to see the relationship between what the child's last teacher in elementary school had said (and implicitly predicted) and how many and what kinds of problems were recorded in his or her folder. For two successive years the evaluation of the child's last teacher was the best predictor of the occurrence of problems in the first year of junior high school.

tary and junior high schools, talking to teachers, principals, and other administrative personnel—we became increasingly aware that junior high personnel view the new student in September rather differently than elementary school personnel did in the previous June. Whereas in June the elementary school viewed the student as a *child,* in September the junior high viewed him or her as a *young adult.* These different views result in different expectations and are an important aspect of the discontinuity between the structure and organization of the two settings. I am, of course, suggesting that meeting these different expectations is frequently difficult for some children, even for many who manifested no problems in elementary school. (Anyone who has any knowledge of, or experience with, college freshmen will not be surprised by this explanation.)

There is another aspect to this problem that is illuminating of the school culture: *the differences in the ways in which pupils are viewed by elementary and junior high personnel are reflections of the differences in the ways in which these personnel view each other.* Many (by no means all) junior high school teachers view themselves as "specialists" in a particular subject matter, while they view the elementary school teacher as a somewhat superficial generalist—much like the differences between the general practitioner and specialist in medicine. Put in another way, the junior high teacher tends to view himself or herself as "higher" and, therefore, better than the elementary school teacher.[9] Although less true today than in previous decades, there is still a tendency for junior and senior high personnel to receive higher salaries than those in the elementary schools. The fact that there are far more men teachers in the junior high school than in the elementary school is undoubtedly a reflection of the view that the elementary school pupil is a child (taken care of by child-care kinds of teachers) while the junior high school pupil (who two months before was in elementary school) is a beginning young adult. These differences in views and expectations sharpen the discontinuities between the two settings.

But why should social studies (in these two junior high schools, at least) be so difficult in the first year? We looked into the curriculum manual and guide (a heavy and imposing document of 200 or more pages), talked to teachers, and sat in classrooms. I do not pretend to know and understand all the factors that would comprise an answer, but I can point to two related factors that seemed important. The first of these factors is that the students were frequently required to engage in projects for which they had to read different sources, use the library (school and community), and organize readings and materials. Many of the pupils were simply not

---

9. This is, of course, identical to the situation in universities where those who teach only graduate courses tend to view themselves as doing a more important, more worthy, or more difficult task than the instructor who only teaches undergraduates. In the public schools, as well as the universities, it is as if the worth of a teacher is determined in part by the age of his or her students.

able to take on this kind of independent responsibility. The task was not made easier by the fact that the degree and content of direction given by the teacher seemed to assume an amount of previous experience with such a task that struck us as unrealistic.

TWO YEARS AFTER THE ABOVE OBSERVATIONS I CONDUCTED A COLLEGE senior seminar for the first time in my teaching life. Up to that time I had only taught graduate students. My attitude had been that parents who sent their children to Yale had a right to expect that they would be given an excellent education, but it did not follow that I had to participate in that education. (Elementary school pupils = undergraduates; junior high school pupils = graduate students.) Midway through the seminar I was aware that I was frustrated and annoyed. Why do *they* know so little? Why is it that when I assign a paper, with a brief but commendably clear explanation of its purpose and scope, I get a barrage of questions (during and after class, in person and on the phone) about what I mean and want? Why are they so dependent and fearful of exercising independent judgment? Where have they been for three years? Who was spoon-feeding them? The principle underlying these thoughts of a teacher is quite similar to that enunciated by Professor Higgins in *My Fair Lady* when he compares men and women and concludes, "We are a marvelous sex!" ■

The second factor I can point to in regard to the social studies finding is that the pupils were required *to organize and write papers* and many of them clearly were inadequate to the task—and I must remind the readers that this population was discernibly above average in ability. This raised questions: In the last year (sixth grade) of elementary school how many times were pupils required to write a paper? How many times did a teacher sit down with a child and go over what he or she had written? My informal polling indicated that some teachers required as few as two "papers" and some required more than four.[10] Although I polled far more children than teachers, I did not hear of a single instance in which a teacher had sat down with a child to go over what he or she had written. When papers were returned to the children there were usually comments, pro and con, written on them, but the matter ended there.

At this point in our discussion it is not relevant to go into explanations of this state of affairs or to explore the universe of alternatives. I have used social studies for the purpose of illustrating how one regularity (i.e., interims) leads one to another regularity (i.e., social studies), the examination

---

10. When my daughter was in the sixth grade in an elementary school (in an adjacent community) that had the best reputation of any school in our metropolitan area, she was required to write only *one* paper.

of which can be extremely productive towards one's understanding of aspects of the school culture.[11]

The purposes of this chapter were to state and illustrate the following:

1. There are regularities of various kinds.
2. Existing programmatic and behavioral regularities should be described independent of one's own values or opinions.
3. Regularities exist because they are supposed to have intended outcomes.
4. There are at least two characteristics to intended outcomes: (1) aspects of them are discernible in overt behavior or interactions, and (2) they are justified by statements of value (i.e., what is good and what is bad).
5. There are frequent discrepancies between regularities and intended outcomes. Usually, no regularity is built into the school culture to facilitate the recognition of such discrepancies.
6. The significance of any regularity, particularly of the programmatic type, cannot be adequately comprehended apart from the universe of "regularity alternatives" of which the existing regularity is but one item. The failure to consider or recognize a universe of alternatives is one obstacle to change occurring from within the culture, and makes it likely that recognition of this universe of alternatives will await events and forces outside the culture.
7. Any attempt to introduce an important change in the school culture requires changing existing regularities to produce new intended outcomes. In practice, the regularities tend not to be changed and the intended outcomes, therefore, cannot occur; that is, the more things change the more they remain the same.
8. It is probably true that the most important attempts to introduce change into the school culture *require* changing existing teacher-child regularities. When one examines the natural history of the change process it is precisely these regularities that remain untouched. Conspicuous by its absence in the school culture, or so low in priority as to be virtually absent, is evaluation of the regularities of the kind we have been discussing. We hear much talk today about "accountability," which reduces to achievement test performance of pupils. If the pupils perform at grade level, the teacher is "good"; if the pupils perform below grade level, the teacher is "bad." I in no way downplay the im-

---

11. The reader will recall that we and school personnel were surprised that mathematics did not produce the largest number of interims. One reason for this may be that mathematics teachers *expect* children to have difficulty and, therefore, either they proceed more slowly or they are more lenient in their grading and evaluations. I present this possible explanation in order to make the point that our understanding of the school culture requires that we try to understand why an expected regularity (or pattern of regularity) does not occur.

portance of achievement when I say that when it becomes overwhelmingly central to discussions of accountability, it is at the expense of recognizing the significance (fiscal and psychological) of behavioral and programmatic regularities in the school culture. For example, I would maintain that to look at achievement test scores independent of the question-asking regularity is short-sighted in the extreme. (There *is* a difference between quantity and quality control.) Similarly, as in the case of interims, to permit the institutionalization of expensive, time-consuming procedures that are supposed to serve important functions and then to have no way of evaluating their intended outcomes is, to say the least, wasteful game playing. The issue is not what priority should be given to evaluation or research, but the seriousness with which one views any behavioral or programmatic feature of the school culture. Current discussions about accountability show an amazing insensitivity to the existence of behavioral and programmatic regularities.

The more our discussion has proceeded, the more evident it has become that a central problem to the understanding of the school culture is how to describe it so that the regularities that characterize it can become apparent. I have already suggested that our usual theories and ways of thinking about individuals are far from adequate for our purposes. We shall pursue this problem further in the next chapter, in which we shall refer to a particular approach that is quite promising, if only because it deals with the problem directly.

Chapter **7**

The Ecological Approach

In our accustomed way of thinking and acting it is extremely difficult, if not impossible, to look at and describe settings independent of the personalities of people. When we spend an evening in someone's home, sit in a classroom, or attend a case conference, we find that our thoughts largely refer either to ourselves or to what we think is going on "inside" someone else's head. That this is so is both reflected in and determined by personality theories, past and present.

Ego, self-actualization, expectancies, defense, anxiety—these and other terms in personality theories are basically conceived as *individual* characteristics or variables, and their variations are understood by looking at other characteristics of the individual as well as his or her interactions with other *individuals*. These theories of individuals have illuminated much and have given rise to techniques and procedures (e.g., therapeutic, educational) of practical value. To suggest that this focus on the individual may prevent us from seeing regularity and psychological structure of the individual does not downgrade or invalidate such a focus. It would be illogical, foolish, and stupidly parochial to deny that there is much to be learned about the school culture by studying individuals. In fact, most of what we know about the school culture derives from what is explicitly or implicitly an individual psychology. But what I suggest is that there are ways of thinking, and questions to be asked, that require, at least temporarily, that we not think in terms of individuals, or in terms of what is good or bad for individuals.

To change one's way of thinking, if only, as a colleague once said, "for the hell of it," is not easy. To do so deliberately for the serious purpose of discovering new questions and problems is even more difficult, because one tends not to want to believe that one's investigative territory can be mapped rather differently and that new "lands" can be discovered by others whose perspective is different. It can be both strange and upsetting to go through most of one's life believing that two parallel lines will not meet in space, and then discover that on the basis of certain assumptions, in the context of certain facts and questions, two parallel lines will meet in space. It is strange because one set of assumptions is not right and the other wrong. It is upsetting because one is forced to recognize that there are productive ways other than one's own of looking at a particular setting or set of problems. Furthermore, if one deliberately tries to adopt another stance, one finds that it is not easy and becomes plagued by such questions as: What questions do I now ask? What do I look at and how? I have no ready answers, but in this chapter I shall describe some of my own attempts at understanding, and those of others who have long concerned themselves with these issues (but who, unfortunately, have not had the influence they should have).

THE KINDERGARTEN

Among the most studied individuals in this country are children in kindergarten. In fact, if a law were passed making it illegal to study kindergarten children, the structure and direction of American child psychology would probably change in a somewhat drastic way. Kindergarten children have been studied for a variety of purposes: separation anxiety, socialization, speech development, discrimination of forms, sex play, and motor behavior, to name only a few. We have learned a great deal from studying individual characteristics of kindergarten children.

How, I asked myself, can I look at kindergartens without thinking of teachers or individual children, because initially, at least, I must not be interested in children as children or teachers as teachers. In fact, it will not make any difference if I look at a kindergarten class this year or next year or if I look at scores of kindergarten classrooms in scores of schools. Are there things I could learn about kindergarten and schools that not only would be revealing of the school culture but would also help us to understand individuals better?

I found myself thinking (without being clear why) about the following question: If on each of a number of days I was randomly to place myself in different parts of the school, how frequently would I see any occupant of the kindergarten? I do not pretend to have done this systematically, but I placed myself in enough places in enough schools to be able to say at least three things. First, there are some places in which I never saw a kindergartner. Second, the frequency of seeing a kindergartner seemed highly related to the distance from his or her room. Third, in each of the places, I saw children from other grades but I was unable to determine how many I could see from each grade. My impression was that the higher the grade, the more likely its occupants could be seen in the different places.

One of the places in which I never saw an occupant from the kindergarten was the toilet, because, as in many other schools, each kindergarten classroom had its own toilet facilities. Overall, the dominant impression I received was that only infrequently does one see an occupant of the kindergarten outside the classroom. Once one gains this impression it is difficult to fail to recognize a corollary statement: *the occupants of the kindergarten relatively infrequently, and sometimes never, see parts of their physical surrounding.*[1] Having come this far, and feeling secure that our conclusion has some merit, we have a basis for asking some psychological questions about children, teachers, and the content of traditions. For instance, why are kindergarten children, in contrast to children in other grades, infrequently found in certain places in the school?

When one starts questioning school personnel, one receives a variety of answers, although the most frequent and immediate response is a mixture of silence and puzzlement, signifying that one is touching upon a tradition that no longer requires reflection and scrutiny. Although the answers are varied, there are certain common assumptions. The most common is that kindergarten children *are* different and these differences require that they be under constant, or near constant, surveillance. Related to this is the view that kindergarten is really not "school," but a preparation for school. A second assumption underlying some of the answers is that if kindergarten children interacted with older children they might be adversely affected; in undefinable ways they might pick up "bad habits" because they are so impressionable, immature, and socially unformed. When I asked one kindergarten teacher if it was really necessary for her classroom to have its own toilet facilities, in light of the fact that all of her children were fully toilet trained when they started the year, she was quite bothered by the prospect of their wandering and getting lost.

What emerges from all this is that school personnel view kindergarten children as different and that the nature of the differences requires a restriction in their sphere of mobility within the school. Equally as important, kindergarten teachers are viewed by others, and they view themselves,

---

1. We all have the tendency to assume that inhabitants of a particular locale (e.g., a building, a neighborhood, a city) know that locale in that they have been to its parts or that they frequently can be found in those parts, an assumption that tends to be challenged only in fortuitous ways. For example, I have relatives who live in Brooklyn, which is part of New York City. I used to envy these relatives not because they lived in Brooklyn but because Manhattan was part of their city and readily available to them. I assumed they went to Manhattan. I was floored one day to learn that they very rarely went to Manhattan and for some of my relatives a year or more would go by without a visit there. We make the same assumption when we look at schools; at least, I did.

as a special kind of teacher *and* person (Hillyard, 1971). The nature of the specialness of kindergarten children and their teachers is not unrelated to the social insulation of kindergartens and their occupants from the rest of the school.

In pursuing the matter I should say at the outset that there is *some* merit to this state of affairs. But the degree of merit is, in my opinion, not so overwhelming as to prevent us from challenging assumptions and examining the always present but rarely recognized universe of alternatives. I should also remind you that in this discussion I am sincerely less interested in the merits of what is or could be than I am in illustrating how one can begin to look at the school culture not with individuals, or with the learning process, or even with goals and values, but rather with what may be termed "ecological concerns."

Let us start the challenging process by suggesting that kindergarten children are viewed and managed in ways that are in the nature of a self-fulfilling prophecy. That is to say, their school experience is organized in ways that end up confirming the assumption that their sphere of mobility within the school should be restricted. If one makes the assumption that kindergarten children (at least most of them) can quickly learn to navigate the building by themselves, and that they should learn to do so, the task then becomes one of setting up the appropriate learning experiences with the intended outcome that a child alone can go to and return from any place in the building. A related intended outcome might be that he or she learn to do so without any overt manifestation of fear.

I MENTION THIS PARTICULAR OUTCOME BECAUSE MY OWN MEMORIES OF kindergarten (and I assume they are subject to the usual sources of distortion) suggest that venturing on my own from my kindergarten room was a fantasy very much associated with fear of those large, cavernous halls and those very big children, and even bigger adults, one would encounter. Then, too, there was the principal, to whom, obviously, God had delegated some of his most important powers. What if I met *him?* I am sure my kindergarten teacher knew all this and, therefore, protected me in ways that guaranteed that I would continue to feel that way! ■

Some readers may say, "Why make such a big deal about the fact that kindergartners live in a restricted physical locale, in light of all the things they have to learn in their own room (e.g., materials, cooperative play)? They will be spending several years in the building and that is ample time to learn all about the building." The primary answer to such a position is that I assume that the children are *very* curious about that building and all that goes on in it, and that such curiosity should be taken account of and utilized for purposes of learning and motivation. They are as curious about the building as they are about their classroom. They are curious not only about its physical dimensions and attributes, but also about all those other rooms and their occupants. Why should the satisfaction of such curiosity be delayed? Can one not satisfy such curiosity in ways that bring to the fore other curiosities and questions? If one takes seriously the goal of broadening the horizons (literally and figuratively in this case) of children, must not one recognize the questions about this "world of the school" that one can safely assume children have?

I wish to emphasize two points. The first is that one can think about kindergartens in a way that would result in activities that do not characterize them now—the intended outcomes of these activities are simply not possible now in most kindergartens. The second point can be put in the form of a rhetorical question: Is a *major* consideration in determining what goes on in the regular classrooms (first grade, second grade, etc.) organized on assumptions about the curiosity of children? Our discussion of question-asking in the previous chapter does not permit a strongly affirmative answer!

A SOMEWHAT ATYPICAL INCIDENT ILLUSTRATES THIS POINT WELL. I WAS meeting each Wednesday with a group of ten new teachers, most of whom were in inner-city schools. One of these meetings occurred after the funeral of President Kennedy. There was no school on the Monday of the funeral. We were meeting, therefore, on the second day after schools reopened. When the meeting began, the teachers continued talking about what they had just been discussing: that it had been difficult, if not impossible, to get the children to attend to their academic tasks, and the children "learned" very little of what they were supposed to learn. The interests and curiosities of the children were seen as *interferences* in learning. ◼

Let us now examine some findings in light of our discussion of kindergartens. The specific findings are that in a large, suburban school system approximately 20 percent of all children repeated either Grade 1 or Grade 2, and in the great bulk of these grade repeaters intellectual level clearly was not an etiological factor (Sarason et al., 1966). There was variation in frequency of grade repetition from school to school, the lowest rate being 5 percent and the highest 29 percent. The most frequently stated reason for grade repetition was "immaturity." I do not maintain that grade repetition is caused by the nature of kindergarten experience. But I do wish to suggest that immaturity (whatever that is) is not a characteristic of a child independent of the environment in which the immaturity manifests itself (e.g., family, classroom). Within the school culture (as well as in a lot of other places) problem behavior is wrongfully viewed as a characteristic of an individual rather than as an interaction of individual and particular setting. Is it foolish to suggest that the highly protected and insulated kindergarten environment helps maintain (not cause) immature behavior? Is the children's inability to adapt to first grade *in part* a function of the sharpness of the discontinuities between kindergarten and first grade? Are the anxieties of these children maintained in part because they remain private, as do their questions about the nature and purposes of the school and schooling?[2]

I am sure that grade repetition is more complicated than those questions suggest, and the validity of these questions can only be determined by future study. What should be kept in mind is that these and other questions we have asked about kindergartens stemmed from the observation that the occupants of kindergartens are rarely, and sometimes never, seen in certain parts of the school in which they live. This observation permitted us to ask the "how come" question, which then directed us to assumption, programs, and outcomes. At the very least, the observation allowed us to suggest that the school life of the kindergarten child could be somewhat different than it ordinarily is. There is a universe of alternatives, even for kindergartners and their teachers.

BIG SCHOOL, SMALL SCHOOL

The heading of this section is the title of a book by Barker and Gump (1964). It is, for our purposes, an extremely important book because it represents the most serious and systematic attempt to date to view schools (high schools) from an ecological standpoint. Its primary focus is not on individuals or groups of individuals. It is not primarily concerned with the psychology of individuals or those sociological variables (e.g., social class, status) by which groups of individuals may be ordered and understood, but rather with stable extra-individual units called *behavior settings*.

IF A NOVICE, AN ENGLISHMAN, FOR EXAMPLE, WISHED TO UNDERSTAND THE environment of a first baseman in a ball game, he might set about to observe the interactions of the player with his surroundings. To do this with utmost precision he might view the first baseman through field glasses, so focused that the player would be centered in the field of the glasses, with just enough of the environment included to encompass all his contacts with the environment, all inputs and outputs: all balls caught, balls thrown, players tagged, etc. Despite the commendable observational care, however, this method would never provide a novice

---

2. From our longitudinal studies of anxiety in elementary school children (Sarason, Hill, and Zimbardo, 1964; Hill and Sarason, 1966) we found that early grade repeaters were more anxious about school than nonrepeaters.

with an understanding of "the game" which gives meaning to a first baseman's transactions with his surroundings, and which in fact, constitutes the environment of his baseball-playing behavior. By observing a player in this way, the novice would, in fact, fragment the game and destroy what he was seeking. So, he might by observations and interviews construct the player's life space during the game: his achievements, aspirations, successes, failures, and conflicts; his judgments of the speed of the ball, of the fairness of the umpire, of the errors of his teammates. But this would only substitute for the former fragmented picture of "the game" the psychological consequences of the fragment, and thus remove the novice even further from the ecological environment he sought. Finally, the novice might perform innumerable correlations between the first baseman's achievements (balls caught, players tagged, strikes and hits made, bases stolen, errors, etc.) and particular attributes of the ecological environment involved (speed of balls thrown to him, distance of throw, weight of bat, curve of balls, etc.). But he could never arrive at the phenomenon known as a baseball game by this means.

It would seem clear that a novice would learn more about the ecological environment of a first baseman by blotting out the player and observing the game around him. This is what the student of light and sound does with elaborate instrumentation, and it is the approach we have taken in the present studies.

It is not easy, at first, to leave the person out of observations of the environment of molar behavior. Our perceptual apparatus is adjusted by our long training with the idiocentric viewing glasses of individual observations, interviews, and questionnaires to see persons whenever we see behavior. But with some effort and experience the extra-individual assemblies of behavior episodes, behavior objects and space that surround persons can be observed and described. Their nonrandom distribution and bounded character are a crucial aid. If the reader will recall a school class period, some of the characteristics of an environmental unit will be clearly apparent:

1. It is a natural phenomenon; it is not created by an experimenter for scientific purposes.
2. It has a space-time focus.
3. A boundary surrounds a school class.
4. The boundary is self-generated; it changes as the class changes in size and in the nature of its activity.
5. The class is objective in the sense that it exists independent of anyone's perception of it, *qua* class; it is a perceptual ecological entity.
6. It has two sets of components: (a) behavior (reciting, discussing, sitting) and (b) nonpsychological objects with which

behavior is transacted, e.g., chairs, walls, a blackboard and paper.

7. The unit, the class meeting, is circumjacent to its components; the pupils and equipment are *in* the class.

8. The behavior and physical objects that constitute the unit school class are internally organized and arranged to form a pattern that is by no means random.

9. The pattern within the boundary of a class is easily discriminated from that outside the boundary.

10. There is a synomorphic relation between the pattern of the behavior occurring within the class and the pattern of its non-behavioral components, the behavior objects. The seats face the teacher's desk, and the children face the teacher, for example.

11. The unity of the class is not due to the similarity of its parts at any moment; for example, speaking occurs in one part and listening in another. The unity is based, rather, upon the interdependence of the parts; events in different parts of a class period have a greater effect upon each other than equivalent events beyond its boundaries.

12. The people who inhabit a class are to a considerable degree interchangeable and replaceable. Pupils come and go; even the teacher may be replaced. But the same entity continues as serenely as an old car with new rings and the right front wheel now carried as the spare.

13. The behavior of this entity cannot, however, be greatly changed without destroying it: there must be teaching, there must be study, there must be recitation.

14. A pupil has two positions in a class; first, he is a component of the supra-individual unit, and second, he is an individual whose life space is partly formed within the constraints imposed by the very entity of which he is a part.

This entity stands out with great clarity. . . it is a common phenomenon of everyday life. We have called it a. . . *behavior setting.* We have made extensive studies of. . . behavior settings and found much evidence that they are stable extra-individual units with great explanatory power with respect to the behavior occurring within them. It is the central hypothesis of our studies that. . . behavior settings constitute the ecological environment of molar behavior, and the theory of them, based upon the earlier work, provides the guides for the investigations.

According to the theory of behavior settings, a person who inhabits and contributes behavior to one of them is a component part, a fixture of a behavior setting. As such, he is anonymous and replaceable, and his behavior is subject to the nonpsychological laws of the superordinate unit. At the same time, however, every inhabitant of a behavior setting is a unique person subject to the laws of individual psychology, where his own private motives, capacities, and perceptions are the causal variables. This is the classical inside-outside paradox, involving in this case persons who are governed by incommensurate laws on different levels of inclusiveness.

One of the sticking points of social and educational psychology is how to account for the consensus, the norms, and the uniformities associated with school classes, business offices, and church services, for example, at the same time account for the individuality of the members. This problem cannot be solved by either individual or group psychology. It requires a different conceptual treatment, the unnamed science mentioned earlier.[3] ■

The ecological theory and methodology worked out by Barker and his associates (Barker, 1968) represent the work of decades. What we need to know about *Big School, Small School* is that it is concerned with the effects of high school size upon the behavior and experience of high school students. The first task was to locate and describe the numerous (and they *are* numerous) behavior settings that make up a school. Having done this, it then became possible to determine the extent to which students participated in each of the behavior settings—not unlike the question I asked about the frequency of appearance of kindergarten children in different places in the school. Still another question asked was the relation of school size to the number of different behavior settings in which the average student participated. Once the behavior settings were identified and their population density determined, then the more psychological kinds of questions could be studied: What satisfactions did students derive from the behavior settings? What were the forces influencing participation in behavior settings?

Barker and Gump (1964) have well summarized the results and their significances:

RESULTS FROM THIS STUDY AND THE PARTIAL REPLICATION YIELDED general support for the theory of the effects of behavior setting size, indicating that the theory is a powerful predictor from ecology to the experience and behavior of individual persons. Students from the small schools, where settings were relatively underpopulated, reported more own forces (attractions) and foreign forces (pressures) toward participation in behavior settings than did students from the large school. Furthermore, a sizable group of students emerged in the large school who

---

3. Reprinted from *Big School, Small School: High School Size and Student Behavior* by Roger G. Barker and Paul V. Gump with the permission of the publishers, Stanford University Press. 1964 by the Board of Trustees of the Leland Stanford Junior University, pp. 15–17.

experienced few, if any, forces toward participation. The small schools in the present study did not contain any such outsiders; all of the small school students reported experiencing many forces toward participation. Preselected marginal students in the small schools experienced as many forces as did regular students, while in the large school, the preselected marginals experienced very few forces, far fewer than the regular students.

Another important finding is that the responses of the small school students reflected more felt responsibility and obligation. Many persons feel that the development of a sense of responsibility is essential to good citizenship, and that it is one task of schools to encourage this sense of responsibility in students. The frequency of responsibility responses in this study followed the same pattern as the data on forces, with extreme differences between schools and the emergence of outsiders, persons in the large school who reported no felt responsibility.

Second, motivation is often seen as purely a function of the person. Attraction and sense of responsibility, especially, are often seen as such "inside-the-skin" variables. Yet, when similar persons were compared in different environments in the present study, attraction and felt responsibility were found to vary with the outside environment also. The data . . . offer some evidence on the question of the comparative influence of ecology and kind of person in determining the experience of forces. Within the limits of the methods used to identify and select regular and marginal students, one would expect, if the kind of person were more important than the ecology of the school, that similar groups of students would report similar experiences in different ecologies. . . . Marginal students from the small schools reported more forces than regular students from the large schools. Marginal students from the large school were a group apart, a group of outsiders. These findings indicate that the academically marginal students had very different experiences in the two ecologies. In the small school, marginal characteristics made no difference; marginal students experienced almost as many forces toward participation as the nonmarginal students. In the large school, however, the marginal students experienced relatively very few attractions and pressures toward participation.

The correlations between forces and participation provide further evidence that ecology is a powerful factor in determining participation. The consistently high correlations between foreign forces and participation suggest that ecology was a powerful determinant of participation among the subjects of the present study. The studies reviewed. . . almost entirely disregarded this variable so strongly associated with size.

Third, there are implications for developmental theory. If it is assumed that "the best way to learn is to do," or "the best way to learn responsibility is to have it," then the implications of the present study are clear. Individual students in small schools, with their relatively underpopulated settings, live under greater day-to-day attraction, pressure, and responsibility felt toward taking active part in the voluntary activities of their school environments. They are more motivated to take part.[4] ■

Barker and his associates did more than study the interrelationships between size of school, behavior settings, and psychological variables. They went on to study the consolidated or regional high school, which requires commuting on the part of students and "attendance at a larger school than the one that had previously existed, or could exist, in the local community." They present the intended outcomes of consolidation put forward by its proponents and opponents.

CONSOLIDATION OF HIGH SCHOOLS, LIKE MOST EDUCATIONAL ISSUES, HAS given rise to considerable controversy. On the one hand, its supporters claim that *students benefit* through better and more varied curriculums, better classifications, better facilities, especially in such subjects as science and music, contact with better teachers, opportunities to participate in better and more varied extracurricular activities, wider social opportunities and experiences, and more regular attendance as a result of being, in some cases, transported from door to school; *parents benefit* through reduced expenditure on education: the *community benefits* through the creation of closer ties with neighboring communities.

On the other hand, the opponents of consolidation claim that *students lose* through increased breaks in their education, loss of contact with local teachers who know the community and the families as well, spending time on commuting which might be spent with greater profit on other activities, and fewer opportunities to participate in the control of their school; the *community loses* through being denied the facilities of an active school, which could serve as a cultural and educational center, and through the breakdown of community cohesion and participation, especially in youth activities.

These and other similar arguments have customarily been advanced by those who enter the controversy on consolidation. However, few systematic attempts have been made to examine the assertions empirically. Apart from studies on school size. . . almost all of the literature on consolidation deals with alleged economies and administrative procedures. The few reports involving student reactions that we found dealt with changes in intelligence quotients and the like. These are important

---

4. Ibid., pp. 133–135.

reports, but our interest lies rather in the experiences and processes that underlie changes such as these, and the published work has been of little direct benefit to us.[5] ■

The findings they come up with on consolidation effects "suggest that the current assumption of consolidated school superiority is, in at least some respects, like the first report of Mark Twain's death—exaggerated." The intended psychological outcomes hoped for by proponents of the consolidated high school are far from realized.

In following our discussion of Barker's ecological approach, some may have discerned a kind of kinship with the approach of our man from outer space, who was parked on his space platform above a school, could observe everything that was going on, was unable to comprehend the meaning of oral and written language, had no way of comprehending "motivation," but, like the fantastic organism he was, had fantastic computers that permitted him to discern and interrelate every conceivable form of overt activity in any part of the school. In short, the man from outer space could not come up with psychological data or questions. He was, by virtue of our fantasied restrictions, forced to adopt something akin to the ecological approach. To requote Barker and Gump:

IT IS NOT EASY, AT FIRST, TO LEAVE THE PERSON OUT OF OBSERVATIONS OF the environment of molar behavior. Our perceptual apparatus is adjusted by our long training with the idiocentric viewing glasses of individual observations, interviews, and questionnaire to see *persons* whenever we see behavior. But with some effort and experience the extra-individual assemblies of behavior episodes, behavior objects, and space that surround persons can be observed and described. Their nonrandom distribution and bounded character are a crucial aid. ■

THE NEED FOR THE ECOLOGICAL APPROACH

There are two major reasons I have for emphasizing what broadly and loosely may be called an ecological approach to the school culture. The first reason is one that is as neglected as it is obvious: there *are* different "positions" from which one can view the school culture and each has much to commend it. However unassailable and obvious this statement is, one is still left with the puzzling fact that the ecological approach is hardly represented in the literature on schools. This is a result of a number of fac-

---

5. Ibid., From the chapter "Some Effects of High School Consolidation," by W. J. Campbell, pp. 139–40.

tors, historical and otherwise, and chief among them is that the major professional influences on American education have come from people and fields—psychology in general, educational psychology in particular, child development, certain aspects of psychiatry, and educational philosophy—that have been dominated by a focus on the individual and individual differences. For example, at the present time the most dominant influence on the field of child development unquestionably is Jean Piaget. It is not surprising, therefore, that many psychologists and educators have begun to apply his ideas to the educational scene—and there is much to apply. It is in no way to deny this man's giant contribution to child development to point out that his theory and studies focus on the individual organism and the ways in which its internal psychological structures develop in response to experience.[6] As in the case of Freud, and somewhat less so of Dewey, the *person* is in center stage, and this has facilitated overlooking the fact that a stage, be it a theatrical or educational one, has what Barker has termed "extra-individual" structured characteristics that affect the actors, even though they are unaware of these characteristics and their effects.

A second reason for the neglect of the ecological approach is that it appears to be dreary stuff. One would not want to be stranded on a desert island with the collected works of Barker and his colleagues (although, come to think of it, they would probably be more useful for survival than the collected works of Freud). The task of defining and describing the "natural" (noninvestigator-produced) aspects that comprise a complicated setting, as well the tasks of determining their population density and the fluidity of boundaries among these aspects, are laborious and extremely time-consuming in their execution. In addition, it is not an approach or methodology that lends itself to the quick recognition of patterns and structure. In short, it lacks the glamor that is ordinarily attributed to scientific investigation.

The third reason for the neglect of the ecological approach is that it requires us to do something that, particularly in relation to schools, is extraordinarily difficult to do, and that is to suspend one's values, one's conception of right and wrong, good and bad, and instead to describe what is "out there." It is probably impossible to do this fully. I am impressed with how difficult it is to do this even to a small extent. As a previous quote from Barker indicated, we have overlearned to such an extent to see persons and not behavior that when we are forced to describe behavior in-

---

6. It is not to contradict this statement to point out that Piaget's thinking and concepts (e.g., assimilation, accommodation) have been very much influenced by biological-ecological considerations and that among his most illuminating contributions have been those concerned with the child's understanding of the attributes of external reality such as time, space, and number.

dependent of what we think about why it occurs and how we personally feel about it, we find it both difficult and upsetting.[7]

A final reason for emphasizing an ecological way of thinking is that one of its fascinating aspects is that one cannot predict the regularities that will be discerned and the significances of these regularities for the problem of change and for the understanding of the motivational and cognitive aspects of behavior. To illustrate this point I would like to return to our man from outer space who is parked in his vehicle above an elementary school, unseen by everyone but seeing everything. Let us assume that he has become interested in a particular room in the school in which a child never, or extremely rarely, appears. It is a room always populated by big people, although it is unusual that more than a small fraction of the big people in the school are ever in that room at one time. For a good part of the school day there is no one in the room. Aside from the one time when they eat it is usually the case that no more than one or two of them are there. In fact, he observes, even during eating time a number of the big people eat in a much larger room with the small people. At the end of the year what does his data say about the amount of face-to-face contact the big people have with each other in and out of the teacher's room?

1. During the course of the average day the teachers spend almost all of the time with small children.
2. Leaving lunchtime aside, during the course of the average day, the amount of time teachers spend in face-to-face contact with each other is extremely small. In fact, it is likely that our space man's computers would show that it is unusual for these face-to-face contacts to exceed one minute.
3. During eating time in the teachers' room there is considerable variation in how much the different teachers talk, and in the degree to which any one teacher will talk to any other teacher.
4. It is extremely rare for a teacher to be physically *alone*.
5. Approximately ten times in the year, and each time after the children have left school, all the teachers meet with someone who ordinarily spends practically all of the time in a room with no children. On these occasions this person—the principal, of course—does most of the talking. In fact, there are some teachers who in the ten meetings never say anything. Most teachers do say something but the extent of their talk is far less than that of the principal.

---

7. The experience of difficulty and upset are expected reactions when one is forced, or has to learn, a new way of listening and looking. For example, if one is accustomed to listening to the sentences of people in terms of literal meaning, it is not easy to adopt a set that gets at other possible meanings and significances, e.g., to follow Freud's dictum that one has "to listen and not listen," a kind of double-bind, which, as he demonstrated, could give one new perspectives and data about human behavior.

The earthling who attempts to replicate the spaceman's findings will, I predict, not come up with markedly discrepant data. And now let us go from these kinds of regularities to their possible psychological significances.

What are the possible consequences of the two facts that during the course of the work day (1) teachers are primarily with small children, and (2) there is very little contact with other teachers or any other adult? (The average mother who is at home with pre-schoolers probably has more contact with adults, e.g., via neighbors, telephone, visiting.) What does it mean to go through a work day with no sustained personal contact with another adult? Being and talking with children is not psychologically the same as being and talking with peers—and I am not suggesting that one is necessarily more satisfying than the other, only that they are different. I am suggesting that when one is almost *exclusively* with children—responsible for them, being vigilant in regard to them, "giving" to them—it must have important consequences. *One of these consequences is that teachers are psychologically alone even though they are in a densely populated setting.* It is not only that they are alone, but they adapt to being alone (and this adaptation, as we shall see in later chapters, does not have desired intended outcomes).

The loneliness of teachers is not something that I became aware of initially by identifying with a spaceman. My awareness stemmed from two considerations. First, anyone who like myself was clinically trained spent a good deal of time in case conferences with colleagues: presenting one's own cases, reacting to those of others, and in concert with others pooling data and thoughts with the aim of arriving at a diagnostic formulation and plan of action. As Murray Levine so well put it, clinics need two staffs: one to go to the conferences and one to do the work. The other consideration was that the tradition of the case conference did not exist in schools, except in certain rare instances.

IN OUR BOOK (SARASON ET AL., 1966) DESCRIBING THE ACTIVITIES OF THE Yale Psycho-Educational Clinic in relation to schools there is a chapter titled "Teaching Is a Lonely Profession." Interestingly enough, it is this chapter that teachers have mentioned most frequently and spontaneously as the one that "hit home." This reaction is one felt most keenly by the new teacher who up until her first teaching position has always worked in the company of peers or other adults. The loneliness of teachers, and again particularly so in the case of the new teacher, is further reinforced by a characteristic of the school culture we have discussed elsewhere (Sarason, Davidson, and Blatt, 1962). I am referring to the expectation, sometimes verbalized by school administrators but in practice shared by most, that a teacher should be equally adequate to the management of *all* children and problems in the classroom. This presumptuous expectation tends also to be shared by teachers, with the result that they have no difficulty finding occasions that prove their inadequacy. Over the years I have made it a practice to ask two questions of teachers: How many children do you have about whom you feel that you are not for them and vice versa? How many times have you gone to the principal with the request that a child be removed from your class because the two of you are not a good mix? Of the scores of teachers with whom I have worked there may have been a handful who never made the request of a principal, although in the case of all the teachers there was always at least one child in the class about whom the teacher felt the match was a bad one. This expectation of which I speak increases the likelihood that the psychological loneliness of teachers will contain a good deal of felt inadequacy as well as simmering hostility to administrators who seem insensitive to the teacher's plight. In this connection it is interesting and important to note that one of the demands being made with increasing frequency of boards of education by teacher unions, particularly in our large urban centers, is that teachers should not be required to have to deal with a variety of difficult children. We shall have more to say about this in a later chapter, but I have mentioned it here in order to make two points: (1) *one* of the many reasons contributing to the rise in strength and militancy of teacher unions is that they have helped dilute somewhat the felt loneliness of teachers as teachers, and (2) over time one can expect that teachers will demand a greater role in determining the criteria to be used in composing a class of children and in transferring or excluding them. ■

It was not until I began to think and observe in a more ecological way that I began to see the dimensions of the problem, for example, that not talking with each other was but one instance of the general tendency for teachers in a school to have very little sustained interpersonal adult contact. But even this general tendency is but one aspect of still another tendency: teachers have very little contact with their principal and others in superior administrative positions. The opportunity—the sheer possibility by virtue of face-to-face meetings—for a teacher to receive a personal sort of "professional message" is amazingly small. Teachers are alone with their children and problems in a classroom, and the frequency and pattern of contact with others like themselves are a kind and quality that make new learning and change unlikely. When in the course of one's day-to-day professional existence the gaining of rewards is dependent almost exclusively on one's relationship with children, and these rewards are frequently indirect and nonverbal, and when the frequency of such rewards is not greater than the frustrations one experiences, it should not be surprising if the well of motivation should run low or dry, or if behavior becomes routinized. To expect otherwise is to assume that one is not dependent to some degree, at least, on contact with and stimulation from one's colleagues. If one further assumes that teachers have a need for novelty, this unmet need may be extinguished, and the process becomes an obstacle to change.

At this point I am less interested in how one interprets the spaceman's findings than in the fact that his findings can serve as a basis for asking and pursuing psychological questions the answers to which can be very illuminating of the school culture. To some readers his findings may have seemed obvious. To others, the nonpsychological (in the sense of being nonmotivational, noncognitive, and unconcerned with individuals and individual differences) nature of the findings may have seemed to lack relevance or interest. The ecological way of thinking and investigating may seem to lack glamor, but there is no question that it is a productive one.

Here is a final example, again from the research of Barker and his colleagues. Indeed, this example stems directly from Barker and Gump's research on big and small schools. I refer here to Barker's discussion of the interplay between people and their environments under different conditions of "manning." Undermanning is the condition of having insufficient or barely sufficient personnel in a setting to carry out the essential tasks and functions. "What," Barker asked, "are the differences for the occupants of a setting when they are in an undermanned, or adequately manned, or overmanned setting?" At first glance it might appear that the answer to this question would be readily straightforward, i.e., what possible advantages could accrue to those in an undermanned setting? Being as they are in an era of shrinking resources, one would expect that as schools enter the undermanned condition the impact on their personnel would only be negative. But, as we shall see, the consequences need not only be negative.

The undermanned setting is, by definition, one in which resources are very limited. Barker's research suggests that "in order to maintain the setting under these adverse conditions, the occupants both receive and produce more frequent, stronger, and more varied messages regarding the carrying out of the setting's essential activities than would be the case if the number of persons available were at or above the optimal level" (Wicker and Kirmeyer, 1976, p. 159). Wicker and Kirmeyer summarize the advantages of the undermanned setting suggested by the research as follows.

1. Greater effort to support the setting and its functions, either by "harder" work or by spending longer hours
2. Participation in a greater diversity of tasks and roles
3. Involvement in more difficult and more important tasks
4. More responsibility in the sense that the setting and what others gain from it depend on each individual occupant
5. Viewing oneself and others in terms of task-related characteristics, rather than in terms of social-emotional characteristics

6. Greater functional importance of individuals within the setting
7. Less sensitivity to and less evaluation of differences between people
8. Setting of lower standards and fewer tests for admission into the setting
9. A lower level of maximal or best performance
10. Greater insecurity about the eventual maintenance of the setting
11. More frequent occurrences of success and failure, depending on the outcome of the setting's functions.

In short, two of the advantages of the undermanned setting are that its occupants interact more with each other and they use more of their different interests and talents. When Conant (see Chapter 3) discussed and strongly recommended the comprehensive high school, he expressed no reservation about the possible negative impact such a large, adequately manned (or overmanned) setting would have on its staff and students. As someone once said, "The large, comprehensive high school had all of the disadvantages of a large, modern factory in which each individual was alone with himself or herself, lost in a sea of specialized functionaries." Barker, unlike Conant, did not start with preconceptions about efficiency or opinions about size or even the goals of education. Nor did Barker, unlike Conant, bypass the question of how people live with each other. Starting with an ecological conception of resources and how people accommodate to them, Barker focused on how resources affect the behavior of people: the diversity of roles they adapt, the quality and quantity of interactions, and the variety of interests and talents they are stimulated to express. Obviously, neither Barker nor I advocate undermanned settings as a matter of policy. And as schools enter this era of shrinking resources I do not refer to Barker's research to sound a note of optimism, let alone satisfaction with the shrinking educational arena. If I emphasize Barker's ideas and research, it is because his ecological approach (not his psychological or educational conceptions) had directed us to issues that are central to the quality and goals of living and working in schools, living and working for staff and students. These issues, it should be emphasized, are independent of whether one is in an era of resource affluence or decline.

THE DEFECTS OF THE VIRTUES OF
STRONGLY HELD VALUES

In this and the previous chapters I have been in different ways emphasizing two themes. One of these has been that we know far less than we should about many aspects of the school culture and that a major cause of this has two facets: (1) we look at and describe the school culture in terms of values and personal experiences, which, however productive of insights, put blinders on what we look at, choose to change, and evaluate; and (2) it is inordinately difficult to adopt approaches that require us to recognize and suspend our values in the quest of achieving distance from our habitual ways of thinking and working. It is most understandable—it is, in fact, inevitable—that we should feel strongly about *our* schools and *our* school experiences. What would not be understandable would be affective and intellectual indifference. *We* have spent years in schools, *our* children's school experiences are of vital concern to us, and in contemporary America concern with schools is in the forefront of our national consciousness. But our strong interests have the defects of their virtues in that they narrow our focus, blind us to the obvious, and rob us of the capacity to recognize that the emperor may be quite naked. Because our values and assumptions are usually implicit and "second nature," we proceed as if the way things are is the way things should or could be. We do not act but we react, and then not with the aim of changing our conceptions—or, heaven forbid, our theories from which our conceptions presumably derive—but to change what is most easy to change: the engineering aspects.[8] Books get changed, new and more specialists are brought in, specialized programs and curricula are added, and new and more meetings (between students and teachers, teachers and parents) are institutionalized. It is meaningless to ask if one is for or against these and other kinds of procedural changes unless one assumes that change in itself is a good thing. What passionate devotion to our values does is to prevent us from asking: *Are these changes intended to change existing regularities or are they new regularities that will exist side-by-side with the existing ones?* Which of these one intends makes the difference between change and innovation.

One of the most illuminating descriptions of American culture was written in the nineteenth century, not by an American but by the Frenchman, De Tocqueville (1956). He saw and described regularities and characteristics that have stood the time test. Like our man from outer space, he did not have our passions and blinders and he did not confuse what we said with what we did, what we intended with what we accomplished. Fortunately, we do not have to await the spaceman to begin to look at the school culture with the freshness of a foreigner, earthling, or otherwise.

---

8. This point is well documented and delightfully discussed by Stephens (1967) in the context of his attempt to show the role of spontaneous psychological forces in learning, forces that long antedate the formal beginning of school. Although his book is not directly concerned with the culture of the school or life in the classroom, it goes a long way in explaining why schools accomplish as much and as little as they do. Stephens is obviously a person who, by taking the obvious seriously, comes up with some important but disquieting conclusions.

Chapter 8

The Principal

In this and subsequent chapters we shall depart from the emphasis of previous ones by looking at certain types of school personnel and attempting to understand them in social psychological or sociological terms; that is, as individuals in roles central to the activities of a school. It might be correct to say that our purpose will be to try to comprehend how these different types of personnel view the school culture. We shall not hesitate, as we did in previous chapters, to state what we think goes on inside the heads of people.

WHY START WITH THE PRINCIPAL?

There are many reasons for starting with the principal, but for our purposes the most important is the principal's relationship to the problem of change. The change may be of two kinds: that which the principal initiates in his or her own school, and that intended for all schools in a system. In either case, the principal plays a fateful role. Particularly in our urban centers where schools have become a battleground involving community groups, city, state, and federal government, teacher unions, and student groups—and where the rate of proposals of change has to be reckoned in terms of weeks rather than months and years—the "leader" of the school would seem to be a good starting point. But, one could argue, while it may be true that the principal is the most influential individual in *a* school, is it also not true that a school is part of a larger "system" that has characteristics, traditions, and a history that determine not only the role of the principal but the activities of everyone in all of its schools.[1] The extreme of this position is that unless one deals with "the system"—unless one's efforts involve changing system characteristics—it is unlikely that one's efforts will be more than shadowboxing with the real problems. This position has been most clearly represented in the New York City school controversies where various groups have concerned themselves with how to change the educational system by realigning the forces and sources of power.

By adopting the principal as our initial focus I do not mean to suggest that system characteristics are less revealing of the school culture or less important in terms of efforts at change. In fact, as I hope to make clear, the role of the principal may well be unique in the light it sheds both on the characteristics of the system *and* life in the classroom. The danger of focusing narrowly on the system and the ways it should or could be changed is that it tends (it need not tend but in practice that is what happens) to bypass the question of how changes are to be reflected in what goes on in the classroom. *If this question remains unanswered or remains in the realm of boring platitudes or unanalyzable abstractions, we stand a good chance of demonstrating that for the child the more things change the more they remain the same.* One could put up a number of arguments for decentralizing large school systems and changing the forces of power and decision-making between its parts and the community; that is, changing the characteristics of the system *qua* system. But if one of these arguments is to effect change in what children experience in classrooms, the changing of power relationships within the system, and between the system and the community, are only the beginning of a process the intended outcome of which is to change life in a classroom. The beginning of the process (like the Supreme Court desegregation decision) may take courage, but let us not confuse initial acts of courage with the achievement of intended outcomes. We begin with the principal because any kind of system change puts him or her in the role of implementing the change in one's school. I have yet to see any proposal for system change that did not assume the presence of a principal in a school. I have yet to see in any of these proposals the slightest recognition of the possibility that the principal, by virtue of role, preparation, and tradition, may not be a good implementer of change. If this turns out to be the case, it clearly forces one to reconsider one's goals of change. It would also sug-

---

1. Overlearned habits of thinking, as well as the requirements of brevity (and the avoidance of awkwardness) in ordinary communication, make it very difficult to avoid talking of the school *system*. I must remind the readers that there are definite drawbacks, too frequently unrecognized, to the concept of the school system, especially when it conveys the impression that what goes on in schools is explainable in terms of factors internal to them. I discussed this in early chapters where I also noted that for certain restricted purposes that conception of a school system can be appropriate.

gest that most of those individuals and groups, both within and without the school system, who clamor for system change are far from knowledgeable about the culture of the school.

THE CLASSROOM AS PREPARATION FOR THE PRINCIPAL'S OFFICE

We begin with a glimpse of the obvious: a person cannot become a principal without first being a teacher for a number of years. The major justification for this seemingly reasonable requirement is that unless a principal has had long experience in teaching and managing children in a classroom, he or she cannot appreciate or understand the goals and problems of a teacher and, therefore, cannot be of much help; in fact, he or she would create more problems than solve. A variant of this justification is that without sustained teaching experience one simply cannot know what a school is all about. Although the different justifications are not without merit, there are other considerations that should cause one to pause before accepting what seems obvious and reasonable.

　　1.　The fact that a teacher has spent a number of years in a classroom *with children* is no compelling basis for assuming that it prepares one for a position in which one's major task is working *with adults.* Put in another way: being a "leader" of children, and exclusively of children, does not necessarily prepare one for being a leader of adults.

　　2.　As we indicated in an earlier chapter, teachers are relatively autonomous in their classrooms, and within a school they have surprisingly little to do with each other. More often than not, the teachers within a school do not feel themselves to be part of a working or planning group. They may identify with each other in terms of role and place of work, and they may have a feeling of loyalty to each other and the school, but it is rare that they feel part of a working group that discusses, plans, and helps make educational decisions.[2] Teachers are "loners"—initially certainly not by their design—and this undoubtedly affects what they think about, and how they view, a school. Over a period of years they absorb and *accept* a tradition, which, if they become a principal, they are not likely to change. In fact, one of the major criteria for choosing a principal is that they were "good" teachers and good refers not only to their quality of teaching, but to their implicit acceptance of the way things are.

---

2. The situation I am describing can best be contrasted to what happens when teachers in a school organize themselves into a union and conduct their meetings. There is a sense of common purpose and responsibility, a sense of belonging, and a give-and-take kind of discussion that they only minimally feel in their usual contacts with each other in their educational roles.

3. What selective factors operate as to who wants to become a principal? There are at least three such factors. The first of these is that the classroom is no longer a challenge to the teacher: it has lost its novelty, next year will be like this year, and the sense of intellectual growth has perceptibly decreased. A second factor is that more money can be made as a principal. Another factor is that one wants to be in a greater position of influence, power, and prestige. These are not unrelated factors. What needs to be said in the clearest terms is that there is nothing wrong or bad about these types of motivation. That one wants to enlarge one's intellectual horizons, or to earn more money to provide better for one's family, or to test oneself in a position of greater responsibility—in our society, at least, these are understandable and desirable motivations. But one has to say in equally clear terms that possessing these motivations is far from an adequate basis for deciding whether one could or should be a principal. The decision to become a principal is almost always a personal one; only rarely does a school system "call" a teacher. Having made the personal decision, the teacher is then required to enroll in a graduate program consisting almost exclusively, and in most instances it is exclusively, of academic courses. (As I pointed out in earlier chapters, the traditional concept of the school *system* facilitates the ignoring how interconnected schools are with colleges and universities. *Surprisingly, the quantity and quality of this interconnectedness have hardly been studied.* That omission in the research literature is not explainable by saying that they are two separate but interacting systems. There is a kernel of truth there, but if my experience is any guide, one cannot truly understand the culture of the school independent of its relationship, present and past, to centers for professional training. These centers, by virtue of being vehicles for the selection and socialization of educational personnel, have an obvious impact on the school culture. The people and organizations who have any degree of influence in determining which people will be selected for training, in formulating the criteria for making differential judgments among trainees, and in recommendations for hiring have to be considered part of the "system" regardless of where they are located. Modern medicine can be dated from the appearance of the famous Flexner Report which studied and criticized how centers of training selected, trained, and socialized their students; and that focus in the report derived from the assumption that one could not meaningfully separate where people were trained from the quality of their practices. One was dealing less with interacting systems and more with symbiotic relations.)

4. Although a teacher and principal are in the same building and they do interact, albeit far less frequently than one would think, it is easy to overestimate how realistic a picture the teacher obtains of the complexity of the role of the principal. The one thing we can be sure of is that the teacher's picture of the role of the principal is primarily determined by *their*

relationship. The teacher may *hear* of the principal's interactions with others (other teachers, special personnel, parents, and children), but it is literally impossible for a teacher to *observe* the principal in the wide variety of relationships in which he or she engages. This point deserves emphasis because it forces us to recognize that the teacher's perception of the role of the principal is based on a narrow sample of experience that may have undue weight in the teacher's decision to become a principal. The narrowness of the experience is certainly not compensated for in those instances where the teacher's experience is limited to one principal and one school. The picture of the principal that teachers have may be gleaned in the following (Sarason, 1969b):

IS IT NECESSARY FOR EACH SCHOOL TO HAVE A PRINCIPAL? I HAVE PUT THIS question to friends who are not connected with schools. There are three types of responses to this question. The first is one of mild surprise that the question should be asked. The second response is that the individual simply has no basis for considering alternatives, although he would not in principle be opposed to alternatives. The third response, and the least frequent one, is one in which alternatives are stated and the pros and cons evaluated. If I have sensed anything common to these responses it is that the question is an open and interesting one. Now how do teachers respond to the question? As you might expect, their response is far more strong than it is to my question about physical education programs. Once emotions were relatively out of the way, a variety of answers were given and they tended to have one thing in common: there are "practical" matters of an everyday sort (that do or could occur) which could bring the operations of a school to a halt if the principal was not present. Who would keep the attendance data? Order supplies? Handle behavior problems and sick children? Supervise fire drills? Talk to parents when they phoned or visited? One could go on listing housekeeping matters which were considered to require the presence of a principal. What is most interesting to me is that teachers rarely, if ever, responded in terms of the factors I presented earlier, i.e., the principal's educational or leadership role, his evaluation functions, his role as representative of the teachers to other administrative bodies, and the importance of personal as contrasted to professional relationships with him. ■

As we shall soon see, this picture of the principal's role is true but disturbingly incomplete.

In making these points I am not only questioning the relevance of teaching experience as a preparation for becoming a principal. *What I am suggesting is that being a teacher for a number of years may be, in most instances, antithetical to being an educational leader or vehicle of change.*

There is little in the nature of classroom teacher, there is little in the motivation of the teacher to become a principal, there is little in the actual experience of the teacher with principals, and there is even less in the criteria by which a principal is chosen, to expect that the role of the principal will be viewed as a vehicle, and in practice used, for educational change and innovation.

THE TEACHER BECOMES A PRINCIPAL

Our understanding of the role of the principal can be approached in a number of ways, but the one we shall begin with requires that we focus on the period between the appointment and the first few months in the job. The major reason for this focus is that in this period the individual is confronted with and experiences a major personal and professional discontinuity, and how this difficult transition is viewed and managed is illuminating of many things. But here we must sharply differentiate between two situations: one in which the principal will be in charge of a new school, and one in which he or she takes over an ongoing school. In these days of shrinking school systems, the frequency of the creation of new schools has been drastically reduced. Nevertheless, descriptions and analyses of new schools, albeit very few in number, have been very illuminating of the culture of the school. The most detailed description is Smith and Keith's (1971) *Anatomy of Educational Innovation.* I urge the study of that book because it is so detailed and thoughtful a case study, illustrating well the major themes I discuss in the present book. For example, their book can be taken as an unusually clear example of how misleading it is to talk about *a* school or *a* school system, as if they are not intimately part of a larger network of settings and groups. That is to say, the failure of the new school they describe is in part (and, in my opinion, a large part) due to the inability of the personnel to take seriously that the school was a creation of, and could be a "victim" of, diverse forces in the community. Another virtue of their book is how it illustrates the dilemmas of principals with teachers, and vice versa, and the conflicts of both with parents and other community forces. And, finally, the Smith and Keith book brings to the fore the significance of power, and conflicts surrounding it, in the culture of the school. One comes away from their description confirmed in the belief that the question most difficult for educators to articulate and think through is: Who owns the schools? For the principal, that question, as we shall see later in this chapter, is similar in principle to the question: Who owns the classroom?

Practically everyone, within and without the schools, automatically assumes that becoming principal of a new school is much to be preferred over assuming leadership of an older school. The reasons seem obvious enough: a new school is expected to have better physical facilities; school personnel, children, and parents will take greater pride in the school; the principal will have greater freedom to organize things his or her way, that is, it will be easier to innovate and to depart from past practices; the principal has more of an opportunity to choose teachers who fit in with his or her plans; the principal will not have to deal with an entrenched faculty who, because of their loyalty to a previous principal (or other reasons), are not likely to change their accustomed way of doing things. The fantasy that one is starting "fresh" is shared both by principal and teachers, a fantasy that engenders a great deal of motivation, enthusiasm, and much hope that *life in this school will be different than life in their previous schools.* But why call this a fantasy? It is a fantasy because it denies certain aspects of reality and because its wish-fulfillment aspects overwhelm and obscure what would be required to achieve change. I shall illustrate this by using a number of opportunities I and others at the Yale Psycho-Educational Clinic have had to observe or participate in the development of new schools.

1. From the time of appointment until the formal opening of the school the new principal spends almost all of his or her time in what can only be called housekeeping matters: ordering books, supplies, and furniture; assigning rooms; arranging schedules; negotiating the transfer of students from other schools; interviewing and selecting prospective personnel; making up bus schedules; etc., etc., etc. Particularly in the case of the principal new to such a role, the complexity of housekeeping is more than he or she imagined and was prepared for. In very quick order, the principal sees as a major goal—a goal determined by others but which he or she fully accepts and in relationship to which one has increasing anxiety—*opening the school on time and in good order.*

2. Up until the opening of school, the bulk of the meetings in which the principal participates are with administrative personnel, not only for the purpose of setting up house but in order for the principal to learn the rules and regulations relevant to whatever decisions one must make and plans that one has. The principal views these meetings—which are frequently with those responsible for his or her appointment or with those who can be helpful with the plethora of housekeeping matters—in terms of accommodating to the roles and power of others ("the system") and not in terms of seeking how to use the system to achieve his or her purposes.

Let us pause for a moment to emphasize a major consequence of what I have just described: up until the opening of the school the principal is not concerned with such issues as what life in a classroom should be, how teachers will be related to decisions and planning about educational values and goals, the role of parents and neighborhood-community resources, the handling of problem children, the purposes of evaluation, and other issues that bear directly on the educational experience of all those who have or should have a vested interest in a school. In fact, up until the opening of school there is precious little discussion of children or education. From the standpoint of the principal, however, the issues I have listed tend not to be issues about which he or she is set to do anything, or very much. It might be more fair, in some instances at least, to say that the principal is concerned with these issues but is acutely aware that he or she does not know what to do about them, a problem we shall have more to say about later. If, in the situation we are describing, the principal was not so totally absorbed with matters of housekeeping and organization, he or she would be faced much earlier with questions that will later arise: *In what relationship should he or she be to what children experience in classrooms? How does one get certain teachers to change their practices and attitudes? What does one do when one feels that a problem child is a reflection of a problem teacher? How should one handle the situation in which a complaint by a parent about a teacher may be legitimate? On whose side is the principal: Child? Teacher? System? Neighborhood?* It is extremely important to note how the principal asks these questions (and other questions) of himself or herself because the form of the question assumes that *he or she alone* must answer the question. It is not in his or her head—and nothing in previous experience would put it there—that these are the kinds of basic issues that the principal *and* the faculty must face, discuss, and resolve because these are the kinds of issues that affect all and, if they remain private, will contribute to the personal and intellectual loneliness of all, including the principal who escaped from one kind of role loneliness to another. To think and act in these ways would be an example of changing certain aspects of life in a school. But we are here also touching on the issue of the power of the principal, and as we shall see later, his or her view of it operates in ways antithetical to changing life in a school. But let us now return to the opening of the new school by the new principal.

3.   There is nothing the new principal in the new school desires more than an "orderly" opening, a desire particularly strong in the neophyte who feels, and who regards others as feeling, that personal worth will be judged by how smoothly things go—identical to what the neophyte teacher experiences when he or she begins to teach one's first class. Smoothness of operation tends to become an end in itself, and anything and anyone interfering with smoothness are not favorably looked upon.

4.   A variety of problems inevitably arises concerning parents, children, teachers, and various assortments of visitors, formal and informal. But of greatest concern to the principal are those with teachers who have changes to suggest, difficult or problem children they wish to discuss

and about whom they want the principal to take action, or emerging conflicts with other teachers about procedures and practices. In addition, it is at this time that the new principal begins to be aware that the teachers, whom he or she may have had an important hand in choosing, are far from a homogeneous group in terms of the way they relate to each other. It is not one big, happy family, but the principal has no basis in thinking and training for realizing that this is inevitable in any organized group. More important, however, the principal has no way to handle these problems except by avoiding them, or handling them, usually indirectly, on a one-to-one basis as they come up.

I can summarize our observations and experiences by saying that by the end of the first year, life in the new school is remarkably similar to that in old ones: what children experience in classrooms; the quality of relationships among teachers and between them and the principal; the relationship among parents, community, and the school; the criteria by which everyone judges themselves and others—in none of these can one discuss a difference that makes a difference.[3]

It is really not necessary for us to go into any detail in the case of the new principal who takes over an ongoing school. We shall do so later. Although the problems, on the surface at least, are somewhat different, the "phenomenology" of the principal, his or her practices and the results are much the same. If there is any difference, it is the speed with which the problem of power and influence comes up.

POWER AND INFLUENCE

When most people think about a school principal they almost always think in terms of what a principal can do, and attribute to him or her a good deal of power and freedom to act in the school. They rarely will think in terms of what he or she cannot do or the numerous restrictions, formal and informal, that limit one's freedom of action. This tendency to think in terms of,

---

3. Those who may think this an unkind or unfair conclusion—or who felt similarly about what we have described in this and previous chapters—should read Goodlad's (1969) conclusions based on the visits he and several colleagues made to 260 kindergartens through third grade classrooms in one hundred schools clustered in or around the major cities of thirteen states. "Neither principals nor teachers were able to articulate clearly just what they thought to be the most important for their schools to accomplish. And neither group was very clear on changes that should be effected in the future. . . . Studies have shown that administrators favor teachers who maintain orderly classrooms, keep accurate records, and maintain stable relations with parents and community. Other studies reveal that middle managers in the educational system, such as principals and supervisors, tend to be recruited from among teachers who demonstrate these orderly qualities. Because they are rewarded for maintaining the system, administrators are not likely either to challenge it or reward subordinates who do."

and to overevaluate, the power of the principal is no less mistaken in the case of the principal than it is when we think of the power of the President of our country. It may well be that we are more realistic about the presidency than we are of the principal, if only because we all were children in a school and viewed the principal as a very powerful person. We have had more opportunity to correct our overevaluation of the power of the President than in the case of the principal.

The tendency not to think of restrictions is a reflection of a rather pervasive tendency to confuse "ownership" of something with complete freedom to use it. For example, we tend to be more aware of what we can do with our car than we are of the scores of restrictions governing its use, for example, speed limits, license and registration fees, stop lights and signs, parking areas and time limits, use of head lights, when and where to pass, and so on. A similar kind of list can be drawn up in regard to what one cannot do with one's house.

The point is that when a person is "in charge," as in the case of the principal, we tend not to think of the restrictions, formal or informal, that are inevitably present. When I say "we" I mean, of course, the outsider. School personnel know otherwise, and no one knows this more than the principal.

Let us begin by asking a deceptively simple question: What responsibility does the principal have for what goes on in a classroom? I have yet to know a principal who could not name several teachers about whom he or she had serious question as to their classroom behavior; for example, this teacher is too repressive, that teacher is too permissive, this one is unorganized, that one cannot teach reading, this one wants to get rid of all of her problems, that one cannot interest his children, this one is always stirring them up, and that one should not be a teacher. Regardless of the "philosophy" of the principal, he or she has no difficulty pointing to teachers whom he or she regards as problems.

There is no doubt that the principal feels a responsibility in these matters, as there is no doubt that we, as outsiders, expect the principal to feel such a responsibility. The problem of the principal is how to discharge the responsibility, and it is here that the principal's experience as a teacher asserts its strong influence. The principal views going into the classroom for purposes of evaluation and change as an act that will be viewed by the teacher as a hostile intrusion. The presence of the principal in a classroom, particularly if it is in the context of a problem in that classroom, is experienced by the teacher with anxiety and/or hostility.

THE DYNAMICS OF THIS SITUATION ARE WELL ILLUSTRATED IN THE JOKE about the man who starts over to his neighbor's house to borrow a rake. On the way over he starts to fantasize about the possibility that his neighbor will not want to lend him the tool. By the time his neighbor has answered the doorbell, the man has decided that his neighbor will refuse the request and so his first and only words to the neighbor are, "You can keep your damned rake." What the joke assumes we know, and what makes it applicable to our discussion, is that the man projects onto his neighbor feelings and attitudes he himself has experienced toward his neighbor or others. ■

Although he or she has the power to do so, and feels a responsibility to do so, the principal prefers not to visit classrooms, a preference very much shared by teachers. But there is more at work here than the principal's past experience as a teacher, and that is that one quickly learns that telling a teacher what is wrong and insisting upon a change is a far from effective means for changing attitudes and practices. The power to legislate change is no guarantee that the change will occur—a principle the principal learned when as a teacher he or she was confronted with changing the behavior of children. From the standpoint of the principal, he or she feels there is little that can be done about what goes on in a classroom, particularly if the teacher has tenure or has been a teacher for a number of years. As a result, the principal tolerates situations that by his or her values or standards are "wrong." Because this toleration is frequently accompanied by feelings of guilt and inadequacy, it frequently has an additional consequence: the tendency to deny that these situations exist in the school.

A FURTHER CONSTRAINT ON THE PRINCIPAL'S POWER

In the next chapter I describe a statewide meeting of principals at which I and a lawyer sophisticated in the process of collective bargaining spoke. Following our presentations, very few questions were directed to me and scores of questions were asked of the lawyer, many of the questions centering on the power of principals to suspend, or expel, or discipline a child. Whereas in earlier decades the school principal could act on the assumption that he or she had the right and duty to take any of those actions, and to be able to count on administrative support, these principals were describing themselves as uncertain either about their power or administrative support. The society had changed and the fiction that schools and school systems were encapsulated and sheltered oasis had been exposed for what it always was (to those sensitive to our social history)—a fiction principals had now to face in two directions: toward schools and toward the "outside." And the principal had now to deal with and, hopefully, assimilate and accommodate to what comes from those directions. All of this at the same time that the principal feels increasingly powerless. Let us look at one relatively new development in the school culture to see how it has impacted on the principal's sense of power. I refer to the rise in strength of teacher unions in the past two decades.

For purposes of brevity, one can say that teacher unions gained strength as teachers generally became aware of and no longer would tolerate powerlessness. From their perspective, they lacked power in regard to setting salaries and increments, administrative arbitrariness, promotional practices, and educational policy. For our purposes here, I wish to emphasize their perceived powerlessness in regard to administrators which, of course, included principals. I am not aware of studies that are relevant to my opinion that teachers had less resentment to principals than to other administrators. But when teacher unions received recognition and began to bargain collectively with boards of education, they sought and frequently gained clauses in contracts that essentially placed some restraints on many administrative actions. Most readers have not had occasion to study contracts between teacher unions and boards of education, but to those who want a glimpse of how teacher unions have influenced the culture of the school and the processes and pace of change, they could do far worse than to read a sample of contracts. Still a better and fairer way would be to read *Arbitration In The Schools,* published monthly by the American Arbitration Association. These publications contain summaries of decisions rendered by arbitrators about grievances brought either by unions or boards of education under existing contracts. Grievance procedures are spelled out in contracts and the hearings conducted by arbitrators have a quasi-judicial atmosphere and standing. I give below three (1978) of literally hundreds of summaries that bear on our present discussion.

Administrative Transfer of Teacher-Personality Conflict

THE DISTRICT DID NOT VIOLATE THE AGREEMENT, WHICH STATES THAT AN administrative transfer must be made for just cause, when it transferred a teacher who had personality conflicts with her principal and with other teachers. The District's action was not punitive where the grievant's conduct was deemed to be uncooperative, challenging and disruptive. "A severe personality conflict may well be the most legitimate basis for administrative transfer."

The evidence supported the contentions that the grievant: (1) was unable to accept and to adjust to her assignment; (2) was uncooperative with her department head; and (3) had irreconcilable differences with her principal.

The grievant objected to being assigned to first period preparation time. This assignment led to the grievant's resigning her stewardship of the reading department and to the alienation of her teaching associates.

In addition, the teacher did not cooperate with her department head. She failed to attend essential department meetings and her relationship with other teachers in her department deteriorated to the point where the reading program was affected.

Finally, she refused to cooperate with the principal, claiming that the first period assignment was the result of her failure to comply with several prior requests of the principal. As to whether the transfer was punitive, the reasons urged by the grievant are "remote and unpersuasive. Feeling wronged, the grievant did everything she could think of to antagonize the principal. That her antagonism was ultimately successful cannot be doubted, but her transfer could scarcely be described as punitive" (p. 4). ■

Evaluation-Change in Rating

ALTHOUGH THE DEPARTMENT DID NOT ACT ARBITRARILY OR CAPRICIOUSLY in its evaluation of a teacher, it did violate three sections of the contract's evaluation provision by its failure to give the grievant written notification of the criteria used, by not actually observing the grievant on the job, and by not listing the names of the teachers who made criticisms or the incidents for which the grievant was criticized. The Department was directed to void the evaluation in its entirety and to give the grievant a satisfactory rating for the year.[4]

The grievant was given the overall "improvement necessary" rating based on: (1) critical comments received from other teachers; (2) the grievant's failure to post his schedule and to mark the equipment in the audio-visual department; and (3) his being observed playing backgammon during school hours. The principal, however, never mentioned any specific names or dates in his written evaluation. This violated language which states that "teacher evaluations . . . [must] . . . be based on documented facts from actual observation" (p. 5). ■

Termination of Probationary Music Teacher

THE TERMINATION OF A THIRD-YEAR PROBATIONARY MUSIC TEACHER WAS not for good cause where the grievant's unsatisfactory rating was the result of her teaching a combined class in piano, guitar and drums. This class was outside her normal teaching routine. For the two other years of her probation, she had been rated satisfactory. The grievant was to be reinstated to another year of probation so that she may be properly evaluated for consideration of tenure.

The grievant was assigned to teach an instrumental music class dur-

---

4. Reprinted with permission from the American Arbitration Association, 140 West 51st St., New York 10020.

ing her third year, a class she had not taught in the two previous years. "This was a class of beginning students and grievant was expected to teach piano/drums/guitar to these students in a single classroom environment." It was with this class that she had problems.

Not being an authority on music, the arbitrator relied on the opinion of a college music professor who stated that "under no circumstances could a probationer teach such a class in her third year as it placed upon her a burden beyond the usual abilities of a teacher" (p. 4).[5] ∎

The significance of these instances lies in the additional constraints principals experience in regard to discharging the duties and powers of their office. If principals experienced hesitations and obstacles (implicit or explicit) in their supervisory relationships with teachers before the era of teacher unions and detailed contracts, those hesitations and obstacles are experienced more poignantly today. Just as principals now agonize about how to handle suspensions and expulsions, and seek to avoid confrontations that can be time-consuming and morale shattering, they are increasingly reluctant to make decisions that would bring into sustained and formal conflict with teachers.

THE PRINCIPAL VS. THE YALE PSYCHO-EDUCATIONAL CLINIC

To concretize some of the general points we have been making, it is appropriate to describe here some of the experiences members of the Yale Psycho-Educational Clinic have had with principals. One of the several reasons for starting the Psycho-Educational Clinic (Sarason et al., 1966) was to have a vehicle for studying the school culture in the role of intervener or changer. In choosing such a role we clearly and deliberately were being guided by our clinical experience, and that of hundreds of others, which demonstrated that the understanding one gains of human behavior when one is in the helping role is extraordinarily difficult to obtain in any other way. One *sees* behavior ordinarily not made public and is forced to the realization (if one had not gained it in other ways) that one's desire to change is more than matched by one's ingenuity in avoiding change, even when the desire to change is powered by strong pain, anxiety, and grief. We were aware that there were different ways we could study the school, but our clinical background was decisive in determining that we would go the clinical route. This is not at all to suggest that we viewed children or school personnel as patients, or that we had any intention of ap-

---

5. Ibid.

plying any of our theories or techniques to whatever problems we encountered. We were far from naive about schools, but we were aware that our views of schools and what we thought they needed were not the results of tranquil reflection and scientific objectivity. We knew we had much to learn and unlearn and that *whatever we had learned about resistance to change would be as applicable to us as to those we hoped to be in a position to help.* (Be assured that these are words much easier to state than to implement!) In order to give more of an idea of the role we wished to be in, I give below the contents of the presentation we always made to the entire faculty of a school with which a helping relationship was being considered:

For a number of years some of us in the Department of Psychology at Yale have been engaged in different research projects involving elementary schools. In addition to our experiences in the elementary schools, some of us have long been interested in various aspects of special education and in the preparation of teachers. As a consequence, we became increasingly interested in the day-to-day problems facing schools in general and teachers in particular. Let me say right off that there are two conclusions to which we have come. The first is that anyone who teaches in the public schools for less than $15,000 per year ought to have his head examined. The second conclusion is that a law ought to be passed making it mandatory for each parent to teach a class by himself for a day each year. Although these recommendations may not solve all problems, they would certainly help bring about changes that all of us would agree are necessary. All of this by way of saying that our experiences have given us an understanding of what is involved in teaching and managing a large group of children, each of whom is a distinct character, for several hours each day over a period of ten months. It is not flattery but rather strong conviction underlying the statement that the classroom teacher performs one of the most difficult tasks asked of any professional person. It would indeed be nice if all a teacher had to do was to teach. You know, and I know, that a teacher is a parent, a social worker, a psychologist, and a record-keeping clerk. Hopefully there is time to teach once the duties associated with these other roles are discharged. We are living at a time when everyone seems to be an expert on the schools and ignorance seems to be no barrier to articulating strong opinions. There is no doubt, as I am sure you will agree, that there is much one can criticize about schools, but there is also no doubt that unless one understands what a school is like and what it is faced with in its day-to-day operation the benefits we would like to see from these changes will not be so great as they should be.

One of the most staggering problems facing our society concerns the degree of serious maladjustment in many people. One has only to look at the size and number of our mental hospitals, psychiatric clinics, reformatories, and the like to begin to grasp how enormous a problem this is. We are talking about millions of people and billions of dollars. What needs to be stressed is that in the foreseeable future we will have neither the personnel nor the facilities to give these troubled people the quality of treatment they need. In all honesty I must also say that for many of these people our knowledge and treatment procedures leave much to be desired.

As a result of our experiences, we at the Psycho-Educational Clinic in the Yale Department of Psychology have come to two conclusions: first, far too little is being done either to try to prevent the occurrence of problems or to spot them at those points in the individual's life where with a little effort a lot may be accomplished. Second, if we believe what we say, we ought in a very limited kind of way to attempt to see what we can do. I do not have to emphasize to a group of elementary-school teachers the significance of a preventive approach to problems in the early grades. As I am sure all of you know as well as, if not better than I, you are faced daily with children whose behavior, learning dif- ficulties, and interpersonal relations (with you or other children) arouse in you concern, bewilderment, anger, and a lot of other reactions. On the basis of all the talks and meetings we have had over the years with teachers there would seem to be in any one classroom of twenty-five children anywhere from three to six children about whom the teacher is concerned in the sense that she has a question about their academic learning and personal adjustment in the school setting.

What do we propose to do? It is easier for me to tell you what we do *not* intend to do. For one thing, we do not intend to come into a school in order to see how many problem children we can refer out to various agencies. There is no doubt that you know a lot of children who could utilize the services of a child-guidance clinic or family service society. To come in with the intent of referring them out is both unfair and unrealistic because these agencies, particularly the child-guidance clinics, are overwhelmed with cases and generally have long waiting lists. *Even if the child-guidance clinic could take the child on, it would take them quite a while to get to first base with the child and in the mean- time you still have that child in your class.* Treatment procedures are neither that quick nor that effective to allow you to expect that *your* dif- ficulties with the child are over once you know he is being seen in a clinic. The question we have asked of ourselves is how can we be of help to the teacher in the here and now with whatever questions and prob- lems she raises with us. In short, we want to see how we can be of help within the confines of the school.

It is not our purpose to come into a school to sit and talk to teachers, however helpful and interesting that might be. When we say we want to be helpful in the here and now within the confines of the school, we mean that in addition to talking with the teacher about a child *we have to be able to observe that child in the context of the classroom in which the problem manifests itself.* For help to be meaningful and practical it must be based on what actually goes in the classroom setting. For example, it is in our experience of no particular help to a teacher to be told that a child needs individual attention, a need which differentiates him not at all from the rest of us. What a teacher wants to know is when, how, and for what goals this "individual attention" will occur, and this requires a first-hand knowledge of what is going on.

We do not view ourselves in the schools as people to whom questions are directed and from whom answers will be forthcoming. Life and the helping process are not that simple. We have no easy answers, but we have a way of functioning that involves us in a relationship to the teacher and the classroom and that together we can come up with concrete ideas and plans that we feel will be helpful to a particular child. We are not the experts who can come up with solutions even though we have no first-hand knowledge of the context in which the problem has been identified.

I hope I have made clear that when we say we want to help it means that we want to talk to the teacher, observe in the classroom, talk again to the teacher, and together come up with a plan of action that with persistence, patience, and consistency gives promise of bringing about change. It is not a quick process and it is certainly not an easy one.

I cannot state too strongly that we are not coming into the schools with the intent of criticizing or passing judgment on anyone. *We are nobody's private FBI or counter-intelligence service. We are not the agent of the principal or some other administrative officer.* In fact, we are in no way part of the administrative hierarchy or power structure of the school system. We have no special strength or power except that which flows from our being able to establish a situation of mutual trust between teachers and ourselves. To the extent that we can demonstrate to you by our manner, gesture, and verbalization that we want to help, to that extent we make the development of this mutual trust more likely and quickly to occur.

There is one aspect of the way we function that I think needs some elaboration. I have already told you why it is essential for us, if our efforts are to be maximally useful, that we spend time in the classroom. Another reason this is essential resides in the one advantage we have over the teacher, i.e., we do not have the awesome responsibility of having to handle a large group of young characters five days a week for several hours each day, a responsibility that makes dispassionate observation and clear thinking extraordinarily difficult. We can enjoy the luxury of being in the classroom without the responsibility of the teacher for managing and thinking about twenty-five or more unique personalities. We do not envy you although I am quite sure that you will envy us for not having your responsibilities. It is precisely because we are "free" that we can observe what is going on in a way not usually possible for a teacher.

In order for us to help in a school it is crucial that we know that school as a physical entity and as a kind of social organization. Consequently, we usually make the request that for the first six weeks or so we visit classrooms and get to know you and what you do in the different grades without any obligation to get involved with any problem. A school and a classroom are not simple settings and it takes several weeks until we get the feeling of familiarity. We will be here on certain days of the week so that you can count on when we will be here. We try to spend a day and a half a week in each school.

We do not know to what extent we can be of help to you. We do not present ourselves as experts who have answers. We have much to learn about this helping process. If our previous work with teachers is any guide, the type of service we want to develop is one that they feel they need. The only thing we can guarantee you is that we want to learn and to help. We have much to learn from you, and together we may be able to be of help to children in school. ∎

For our present purposes the most important aspect of this presentation was that *we were going to be in classrooms*. Although we expected that our role would cause discomfort for the principal, we did not expect the degree of difficulty we in fact encountered in most but not all instances. The following summarizes our experience:

1. In diverse ways the principal would attempt to structure our role so that we would work with children rather than teachers. With us, at least, the principal tended to describe problems as existing inside the child's head independent of the classroom he was in or the teacher he had. It was children who were problems and needed help.

2. Principals were bothered and puzzled by the amount of time we spent "observing" in classrooms. Were we observing children? The teacher? The whole classroom? But amount of time was less puzzling than what we did with our observations. Since we had and wanted no power to tell anybody what to do, and we were not evaluators, how did we use our observations? What did we talk about with teachers?

3. In a number of instances the principal became visibly upset when he found out that in order to cope with certain classroom problems the teacher and clinic member had worked out and implemented a new procedure or approach. If the teacher had made these or other changes on her

own, as is frequently the case, she would have felt no need to check with the principal who would then have nothing to be upset about. What seemed to be the chief basis for upset was that in some way the relationship between the teacher and clinic member had resulted in the teacher changing something about *her* procedures, practices, and thinking, i.e., in each instance the teacher had willingly changed in some respect.

4. In some instances the principal suggested, and in some cases demanded, that we not go into the classrooms of the new teachers, claiming that the new teacher is very anxious, that she usually has difficulty in matters of discipline, and that she would become more anxious and ineffective if an "observer" was in the room. Interestingly enough, it was always our experience that in contrast to older teachers the new ones were more likely to seek us out, invite us to their classrooms, and more quickly and openly present their problems. As we have pointed out elsewhere (Sarason et al., 1966), where for a period of months we had to stay away from new teachers we spent the last half of the year trying to help the teacher undo what had been done in the first half.

5. Much of what has been said above was put spontaneously, and in the context of heated discussion, by two different principals: *"You are doing what I am supposed to be doing."*

From the standpoint of many principals, the conflict with the clinic member did not stem from a perception of differences in roles but rather from a perceived similarity in which we seemed to be able to relate and work with teachers in ways in which the principal would like to function but cannot or does not know how. It was very difficult for the principal to recognize that our relationships with teachers did not develop in the context of power and evaluation. Although the principal and the teacher are acutely aware that their relationship takes place in the context of power and evaluation, neither of them knows how to minimize the negative consequences of such a context except by minimizing contact. In an informal study I conducted in several schools the average frequency of appearance of the principal in a classroom during a two-week period was between one and two times (for some classrooms it was zero) and the duration of such appearances varied from two to ten minutes.[6] In a fair proportion of the times there was no subsequent communication about the visit, and this was

---

6. These figures are based on observations in elementary schools. In the junior and senior high schools, which have many more pupils and classrooms, the principal and his or her assistants rarely visit classrooms in other than the most perfunctory ways. Since these schools tend to be organized along departmental lines, one would expect that the departmental chairperson would play the role of educational leader, but since he or she is a teacher, the chairperson literally has little or no time to visit classrooms.

to be interpreted that all went well. Where there was communication, it was
the rare teacher who would state that the communication was helpful.

THE PRINCIPAL AND SPECIAL SERVICES

There used to be a time, we are told, when a school was a relatively simple
affair consisting of children, teachers, principal, janitor, secretary, and, on
certain days, a nurse. Not only was there consistency in type of personnel
but one could also count on the particular individuals in these roles being in
the school over long periods of time. In our large urban settings, at least,
this situation no longer obtains. As we indicated in an earlier chapter, the
percentage of children who are in a school in September but are no longer
there in June is high. However bothersome this may be to a principal, it
presents far fewer problems than the increasing presence of a wide variety
of special people or services who have duties to perform in the school.[7]
School psychologists, psychiatrists, social workers, remedial reading
teachers, speech and hearing specialists, special class supervisors, curriculum supervisors, representatives from different social agencies, a wide
assortment of volunteers, class mothers, teachers' aides—these are only
some of the special services that are represented in a school. During one
week, ninety-three different people (not counting personnel full time in the
school) performed a service in one of the inner-city schools in New Haven,
Connecticut, and we had no reason to believe that it was an atypical week.
Undoubtedly, there are fewer such people coming into suburban schools,
but this does not controvert the fact that more people, representing services, come into our schools than ever before.

 This situation exacerbates almost every problem of the principal we
have thus far discussed. The fact that so many different people come into
the schools bears witness to at least two things: there are problems in the
school, and the usual personnel cannot, or have not been able to, resolve
them. In addition, the titles of many of these people convey that they have
knowledge or competencies that regular school personnel do not have. In
short, these specialists are a constant reminder that regular school personnel, including the principal, cannot do the job themselves. Up to a point,
the principal agrees with and accepts this formulation, and indeed there are

---

7. The problem has become even more difficult as a consequence of Public Law 94-142,
popularly known as the "mainstreaming" law. I devote a later chapter to the substance and
consequences of that legislation. Suffice it to say here, 94-142 requires placement teams, consisting of diverse educational specialists, whose major responsibility is to develop an individual
educational program for each handicapped child. The role of these specialists was, heretofore,
a matter of custom and administrative regulations; 94-142 now gives a legal legitimacy to their
roles and introduces new sources of conflict between them and principals. And because the
legislation gives dramatically new legitimacy to the role of parents of handicapped children,
the principal has an additional problem with "outsiders."

principals who are constantly pressuring for more special services. But the conditions for conflict are present and we detail some of them here:

1. The relationship between the principal and the specialist is unlike that between principal and teacher in that the specialist is expected to have knowledge and skills not possessed by the principal. Consequently, the principal cannot determine or tell the specialist what to do. The principal, however, being acutely aware that it is *his or her* school and he or she bears responsibility for what takes place in it, feels a strong need to know what the specialist will do. The principal feels even a stronger need to decide whether or not the recommendations of the specialist should be implemented and in what ways. A person with the greatest amount of power is dependent on a person with greater knowledge and skill. Although this type of relationship does not necessarily have to result in conflict, and too frequently such differences are used as if they explain everything, but one cannot overlook the existence of conditions of role conflict.

2. The specialist is acutely aware of a problem that is compounded of administrative and professional aspects. On the one hand, in almost all instances he or she is *not* administratively responsible to the principal—one is usually part of a pupil personnel services department—and, on the other hand, he or she knows that in a real way one is also responsible to the principal. At the very least, the specialist is accountable to the principal. The specialist is frequently in the situation where one cannot act in accord with his or her professional knowledge and standards (i.e., one cannot do what one thinks is best to do) because the principal is determining what he or she can or cannot do. As any specialist will attest, there are some schools to which one goes with the greatest reluctance because of the feeling that he or she cannot perform one's duties according to professional standards. The specialist would like to feel that what he or she has to say and do is respected and followed; the principal would like to feel that he or she is not merely a servant of the specialist but an important participant in and determinant of what goes on.

3. From the standpoint of the principal the specialist is a transient whose expertise does not include an intimate knowledge of what is distinctive about *that* school and its occupants, and if for no other reason the principal must be vigilant about what the specialist does and recommends. This is difficult for the specialist to comprehend and when it happens that his or her work and recommendations are not accepted or followed, there is a tendency to explain such behavior in terms of narrowness, obtuseness, and rigidity. Such attributions may be true, but when it is not seen in the context of the principal's perception of his or her role, the response of the specialist tends to increase conflict and psychological distance.

4. The nature of most problems referred to the specialist involves one with teachers. To the principal for whom relations with teachers is a

source of conflict and personal dissatisfaction, the relationship between specialist and teacher can be one more source of trouble. Messy triangular relationships are by no means infrequent, and it is not unusual for the teacher to feel caught in the cross-fire.

A MAJOR DILEMMA

To understand the dilemma of the principal, one must begin by recognizing that the principal views his or her role, as do many others, as implying leadership. Whatever the motivations for seeking the position, they did not include being a housekeeper, or highly paid clerk, or embattled figurehead. Initially, at least, the principal expects and wants the school to bear the stamp of his or her conception of what good education and a school are. This conception may be vague, and depending on one's point of view, it may be regarded as liberal, conservative, progressive, punitive, permissive, and so on. The principal wants to be and to feel influential. The dilemma begins when the principal realizes that words and power, far from guaranteeing intended outcomes, may be ineffectual and even produce the opposite of what is desired. When hostility and resistance to his recommendations or ideas for change is encountered (e.g., with a teacher), the principal feels there is one of two alternative means of response: assert authority or withdraw from the fray. The usual consequence of either response is to widen the psychological gap and to increase the feelings of isolation of those involved.

WHEN I LOOK BACK AT ALL THE NEW PRINCIPALS I HAVE KNOWN OR observed, their "administrative styles" vary, but two of the most frequent types are relevant here. One of them includes those principals who, as one teacher said about her new principal, "acts as if everything before him was lousy and we should be thankful that the truth is here." The other type is far more favorably viewed because the principal does not impose personal ideas on anyone, i.e., he or she leaves the teachers alone. There is a third type which, in my experience, I have only observed in our urban centers, and this is the principal whom everyone considers favorably because the individual is "strong" with the children. A number of these principals were, in fact, strongly for "law and order" at the same time they were highly effective with difficult children in the sense of being able to listen to them, talk with and not at them, and conveyed to them a desire to help. But as one of these principals said to me: "*I* know how to handle these poor kids in *my* office. But there are about 300 of them in this school (which had an enrollment of 1,200) and I can't do it myself. How do I get some of my teachers to be able to change what and how they are teaching them?" This principal, who spent most of his time handling pupils sent "to the office," literally had no time to spend in classrooms or with those teachers he regarded to be as much of a problem as he did the children. ■

The dilemma of the principal is further complicated when one has to deal with people who have a different type of expertise and with whom the principal is not in the role of leader. What is important is that the principal's problems of leadership with "his" or "her" people interact with the same kinds of problems encountered with special services. The consequence of this interaction is that the principal is constantly wrestling with the problem of leadership with the feeling, which increases in strength over time, that the battle is being lost, that the individual is not the leader he or she expected to be, or would like to be, or that others expect him or her to be.

In large measure we have been discussing the principal in the context of one's experience in matters one would like to affect, or changes one might want to make; that is, matters in which the principal would like to be influential because they reflect *his or her* conception of what life in a school should be. The dilemma in leadership is further aggravated by the fact that often proposed changes for the school (e.g., the introduction of a new curriculum) do not come from the principal but from sources in the system ("downtown"). The point that we must not overlook is that regardless of whether or not the principal likes the proposed changes, he or she is in large part responsible for implementing these changes *in fact and in spirit*. When in favor of the proposed changes, one is faced with the task of leading the process of change so that its intended outcomes are realized, which is another way of saying that the principal has to help and insure that other people change. As we have seen, this is precisely the problem about which the principal feels most inadequate or, in practice, does inadequately. When not in favor of the proposed change, the dilemma may be simultaneously increased and decreased: increased because the principal must do something he or she does not favor, and decreased because he or she does not personally feel responsible for the change and can be so represented to others in the school who are also affected by the change.

THE INCOMPLETE PICTURE

In this chapter we tried to make a number of points. First, as an initiator or implementor of change the principal is in a crucial role. Second, neither by previous experience nor formal training nor the processes of selection is the principal prepared for the requirements of leadership and the inevitable conflicts and problems that beset a leader. Third, these background factors may not only be inadequate as preparation, but they may be antithetical to appropriate performance in the role. Fourth, with increasing frequency the principal is involved with a variety of special services that are beyond areas of personal knowledge and expertise and, because they are administratively not under his or her jurisdiction, complicate problems with leadership, responsibility, and power.

This is not a happy picture. Although what I have described is based on the extensive experience of myself and others at the Yale Psycho-Educational Clinic, I would like to emphasize that our experience includes candid discussions with principals, discussions that could only take place after we had demonstrated that we were not in the schools to judge or criticize; that is, *really* we were not in a school to compete with or supplant or undermine the authority and functions of the principal. There was conflict, there were differences of opinion, there were battles—some of them quite stormy—but in a number of instances these confrontations brought issues out into the open, which were then worked through and resulted in productive and enduring relationships. (As we shall see in the next chapter, the "psychology of confrontation," which we consider to be a most important aspect of the problem of change, is where the principal feels most at sea.) What I consider to be the most important points made in this chapter could have been written using little else than what some principals actually said in the context of confidential discussion. But for obvious and understandable reasons principals do not and will not make their dilemmas public.

What I have just said is a consequence of the anticipation that some people would view the contents of this chapter as critical and derogatory. Verbal disclaimers are usually held suspect and are rarely effective. Nevertheless, I have to say that the intention of this chapter was to describe a particular educational role and the dilemmas and problems encountered in performing the role, independent of the personalities one finds in this role. When I have used judgmental terms (e.g., inadequate) I was referring not only to my perception of the relationship between theory and practice of the role, but to that of principals as well.

The picture we have attempted to describe is incomplete in at least two respects. For one thing, we have only alluded to the principal's perception of "the system" and how this perception affects what he or she does and, more important, what the principal does not do because of feeling that he or she cannot do it. A related aspect, and one we stated and bypassed in the beginning of this chapter, is the legitimacy of using the concept of "the system" as the sole etiological scapegoat for whatever one may think is bad in the school culture, and no role allows this question to be raised with greater cogency than that of the principal. These aspects are the focus of the next chapter.

Chapter 9

The Principal and the Use
of "The System"

Particularly in our larger urban centers one quickly finds in conversation with all school personnel, from janitors to the school superintendent, that they are acutely aware that they are part of a very complex arrangement of roles and functions, purposes and traditions, that are not entirely comprehensible either as a whole or in part. Where it is comprehensible, it is often not viewed as "rational." The dominant impression one gains is that school personnel believe that there is *a* system, that it is run by somebody or bodies in some central place, that it tends to operate as a never ending source of obstacles to those within the system, that a major goal of the individual is to protect against the baleful influences of the system, and that any one individual has and can have no effect on the system *qua* system. There is no doubt in anyone's mind that the system "works" in the sense that children are in school, teachers teach, administrators administrate—everyone is doing something for or with someone else—but rarely does one meet someone who believes it is working well and that one's own job could not be done better if the system operated differently.[1]

---

1. This view is not peculiar to schools and school personnel. It is a view expressed by individuals who work in large, bureaucratic, hierarchically structured organizations, e.g., the armed services, government departments, and large business and industrial institutions. The New York city school system is very large, and its problems probably have received more attention in the national media than any other system, but that should not obscure the similarities that exist among urban school systems. Rogers' (1968) *110 Livingston Street* (the site of the New York City Board of Education) remains one of the best descriptions of the degree to which the urban school system has become bureaucratized. That book has at least three other major virtues: it demonstrates the problematic nature of the school administrator's role, it

The important point is not that everyone has a conception of the system, but that *this conception governs role performance even though it may be a correct or faulty conception.* Although in this chapter I shall be emphasizing the ways in which faulty conceptions affect role performance (i.e., by constricting the range of activities and the capacity to act), I am not unmindful of the fact that the consequences of a correct conception may be very similar to those of a faulty one. While I do not in any way question that characteristics of the system can and do have interfering effects on an individual's performance, it is the major theme of this chapter that "the system" is frequently conceived by the individual in a way that obscures, many times unwittingly, the range of possibilities available to him or her. Too frequently the individual's conception of the system serves as a basis for inaction and rigidity, or as a convenient target onto which one can direct blame for most anything. The principal illustrates this point as well or better than anyone else in the school system.

VARIABILITY AMONG PRINCIPALS

Let us start with a simple but actual instance:

AN OUTSIDE AGENCY OFFERS A SERVICE TO SEVERAL SCHOOLS. THE SERVICE involves a weekly, one-hour meeting with groups of teachers around problem cases in their classrooms. It is necessary that these meetings take place during school hours. Each of these elementary schools has two teacher aides who can take over the classrooms of the teachers who will attend these weekly conferences. Since the outside agency feels that it would be better if more teachers could attend, each principal is asked if there is not some way by which more could be accommodated. Most of the principals respond by saying that there is really no way to free more teachers. One principal says that she could take a classroom for the hour and her secretary could take another. One other principal says that two more teachers can be freed and that their classrooms would be unattended for the hour, i.e., the children would be on their own doing assigned work. ■

For a principal to take over a class is, of course, not an unusual matter, particularly under certain emergency conditions. It is unusual for a principal to do this once a week over a period of months; it is more unusual to assign a secretary to a classroom on a regular basis; and it is extremely rare, again on a regular basis, to leave a classroom unattended for one hour

---

realistically brings to the fore the role of power in the school culture, and it exposes as nonsensical the traditional concept of the bounded school system.

each week. The reasons for the rarity of these instances are several, among them being the feeling of most principals that these represent bad practices and that they are unfair to the educational progress of children. But more important and pervasive than these reasons is the feeling that these are not "legal" or permissible or responsible practices. When the principal is occupied in a classroom, or a secretary takes over a class, or children are unattended by a "responsible" educator, many untoward things can happen for which the principal will be held responsible, and it is a major concern of most principals that they not permit a practice that may produce criticism by administrative superiors or others. The major basis for this attitude is that "the system" does not view these practices either as permissible or desirable, and most principals do not question this position. However, one also finds principals who have seriously considered such practices but who refrain because of their conception that the traditions of the system are wise and not to be countered. The fact that some principals within the same system do permit these practices and spontaneously develop and support them, and that these practices become known to and tolerated by "the system," indicates that as important as the system itself is the conception of it held by the principal.

To further illustrate this point I shall present below part of an extended discussion of how "the unmanageable child" can be handled by classroom teachers. The excerpt concerns a way of thinking and a procedure that one member of the Yale Psycho-Educational Clinic was able to implement in one inner-city school. The question to keep in mind is why most principals have been opposed to trying the procedure.

THE ENORMOUS EFFORT AND INVENTIVENESS REQUIRED OF A TEACHER IN fostering good relationships both between herself and her children and among her children is sometimes defined as a distraction from her educational role by even the most kindly teachers. After all, she has a curriculum guide to cover and her children are evaluated against local or national achievement test norms. The psychologist can be of some help by pointing out how neglected emotional undercurrents festering in the class considerably reduce the teacher's educational effectiveness as much as they work against a child's developing his most human character traits. To neglect emotional factors in the classroom with an unmanageable child is to invite upheaval.

Relationship-building techniques for influencing the unmanageable child are indispensable to involving him constructively in the classroom, but they are usually insufficient to produce the dramatic suppression of hostile defiance that is necessary if he is to be allowed by the principal to remain in school. For the child's own welfare, therefore, it is necessary to work out with the teacher influence techniques that effectively suppress the child's defiant outbursts almost at once, unless teacher and psychologist feel that he would profit from a brief exclusion from school. The use of exclusion from school as an initial influence technique, however, is usually not nearly so effective with the defiant child as other measures. One of three techniques for suppressing defiant outbursts is implemented along with the relationship-building techniques in the case of each unmanageable child.

The most commonly recommended technique for suppressing defiant behavior is that of excluding the disobedient child from his classroom and placing him for half an hour in a classroom nearby. The success of exclusion depends on the preparation given by the psychologist to the teachers and school personnel involved, the support or toleration of the principal, and the precise manner in which the teacher prepares her class and implements the technique. Any such dramatic recommendation, of course, requires the approval and comprehension of the principal, whose begrudging acceptance of the plan could undermine teachers' use of it. The principal must also participate in selecting the relatively experienced teacher with whom the unmanageable child's teacher pairs. Teachers have an antipathy to imposing on each other: the excluding teacher usually feels embarrassed about depending on another teacher, and the receiving teacher is concerned about her class being unsettled by the visitor. These understandable concerns must be recognized and assurance given that the play may be stopped if it creates more problems than it solves. The participating pair of teachers must be fully briefed on the rationale and dangers in the plan so that they experience as few surprises as possible in implementing it. From our experience with the exclusion plan we now routinely brief participating teachers on several points. When a child is received in another room, he is to be given a seat at the back and excluded from any form of participation or interaction in the class. Before making this clear to teachers we occasionally found the excluded child excitedly participating in the receiving teacher's classroom activities. We also now prepare the excluding teacher for the problem of a child refusing to leave the room. He is to be carried out by the pair of teachers if he is in kindergarten through second grade. Older children refusing to leave their rooms are to be informed that unless they do so their parents will be phoned immediately. Never has a child refused to respond to either pressure. Never has an excluded child posed the slightest problem in the receiving classroom. Never has a child greeted the exclusion with anything but distasteful embarrassment.

So far the exclusion plan has the ingredients of an effective technique for suppressing defiant outbursts: it immediately terminates the disobedient behavior without introducing complications in either the receiving or excluding classrooms. Its unpleasant quality for the child renders it an effective influence technique in shaping more compliant subsequent behavior. The most significant source of power adhering to the plan, however, is probably not its unpleasantness per se but its decisive ability to force on the consciousness of the child the limits beyond which he may no longer go; in short, to underline by dramatic action those rules that other children remember and obey through verbal injunctions alone. It also gives the teacher a measure of authority she had been lacking in verbal injunctions. If the plan is to maximize the child's chances of remembering and following classroom rules, it must be introduced to the whole class not as an angry punitive retaliation by a distraught teacher but as a way of helping children to remember to follow rules that allow them to enjoy learning. It should be explained to the children repeatedly that a child will be excluded not because he is unwanted or disliked but because he needs the brief opportunity in another classroom to reflect on the rules he has been disobeying. By introducing the procedure to the entire class in a group discussion it does not appear as though the defiant child is being singled out; the shock of implementing the technique is reduced to more manageable proportions; and its rationale is communicated during a period of relative calm in the classroom. In their actual implementation of the plan teachers are cautioned against excluding children when they are furious with them, waiting instead until they have regained their composure. At that point the child is to be given one private, unembarrassing warning that clearly states that if a specific behavior does not cease he will be excluded. If several children are acting up defiantly they are to be warned publicly, but in no case is a child excluded unless he has had one and only one private warning from the teacher to remind him clearly of the rule he is breaking and of impending exclusion if he does not stop disrupting the class. Contained in such private warnings must be the teacher's attempt to explain to the child how he is disrupting the class, together with whatever relationship-building techniques she feels appropriate and feasible. Should the child subsequently defy the warning intentionally, he is to be led out of the classroom by the teacher who explains to the entire class in the presence of the child why he is being excluded.

On returning to the classroom after delivering the child to the receiving teacher, the excluding teacher reviews the situation with her class, emphasizing the reasons behind the relevant rules and alternative ways in which the excluded child might have acted. Whenever possible her remarks are channeled into a group discussion that can be used to marshal the support of the class in helping the excluded child. Once children have expressed their expected bitterness toward the defiant child in such discussions, the teacher can elicit more sympathetic interest from them in helping him, especially when she points out that she needs help from the class in teaching the excluded child to follow class rules. Such discussion that can be used to marshall the support of the class in a meaningful basis for the teacher to develop with her children a casual and change-oriented view of surface misbehavior. If the excluded child is to derive from his exclusion the maximum incentive and minimum discouragement to changing his ways, the teacher must schedule a short after-school interview with the child on the day of his exclusion. Like the class discussion, the follow-up interview is an essential ingredient in effecting a rapid suppression of his defiant outbursts. During the interview the teacher can explain how she excluded the child to help him remember class rules rather than to embarrass him, how she hopes that in the future a warning will be sufficient to induce the child to control his behavior, how it is the child himself and not the teacher who decides whether he is to be excluded from the room. Finally, the teacher can use the interview to explore with the child whatever difficulties he is experiencing in the classroom, promising the child confidentiality if he wishes to reveal something personal. Throughout the interview the teacher makes clear her affection and respect for the child, indicating how his misbehavior is at least as discrepant with his own hopes for himself as it is with hers for him. The psychologist can be helpful in reducing the aversion some teachers express about "psychoanalyzing" their students. As long as they do not probe deeply and listen warmly and acceptingly to any problems the child discusses, their common sense and professional ethics, he tells them, are adequate guides. Most of the inner-city children who require psychotherapy will never receive it; thus the teacher's may be the only interest ever expressed in their emotional lives. Of course, the psychologist is always available to review with a teacher any material that baffles or disturbs her. We have never regretted encouraging teachers to conduct such therapy-like interviews, though we have played down the suggestion with some teachers more than others. One outcome of such interviews is that they establish an open line of communication between child and teacher by dramatizing the teacher's wish to help him by talking with him rather than by forcing him to change.

The exclusion plan has proved an effective defiance-suppression technique for influencing children through the fourth grade. Especially when applied as calmly and consistently as possible, in a program of relationship-building, the exclusion plan can greatly reduce mounting classroom tension in a relatively antiseptic way. We have not yet experimented with its use for unmanageable children above the fourth grade.[2] ∎

This description allows us to raise two questions: What objections to this procedure have principals raised? Why did one principal accept and

2. S. B. Sarason et al., *Psychology in Community Settings* (New York: John Wiley and Sons, Inc., 1966), p. 143.

warmly support the procedure? The most frequent objection raised by principals was a variant of the "legal" question and goes like this: "I personally do not see anything wrong in the procedure except that we are not supposed to lay our hands on children, and if we have to carry a screaming child from one classroom to another we are breaking the rules. I would be accused of poor judgment, to say the least, and I stand a good chance of having the parents on my neck with all that implies. This is not something the school system would tolerate." In short, the principal's view of the system—what it will or will not tolerate—was a decisive factor. I should emphasize that a number of principals were sincere in saying that they *personally* had no objections but that they could not agree to the procedure because it was counter to rules and regulations, i.e., the system and its traditions.

How can we understand why one principal went along with the procedure? Another principal answered that question in this way: "He is a fool and he is asking for trouble." The tendency to anticipate trouble *in relation to the system* is characteristic of many principals and one of the most frequent and strong obstacles to trying what they conceive to be an atypical procedure. But the principal who went along with the procedure saw things somewhat differently: "Right now the only thing I can do with those kids, and I have a lot of them, is to send them home. The system says I can do that, except that it doesn't do any good. You can't teach a child who is not there. We are not going to hit the child or manhandle him. We are not going to descend on him like a bolt out of the blue. There may be trouble but that's what we have now. This is not being done to make life easier for us—in fact, it means more work—but to help a child in school. What are we here for? Certainly it is not to send kids home." It is not important that the procedure worked beautifully in this school, for which the principal's unequivocal support was no small factor. What is important is that he did not conceive "the system" as preventing him from discharging what he saw as his responsibility to extremely difficult children. In fact, it was his strong sense of responsibility that frequently put him in opposition to the "system," and he won far more battles than he ever lost. Rather than saying that he won battles, which is the way he saw it, it would be more accurate to say that what he demonstrated was that the system could "tolerate" diversity. But to test tolerance requires that one assume that "the system" can be or should be or will be malleable. Without this assumption one begins with a conception of the system that, in the tradition of the self-fulfilling prophecy, one ends up confirming.

Let us take one more example:

IN A PARTICULAR INNER-CITY SCHOOL THERE WAS A MAJOR PROBLEM IN controlling a rather large group of first and second graders during the recess period following lunch. In the fall and spring the recess was held in the school playground, and in bad weather it was held in the gym.

Two teacher aides had been assigned to organize and oversee the activities of the seventy or so children during the recess. Chaos was the norm, in part due to the absence of any meaningful or interesting play materials. As part of his work in a clinic seminar, a Yale senior had been assigned to work with one of the first grade teachers, and shortly after he began he became aware, like everyone else, of the chaos during this particular recess. After several months, during which he tried to be helpful with the recess problem, the student suggested to the principal that a couple of seventh or eighth graders from an adjoining school be gotten to help out during recess by organizing smaller groups around certain games. The first response of the principal was that insurance policies might not cover the seventh and eighth graders if they were somehow injured. The second response, upon which the principal dwelled for some time, was that the superintendent would not accept students functioning as teachers. Close questioning by the undergraduate produced nothing to indicate that the principal was not sincere in her belief that using students in the proposed way was frowned upon, if not directly against the rules. *The fact of the matter was that other principals in the same system had been using older students in the proposed way for some time.* ■

In choosing examples I have deliberately selected those that had either or both of two characteristics: an element of risk and, in the mind of the principal, a possible legal question. In each of these instances (many more could have been presented) at least one principal did something that most principals could not do because of their conception of what the system would allow or tolerate. The fact that at least one principal conceived of his responsibility and the system in a way that permitted him to take an action accepted or tolerated by the system indicates that for the other principals the decisive factor was their conception of what the system would permit.

The role of the principal cannot be understood by a listing or description of what he or she can or cannot do, if for no other reason than that conditions change and new problems arise. Any job description of a principal consists essentially of a set of generalizations, which, if anything, states or implies the *minimum* limits or scope of the position. It does not describe the maximum limits or scope of the position. For example, the job description may state that the principal is responsible for the quality of instruction in the school; it will not state the myriads of ways by which the principal should or could discharge this responsibility. The job description may state that the principal is responsible for insuring that parents are informed about progress of their children; it will not state the numerous ways by which this may be accomplished. The description may state or imply that the principal is responsible for keeping "law and order" in the school; it will not state the many different ways in which this may be viewed or done. The scope a principal permits himself or herself, so to speak, is a function of several things (e.g., personality, imagination, etc.) and the one I am emphasizing here is the conception of the system and its relation to what the system permits and tolerates. I have, of course, stated the opinion that too frequently the principal's conception of the system does not square with what the system in fact permits or would tolerate. Why this should be so is less important at this point than the fact that it is so. I have discussed some of the causative factors in the previous chapter, and we shall return to the problem at the end of this one.

It is perhaps necessary that I make clear what I have *not* been saying or describing. I have not said or implied that the modal urban school system (its traditions, structure, practices, role relationships, and "atmosphere") encourages or facilitates innovative or bold thinking and action on the part of the principal. I have not said or implied that the system does not present numerous obstacles in the path of a principal who may want to venture in new directions. In short, the modal urban school system does not have the soil in which the seeds of new ideas can grow and thrive easily or well. To argue otherwise requires a capacity to deny reality that goes well beyond ordinary psychopathology.

But having said this, one runs the danger of overlooking three important considerations. First, the knowledge on the part of the principal that what he or she wants to do may and will encounter frustrating obstacles frequently serves as justification for staying near the lower limits of the scope of the role. Second, the principal's actual knowledge of the characteristics of the system is frequently incomplete and faulty to the degree that his or her conception or picture of what the system will permit or tolerate leads the principal to a passive rather than an active role. Third, and perhaps most important, the range in practices among principals within the same system is sufficiently great so as to suggest that the system permits and tolerates passivity and activity, conformity and boldness, dullness and excitement, incompetency and competency. One of the most distinguishing characteristics of the modal urban school system is the diversity in quality and practice it contains. If "the system" is to be blamed for whatever one considers its defects, it would seem that it also should be blamed for its virtues, however occasional and infrequent they may be. But diversity within the system is not explainable by the system *qua* system. One has also to take account of the variations in the way in which individuals conceive of the system.

LOCUS OF CONTROL

To understand diversity in role conception and performance requires that we look at factors ordinarily relegated to a secondary status when we think in terms of the school system or the culture of the school. One such factor, which has emerged rather clearly from our work with and observations of principals, concerns the degree to which principals feel that they are what they are *as individuals* because of forces external to them in contrast to those perceived as internal. That is to say, there are principals who act as if *they* are primarily in control of their destiny, and there are those who act as if what they have been, are, and will be largely a function of external conditions and forces over which they have had or will have little control. I know that I am drawing too sharp a distinction and perhaps conveying the idea that there are "types" according to which people can be conveniently labeled and pigeonholed. I do not intend such a typology, but overdraw the distinction in order to emphasize a factor that has clarified for me the diversity in role performance among principals. I should hasten to add that I do not attach goodness or badness to this factor. Because a principal acts on the basis that one must be governed not by outside forces, changes, and demands but rather by considerations that internally govern him or her in no way means that the consequences of the actions are good or bad. One's actions are mediated not only by how one views "locus of control," but by a set of values as well.

A PRINCIPAL WAS DISCUSSING WITH ME A CHILD WHO HAD BEEN AND STILL was presenting behavior problems in his classroom. She related to me that a month earlier the child did something the principal did not like and she slapped him. The child's father complained to the superintendent. In discussing this with the superintendent the principal said that if he, the superintendent, would send the father to her he would also get his face slapped. ■

I could write a fair-sized monograph on this principal demonstrating in diverse ways how her actions were determined not by external conditions or requirements or demands, but by her view that *she* would determine what she did, when she did it, and how she did it. One may conclude that I am merely describing an authoritarian personality, but this conclusion can obscure the fact that the same view of locus of control can be found in nonauthoritarian individuals. I do not question that this principal was authoritarian, but I also do not question that she viewed herself as the primary determiner of her destiny as a principal and person. That the relationships I am discussing are far from simple are illustrated in the following, which concerns not a principal but a teacher who unknowingly taught me a great deal.

THIS WAS A WOMAN WHO HAD BEEN TEACHING IN THIS SCHOOL FOR FORTY years. She was four years away from retirement. The school had changed drastically in the previous decade. In earlier years its student body was primarily Jewish and Italian but now it was almost exclusively black and Puerto Rican. When I began to work in this school this

Jewish woman was one of the first teachers with whom I had a discussion and it was not one to generate happy thoughts about the future. She struck me as somewhat aloof and cold, very reserved and proper, and not someone who would easily change her mind about anything. These personality characteristics bothered me less than her organized presentation about how the neighborhood and its people had changed (all for the worst), and how the nature of schooling could no longer be considered as serving educational goals. Whereas it had once been a joy to teach the children who came to this school, it was no longer so. I concluded from this discussion that for this teacher the world had changed and that there was nothing she would or could do about it, i.e., she was now in a situation where a changed and still changing world were the primary determinants of what she did.

I did not look forward to visiting her classroom, expecting, as I did, that it would be the modal, unmitigated, boring disaster characteristic of most other classrooms in that school. What I found over a period of months was quite the reverse. To see how this woman put out for her pupils, the ways in which she managed to work individually with children, the interesting home-made instructional materials she used and the interesting and sometimes exciting ways she used them, the complete fairness with which she set and enforced rules, the games they played (there was no gymnasium) and her own physical involvement (despite her age and poor health)—my amazement was only matched by my puzzlement. Two other facts: at the end of each year the academic achievement of her second-graders was, on the average, above national norms, and in the four years we were in that school no child in her class was ever referred by her as a behavior problem. My puzzlement was simply that I did not understand what kept her going in this remarkable fashion. The more I thought about it the more I began to understand that, despite her perception of how the school, the school system, and the neighborhood changed, she could not or would not change her way of conducting herself as a teacher. It is almost as if she had said to herself: "I do not care how much things have changed, or what other people do about these changes, I can (must?) only continue to function in a certain way and if I do I'll achieve my goals. I can make these children learn." She had to feel that she was the primary determiner of her behavior in her role and that she was not going to be unduly influenced by external factors, forces, or changes. ■

Thus far in this chapter I have attempted to bring several factors into relationship with each other:

1. There is a marked tendency for school personnel to view the school system in negative terms.

2. In the case of the principal there is an equally marked tendency to view the system as the primary determinant of role performance.
3. The principal's view of what the system will permit or tolerate tends to be faulty and incomplete and obscures the diversity in role performance.
4. An important factor shaping the principal's view of his or her role and the system is, in part at least, determined by the degree to which the principal feels he or she rather than external factors will govern the course of action.

In trying to understand diversity in role performance among principals we should not overlook the obvious and momentous significance of the diversity, and that is that the potential scope of the role is far more broad and important than modal performance would suggest. What the principal could do should not be confused with what the principal does do. What the modal principal does should not be confused with what the school system would permit or tolerate.

A PRINCIPAL AND HIS FACULTY IN A SUBURBAN SCHOOL FOUND THEMSELVES in agreement that they would prefer not to have report cards except at the end of the year. They felt that the anxiety and competitiveness that surrounded report cards were unwholesome, and they also felt that what was communicated to parents by report cards was as frequently misleading as it was helpful. What they preferred was to take the responsibility of talking to parents whenever they felt a discussion was necessary and also to encourage parents to take more initiative in coming to school whenever they wanted to know how their child was doing. The group was ready to terminate the discussion because it was the feeling of all that the school system required report cards and that there was no point in taking on a losing battle. The principal wondered aloud whether they should not take the issue up with the PTA, if only to find out how they viewed report cards. The meeting was held and a majority of the parents not only agreed with the principal and teachers but urged them to try to implement the plan. The principal then took the matter up with the superintendent, stressing the feelings and support of the parents, and he was told to go ahead and try it. ■

The school system sets the lower limits of the scope and responsibility of the principal. The upper limits of the role are far less determined by the system than one might think by looking at modal performance.

In this connection I recommend Wolcott's (1973) ethnographic study, *The Man in the Principal's Office.* One can only wish that the type of detailed study Wolcott did was more frequent so that we would obtain a more comprehensive picture of how what principals do varies with the school's size, regional placement, tenure in office, and gender. What we are also lacking is how the role of the principal has changed as a function of changes in the larger society. So, for example, how have the school and the principal that Wolcott studied changed in the decade following the study? (His study was published in 1973 but it was done several years before.) Would the picture have changed in line with Wolcott's 1977 ethnographic *Teachers vs. Technocrats?* Although somewhat more frequent than in earlier decades, the ethnographic approach to schools and school personnel has hardly been mined as a way of describing and understanding the school culture. Why this is so can be deduced from Porter-Gehrie's (1979) summary description of ethnographic methodology:

TRADITIONALLY, ETHNOGRAPHERS OBSERVE AND RECORD EVENTS IN THE daily lives of people conducting their normal activities. Although their subjects are aware of being watched, ethnographers attempt to interfere as little as possible with the flow of events at the research site. They attend to the details of ongoing events in order to gain an in-depth understanding of the subjects, their interrelationships, and the social context in which they interact. Because ethnographers usually observe subjects for one year or more, they obtain longitudinal perspectives on the relationship of people and events.

The primary data produced by ethnographers are the written records of events observed in natural settings. They attempt to make their "field notes" as detailed as possible, including specific description, exact wording, diagrams, and time sequence. These observations of events in process may be supplemented by taped or written records of interviews, documents and memoranda collected at the site, photographs and films of events, and survey instruments designed to elicit uniform information from research subjects. Traditional ethnographic data are the product of those methods. ∎

There are few researchers willing and able to devote a year or more observing and recording events in the daily lives of people in a complicated setting, and then spending a year or more integrating voluminous and heterogeneous data into a form that can be understood and tested by others. The ethnographic-anthropological approach to people and settings has been very productive of new ideas and perspectives in the social sciences. Indeed, in my opinion, that approach, despite its infrequent use, has been more illuminating of the school culture and the problem of change than any other approach. So, for example, when I read Wolcott's *Teachers and Technocrats* (1977), it confirmed and further illuminated what I had observed and experienced about the school culture, but with a detail and within a longitudinal framework that my own written observations often lacked. And that is the potential of the ethnographic approach: it culminates in a "picture" containing diverse details ordinarily not studied in relation to each other (e.g., Porter-Gehrie, 1979).

IDEAS: THE NECESSARY INGREDIENT

It is very likely that some readers will have concluded that I am advocating that principals should view themselves as the primary determiners of their courses of action rather than view themselves as kinds of victims of external forces and changes. I intended no such conclusion, and if I had, it would not have been justified for one very obvious reason: there are principals (just as there are many other kinds of people) who do view themselves as the primary determiners of their courses of action but whose ideas and values—the ingredients that empower and give substance to their actions—can be questioned on numerous grounds. Actions, regardless of whether they reflect an internal or external orientation, are always mediated by a blend of ideas and values.

THE PRINCIPAL OF A JUNIOR HIGH SCHOOL WAS INDISPUTABLY A PERSON who viewed it as necessary that he feel that his actions and decisions were primarily controlled by factors internal to him rather than by the way things happened or changed "out there in the world." When he became aware that boys' hair styles were changing, he was quite bothered although he did nothing when these styles started to be evident in the school. He stewed over the matter for some time. The school did have explicit rules about what was proper attire and he did not consider the new hair styles as falling within these rules. He was also aware that some of the parents were permitting or tolerating the new fashion. One day he decided that he had to take a stand and so he instructed each teacher to send to his office any boy whose hair style was clearly long. Approximately twenty boys appeared at his office where he informed them that they were to go home and not return until their hair was cut. This they all did. ■

There are those who would applaud this principal for viewing himself as he did *and* for the specific ideas and values reflected in his actions. There are others who would applaud this principal for viewing himself as he did *but* who would disagree with the ideas and values giving rise to the course of action, in terms both of means and ends. And so we come to the heart of the matter: the fact that a person has a particular orientation toward himself or herself and the world is important, but equally important are the ideas and values to which the orientation is related. When I say ideas and values I refer to a number of things: one's knowledge and conception of what children are and the kinds of problems they inevitably have in the course of growing up; to what extent and how the interests, problems, and characteristics of children should be reflected in and determine the school experiences; to what extent and how decisions and planning in the classroom are discussed and made; how a faculty should think about how it confronts and resolves problems concerning their relationships with each other, administration, pupils, and parents; how should a faculty avoid the usual situation in which they feel intellectually and personally isolated and lonely; and what makes a classroom interesting for the teacher? Is the intellectual growth of teachers less important than that of pupils? Can pupils learn and change if teachers are not continuing to learn and change? Many more statements and questions could be formulated and asked concerning what the nature of life in a school should be, but they would only underscore two facts: life for everyone in a school is determined by ideas and values, and if these are not under constant discussion and surveillance, the comforts of ritual replace the conflict and excitement involved in growing and changing. The principal may be this or that type of personality, experienced or inexperienced, likeable or otherwise, intellectually bright or average—if the principal is not constantly confronting one's self and others, and if others cannot confront the principal with the world of competing ideas and values shaping life in a school, he or she is an educational administrator and not an educational leader.

Most principals are administrators.[3] That this is so is not entirely explained by the characteristics, traditions, and practices of "the system." The fact that one cannot say that all principals are administrators should make one pause about using the concept of the system as the sole etiological factor. That there is some (not much) diversity among principals is a characteristic of the school system that requires recognition and explanation. What I have been suggesting in this chapter is that the modal school system permits and tolerates diversity, and that limits of this tolerance are *in part* determined by the principal's conception of himself or herself in relation to the system and how this conception is powered by ideas and values. That one may not agree with a particular blend of ideas and values should not blind one to the more general point that the ultimate fate of ideas and values depends on the principal's conception of himself or herself in relation to the system.

---

3. The problem of the school administrator has been briefly but well discussed by Usdan (1968). For a more detailed discussion, consult Gross and Herriott (1965) as well as Goldhammer, Suttle, Becker, and Aldridge (1967). As I indicated earlier, Wolcott's (1977) *Teachers and Technocrats* is one of the most revealing studies of administrators and the process and problem of change.

WHEN "THE SYSTEM" IS CHALLENGED

I have been discussing the role of the principal from the traditional view of a school system: a bounded social organization that is largely autonomous in determining its functions, structure, goals, distribution of power, personnel, and role definitions. So, when I was emphasizing the centrality of the principal to the process of change or the importance of how the principal understands and deals with the system, I was assuming what school personnel have long assumed: there is a bounded system that may have all kinds of contacts with outside forces, but those contacts do not and should not alter the characteristics of the system. Those who hold this view recognize the "outside" world, and support diplomatic relations with it, but strenuously protect the system's sovereignty over its own turf. It is a view that propels the attention of school personnel to what happens within the system. Unless one understands the strength of the hold of this traditional view, and employs that point of view as an initial basis for studying the culture of the school and the processes of change, one will gain only a very partial understanding of what has happened and continues to happen to and within schools. The fact is that the absorption of school personnel with the internal nature and workings of the school system, in addition to an ahistorical stance that prevents questioning the traditional concept of a school system, has had the effect of blinding them to what was happening "outside" the system. When they, so to speak, woke up to what was happening outside the system, they were forced to recognize that far from being walled off from its surroundings, the autonomous school system had never been as autonomous as rhetoric had suggested. More than that, they began to recognize that the culture of the school reflected *and* was sustained by the culture "outside" of it. *The view of the school as an autonomous system has long been the basis for the belief that schools were vehicles for societal change. How could one hold such a belief unless it rested on the assumption that schools were independent of outside forces; i.e., they were sovereign systems?* What events of the last two decades have exposed is that the reverse comes closer to the truth: far from being a sovereign system, the schools have always been creatures of outside forces. If there have been periods when it seemed as if schools were sovereign over their territory, they were the exception rather than the rule, periods of truce between wars over sovereignty.

Let us now return to the role of the principal when he or she is forced to deal with problems that have two characteristics: they represent a challenge to school practices and the power of the principal, and they derive, or appear to derive, from outside the schools. What do these instances tell us about the culture of the school generally and the school principal in particular? Let me begin with a personal experience.

Several years ago I was asked to address a state association of school principals. As it turned out I was one of two speakers, the other being a lawyer who spent most of his working time representing boards of education in collective bargaining with different unions, e.g., teachers, administrators, custodial, and food services. I spoke first about some of the things contained in this book. The lawyer then spoke about the dilemmas and opportunities in collective bargaining. Each of us spoke for about thirty minutes, leaving forty-five minutes for a question and answer period. During that forty-five- minute period I was asked two questions! The rest of the time the lawyer was bombarded with questions almost all of which had to do with the legal issues involved in suspending or expelling students from schools. These questions were of various types: What were the legal rights of students and parents? What constituted due process in regard to suspension and expulsion? Under what conditions could a principal be sued by parents? Were the policy issues involved in suspension and expulsion subject to collective bargaining? No less impressive than the kinds of questions that were being asked was the obvious bewilderment, anxiety, and anger that accompanied these questions. It was understandable if an outsider at this meeting came to two conclusions: each school principal needed a personal lawyer; and a shooting war was going on between school principals on the one hand, and parents and students (and their lawyers) on the other hand. A third conclusion would also have been justified: the school principal felt somewhat alone with these problems. He or she was uncertain what kind of support "higher-ups" would give the principal, in the same way that the principal was uncertain how far he or she should go in supporting a teacher who was pressuring for a student's suspension or expulsion.

From the standpoint of parents and school personnel, the core issue was the scope of the power, in law and custom, of school personnel. More concretely, parents were challenging the school's right and manner to suspend and expel; i.e., parents and students had *rights* that school personnel would have to recognize. And behind that challenge was a more basic issue: Who owned the schools, and who had the final power to decide school policies? There was a clear answer from the parents: school policy was not made by educators but by representatives of the community; the school system was not an encapsulated one within which educators were the sovereigns. The problem for the educators was that they could not disagree with that answer, even though psychologically they were used to seeing themselves as rulers of the system. In point of fact, the parents were not challenging the power of school personnel, they were seeking to assert the power they possessed. It would be surprising if school personnel did not perceive the assertion as a challenge and seek to deflect and dilute it, but in trying to do so they were holding on to a conception of a school system that contributed to the problems they were faced with. *No less remarkable than the contents of the meeting I described was what the school principals*

*related afterwards in informal conversation: suspension and expulsion were
but two examples of a more general assault by parents and others on the
worth and competency of school personnel.* "How can we do our jobs if
everybody has the right to control and criticize us?"—that query summed
up the beleaguered stance of the school principals.[4] Crowson and Porter-
Gehrie (1980) make the following conclusions on the basis of studying ten
urban school principals over a period of a year.

MORE THAN ANY OTHER SINGLE POSITION IN THE AMERICAN SCHOOL
hierarchy, the principalship represents the pivotal exchange point, the
most important point of connection between teachers, students, and
parents on the one hand and the educational policy-making structure—superintendent, school board, and taxpayer—on the other.
Through the principal's office pass both the needs, problems, and issues
of the local community and the problems and issues that accompany the
implementation of policies flowing downward from the top of the school
bureaucracy. Griffiths has recently observed: "School principals, long
considered men-in-the-middle, have been deprived of virtually all
authority, and now only the most astute survive through a finely tuned
political acumen." Although the school principalship is not quite devoid
of all authority, it is clear that the principal is called upon to play a
most difficult organizational role—one which demands very highly
developed skills of staff leadership, client sensitivity, facilities management, crisis intervention, community savvy, and bureaucratic adaptabil-
ity (pp. 65–66). ■

That the principal is in a most difficult organizational role goes without
saying, but the difficulty stems to a significant degree, as Crowson and
Porter-Gehrie's ethnographic data indicate, from the inability of "the

---

4. If principals by virtue of their role as gatekeepers between school and community feel particularly beleaguered, let us not overlook how general such a feeling is among school personnel.
And why not? Take but three recent instances that confirm such feelings. In the 1980 presidential campaign the candidate who ultimately won promised to eliminate the new Department of
Education. President-Elect Reagan appointed a task force on education and I obtained a copy
of the first draft of its report and there is nothing in that report that would give educators the
feeling that their problems are understood and the difficulties of their different roles appreciated. (For example, the first recommendation is the elimination of funding for Teacher
Centers, on the basis that "there is no evidence that they promote quality education.") Then
there is the report (1980) *The Humanities in American Life* which catalogues the general
deterioration of our schools and criticizes many of its practices. Kramer's (1980) review of that
report is very much worth reading. I could go on and on, but the point remains: school personnel not only feel unappreciated and misunderstood, but they bitterly resent the implication in
the utterances of public officials and by the writings of many professionals that the attitudes
and practices of school personnel "explain" what is wrong with schools; more correctly, why
schools have changed in such an educationally defeating way. As I suggested in an earlier
Chapter, the failure to see the present situation in terms of social-history contributes mightily
to the polarization between school personnel and "the rest of the world."

system" to recognize that it is not and has not been a bounded one. This is especially clear when Crowson and Porter-Gehrie describe four coping mechanisms used by principals, of which we present one:

Coping Mechanism: Redefining the Supervisory Role

A FIRST COPING MECHANISM WE OBSERVED INVOLVED AN EFFORT TO address the very commonly held expectation that it is the principal's job to supervise closely the instructional work of the school. Principal Jenkins, below, speaks to the nature of the problem.

Jenkins says that when she took her graduate work, there was very little that was talked about in administration courses which related to the urban school system. She said there was a lot of information about things like how to deal with school boards and how to get tax assessments made, but these were issues which relate very little to the job of the city principal. Then, she says another misconception in the administration curriculum is "all of those studies that have been made of principals, giving the impression that my job is doing something out there in those classrooms. That really doesn't fit." Jenkins says that the way principals have to allocate their time, there is no way they can spend huge amounts of time sitting in classrooms and that, if they do, they're going to neglect the other important things that have to be done in the school. She should be spending 60 percent of her time in teacher supervision. That just isn't possible. But, she says, if she sat in classrooms all day long she would not do that much good and there wouldn't be anybody here to meet the people who come expecting to see and talk with the principal.

Principal Jenkins and her fellow principals face very stiff constraints of time and procedure in fulfilling an element of their role (instructional supervision) that is generally considered very important to the work and welfare of the school system. Procedural difficulties abound in any effort to dismiss an incompetent teacher and, although some principals do work hard to weed out their poorer faculty, the more common response seems to be to redirect much of the supervision component of the principalship role into other endeavors which relate *in some way* to the supervisory role expectation but appear to have a better chance for some payoff. Some principals spend a good deal of their own time tutoring underachieving pupils, others give themselves to curriculum improvement (e.g., inservice meetings or textbook selection), and still other principals pursue program development in order to increase resources available to the school (pp. 63–64). ■

What this principal is illuminating are the dilemmas that are created when a role is defined in terms of a conception of a system that does not recognize the porousness of its boundaries, or the degree of commerce it has or should have with its social surroundings.

In earlier pages I attached special importance to how principals conceive of "the system" as one factor in understanding variations on how they deal with problems *within* the system. And we said that the traditional conception, based as that is on the principal's experience as a teacher and socialization into his or her role as principal, produces restraints (internal and external, valid and invalid) on his or her exercise of power and reaction to change. That conception and its consequences are not only fateful for how the principal thinks about and reacts to issues of power coming from outside the system, but these external challenges exacerbate further the dilemmas of the principal within the system. On the one hand, the principal has to decide the range of actions permitted him or her by those in higher positions as well as how to deal with teachers who look to the principal for support and leadership. The root cause of the dilemma is the principal's assumption that his or her constituencies are those within the system; i.e., the principal is more responsible to those within than to those without the system. The principal, of course, is not alone in this respect; it is an assumption held by people in every role in the system. When the validity of that assumption is challenged, it is a direct challenge to the educator's conception of what a school system is or should be. It is no wonder that the principals in the meeting I described reacted as they did. What would be surprising is if they had felt and reacted differently. After all, what was at stake was how to answer the question: Who owns the schools?

From the standpoint of the principals at the meeting, the challenge was an external one. From another perspective, it would be more correct to say that the new challenge was external, but the longstanding one was internal. I refer to the fact that "discipline" and "law and order" have always been problems in schools. Few situations are more upsetting to school personnel than rule-breaking behavior of pupils, and that kind of behavior has always been a feature of the school culture, increasing steadily from the elementary to the high school. School personnel have always reacted to these "internal" challenges from the standpoint of rules they deemed necessary and appropriate; they were not rules that were, so to speak, "negotiated" between pupils and school personnel. It seemed right, natural, and proper that behavioral rule making should be the prerogative of school personnel. That rule-breaking behavior (minor to flagrant, covert to overt) has never been miniscule in frequency in schools has largely, if not always, been explained in terms of the characteristics and background of individual pupils. And it was also the case that the manner in which penalties were meted out was the right of school personnel. Given the traditional stance of school personnel, one question could never surface in a direct way: What was the culture of the school contributing to the types and frequency of rule-breaking behavior? That question did not surface as long as school personnel could contain rule-breaking behavior and there were no external challenges to the rules that in effect said: "You are not a law onto yourselves, you are part of the problem not part of the solution, you will have to change."

How do we understand the rise and force of the external challenge to schools and how that interacted with the internal challenge to require one to question the concept of the bounded school system? That question requires a separate book and I will only indicate here the highlights of an answer. One can begin with a summary statement: the post-World War II era has been one in which diverse groups in the society began to *redefine* their conception of themselves; i.e., they began to challenge the ways in which society had been used to defining them (Sarason and Lorentz, 1979). Blacks, women, gays, handicapped people, and a host of other minorities were no longer content to stay within the social confines of the roles society had accorded them. Initially, the process of redefinition was largely based on personal-social-moral considerations, but it was not long before the process was bulwarked by use of the legal system. Another way of describing the post-World War II era was that it brought to center stage the civil rights of individuals and, consequently, the ways in which social institutions had to respect those rights. It was not surprising that the rights of children began to occupy legal scholars and others. What was the standing of children in law? Still another way of describing this era is that it was one in which traditional authority and the major social institutions were under attack to change in the direction of becoming more responsive to the rights and needs of individuals. The authority-power basis of every major institution was questioned. It was an era of redefinition and challenges. And, finally, it was an era in which our urban-metropolitan areas were undergoing sea-swell changes in population composition, economic instability, juvenile delinquency, and everything else subsumed under "the urban problem."

If the principals seemed preoccupied with suspension and expulsion, it was because an internal problem to which they were ever vigilant had increased and had become related to external social changes, one of the consequences of which was a challenge to the authority and power of school personnel. The principals were absolutely correct in their informal comments about the variety of challenges that were being directed at schools. They were also correct in their conclusion that the role of the principal had become much more vulnerable precisely because the principal is such a convenient target for criticism and challenge from within and without. Even when principals could act on the basis of a narrow conception of the school system, it was all too easy to see that system as not permitting much room for change. But when in addition the principal perceives and deals with external challenges, risk taking and initiatives for change become even more problematic than ever. (And in times of shrinking school populations and the closing of schools, survival rather than change will tend to get top priority.)

There seems to be a consensus that the principal occupies a key role in the educational change process. More correctly, the potential of that role for the change process is greater in theory than it is in practice. I should point out that that consensus derives from studies of efforts at change that originated within the system; i.e., efforts that came from the principal, teachers, or administrators. But is the substance of that consensus applicable when proposals for change come to the principal from external sources, e.g., parents and other community groups? Is the potential of the role of principal in regard to these proposals as great in theory as it is when the proposals are internally generated? We shall return to these questions in a later chapter when I will outline a conception of what the change process might look like. Suffice it to say here that it is a conception that begins with the question: Who has or should have responsibility for schools? Too frequently that question comes up after conflict, failure, and polarization, a situation not likely to support or sustain change.

The Teacher: The Role
and Its Dilemmas

In all the previous chapters we have, in varying degrees, discussed the classroom teacher. Although in this chapter we shall concentrate on communalities among teachers, one should not forget how diverse a group classroom teachers are. Teachers vary on a number of dimensions; for example, the grade level they teach (kindergarten, elementary, junior, and senior high), the kind of child they teach (retarded, disturbed, physically handicapped), area of subject matter specialization (physical education, math, etc.), length of teacher experience, type of teacher training background, and sex.[1] Each of these dimensions could serve as a basis for understanding the role of the teacher in the culture of the school. In fact, the diversity is of such a degree as to rule out the possibility that any one individual can know the culture of the school in terms of all or even most of these dimensions. We will have to content ourselves with the modest goal of trying to see some of the communalities underlying obvious diversity. In this attempt I shall inevitably be influenced by my own immersion in schools as well as my interest in the problem of change. Precisely because of the problem of change, we must not overlook how the role and ex-

---

1. Teaching in an elementary and a high school are two very different experiences. The phenomenology of the elementary school teacher is better described and understood than that of the high school teacher. In general, research of all kinds has focused far more on elementary than on high schools, perhaps because the latter are so much bigger, more bureaucratized, and more difficult to understand than the latter. This point is made with force in a manuscript of a forthcoming book *Teachers: Their World and Their Work* by Anne Lieberman and Lynne Miller of Teachers College, Columbia University.

perience of teachers have changed with the passage of time. So, if you compare Waller's (1932) classic *Sociology of Teaching* with Lortie's (1975) more recent book *School Teacher,* one cannot avoid the impression that they were describing two different worlds. Not totally different, of course, and in some important respects not different at all, but where there are differences they bespeak of vast changes in the larger society. In 1932 you would have been derided if you predicted that labor unions would successfully organize teachers, that there would be long strikes, that teachers would be less intimidated in their personal lives by the proclaimed morality of the community, that handicapped children of all kinds would become an obligation of the schools and alter the composition of the classroom, that preparation of teachers in two-year "normal schools" would be supplanted by preparation in a four-year liberal arts program, that urban school systems would primarily serve minority children, and that the substance and severity of school problems (and, therefore, teachers' problems) would vary as a function of dramatic increases and decreases in the number of school age children. When we talk about "the problem of change," we usually mean a deliberate, focused effort to change something in schools. *The fact is that some of the most dramatic changes in schools were unintended consequences of what was happening in the larger society, not the intended consequences of an articulated policy.* The school teachers who today are in their late forties and fifties can talk at length about how schools have changed, but it is the rare teacher who can place these changes in the context of changes in the larger society that, although not directed at schools, had an enormous impact on them. So, for example, as World War II went on and required an increasing number of industrial workers to sustain an unprecedented war effort, a very deliberate effort was made to attract people from different rural·regions of the country to urban industrial sites. Thus began (or accelerated) a change in the size as well as in the social, ethnic, cultural composition of urban populations that was to set the stage for new pressures on schools. It is understandable (albeit unjustifiable) if school personnel reacted to these pressures by derogating these new populations, as if "they" were only a cause of school problems and not themselves an effect of other societal forces.[2] But if it is understandable, it was at the same time a misreading of what was going on and why, of how pressures for educational change tend to arise. It is another example of how poor we are at thinking through the intended and unintended consequences of social policies. The feeling of necessity interacting with passionate com-

---

2. As I pointed out in an earlier chapter, throughout the nineteenth and twentieth centuries *every* immigrant group had been derogated and perceived as a threat to the existing social fabric. School personnel and the controlling groups and classes in the society saw the immigrants as culturally and intellectually inferior, as "material" that had to be given a new but familiar shape and substance. When I use the word *immigrant* I refer both to large scale movements into the country, and from one part of the country to another.

mitment to a particular policy makes it extraordinarily difficult to try to fathom unintended consequences. Only rarely are we aware that in solving one problem we are creating other ones. Problem creation through problem solution!

Let us now examine aspects of the teacher's role, keeping in mind that it has changed from the past no less than it will look different in the future. One can only keep that in mind, however, if one grasps that what we call a school system has been, is, and will be a creature of its social surroundings. Once that is understood, one is not as likely to rivet attention on *the* system, and more likely to look at the variety of ways schools and communities are integral parts of larger contexts.

THE PERENNIAL PROBLEM: NUMBER AND DIVERSITY OF CHILDREN

From the standpoint of teachers the complexity of their task reflects in large measure the fact that a classroom of twenty-five or more children *is a lot of children for any one person to handle.* In addition, the children vary enormously in terms of academic achievement, intelligence level, behavior, interest, likeability, and maturity. The modal teacher divides the adult world into two groups: those who understand this complexity and those who do not, and in the latter group they place many school administrators and most parents. However, the complexity of the teacher's task is not easily understood by pointing to numbers and diversity of children. Perhaps the major reason that causes the teacher to point to these factors is something that intrinsically or logically has nothing to do with the process of education. I am referring here to the fact that the teacher feels, and is made to feel, that one's worth as a teacher will be judged by how much a class learns in a given period of time. The strong feeling that teachers have about the complexity of their task stems from the awareness that they are expected to bring their children (if not all, most) to a certain academic level by a time criterion in regard to which they have no say. Faced with numbers and diversity of children *and* the pressure to adhere to a time schedule presents the teacher not with a difficult task but an impossible one. *I say impossible because I have never met a teacher who was not aware of and disturbed by the fact that he or she had not the time to give to some children in the class the kind of help they needed—and the need for help, it should be emphasized, is frequently not due to any basic intellectual defect.* There are, of course, other reasons why a teacher cannot help certain children, but none of them is more important than the felt necessity to have the class reach a particular level of skill and knowledge in a fixed period of time.

What is deserving of note here is that, by and large, teachers accept this state of affairs. They may criticize the amount of material they are expected to cover, they may feel badly that in the process certain children fall by the wayside, and they may bitterly resent that their worth as teachers is judged primarily by the average achievement level of their class, but they do not question that a time criterion is necessary. One alternative to this situation is the concept of the ungraded classroom in which children move along at their own pace and not all are expected to reach a certain level at a certain time. But in the instances where I have observed ungraded classrooms I have been impressed by several things. First, principals and other administrators still judged the worth of teachers by how much material was covered in a fixed period of time. Second, teachers, no less than before, felt under pressure to show the usual rate of progress. Third, I could discern no difference, favorable, or unfavorable, between graded and ungraded classrooms. Fourth, as one teacher put it, "You can ungrade a classroom of twenty-five to thirty distinctly different children, but you still have one teacher to handle it all." I am not calling the concept of the ungraded classroom into question. All that I wish to indicate is that teachers and other school personnel have inordinate difficulty in thinking other than in terms of covering X amount of material in X amount of time. It would indeed be strange if they thought otherwise. After all, the school is organized according to grade levels, children are expected to be promoted at a certain time on the basis of achievement, and teachers at one grade level expect that the teachers of the previous level have adequately prepared their pupils, just as they know that the teacher to whom their children are passed on will expect that a particular amount and kind of material will have been covered. One of the major sources of psychological distance or interpersonal conflict among teachers in a school is when a teacher feels that the previous teacher of his or her pupils did not adequately prepare the children or did not cover an adequate range of material.

The effects of time pressure, as well as one of its potent sources, are seen in its most clear form in the new teacher who comes to school armed with the concept of lesson plans and the knowledge that these plans will be scrutinized and evaluated by the principal and other supervisory personnel. There seems to be wide agreement that keeping control of the class is one of the new teacher's major problems and about which he or she has much anxiety. Superficially, this appears to be the case on the basis of my own experience. Although difficulty in keeping control has several sources, one of the most important of these is the preoccupation with lesson plans and the need to cover them by a certain time. Time and again I have seen new teachers successfully complete a forty-minute lesson—in the sense that the points to be covered were covered—only to have lost the children somewhere around the ten-minute mark—and "lost" could mean lost in behavioral chaos or a fog of confusion. On those occasions when I have asked the new teacher why he or she persisted with the lesson plan when it was clear to the teacher (as it often is) that he or she was losing the class, I have met with several reactions, the two most frequent of which were: the teacher could think of no alternative to continuing, and relief that someone else verbalized what he or she would have liked to have verbalized and acted on.

I have been stressing the point that a major problem of the teacher inheres in the interaction between number and diversity of children, on the one hand, and the felt need to adhere to a time schedule, on the other hand. There are two types of time pressure, short and long, and I have only been referring to the one that may involve weeks, months, or the span of the school year. If one focuses only on the single day and attempts to understand why the classroom day is organized the way it is, one quickly sees that time considerations again are fairly decisive in determining how the class day is to be apportioned. A certain amount of time is apportioned to social studies, math, and so forth. The amount of time any one activity receives is a function of some scale of value and the number of activities that have to be represented. In short, the absolute amount of time any one activity receives is generally predetermined and is not a function of what teachers feel their class of pupils requires. As we shall see later, few teachers feel free to depart from the predetermined time allocations.

The graded school system was essentially in place in this country by the end of the nineteenth century. But as soon as it was achieved, difficulties appeared and they were remarkably similar to what plagues teachers today, especially when a faltering economic system interacts with a declining school population and with a federal policy requiring schools to integrate handicapped children. A graded school system, taking a new crop of children every year at five to six years of age, moving them through their studies in "lock-step" fashion till graduation, makes an assumption about the equality, motivation, and performance for children of similar age that the reality of individual differences rudely challenges. I have long been puzzled by the failure of the early proponents of the graded school system to anticipate the problems that were easily predictable. Certainly part of the answer is that they were so taken with the rationale for the graded school that they were oblivious to the obvious. Another, no less important, reason was the concern with efficiency in instruction. One could also argue that far from being oblivious to the obvious, the proponents were painfully aware of the problems facing the teacher who had to deal with large numbers of children (e.g., sixty, seventy, or more) who were quite heterogeneous. For example, William Torrey Harris, the Superintendent of the St. Louis school system first raised the issue in his report for the school year 1868–1869, and it was a prominent feature of his reports in subsequent years. Harris was clearly aware of the advantages of graded schools, such as increased efficiency in instruction and recitation afforded by the classification of pupils. He also prized the social stimulation that was added to the learning process when children were taught in groups of similar age and ability. But at the same time he maintained that grading and simultaneous instruction provided a kind of Procrustean bed, holding back and cramping the talented students at the same time it overstretched the abilities of duller children. In the case of talented children, there was the danger that boredom would lead to the development of poor habits of study and application. The duller child would suffer from discouragement and lowered self-esteem that might even lead to withdrawing from school.

Harris was aware of the many factors making for different levels of performance in the graded classes. Children differed in ability and in perseverance for study. Children were started at different ages, with some more mature and better able to cope with the course of studies. Attendance figures indicated high rates of absenteeism. A child returning to school after several weeks' absence could hardly be expected to catch up on the missed work while trying to keep abreast of the new work. And if the child could cover the missed work on his or her own, would that not disprove the efficacy of group teaching? The economic conditions of families forced some of the children to work and attend for only part of the school year. All of these factors made it impossible for a class to move along in its studies with even pace. And if a child fell behind, should the whole year be repeated even though the child might have already mastered 50 or 75 percent of the work? If it happened once, it was a bitter disappointment to the child and family. If it happened twice, the discouraged child might withdraw. There was no doubt—and subsequent investigators would bear it out—that grade retardation was correlated with withdrawal from school.

Harris's solution to the problem was to make classifications of finer gradation: to develop a system of classes not by steps of a yearly interval of work, but by irregular intervals of six to twenty weeks. Thus, a student would be moved up or down, or fall behind, by only small steps. Reclassification of the pupils would be made throughout the year. The stability of class groupings would not be too threatened because with each reclassification period a part of the more advanced students in a class would be moved up to the next higher class at the same time that a number of students would join the group from the class one step below. Harris thus envisaged a flexible, fluid progress of pupils through the graded school (Harris, 1900, pp. 303–330).

Harris's system was similar to several other systems adopted in various cities during the last quarter of the nineteenth century. However, the irregular intervals for reclassification was not a feature of the plan that achieved any wide acceptance. The need for somewhat closer intervals between classes was more readily granted, and a survey included in the Report of the Commissioner of Education for 1890–1891 indicated that of 465 responding cities, 237 had adopted class intervals of less than a year with the modal interval among these being one-half year (Boykin, 1894).

I have gone into detail about Harris's thinking and recommendations because they reflect a view of teachers and classrooms that is still the prevalent one: a classroom is a place with *a* teacher and *many* children, and it is the teacher's responsibility to move them along in their academic development. Within that view the teacher can organize the children in diverse ways, but here too what a teacher does must be justified in terms of the academic growth of children. It did not seem to occur to Harris that making classifications of finer gradation would put clerical and diagnostic burdens on teachers that would take time away from actual instruction. I must confess that what gets conjured up in my mind is a picture of Harris sitting in his office, like a modern efficiency expert, devising schemes that on paper, at least, "answers" the problem of dealing with individual differences, unaware that his refinements of the grade system increased rather than decreased the pressures on the teacher, making time a more precious commodity than before. More than a hundred years later, similar efforts to change the schools were no less vulnerable than those of Harris. Here, for example, is what Cohen and Farrar (1977) report about the Alum Rock educational voucher program:

. . . THE DEMONSTRATION MEANT MUCH MORE WORK: ADMINISTRATIVE AND fiscal procedures were redesigned, new budgeting systems were created, and mini-schools curriculums were established, placing greater burdens on teachers and principals. Many teachers reported they had never worked so hard and had not expected that the demonstration would require so much effort. Especially in the early stages, there was an avalanche of meetings, and many teachers felt overwhelmed and exhausted.

Thus, although the working conditions of the teachers improved in some respects, in others they declined. There was more work and more worry, but no less teaching, nor more hours in the day. And while there was more money to spend on materials and resources, teachers were not paid much more for their extra duties. They received some compensation for in-service training, but it amounted to a very modest annual salary increase over the course of the demonstration. If this was an incentive, it certainly was not awfully enticing. Indeed, the whole demonstration was a terrible tease: It offered some opportunities and encouragements to teachers, but made only marginal allowances for the personal and professional sacrifices involved.

It was no surprise, then, that as the demonstration progressed energy flagged. Teachers had less time for meetings, less patience for the demands of innovation, less desire for the rigors of collaboration, and more appreciation of the lives they could once again lead separately and individually behind classroom doors. Because the voucher demonstration offered some encouragements for innovation, and because many professionals desired change, things began with energy, hasty improvisation, and excitement. But because the scheme had not been designed with much appreciation of the classroom experience of teachers—because it assumed that teachers should be reshaped by a stiff dose of competition—there were only partial and sometimes accidental incentives for professionals. As the demonstration moves toward a close, many innovations have begun to slip away (pp. 90–91).[3] ■

And if the Cohen and Farrar report is not convincing, readers should peruse Wolcott's (1977) *Teachers and Technocrats*. It is as clear an example as I have ever seen of how proponents for educational change were insensitive to the importance of time in the phenomenology of the classroom teacher. Is it any wonder that teachers have such fond fantasies of fewer children in the classroom?

THE FANTASY OF REDUCED CLASS SIZE

Fantasy is a double-edged sword in that it solves problems and gives expression to wishes at the same time that it denies external reality. One of the most frequent fantasies in which teachers indulge—and it is by no means restricted to teachers—is how enjoyable life in a classroom could be if class size were discernibly decreased. Like the heavens of religions, reduced class size is a teacher's ultimate reward in comparison to which inadequate salaries pale in significance. The reason I label this a fantasy is not only because it is incapable of fulfillment, but because those who hold it tend to be unaware that it is unrealistic. Let us put it this way: if Congress in its infinite wisdom were to pass legislation making it financially possible to reduce class size in half, *the legislation could not be implemented.* It is conceivable that over a period of a decade the necessary physical plant could be built—our society has rarely failed in crash programs of a technological nature. What would be impossible would be to train teachers and other educational specialists in numbers necessary to implement the legislation, especially if one employed more demanding criteria for selection than has been true in the past. During the sixties when schools were experiencing the height of the consequences of the post-World War II population explosion, training centers could not keep up with the demand for teachers and they were quite aware that they were not doing the quality job required in terms of selection of students and quality level of faculty. And that was at a time when discernibly cutting class size in half was recognized as an impossibility! The goal of dramatically reducing class size is far from being only a financial problem.

---

3. Reprinted with permission.

What I call the "fantasy of numbers of professionals" is not peculiar to the culture of the school. Following and in large part because of World War II, the mental health professions convinced themselves and the public that the solution to the problem of mental disturbance was to engage in a crash program in the training of psychotherapists. That there was a good deal of governmental support for these programs had the effect of maintaining the illusion that university training centers could in fact meet the demand, an illusion recognized as such by only a few people. It took two decades for this illusion to be shattered on the rocks of reality and social change. As a consequence, and one that has direct relevance for the culture of the school, there is beginning to be an accommodation to the idea that the solution cannot be based on the assumption that the traditionally trained professional will ever exist in adequate numbers. Other human resources will have to be tapped and developed. But in the case of the school, as we shall now see, this accommodation has not been without its major problems and is inevitably a reflection of the modal way in which change occurs in the culture of the school.

In the past two decades, and particularly in our urban school systems, the use of teacher aides has increased perceptibly. More often than not these aides have a high-school education or less, are indigenous to the area served by the school, and are given a modicum (at best) of preparation for being in a classroom. When these programs have been initiated it has usually been with a good deal of fanfare proclaiming that teachers are finally going to receive some of the help they long asked for and needed. I have been in the position of observing these programs and talking to many teachers who received aides. Why do so many teachers view teacher aides as being quite far from an unmixed blessing? Some teachers, by no means all, rather bitterly resent the implication that someone without college education and training can play a significant role in the education of children—a position identical in principle to that held by the field of psychiatry two decades ago that someone who did not have a medical background could not be an effective psychotherapist. Some teachers complained that while the aides were appropriately motivated and eager to work with children, the teacher simply did not have the time to instruct and supervise the aides and, therefore, used them primarily for clerical purposes. Some teachers frankly said they could not work with another adult in the room—they anticipated that it would be distracting both to them and the children—and, therefore, did not request an aide. There were, of course, some teachers who were enthusiastic about having an aide, although the number of such teachers was definitely small.

The negative or lukewarm reactions of the teachers can be understood from several standpoints but the one that can be easily overlooked—and it certainly is by administrative personnel—is the one that focuses on the role of the teacher in formulating, developing, and carrying out the aide program. *In every such program I observed, the teachers were presented with a ready-made program, and in some instances they learned about it in the local newspaper.* The advice of teachers was never sought, the problems that could occur were never discussed, teachers were given no role in formulating a training or selection program, and, needless to say, teachers had no opportunity to express the professional and personal problems and questions they might have about the use of aides.[4] The change process in regard to aides was as "modal" as the change process in regard to the new math. What I think deserves special emphasis is the difficulty many teachers had in verbalizing their resentment about having little or nothing to say about decisions that could or would affect their work. It may well be that this difficulty in recognizing and verbalizing resentment reflects the degree to which teachers are accustomed to being treated as lowly proletariats. It may also be that it reflects a kind of preconscious awareness that they should do something about the conditions that produce such resentments, but doing something that would change their perception of themselves and their role is not easy for teachers or anyone else. As a teacher once said to me: "Teachers are not militant by nature, only from sheer desperation."

Zax and Cowen (1967) have done some of the most systematic research on the training and introduction of teacher aides, and they have well demonstrated that when teachers are an integral part of the development of the program, have an important role in the training of aides, and come to know them before they are introduced into the program, the teachers and the aides not only find it a mutually productive experience but the gain to children is great. The single best description of the sustained use of teacher aides is that by Cowen et al. (1975) in *New Ways in School Mental Health.* That book describes a program in the Rochester (New York) schools, now into its third decade, on early detection and prevention of socio-emotional and educational problems in young children. It is the best example I know of how an extremely initiated effort to introduce a behavioral and programmatic change in schools was productively assimilated by the schools. What is particularly instructive about this report is that in pilot studies they proceeded with the training program for the aides with little or no involvement of teachers. After the aides were introduced they quickly sensed the sources of teacher dissatisfaction, they realized that as people from outside the school system they had excluded teachers in planning in much the same way as insiders do, they changed

---

4. As we shall see in the next chapter, the relationship of teachers to program planners is similar to, if not identical with, that of the teacher to the children in the classroom.

strategies, and the level of cooperation and enthusiasm of everyone markedly increased.[5]

In the case of the classroom teacher what is at issue is not involvement for the sake of involvement or to satisfy the elementary requirements of courtesy. What is at issue, but rarely clearly stated, is how the change process can enable the teacher to perceive his or her role differently; that is, to perceive the role not as threatened or derogated but as expanded in scope and importance. Any conception of change that does not explicitly recognize that changing the perception of role is never an easy task, and that it cannot be accomplished by legislation or regulation—or by virtue of laudable goals or the pressures of external reality—is likely to result in strengthening the rigidity of role boundaries. Involving teachers in those decisions or plans that will affect them can be justified on several grounds. First, involvement makes it more likely that responsibility will be assumed and not be attributed to others. Second, it makes it more likely that problems of attitude and goals will surface and be dealt with. Third, and of crucial importance, it increases the chances that the alternative ways in which problems can be formulated and resolved will be scrutinized and act as a control against premature closure and the tendency to think that there is only one way in which problems may be viewed and handled. There is another factor, and precisely because it is so rarely recognized and discussed, and because of its importance in understanding the classroom teacher in the context of the culture of the school, I shall deal with it separately in the next section.

THE EFFECTS OF BOREDOM AND ROUTINE

As in earlier chapters, we shall imagine that we are someone from outer space parked in a space platform, incapable of comprehending language or writing, capable of seeing everything that goes on in the school, and possessed of a mind and advanced computers that allow one to record anything in the nature of a regularity. Let us further imagine that we have been parked above the school for a long time, perhaps two years. Readers may recall from earlier chapters that one of the things that the man from outer space discerned as a regularity was that the frequency with which

---

5. It should be emphasized that recent efforts to utilize so-called nonprofessional personnel in the schools (particularly in urban schools) are far from being the first of such concerted efforts. Levine and Levine (1970b) have documented the visiting teacher movement at the turn of the century, a movement that largely involved nonprofessional workers from settlement houses. The school social worker of today is a direct descendant of the visiting teacher except that, as the Levines point out, in the process of "professionalizing" the work of the visiting teacher most of what was distinctive in their role went by the boards. The readers are urged to become familiar with the Levines' account.

"big people" engaged in face-to-face contact for more than a couple of minutes was amazingly low. His computers also told him that on those infrequent occasions when all or most of these big people would be together in one room (e.g., faculty or PTA meetings), the frequency with which sounds emanated from their mouths was fantastically less than when each big person was alone in a room with the small people. We discussed these findings in terms of "teaching is a lonely profession" by which we meant that the teacher is alone with problems and dilemmas, constantly thrown back on personal resources, having little or no interpersonal vehicles available for purposes of stimulation, change, or control against people's capacity to act and think foolishly.

But what are some of the regularities that our man from outer space would observe about the teacher in the classroom? One of the more obvious regularities he would observe is that the teacher does much the same thing on each of the 180-plus days of the school year with much the same children and in exactly the same classroom. From the rituals associated with the beginning of the school day to those associated with the end, each day is very much like every other day. Occasionally there are variations that the man from outer space might have difficulty comprehending because they are so infrequent; for example, fire drills, assemblies, shortened days due to snow storms, visiting police officers and firefighters, business-in-education week, Christmas parties, and so on. These occasional events causing some kind of change in the daily routine only emphasize that there is a routine.

We have to leave the man from outer space because he can only (*only*?) discern overt behavioral regularities and he cannot help us in understanding the covert significances of what we have learned from him. In leaving him, let us note that as a result of making observations for more than one year he saw something else: there was a marked tendency for the same teacher to be with the same *kinds* of children; in successive years the same teacher tends to teach the same kind of child. We now have to ask the crucial question: To what extent and in what ways does this routine—this identity among days, the degree of age specialization—affect the thinking and feelings of teachers? What enables a teacher to resist the effects of a routinized existence? Before attempting to answer these questions I should hasten to point out that the regularity we are describing is about the elementary school teacher whose degree of routine contains far more diversity than that of the junior or senior high school teacher who teaches *a* particular subject; for example, math, English, French, and so on. Whereas the elementary school teacher tends to teach all the major subjects, the junior and senior high school teacher within the course of the day tends to teach the same subject matter to five or more different groups of students.

The questions I raised earlier are not easy to ask of teachers and they are far less easy for teachers to think about and answer. After all, if one's job is not very interesting, if it is the only type of job that one is likely to have in life, and if in the public's mind it is a job that is thought to be interesting, it should not be easy to talk freely about how one thinks and feels about that job. On the basis of my discussions with teachers it seems clear that how teachers respond to these questions in part is related to the length of their teaching career. Without exception those who have been teaching for five or more years admitted that they no longer experienced their work with enthusiasm, excitement, sense of mission, and challenge that they once did.[6] (I should make it perfectly clear that these teachers were *not* saying that they disliked being a teacher, although in a minority of instances I felt that to be the case.) For the most part they felt as competent as they ever were going to feel, and they verbalized no expectation that they would be teaching or thinking differently sometime in the future. Almost without exception each teacher had at one time considered, or was still considering, moving out of the classroom and even moving out of education. Some teachers were clear that this consideration was motivated by the knowledge that there was much to learn and do in education and the rest of the world and they were not going to learn this by remaining in the classroom. In one way or another these teachers indicated that they rarely experienced anymore the sense of personal or intellectual growth. The shape of the future was quite clear and there were aspects of it that bothered them. The future contained a routine with which they were already quite familiar.

All these older teachers had taken or were taking advanced courses in education in local colleges and universities, and their motivation for taking these courses was not simply to meet a requirement in order to gain a salary increase. There was a passive desire or need to be intellectually stimulated and to have horizons expanded; they knew well that there was much to learn. There seemed to be the unverbalized hope that by virtue of these courses something new would be injected into their working lives. What I learned from these discussions, which I did not fully realize before, was that in a fair number of instances these courses did serve as a source of intellectual stimulation—it did confirm to the teachers that there was a world of interesting and conflicting ideas—but they did not, or could not, see the relevance of these courses to their daily work in the classroom. On the basis

---

6. Green (1968) has written an extremely stimulating general discussion of the concepts of work, labor, and play, and the different consequences of each on the individual. In the last chapter of his book he relates this discussion to the schools, with particular attention to the teacher as a producer. "Our understanding of teaching as an activity has tended to become focused primarily on the results; what counts is not the process, but its outcome. The tendency is therefore to view teaching, to assess its excellence, in terms of its product." What I am describing about teachers, what they have told me, are consequences of viewing what one does as work; i.e., as a kind of activity that makes sense only when it has a connection with a result or a product. This is radically different from play and, as a result, it is difficult, if not impossible, for someone who views one's role as work to maintain enthusiasm, excitement, sense of mission, and challenge.

of nearly three decades of teaching and working with teachers I cannot refrain from pointing out that, as a group, teachers have long been living with the knowledge that their college experiences were for the most part irrelevant to their work. If one thinks one understands and sympathizes with what so many in the university community, students and faculty, call irrelevance and alienation, one then understands a good deal of the phenomenology of the classroom teacher.

The picture that emerges from discussion with the younger teachers is more complex and somewhat less clear, and primarily for two reasons. First, to oversimplify the matter, they grew up and went to school in a society rather different than that experienced by older teachers. Second, the discussions took place at a time in their careers when problems of identity, professional and personal, were ever present and poignantly so. A surprising number of these younger teachers were already convinced that they did not want to remain in the classroom.[7] There were many reasons for this, but for the purposes of our present discussion the one requiring our attention is that they did not see the school as an intellectual community in which they could look forward to growth and change. *In fact, some explicitly pointed to some older teachers in the schools as examples of what they feared they might become.* Here, too, I must emphasize (and shall discuss later) that these teachers were not complaining about being teachers of children or that there were no rewards in what they were doing, but rather about the painful awareness that their present and future seemed all too similar. By and large they had all the commendable features of youth: the need to give to others, to eradicate injustice, to question tradition, and to experience the sense of learning, changing, and growing. Some of these needs could and were being met, but neither in relationship to their colleagues or to children was the need for new ideas and intellectual growth met.

AFTER WORKING FOR SOME TIME WITH A YOUNG, UNMARRIED WOMAN WHO taught French in a junior high school, I finally got the courage to say to her: "You teach French each day to six different groups of children. You have been doing it now for three years. It occurred to me the other day that if I had to do what you do, even if it were psychology, I would go crazy. What keeps you going? And you are a good teacher. Where are the kicks?" I was surprised by the speed with which she responded—obviously, my statement and question touched on something about which she had been thinking. "Two weeks from this Saturday I have appointments at the UN and the French Consulate to find out about job

---

7. Readers will recall that in the study by A. Levine (Chapter 4) of a MAT program, a rather large number of students said that they were not going to pursue a teaching career.

possibilities, and it well may be that if it is necessary for me to learn shorthand and really be able to type for these kinds of jobs, I will do it. As to kicks, there are some. For instance, when you get a student in beginning French who for some mysterious reason has just the right intonation and pronunciation, it is a real pleasure to see him or her blossom. Or the student who went on his own to the library and got out some French books he wants to discuss with you. I enjoy their interest *in me,* and I get a good feeling when they want to talk with me alone and tell me something personal. But most of the time it's push, push, stimulate, stimulate, and sometimes *I* get the feeling that I think many of the kids have: Is it all that necessary and important? I have learned a lot and probably could and will learn more but I am not honestly convinced of that. It has turned out to be much more of a grind than I ever imagined. What do other teachers tell you?'' ■

Not all the younger teachers were as frank with me as this young woman, and they certainly did not talk over these matters very much (if at all) with each other. Overall I gained the distinct impression that the younger teachers were acutely aware of a discrepancy between what they were personally and intellectually experiencing as teachers in classrooms and their earlier fantasies or expectations about what life in school would be like. If they experienced the sense of intellectual growth and excitement except on occasion, I did not pick it up.

TOWARD THE END OF A YEAR-LONG SERIES OF WEEKLY MEETINGS WITH A group of young high school teachers, organized around whatever problems they were having as teachers, one of the teachers said that he was seriously thinking of leaving teaching. There were several reasons why this and the other teachers would not have wanted to remain at this school (and indeed two were making arrangements to go to another system), but the discussion centered on the lack of intellectual stimulation, which all experienced. They complained that their days were not varied, school was a well-insulated fortress, and that they felt locked into a system that had some characteristics of a factory. ■

There are, of course, teachers who give no indication that they are bothered by an awareness that their working lives are fairly routinized or that they have settled into a mold about which they should be disturbed. They do not view the classroom, now or in the future, as something closing in on them. I cannot estimate the size of this group, although it is probably not as large as some critics would have us believe. As I said earlier, if teachers are intellectually dissatisfied with their lot, if they come to view teaching as a job lacking the attributes of excitement and personal growth, one should not expect them to parade such feeling in a very public manner.

If my observations have merit, they force one to raise a most serious question: *If teaching becomes neither terribly interesting nor exciting to many teachers, can one expect them to make learning interesting or exciting to children?* If teaching becomes a routine, predictable experience, does this not have inevitable consequences for life in the classroom? The modal classroom does not allow me other than to conclude that children and teachers show most of the effects of routinized thinking and living.[8] It would be strange if it were otherwise.

There is still another factor, again infrequently recognized, which often has the effect of facilitating the development of a protective routinized existence. This factor is the obvious one that inherent in teaching is *giving;* that is, the teacher is required to give of himself or herself, intellectually and emotionally. At the beginning of one's career this presents no particular problem because most new teachers come to their task with that sense of mission and enthusiasm that makes giving a natural, unreflective act. But even where this feeling is weak, or even absent, children, in different ways, need, want, require, and demand giving by the teacher. Constant giving in the context of constant vigilance required by the presence of many children is a demanding, draining, taxing affair that cannot easily be sustained. Even where it is sustained on a high level, it still does not always prevent guilt feelings because the teacher cannot give all that he or she feels children need. To sustain the giving at a high level requires that the teacher experience *getting.* The sources for getting are surprisingly infrequent and indirect. One can get from children, but this is rarely direct; one can get from colleagues and administrators, but this is even more infrequent. One can get from oneself in the sense that one feels one is learning and changing and that this will continue, but this crucial source of getting is often not strong enough to make for a better balance between giving and getting. One of the consequences of a marked disparity between giving and getting is development of a routine that can reduce the demand for giving.[9]

---

8. This is not a conclusion that should be restricted to the modal public school. Among the many different things our college students told us in the sixties, and (literally) demonstrated for us was that their life in the classroom was often all too dull and predictable. Although the extent of my direct observations of college teachers is far less than those of public school teachers, I have no basis for contradicting the assertion that the modal college teacher is no more stimulating than the modal classroom teacher. If someone ever determines that the college teacher is more stimulating, it will not be unrelated to two facts: the college teacher (particularly in our major universities) is in a classroom far less than the public school teacher (ordinarily he or she is not expected to teach the same course year after year), and the college teacher has the time *during the working day* to talk and be with colleagues and others. The point is that in talking about the public school we should not allow ourselves to forget that the "teacher problem" is by no means peculiar to the public school.

9. One sees the same process among physicians despite the obvious fact that they enjoy more getting, psychologically (probably) and materially (certainly), than teachers do; they generally feel under strong pressure to give more than they think they can, or should, or are able to.

DR. MURRAY LEVINE HAD A STUDENT KEEP A DIARY DURING HIS FIRST year of teaching in an elementary school. In the diary the student makes quite clear the guilt and conflict a teacher can experience around the problem and necessity of giving. To illustrate the point the student describes a five-minute interval during which one child broke a class rule, one child joyfully completed an assignment he showed to the teacher, and one child needed the teacher's help with something he did not understand. Each of these required of the teacher a different cognitive orientation, each engendered different emotions, and in sequence they necessitated the teacher, chameleon-like, quickly to change thought, feeling, and action. Not all five-minute intervals are like this one but it is not as infrequent as the lay public imagines. It is frequent enough within the course of a day to emphasize not only the extent of giving required of the teacher but also the difficulty the teacher has in sustaining a high level of giving and not resorting to strategems of routine that reduce giving at the expense of meeting the needs of children. I have often said, only somewhat facetiously, that we ought to pass a law requiring each parent alone to teach or to manage a class of children for one day. At the very least, it would educate the public to what a teacher is confronted with day in day out, year in year out. It might also raise the level of discussion about where and what kinds of changes we should be thinking about in our efforts to "improve" our schools. ■

What I am describing here is no more than what many teachers have told us in the context of our working relationship with them (Sarason et al., 1966). At the beginning of the relationship, usually initiated by the teacher around a problem child, we would frequently sense an ambivalence: wanting discussions and help, and yet fearful that *we* would be putting more demands on the teacher to do and give more. This ambivalence would not dissipate until the teacher recognized that we were asking for more giving, but we were prepared to give as well—by being in the classroom, giving time, being available, and obviously being interested and concerned. It was only after the dissipation of the ambivalence that some teachers could tell us what it was like to constantly feel that one has to give with little expectation either that one will get or that what one will get will be direct or predict-

---

Like teachers, they frequently do not know what to do for a patient, or they feel they do not have enough time to handle all problems in the way they would like. Frequently this results in a style or routine or rationalization that reduces the guilt associated with not meeting the external or internal demands to give. Those who are especially interested in the dynamics and frequency of career change among highly educated, professional people might wish to consult my book *Work, Aging, and Social Change. Professionals and the One Life—One Career Imperative* (1977). Although that book is largely based on studies of physicians and lawyers, the dynamics and social-historical context of career change that I describe are applicable, in my opinion, to professionals in education.

able. One member of the Yale Psycho-Educational Clinic has maintained that a good part of whatever success we have had in working with teachers was due to the fact that we were giving to them and this was atypical in the working lives of the teachers.

There is nothing evil about a routinized day. But as each succeeding routinized day passes and it adds up to years—sometimes in the same classroom with the same kind of child with the same subject matter—one is justified in asking what are the internal and external factors that prevent what is overtly a routine from resulting in routinization of thought and action? I have suggested that in the culture of the school where the teacher is alone with many and diverse children, subject to all kinds of internal and external demands to give and do, and where the level of giving tends to far exceed getting, the modal teacher is hard put to escape the psychological effects of routine.

We are currently into a period when school systems are contracting in size: schools are being closed, teachers and administrators are being laid off, and those who continue to be employed fearful of what the future might bring. No issue between boards of education, on the one hand, and the organizations that represent teachers and administrators, on the other hand, is more sticky and scrutinized than that involving seniority. The fact is that the average age of teachers who are teaching is increasing even though teachers who retire tend to be replaced by much younger people who, of course, get lower salaries.

What are the possible effects of what is happening at this time on the classroom teacher? For one thing, it has reduced the teacher's mobility; i.e., if the teacher is dissatisfied, he or she cannot pick up and expect to get a position elsewhere. The feeling of "being stuck" tends to feed on itself and it would be surprising if such a persistent, dispiriting feeling did not directly or indirectly manifest itself in the classroom. If it is by no means easy to shift from one system to another or from one place to another in the same system, it is also true that this is a time when it is far from easy to leave teaching and to get a desirable position in a very different type of work. In the past, teachers have left teaching for many reasons, two of the most important being the need for a higher income and the desire to experience new challenges. *But it was also true that many people entered teaching as a second career because of their desire to experience new challenges.* That direction of career switching has practically stopped and one cannot assume that it will be without effect on the culture of the school. Fountain (1970) found that job satisfaction among those for whom teaching was a second career tended to be higher than among those who had only had a career in teaching. But this type of finding raises an even more fateful question: Who seeks to become a teacher today when the opportunities of employment are bleak and the possibility of sustained employment in shrinking school systems are not high? We have no data to answer this and previous questions but one does not need data to suggest that selective factors are at work that will alter the outlook, experience, and motivation of the classroom teacher. The role of the teacher is not changing, and neither is the basis by which teachers will be judged, but it is hard to see how the selective factors determining who *remains* a teacher and who *becomes* a teacher in this era of shrinking resources will be unimportant.

TEACHER BURNOUT

The word *burnout* has become quite fashionable these days, although it is obvious that different people mean different things by it. Without doubt the best discussion is that by Cherniss (1980) in his book *Professional Burnout in Human Service Organizations*. That book describes and analyzes what happens to people when they become professionals.

MORE SPECIFICALLY, IT IS A STUDY OF NEW PROFESSIONALS WHO HAVE BEgun their careers working in public human service agencies such as mental health clinics, schools, public health departments, and poverty law agencies. It is these professionals on whom many rely for education or aid, especially when under physical or emotional stress; it is these professionals who seem to have much influence on important life decisions and events. Yet all too often, the person-in-need encounters "helping" professionals who are distant or disdainful, "human service" workers who seem unresponsive to human need and pain (p. IX). ∎

High school teachers were part of the sample Cherniss studied longitudinally and in depth, and his overall conclusions are no less applicable to teachers than to the other groups. Let us first listen to Cherniss's description of burnout:

BURNOUT INVOLVES A CHANGE IN ATTITUDE AND BEHAVIOR IN RESPONSE TO a demanding, frustrating, unrewarding work experience. The dictionary defines "to burn out" as "to fail, wear out, or become exhausted by making excessive demands on energy, strength, or resources." This term all too aptly describes the experience of many human service professionals. However, the term "burnout" has come to have an additional meaning in recent research and writing on the topic; it refers to negative changes in work-related attitudes and behavior in response to job stress. What are these negative changes? A major one is loss of concern for the client and a tendency to treat clients in a detached, mechanical fashion. Other changes include increasing discouragement, pessimism, and fatalism about one's work; decline in motivation, effort, and involvement in work; apathy; negativism; frequent irritability and anger with clients and colleagues; preoccupation with one's own comfort and welfare on the job; a tendency to rationalize failure by blaming the clients or "the system"; and resistance to change, growing rigidity, and loss of creativity.

In moderation, some of these changes associated with burnout may not be entirely negative. For instance, it is probably desirable for an extremely idealistic and naive new professional to develop a more realistic and balanced view of clients and their problems. Also, adopting more modest goals and expectations for one's self and one's clients is certainly desirable if one's goals were unrealistically high. Tempering one's involvement in work with outside commitments, rather than remaining totally absorbed in the job, is to be recommended. Even assuming a somewhat detached, objective, and "professional" stance toward clients is probably useful in many helping occupations. However, there is clearly a point at which these desirable changes in attitude and behavior become undesirable for all concerned. Burnout has come to be associated with that point at which the changes are no longer positive.

On a concrete day-to-day level, there are many signs of professional burnout. For instance, one might feel great inner resistance to going to work each day. Frequent "clock watching" is another sign, as is postponement of appointments with clients. An inability to concentrate on or listen to what a client is saying may be a sign of burnout. Increasing reliance on rules in dealing with a client demands may be a sign.

In addition to these negative changes in thought and behavior related to the job, there are physical and behavioral signs. These include chronic fatigue; frequent colds; the flu, headaches, gastrointestinal disturbances, and sleeplessness; excessive use of drugs; decline in self-esteem; and marital and family conflict. Of course, not all of these symptoms need to be present to say that a person is burning out. Some may be present and some not in any particular case. However, when there are several of these signs and changes in a professional, the work situation is all too likely the source of this burnout. This will be elaborated upon in later chapters of this book (pp. 6–7).[10] ■

Cherniss emphasizes that burnout is not simply fatigue or strain, and it is not the same as socialization or acculturation which are processes by which colleagues and others exert a conforming influence, and burnout is not turnover. Burnout may cause staff members to quit, but they may burnout and remain on the job. Burnout is an adaptation to overload, stress, and the perception that conditions are not likely to change. Cherniss's major conclusion is that most of the new professionals he studied were clearly ex-

---

10. Reprinted with permission.

periencing burnout, a conclusion quite clear in the case of the high school teachers.

On June 13, 1980, the MacNeil/Lehrer report on public television (WNET and WETA) devoted the program to Teacher Burnout. With permission of the MacNeil/Lehrer report, I present several excerpts from the transcript.

Teacher Burnout

TEACHER: When I got to the point I thought "thirty years from now I could be in the same room, with the same blinds and the pencil sharpeners that don't work" and I was going nowhere—so frustrating. You have emotionally disturbed children. You have physically handicapped children. Learning disabilities. You're a teacher, and you want to see that these children are taken care of. That's what you're there for. The process is so involved. It's sad, sad—and frustrating to me. I couldn't deal with it any more.

ROBERT MACNEIL: They call it an occupational hazard, stress, battle fatigue, burnout. Whatever the name, the bottom line is the same. More and more teachers who quit teaching.

MACNEIL: Good evening. My nine-year-old son said this morning, "Great. Only four more days of school." And knowing we were doing this program tonight, I wondered how many thousands of teachers were saying this morning, "Great. Only four more days of teaching— forever." No one has good figures on how many, but it's believed that a growing number of the country's 2.2 million public school teachers are walking out of their careers. They are the victims of a syndrome that's being called teacher burnout. Teachers, often the most dedicated teachers, are fed up with years of long hours, low pay, turned-off students, indifferent parents, red tape, physical danger, and so on. Some say they suffer from illnesses related to stress. Other surveys show that teachers have almost the lowest job satisfaction of all the professions. Tonight, what is creating this so-called teacher burnout, and what can be done with it? Jim?

JIM LEHRER: Robin, the teacher used to be one of the most respected and revered figures in American society. No more. There is clear evidence the public thinks the schools aren't doing the job any more, and they lay much of the blame on the teachers. In a Gallup Poll last year, the public put "improving the quality of teachers" number one on their list of ways to improve the education system. That same poll showed a decreasing respect and regard for the public schools generally, a concern over declining test scores and high school graduates who can't read or write very well, specifically. Rightly or wrongly, the teacher's getting much of the heat for it. This week's *Time* magazine, for instance, goes right at that problem in a cover story entitled "Teachers Can't Teach." This new negative attitude toward them and their profession, say some, only makes the burnout problem worse. ■

The second excerpt is the discussion between Mr. MacNeil and Carolyn Mihalko-Bakinow:

MacNeil: One teacher who says she is burned out after nine years of teaching, and is wrestling with a decision on whether to quit, is Carolyn Mihalko-Bakinow. She is an eighth-grade teacher in Southington, Connecticut. She is also active in the Connecticut Education Association. Ms. Mihalko-Bakinow, what have you experienced as a teacher that makes you feel you are burned out? What has happened to you?

Carolyn Mihalko-Bakinow: When I went into it nine years ago, I did not feel that I was expected to be more than a teacher. Today, society, the community, administrators expect us to be counselors, social workers, clergy, and also sometimes to take on the role of parents. When I went into teaching nine years ago, the students that I had were much different than the students I have today.

MacNeil: In what way are they different?

Mihalko-Bakinow: In some of my classrooms, up to 50 percent of the students come from families where there is only one parent present. Many are students—there's an increase in drug use. Now, I'm not saying the majority of students, but it is on the increase. School violence is on the increase. By the time my students reach me, they are thirteen years old and they're in eighth grade, they've spent thousands—and I mean thousands—of hours unsupervised in front of TVs. I have students who come to school in the morning who are hungry, who are physically, mentally, and emotionally abused. And in between dealing with all these kinds of problems that these children have, I—my job is to teach. And that's very difficult.

MacNeil: Being burned out—we've heard the other description of it—what do you actually feel? I mean, do you feel physically ill with it, do you feel depressed, or do you just feel fed up, and you want to change to something different. What does being burned out make you feel inside?

Mihalko-Bakinow: In my own personal experience, there was several years ago where I got sick to my stomach, or I had headaches, and I learned how to cope with those. Sometimes it's mental depression where you feel that you just can't take any more, but you feel frustrated because you want to help all the different kinds of students that you have in your classroom, and it's literally and physically impossible to get to each and every one. And I know that there are teachers who just don't come in, who just call in sick because they just can't walk into the classroom. They just can't face another day.

MacNeil: How much of it is fear of physical violence from the students, which we read a lot about, hear a lot about?

Mihalko-Bakinow: In my town, I don't think it's a great deal. I think it does exist. I myself am not afraid to walk into my room, or into my building. But I know it does exist in the high school to some extent.

MacNeil: What did you hope that teaching was going to be as a career?

Mihalko-Bakinow: Well, I had spent summers working with students in the remedial programs in my town, in Head Start, and I had a knack for helping the slow learner, and I really enjoyed it. And when I went into it, I had very high hopes of being able to help the students.

MacNeil: Did your teacher training prepare you for the reality of the classroom that you have experienced over the last nine years?

Mihalko-Bakinow: When I went through college, there was not a term "learning disabled." There were not the handicapped children we have in schools today. With Public Law 94-142, which is the Education of all Handicapped Children Act, it does not say "mainstreaming." The words are "least restrictive environment." Well, administrators are taking it to mean mainstreaming, and they are placing a lot of handicapped children, learning disabled children, in classrooms. And not giving the teachers the support, the aid. For example, I have a classroom of twenty-four. They are below average in academic ability. In that classroom, there's one handicapped child, there are eight children with learning disabilities. They read anywhere from second to sixth grade level. And there are some days that I just can't get to them to make sure that they know what is going on. Besides preparing a regular lesson plan for the fifteen students who are not learning disabled or handicapped, I must prepare individual programs. That's just one class.

MacNeil: Is it the federal government's insistence that schools include handicapped children in the last couple of years which has really tipped the scales for you, or is it just the general situation you're in?

Mihalko-Bakinow: That's just one situation. I feel the way the administrators are interpreting the law, it's not necessarily the federal government, the onus is not on them. It's also the growing number of disruptive students. That is a major problem. I think, in any school, there are three areas that I feel that teachers need more support from the administration. They must be firm and consistent. I am firm and consistent in my classrooms, and I don't feel that administrators always are. But then, sometimes too, they're hampered by legal restraints. And

then, underlying it all, is a growing lack of parental concern or cooperation. When you get a note from a parent that says, "My child will not
stay after school for you. I told my child they do not have to listen to
you."

The final excerpt centers around this teacher's reaction to a plan of another
program participant to reduce or prevent burnouts:

LEHRER: Ms. Mihalko-Bakinow, would you—Does the program that
Mr. Sparks laid out, do you think that would be any help for you? Help
to you?

MIHALKO-BAKINOW: I think that I'm beyond that. I got through the
past five years with the help of the Southington, Connecticut National
Education Association, through the work I've done with them. He was
talking about time management skills. Well, I teach them as a part of
the Women's Leadership Training Program in the CEA. I started my
own—not my own, but it's a community newsletter for the Southington
Education Association which I write and edit. And that's my own way
of trying to reach out to the community. I feel that my—I do not utilize
all my skills in the classroom. I have developed skills that go beyond the
classroom, and I wish to change my goals in life. My goals in life have
changed.

LEHRER: But in other words, you've done—already done what Sparks
here offers, and you still want—you're still thinking seriously about getting out of it because of structural things, right?

MIHALKO-BAKINOW: Quite definitely.

Finally:

LEHRER: Mr. Sparks, let me ask you. You heard what Ms. Mihalko-
Bakinow just said a moment ago, that one of the real problems she
faces is the students in the class who are disruptive, students in the class
who are slow learners, handicapped, etc. There's nothing you can do to
help her on those problems, is there?

SPARKS: Well, I don't think that we can totally turn that problem
around, but our Professional Development Center is addressing a whole
range of issues besides the issue of stress and burnout. We teach
teachers to be effective teachers, and that involves a whole range of
things. David mentioned classroom management. It can be other kinds
of effective teaching skills that are going to make a difference for them
in the classroom and help them feel more competent, and increase their
own feelings of self-worth.

LEHRER: Beginning with you, Carolyn, there's one thing that none of the four of you have mentioned, and that is, that the teachers themselves have any responsibility for their collective problems. Is that just an omission, or is that the way you all feel? Is that the way you feel?

MIHALKO-BAKINOW: That we are responsible for all the problems that are going on?

LEHRER: No. No, no. That you have no responsibility—that, as a teacher, you have no responsibility yourself for whatever problems you feel about teaching or whatever. They're all problems that society has thrust upon you, or lack of training, or whatever.

MIHALKO-BAKINOW: No. I don't think we're totally blameless. I think one thing that teachers have to realize is, they have to do some public relations themselves. They have to tell the community the good and the positive things that are going on in the classroom. And I don't think that we've done enough of that.[11]

Indirectly, but nonetheless compellingly, this TV program makes a point congruent with a major theme of this book: the characteristics and experiences of school personnel cannot be understood only, or even primarily, in terms of individual personalities or of the encapsulated school or school system, but rather has to be viewed in terms of the changed and changing nature of transactions between training centers and prospective educators, between school and community, and between professional organizations (unions) and schools and community. And, no less important, is another point congruent with another theme in this book: the phenomena that are so troublesome about schools today were not created yesterday, or last year, or a decade ago, but rather are the latest eruptions and disruptions that have long characterized schools in our social history. Today the actors are different, the problems are differently diagnosed and formulated, and certainly these problems have received *national* attention as never before. Nevertheless, two facts remain: there has always been serious conflict between school and community, and the "solutions" adopted to deal with these conflicts have not only been far from successful, but amazingly similar in terms of underlying conceptions of what schools are and should be, and to whom in practice they belong. As I have indicated earlier, and shall return to later, it is these underlying conceptions that we can no longer afford to remain unchallenged in their presently inarticulate form.

---

11. Reprinted with permission of WNET/Thirteen, 356 West 58th St., New York 10019.

If only to alter the mood (albeit temporarily) of this discussion, let us turn to the "outstanding teacher." It is too easy to overlook the obvious fact that there are outstanding teachers. The question is: Have they become in shorter supply than in earlier decades? If that question cannot be satisfactorily answered, it nonetheless must be posed and discussed.

THE OUTSTANDING TEACHER

In a highly recommended book entitled *Life in Classrooms,* Jackson (1968) presents conclusions based on interviews with a group of outstanding teachers, so labelled and chosen by administrators and supervisors who presumably knew their work well. Four themes emerged from these interviews, and Jackson, skillfully using the teacher's own words, illustrates how these themes are verbalized in the interviews. The first of these themes is immediacy, which can be described as an acute sensitivity to the "here-and-now"—what I have earlier described as the need for a state of constant vigilance. The second theme is informality, which is not easy to summarize or characterize, but can be described as the opposite of an emphasis on undue routinization; that is, an emphasis, relatively speaking, on the importance of freedom of movement and thought for children. A third theme is individuality, which "deals with the teacher's interest in the well-being of individual students in his class and becomes particularly evident when the teacher is asked to describe the satisfactions he derives from his work. Although he confronts an entire class, it is what happens to individuals that really counts." A fourth theme is autonomy, which was most clearly verbalized in response to at least two hypothetical conditions: the possibility of an inflexible curriculum and the "possible invasion of the classroom by administrative superiors bent on evaluation"—to both hypothetical conditions they were quite emphatic about how strong their resistance would be.

At this point I would like to make a comment that is a glimpse of the obvious: Jackson's teachers do not *talk* in ways that suggest that they have suffered the consequences I have described earlier in this chapter. They certainly talk as one would imagine outstanding teachers would talk. Let us leave aside the unanswerable question of the relation between what these teachers say and what they actually do. The fact is that I have met and worked with these kinds of teachers in their classrooms. In my experience they exist in very small numbers. Jackson makes no claim that his sample of teachers is a representative one. He points out that at best his sample comprises the top 5 or 10 percent of the instructional staff as perceived by administrators.

How do we account for the fact that so few teachers are considered outstanding? Is it that outstanding teachers were outstanding in the relevant characteristics *before* they became teachers; that is, are they a special breed of people who are always in short supply? How many young teachers left the classroom and teaching precisely *because* they had the relevant characteristics and could not tolerate the interferences or constraints they experienced? How many "average teachers" had the potential to be much better teachers, but either because of the lack in training or the schools in which they worked this potential could not be developed? Is the quality level of a teacher completely or largely independent of the school in which one works? Would Jackson's outstanding teachers, who were from suburban schools and one private school, be outstanding in inner-city schools? By these questions I am, of course, returning to a dominant theme of this book: *characteristics of individuals are always, to some extent, a reflection of the setting in which these characteristics are manifested.* "Outstandingness" may be seen by others as a characteristic of an individual, but the very fact that it is seen and responded to by others *in the setting* indicates that we are dealing with more than the characteristic of an individual.

I, for one, have no difficulty accepting the idea that the characteristics of outstanding teachers, as Jackson so well describes, probably characterized them before they became teachers. I do have difficulty accepting the notion that their becoming good teachers was independent of where they were teaching. My experience with very young teachers has brought me to several conclusions:

1. By and large they are an eager, anxious, malleable group searching rather desperately for some kind of acceptable compromise between the realities of the classroom and their fantasies about being able to help all children.
2. They are often torn between the perception that they must adhere to a schedule and a curriculum (and in some instances daily lesson plans are required) and their frequent feeling that they should depart from the routine.
3. They are quite unprepared both for the loneliness of the classroom and the lack of relationships in which questions and problems can be asked and discussed without the fear that the teacher is being evaluated.
4. When an evaluation-free relationship is available—such as that we have tried to develop at the Yale Psycho-Educational Clinic—a fair number of these young teachers are able to change, and sometimes dramatically so.

As we have pointed out elsewhere (Sarason et al., 1966), the direction in which the teacher changes (in matters of discipline, curriculum, and handling of administrative personnel) often involves doing what the teacher wanted to do, but for which there was no "authoritative support." The first two years of teaching are a baptism of fire in which many things can be consumed, including some of the ingredients that make for a good and even outstanding teacher. The important point is that what happens in these years, *for good or for bad,* cannot be understood by narrowly focusing on the teacher, but by seeing the teacher as part of a matrix of existing relationships, practices, and ideas.

I suppose I feel strongly about these matters because a lot of my experience has been with the young teacher in the inner-city school about which a number of people have written a good deal (e.g., Kohl, 1967; Kozol, 1967). I am thinking particularly of those who were becoming outstanding teachers, and those who had the potential to become good teachers. All of them chose to teach in inner-city schools. Some left teaching after a year or so, others stayed on with the knowledge that they would someday leave, and some succumbed in the sense that they retrogressed rather than progressed as teachers and as individuals. To understand their development and fate in individual terms would be grossly incomplete. Similarly, to look only to external factors ("the school or the system") would also be a partial explanation, although these young teachers tended to explain everything in terms of such factors. What became clear to me, as a participant observer and helper, was that the problem could not be formulated in cause and effect terms or by dichotomizing factors into external and internal. Their inadequate formal training for the realities of the classroom, their sheer ignorance of and lack of preparation for what life in a school would be, the demands and willingness to give and the consequences of sustained giving in a context of constant vigilance, the absence of meaningful helping services—all of these and other factors interact in ways that should make simple explanations suspect. I have by now seen many inner-city schools demolished and new ones built with the not surprising result that the more things change the more they remain the same. Why this should be so I have only partially discussed in the chapters on the principal. We shall take this problem up again in a later chapter. I wish here only to make one observation: in all the new schools and new programs I have seen (inner- and outer-city) I rarely heard any discussion about how life in the classroom for teacher and child would be or should be changed. There was discussion of special services to teachers and children and the need for teacher aides, but this discussion hardly seemed to reflect other than the most superficial recognition of the problem of the effects of teaching on the modal teacher in the modal classroom. There was much talk about the need for teachers to be flexible, creative, stimulating—everyone was against sin and for virtue—but no one, in my memory, asked the question: To what extent may the development and maintenance of these virtues be hindered by what we know about the modal teacher in the modal classroom?

But how do we understand how Jackson's outstanding teachers, albeit in suburban and private schools, did it? The answer is a simple one: we do not know and it has barely been studied. We know some of their characteristics, but surely there is more to it than that. When we listen to a symphony we are set to pick out and respond to the melodic theme, and it is all too easy to forget that the way we hear that theme is very much determined by literally scores of instruments that are not playing that theme, but nevertheless are part of the whole. If we look at teacher characteristics in this way we can learn much—just as we can enjoy the melodic themes in a symphony—but just as the melody is not a symphony, teacher characteristics are but one aspect of a more complicated orchestration of factors. That we are set to respond to and think about teacher characteristics probably tells more about our accustomed ways of thinking than it does the complexity of the culture of the school. All of this would be no more than an interesting problem in theory were it not for the fact that our actions and proposals for change are determined by the way we formulate problems.

As I noted, Jackson's comments were based on interviews with teachers in suburban schools. His book was published in 1968, meaning that his study was done somewhat earlier in a period of an increasing school population, economic growth and affluence, community support for educational innovation, and a shortage of teachers. To what extent were his conclusions applicable then to urban schools experiencing racial conflict, limited resources, and school-community conflicts? My experience at the time in urban schools in part confirmed Jackson's conclusions: regardless of the overall disorganizing and morale lowering atmosphere of a school, I could always find at least one teacher who fitted Jackson's definition of the outstanding teacher. I say "in part" because it was obvious then that these rare teachers were experiencing some of the features of burnout. As a group, they knew their worth, would not compromise with their standards, and appreciated the fact that their peers and superiors regarded them highly. But increasingly they were feeling that life in the classroom was being adversely affected by life in the school and by their perception that conditions would worsen. Discipline problems, personal safety, and vandalism were seen by them as portents of more difficult days ahead. How many of them (and, as Jackson noted, outstanding teachers are few in number) left teaching or despairingly became less "outstanding" I cannot say. But let us ask more current questions: To what extent is Jackson's picture applicable to suburban teachers today? To urban teachers today? In the previous section I summarized the comments of a teacher participating in a televised program on teacher burnout. That teacher was working in a suburban school system and none of the other participants disagreed with the major implication of her remarks: to be an effective, let alone outstanding, teacher in schools today has become more problematic than ever before. Her description of life in a suburban school is only somewhat different from the one given by urban teachers today. The scene is a very different one from the mid-sixties, and it would be surprising, albeit mammothly encouraging, if someone repeating Jackson's study came to similar quantitative and qualitative conclusions. *The one educational setting today where Jackson's conclusions are confirmed in my experience is the alternative public school.* I have known several alternative urban schools and, generally speaking, they contain a higher percentage of outstanding teachers than Jackson found. Let me list the characteristics of these schools:

1. Teachers were usually self-selected; ie., they wanted to be in a different type of school, they were dissatisfied with life in the traditionally organized school.
2. The schools (middle and high schools) were explicitly created to foster and sustain more equality in the power relationships between teacher and pupil and between parent and school.
3. There was a minimum of hierarchalization; i.e., there was by consensus a "leader" but all teachers and student and parent representatives had a voice in formulating policy.
4. The number of students was far less than in the usual school, but the formal resources available to them seemed proportionately *less* than was available to other schools.
5. These schools were "allowed" to be created because they would serve students who in the traditional schools tended to be problems of one kind or another.

These schools were not educational paradises. There were discrepancies between their theories and their practices. But two conclusions were inescapable: the teachers were by and large committed, flexible, and treasured the sense of community they had with each other and with students. They tended to be rugged individualists who, nevertheless, knew they needed each other. Power was not an issue kept under the table, its dilemmas and opportunities were always on the table. And these schools were extraordinarily clear examples of the benefits of what Barker (1964, 1968) has described as "undermanned" as opposed to "overmanned" settings. The culture of these alternative schools is markedly different than the traditional schools in terms of behavioral and programmatic regularities. If these schools had more outstanding teachers than one would expect, it is in part because they were in settings outstandingly different from those from which they came.

Chapter 11

The Teacher: Constitutional
Issues in the Classroom

In the previous chapter our primary aim was to convey how in the modal school certain internal and external forces, extending over time, are experienced by and influence the modal teacher. In this chapter our focus will shift to what teachers think and do in regard to a number of specific and predictable events or issues that arise in any classroom. We can consider only a few of these events or issues, and they have been deliberately chosen to illustrate the general and obvious point that life in the classroom is a function of what and how teachers think about children, and how such thinking reflects the teacher's conception of his role. In a real sense this chapter is concerned with the teacher's "theories" of human behavior and group living. As we shall see, it is only when these theories are made explicit, and are seen in contrast to alternative conceptions, that we get a deeper understanding of certain behavioral regularities in the culture of the school. Let us not forget that the existence and pervasiveness of a behavioral regularity are two of the best indicators of a covert regularity involving the relationships between thinking and conceptualization, on the one hand, and a scale of values (what is good and what is bad), on the other hand.

CONSTITUTIONAL ISSUES

Almost all teachers meet a new group of pupils on the first day of school. The beginning phase of the school year certainly extends beyond the first day, but by the third or fourth week a routine is established, and teacher and pupils have, so to speak, sized up each other; the rules of the game by which everyone will be governed are fairly well known. How does this come about? How do teachers present and explain these rules of group living? Are these rules discussed? Are they for children only? What role do pupils play, if any, in the formation of rules? These questions and others comprise what I like to call the constitutional questions because in each classroom there is a constitution, verbalized or unverbalized, consistent or inconsistent, capable or incapable of amendment, that governs behavior. Constitutions tell us a good deal about history, tradition, and conceptions of human behavior.

We did an informal observational study of six classrooms, two each in grades 3, 4, and 5 in a suburban school system. In each of these six classrooms we had an observer who sat in the classroom for the first month of school beginning on the first day. The task of the observer was to record any statement by teacher and child that was relevant to "constitutional issues." The results were quite clear:

1. The constitution was invariably determined by the teacher. No teacher ever discussed why a constitution was necessary.
2. The teacher never solicited the opinions and feelings of any pupil about a constitutional question.
3. In three of the classrooms the rules of the game were verbalized by the end of the first week of school. In two others the rules were clear by the end of the month. In one it was never clear what the constitution was.
4. Except for the one chaotic classroom, neither children nor teachers evidenced any discomfort with the content of constitutions—it was as if everyone agreed that this is the way things are and should be.
5. In all instances constitutional issues involved what *children* could or could not, should or should not, do. The issue of what a *teacher* could or could not, should or should not, do, never arose.

On a number of occasions I have presented these findings to groups of teachers with the question: How do we explain them? In every group the question produced silence. In one group a teacher responded in a way that I think verbalized what most teachers were thinking: *What* is there to explain? I would then follow my initial question with another question: What do we have to assume to be true about children and teachers in order to justify these findings? These discussions were by no means easy or pleasant, and understandably so, if only because the teachers had never been called upon to make explicit the conceptions and values upon which these practices were based. But what were some of the assumptions that teachers could, after prolonged discussion, recognize and state?

1. Teacher knows best.
2. Children cannot participate constructively in the development of a classroom constitution.
3. Children want and expect the teacher to determine the rules of the game.
4. Children are not interested in constitutional issues.
5. Children should be governed by what a teacher thinks is right or wrong, but a teacher should not be governed by what children think is right or wrong.
6. The ethics of adults are obviously different from and superior to the ethics of children.
7. Children should not be given responsibility for something they cannot handle or for which they are not accountable.
8. If constitutional issues were handled differently, chaos might result.

If one does not make these assumptions, which is to say that one thinks differently about what children are and can do, one is very likely to think differently about what the role of the teacher might be. In this connection it is instructive to note that as I pursued the issues with the groups of teachers, and the assumptions could be clearly verbalized, *many of the teachers found themselves disagreeing with assumptions they themselves recognized as underlying their classroom behavior.* Equally as instructive was the awareness on the part of a few that if one changed assumptions one would have to change the character of one's role, and this was strange and upsetting, as indeed it should be because they realized that life in the classroom for them and the children would become different.

The problem we are discussing goes beyond the classroom, and its generality hit me with full force during one of these discussions with teachers. That it hit me with such force in this particular group was in part due to the fact that several of the teachers were quite adamant in maintaining that young children had to have their lives structured for them by adults because they were too immature to participate in and take responsibility for important decisions governing classroom life. *What I became aware of during the discussion was that these teachers thought about children in precisely the same way that teachers say that school administrators think about teachers; that is, administrators do not discuss matters with teachers, they do not act as if the opinions of teachers were important, they treat teachers like a bunch of children, and so on.* And should not these analogies be extended to include the way in which school personnel regard community representatives in relation to participation in educational policy? In earlier chapters I emphasized the significance of power, and people's view towards it, in understanding relationships within the school culture and between those within and without the school setting. The failure of efforts to introduce and sustain educational change have foundered largely because they have not come to grips with the power aspects of existing relationships, and by coming to grips I obviously do not mean change by fiat or appeal to people's good will or to token gestures that everyone recognizes as a degrading charade. Readers will recall that one of the major findings of Berman and McLaughlin was that successful educational change required the serious and active participation of the classroom teacher. Similarly, Cowen (Cowen et al., 1975), whose program in the Rochester schools is the most long-lived successful intervention that will be found in the research literature, emphasizes the centrality of the classroom teacher in planning and implementation. Unlike most proponents for change, Cowen altered the teacher's accustomed feelings of powerlessness, a change that had remarkable effects on the teacher's motivation, creativity, and industry. The point that must not be overlooked, however, is that teachers tend to regard children in a way that arouses hostility and lowers motivation in teachers when others regard them in that same way. The use and militancy of teacher organizations have a complex history, but one of the most important factors was the unwillingness of teachers to be governed by a tradition in which they had no part in decisions and plans that affected them. During the turbulent sixties and early seventies, a period during which teacher militancy dramatically increased in strength and consequence, there was a similar militancy on the part of pupils (largely in middle and high schools) centering around dissatisfaction with the powerlessness of students in regard to life in schools. Students no longer were content to be the traditional students—passive receptacles of learning. They clamored to be regarded as capable of participating in and taking some responsibility for their formal education. Just as teacher militancy was perceived as a threat to the decision-making power of administrators and boards of education, and just as the militancy of community groups was perceived as a threat to the power of educators, so was the militancy of students perceived by school personnel. The creation of alternative schools has to be seen in the context of the different power struggles that were going on.

One should not overlook the fact that what was going on in the public schools was also going on in college and universities: students were challenging their accustomed role of powerlessness in the classroom. A constitutional change seemed to be occurring. The amending of constitutions has been and always will be accompanied by strong conflict for two reasons: there are differences in conception of what people (teachers, students) are, and it is recognized that what is at issue is what life in a school is and could be. The conflicts wax and wane depending on what is happening in the larger society. The issue of power has long been the basis for competing educational theories, but it requires sea-swell forces in the society to illuminate dramatically the practical significances of these competing theories for institutional change. To change the quality of life in a classroom, especially when that change involves changes in power relationships, involves no less than a basic change in the culture of the school. It is not a change that can happen quickly. It is certainly not a change that can take place only from within what we traditionally call a school system. It is a change, in whatever degree, that will occur through alterations in the transactions between school and society.

It is not the purpose of this book, except in a very secondary way, to say how things should be. The primary purpose is to describe some of the important regularities in the culture of the school and to relate them to the conceptions and theories that "justify" these regularities. In order to do this I have tried, wherever possible, to contrast these existing relationships with the ever present but neglected universe of alternatives of conceptions from which derives a universe of alternative actions. This tactic not only serves to make one aware how the weight of habit and tradition can obscure the difference between what is and could be, but it also helps force those who want to introduce changes to be more precise about what it is they want to change. The "constitutional problem" is a case in point. I have known many teachers, principals, and school administrators who pride themselves on their adherence to democratic principles and feel strongly that the needs and rights of children have to be taken into account. In addition, these same people can point to colleagues whom they label as authoritarian or restrictive, with the implication that these characteristics are antieducational in spirit and effect. Without denying in the slightest that these differences exist, I have also to say that, constitutionally speaking, the differences are not all that great; in terms of how and on what basis the classroom constitution is determined, the "democratic" and "authoritarian" teacher are not as far apart as one might think.[1]

In both cases I have been impressed by three things: constitutions are for children and not teachers, complete power is retained by the teacher, and children passively accept the constitution developed for them. Those who wish to change life in the classroom are dealing with constitutional issues and not, as is too frequently the case, with highsounding slogans whose conceptual underpinnings remain unexamined with the usual result that there is a discrepancy between what is said and what is done.[2]

1. This conclusion is similar to that made by Jules Henry (1963), based on his observations of life in the suburban classroom. Henry is one of the very few anthropologists who has directly studied the classroom. His description and discussion of life in the classroom are illuminating and provocative. Given the emphasis in anthropology on foreign and so-called primitive cultures, it is not surprising that this important discipline has not focused on the classroom in our society (e.g., Spindler (ed.), 1963).

2. The constitutional issues, as well as others to be raised in this chapter, could be regarded as relevant to, or subsumed under, a theory of instruction. This would be a matter of indifference to me were it not that theories of instruction do not deal with constitutional issues, but rather

As a reminder, in this chapter we are attempting to understand the relationship between what teachers do (or do not do) and how they think about children and themselves, to understand the "theories" of teachers—not their feelings or values, but their conceptions of what people are. And teachers, like the rest of us, have such conceptions, which, again like for the rest of us, are usually implicit rather than explicit. In this connection we now turn to another issue that was the major reasons we did our little observational study.

THE STUDENT'S AND TEACHER'S CONCEPTION OF LEARNING

Prior to the observational study, I had, in connection with numerous studies on anxiety in elementary school children (Sarason et al., 1960), sat in scores of classrooms. It took quite some time for me to become aware that something was missing, and that was discussion in class of why and how people learned. It is obvious enough that however one defines such words as *learning, schooling,* and *education,* they refer to things or processes that take place in a school. They can and do take place outside of a school, but they are involved in what goes on in a classroom. What do children in a classroom think about the business of learning? Do children have their own theories (as indeed they do) about how and why one learns? Are there discrepancies between the theories children think about and the theories they are asked or required to adopt? Would children like to talk about these matters? Are they able to talk about them? How do teachers explain and discuss their theories of learning and thinking with their students? In short, to what extent were the whys and hows of learning and thinking an explicit focus and subject of discussion in the classroom? My observations left no doubt that how children thought about the processes

---

focus on the cognitive characteristics of the individual child, and on how these characteristics develop and could be taken account of in curriculum building. As often as not the theory talks about *a* child, and not a child in a group of children. Any theory of instruction that does not confront the reality that the teacher does not instruct *a* child but a group of children is not worth very much, to teachers at least. Even where the teacher intends to instruct a particular child, it takes place psychologically (for the child, teacher, and the other children) in the context of being part of a larger group and set of relationships. I quite agree with Jones' critique (1968) of Bruner's (1966) theory of instruction; that is, his overemphasis on cognitive skills and curricular skills and underemphasis on the affective. Jones comes close to including the constitutional question in his theory of instruction, but it is far from as explicit as I think will be found to be necessary. This may be because Jones, in reacting to Bruner's overemphasis on the cognitive side, gets riveted on the expression of the affective side, and what tends to get sidetracked are the constitutional arrangements between teacher and class that maximize such expression. Depending as Jones does on Freud's and Erikson's conceptions about individual development, he cannot develop what is needed: a truly social psychological theory of instruction. These objections aside, I consider Jones' book a distinct contribution.

of learning and thinking rarely came up for scrutiny in the classroom, but I was not as certain that the teacher's theories were as rarely presented and discussed. Therefore, we placed observers in classrooms to study this, and we chose the first month of school on the assumption that it would be during this interval that a teacher was most likely to make his or her own thinking explicit to the students. The most general instruction given to the observers was to note anything that a teacher said bearing on the whys and hows of learning and thinking. More specifically, they were asked to record anything relevant to the following questions:

1. When a child did not know or could not do something, did the teacher's response in any way attempt to find out how the child had been thinking or how the child might think—in contrast, for example, to telling and showing *a* correct procedure.
2. How frequently did a teacher say, "I don't know," and go on to discuss how he or she would think about going and *knowing*.
3. How frequently and in what ways does a teacher take up and discuss the role of question asking in intellectual inquiry or problem solving?

There were other questions, but I expect from these that one will understand that we were interested in the degree to which such topics as thinking and problem solving were discussed in the classroom. The results were quite clear: such discussions did not take place. Although unverbalized, the ground rules were not difficult to discern. First, the task of the student was to get the right answer and this was more important than how one arrived at the answer. By "more important" I mean simply that the right answer was what teacher and student obviously treasured. Second, for any one problem or question there was *a* correct way of thinking about and answering it. Third, *thinking was really not a complicated affair.*

There is nothing new or surprising in this. For example, Wertheimer (1945) well described, in the case of a geometry class, how the students were taught by their teacher to solve the parallelogram problem. When Wertheimer then tried to get the students to consider alternative ways of solving the problem, they were hardly able to grasp the idea that there was more than one way one could think about the problem. When he demonstrated alternative proofs, the students said he was wrong because he did not do it "the right way."[3]

---

3. One of the several justifications for the development of the new math was to counteract the kinds of things Wertheimer and others have described. That is to say, one wanted children to grasp the idea that there were different ways one could use and think about the world of numbers. As we pointed out in an earlier chapter, the new math is taught in much the same ways as the old math. It could not be otherwise if for no other reason than those who pushed for the change seemed unaware that the theories of learning and thinking that guide teachers, in addition to the constitutional issues discussed earlier, do not permit the processes of thinking to be an object of inquiry in the classroom.

What happens when I take up these observations with teachers? One of the most frequent reactions is similar to what Susskind reports when he presented to his teachers the discrepancy between the number of questions they asked of students and the number students asked of them: distress signifying that perhaps something was wrong. Another reaction is again similar to what only one of Susskind's teachers said, although I obtained it more frequently: "That is the way things should be." In a real sense these teachers were responding in a manner identical to that of Wertheimer's students, who could not accept the idea that there were other ways of thinking. But most instructive of all were those occasions when I could raise these issues with teachers *after* a discussion in which they had critically examined their experiences as students in their college courses. *What I confronted them with was the startling identity between their complaints as students in college and what their own students might complain about if they could but talk.* Some teachers could immediately see the possible connection. Other teachers could not accept the idea that how they felt could bear resemblance to how their students felt; that is, children did not think about thinking or learning the way teachers did. Leaving aside these reactions, there were two reservations that teachers verbalized. First, there was little or nothing in their training that would enable them to handle the issues in the classrooms. Second, even if they wanted to or could handle them, the demands of curriculum coverage leave little time for such matters.

Life in the classroom can be viewed and understood from different vantage points, but in my opinion, one of the most important ones is that which looks at the implicit theories teachers have about thinking and learning. What I have tried to suggest in this section is that many teachers have two theories: *one that applies to them and one that applies to children.* Put in another way, many teachers are quite aware from their own experiences of the differences in characteristics between dull and exciting conditions of intellectual activity. But their inability to see or assume some kind of identity between their pupils and themselves leads them unwittingly to create those conditions that they would personally find boring. Classroom learning is primarily determined by teachers' perceived differences between children and adults, a fact that makes recognition of communalities almost impossible.

CLASSROOM SEATING

In asking how teachers think about and what they do with children in relation to predictable issues or events, we started with what are obviously two important issues: the constitutional question and the teacher's conception of the role of discussion of the whys and hows of inquiry.[4] A study by A. Schwebel (1969) allows us to pursue the discussion in terms of a question that, on the surface at least, would not seem to be for our present purposes very important or productive. But complex questions tend on examination to remain complex at the same time that simple questions on examination tend to become complex.

Schwebel's study started with his observations, stemming from his work with teachers in their classroom, that children in the back of the room tended to behave differently than those in the front of the room. He did a small preliminary study (using independent observers who did not know the purposes of the study) and found confirmation for his own observations. He then developed a more elaborate study around the question: How are the seating arrangements in a classroom determined and what are their effects? Schwebel summarizes teacher descriptions of their procedures as follows:

FROM THE POST-EXPERIMENTAL INTERVIEWS WITH THE PARTICIPATING teachers it was learned that seat assignment procedures as a social-psychological problem is not included in teacher training programs or discussed by elementary school teachers. Nonetheless, the procedures the teachers described using were highly similar, suggesting that they were reacting to common psychological and/or environmental demands. The one demand they spoke of in particular was that of *achieving classroom control*. . . .

The procedure which teachers typically reported using to prevent disruption was to separate those children they had judged as "disruptive" and to assign them to seats in various parts of the room. Most teachers stated that they could identify the "disruptive" children in the

---

4. Fuchs' (1969) *Teachers Talk* is relevant here. Most of Dr. Fuchs' book consists of excerpts from journals kept by fourteen new teachers during the first semester in the classroom in city schools. These excerpts constitute compelling confirmation of many points I have made in this and previous chapters. My favorite excerpt (because of the importance I place on constitutional issues) is from a teacher's report of the first day of school: "Then I established class routines: how we would put away our clothing; how we would get our clothing; raising your hand when you have something to say, not calling out; not talking when I'm talking; not talking when I haven't given permission to talk; not talking when you are doing something. I told them that we would have free time for talking. Then we discussed fire drills, what we would do and how we would line up, and our behavior in the hall and in the yard. I also covered supplies, the things that I requested that they bring in, and any problems. I complimented them on how they were dressed and how I would like them to come to school from now on, dressed neatly and clean; we discussed routines at home, the time we go to bed at night, how we take our bath, what happens when you get up in the morning. We discussed why breakfast is called breakfast and why we eat breakfast. Before we knew it the whole morning had gone and it had been a very good morning." The book is a storehouse of accounts of life in the classroom and school.

first day or two of school. "Good" children were typically seated by the teacher next to those judged as "disruptive." While this suggests that teachers use physical proximity to certain types of children as a control mechanism, it raises the question of why the teachers do not assign several or all of those they judge as disruptive to seats in the front of the room where they as teacher could act as the control agent (Schwebel, 1969). ■

Among his major findings were:

1. Although individual teachers were consistent, as a group they varied with respect to the location in which they assigned pupils whom they judged as attentive, shy or likeable.
2. Those children assigned by teachers to the front row are more attentive to classroom activities than their classmates in the middle and back rows.
3. Occupancy of seats in the front, in contrast to those in the middle and back, affects in a positive manner, the way in which pupils are perceived by their teacher and peers, the way in which pupils evaluate themselves, and the way in which they behave.

Schwebel also points out, on the basis of his interviews, that "seat assignment procedures as a social psychological problem are not included in teacher training programs or discussed by elementary school teachers." Furthermore, although teachers were aware that they had assigned some "good" and some "bad" pupils to the front, and others to the back, the teachers could not verbalize their reasons. "Either they were less aware of the considerations which they had taken into account in making these decisions or, for one reason or another, they were hesitant to report them."

Why were teachers rather unclear about how they consider seating procedures? Or was it that they were clear in that discipline and control were the primary considerations that governed their thinking and decisions? What complicates answering these questions is what may be Schwebel's most intriguing finding: teachers with a high need to please other people (according to the Marlowe-Crowne Social Desirability Scale) rated pupils who sat in the front of the room more positively than those who sat in the back; teachers with a low need to please others rated pupils in the front of the room less positively than those in the back. These findings suggest that characteristics of teachers may be as important in determining seating (and, therefore, behavior) as characteristics of children.

That a classroom is a social organization is a glimpse of the obvious. What is not so obvious and is suggested by Schwebel's other data is that children seem to be more aware of, or attach more significances to, the social aspects of classroom organization than do teachers. To the extent that the teacher's thinking about seating is oversimple (i.e., oriented almost exclusively toward control of disruptive behavior) or determined by his or her personal needs, *it is almost impossible for the teacher ever to recognize that the pupils view seating differently.* That seating may not be high in the hierarchy of important problems facing a teacher requires no discussion, but this should not obscure the fact that in small as well as large problems two things are decisive: how one formulates the problem, and, equally important, how one structures the situation so that the problem can be reformulated on the basis of new information provided by others. The relatively unimportant problem of seating contains within it all the constitutional issues raised earlier.

THE TEACHER AS A THINKING MODEL

Thus far in this chapter I have been, in one or another way, raising a descriptive type of question: What and how much do children know about what a teacher thinks? It is inevitable that children will know something about how a teacher thinks—how much depends on the teacher. I have never heard anyone argue that a teacher is not a model for children of how one should think and act. It is not a matter of *should* a teacher be a model, but rather that he or she *is* a model. But the fact that the teacher is a model of a particular kind and degree very definitely involves a variety of "shoulds," such as what children should learn, what a teacher should do, and so on. The point I wish to emphasize is that it appears that children know relatively little about how a teacher thinks about the classroom; that is, what the teacher takes into account, the alternatives the teacher thinks about, the things that puzzle the teacher about children and about learning, what the teacher does when unsure of what should be done, how the teacher feels when he or she does something wrong—there is quite a bit that goes on in a teacher's head that is never made public to children.

Am I advocating that teachers act like patients on an analyst's couch and give forth with all that is inside them? Obviously not, in addition to which I am not advocating *anything.* I am merely pointing out that the degree to which teachers make their thinking public inevitably reflects the kind of "thinking model" to which they adhere. Put in another way, it reflects a conception of what is helpful to children. How does one decide what is helpful? For example, if it were true that how a teacher thinks about the classroom is something about which children are curious, is it helpful *not* to satisfy this curiosity? Is there any reason to believe that it is helpful to children to know how a teacher thinks? Unfortunately, we do not have a truly firm foundation for answering the question. However, there is a good deal of anecdotal evidence strongly indicating that the more a teacher can make his or her own thinking public and subject for discussion—in the same way one expects of children—the more interesting and stimulating the classroom becomes for students, and I assume that is a helpful state of affairs. Phillip Booth (1969) put it beautifully in a review of a book by the teacher and poet, Mark Van Doren: "His unique genius as a teacher was to speculate publicly; in opening the play of his mind to students, he gave each student a self-assigned role in resolving these questions his teaching dramatized." I would be quite surprised if Professor Van Doren's "unique genius" was not in some measure a reflection of a clear conception of what would be helpful to his students.

The issue I am raising is well illustrated in the research endeavor. If one reads professional research journals, it is easy to gain the impression that research is conducted by rational people in rational, planned ways. In the modal research paper one finds hypotheses that are related to or stem from a theory, defined procedures, results, and then a discussion section in which one explains why things happened as they did. As often as not (probably more often than not) the discussion section is an implicit tribute to the researcher's ability to predict. It is hard, particularly for those who are not researchers, to avoid concluding that research is a cold, cut-and-dried set of logically related cognitive processes in which the personal and subjective are not allowed to intrude. That this is a partially true but horribly misleading model of how a researcher thinks and acts is something that researchers themselves well know (e.g., Taylor, 1959; Watson, 1968). Graduate students who are being introduced to the research endeavor frequently suffer trauma when it dawns on them that published research is a most inadequate and incomplete representation of how the researcher thinks. The public and private model are far from congruent. *What I have tried to indicate in this section is that the modal teacher in the modal classroom presents a "model of thinking" to students that is as unrepresentative of his or her thinking as a published piece of research is of its author's thinking.* It may be that the similarity does not end there. I would venture the opinion that the similarity between teacher and researcher rests, among other factors, on their implicit belief that their audience would not be interested in or would not comprehend a more realistic presentation of their thinking. If my experience with school children—in fact, with all levels of students, from elementary through graduate school—is any guide, that large part of a teacher's "thinking about thinking," which is never made public, is precisely what the children are interested in and excited by on those rare occasions when it becomes public.

THE PREPOTENT RESPONSE TO MISBEHAVIOR

No discussion of how teachers think can long avoid the problem of discipline. Particularly in the case of the new teacher, nothing rivals discipline as a problem (Sarason, Davidson, and Blatt, 1962). It is interesting to note that in our observational study of the first month of six classrooms, discipline as a problem in group living was never discussed. Most teachers made clear what was good and bad behavior—what the characteristics were of crime in the classroom—but these were not discussions.

We might begin by asking the following question: What is a teacher's prepotent response to a child's misbehavior? The answer is rather clear: the teacher reprimands the child in one way or another; that is, the child is told (many times gently and nonpunitively) that what he or she is doing is wrong. The more serious the infraction, or if it involves a child with a notable classroom criminal record, the stronger the teacher's response and the harsher the punishment. This is all very obvious. What is not so obvious is the content of the thinking that gives rise to this type of prepotent response. I say this because when on scores of occasions I have asked teachers to explain to me the justification for the prepotent response, they have been puzzled by the question. From their standpoint the answer is obvious and not necessary to justify: if a child does something wrong, you tell the child so that he or she will then do the right thing. If I then ask why it does not always work, the answer is almost always in terms of characteristics of the child.[5] (The "theory" is correct but the child does not know that!)

ONE TEACHER (IN A SUBURBAN SCHOOL) HAD BEEN DISCUSSING WITH ME A particularly troublesome boy. I said that I would be back in three days to see how things were going. When I returned the teacher gleefully said, "I am not superstitious but I don't want to say anything. He has been absolutely no problem for the last two days." I then said to the teacher, "Have you told *him* how pleased you are at how well he is doing?" His facial expression was sufficient to tell me that it did not occur to him to reward the child. His theory was explicit about when one punishes, but not about when one rewards. One might say that the principle underlying his thinking was: you let well enough alone until well enough becomes bad enough. ■

Wherein was the approach to this troublesome boy different from that of the teacher's? Let me paraphrase what I said to this teacher, although this summary should not be viewed as a cookbook recipe:

WHAT YOU ARE DOING WITH THIS BOY IS NOT WORKING. WE DO NOT know why it is not working and we really don't have the time to find

---

5. The experiences I shall be relating here are based on those contacts with teachers who asked to see me about a misbehaving child. In almost all classrooms there is at least one child who is a chronic misbehaver, although teachers vary markedly in seeking help with these children. The frequency of such children is quite high in inner-city schools where I have spent most of my time, and it was my experiences in these schools that forcibly brought to my attention the significance of the prepotent response to misbehavior.

out why. The longer this continues the worse for you and the boy. What about trying this: Tomorrow morning before school opens get this kid alone and tell him that you are quite aware that your way of trying to help him in regard to misbehavior is not working. He knows it and you know it. What he may not know is that you are puzzled and bothered. You do not enjoy punishing him, although that may be hard for him to believe. You have two questions to put to him. The first is what ideas does he have about how you can help him. The second is what does he think about this: from this point on when he misbehaves the two of you are going to leave the room and the two of you are going to discuss what had just happened and why, and how it could have been avoided. This does not mean that you are throwing punishment out of the window. You will have to punish, much as you, the two of you, may not like it, but that is less important than figuring out ways in which you can help him avoid trouble and that is what you are most interested in.[6] ■

It is not easy, nor is it our present task, to explicate the thinking from which the above is or can be derived. That it is different than what underlies the prepotent response is obvious. Readers may have noted that one of the differences reflects the content of the discussion in the previous section; that is, *teachers make public what and how they think about a problem.* A related difference, of course, is that *one assumes that children are really interested in what goes on in a teacher's head, particularly as that does or will affect children.* There is much more to it than these differences. The important point is that the prepotent response, which is so typical an aspect of life in the classroom, reflects only one way one could think about the problem.[7]

---

6. I must emphasize that this is a paraphrase and has to be viewed in the context of a relationship of weeks with this teacher in his classroom. What I presented above was not for the purposes of describing a procedure, but simply a way of thinking.

7. The work of Kounin, Gump, and their colleagues (Gump and Kounin, 1959; Kounin, Gump, and Ryan, 1961; Kounin, Friesen, and Norton, 1966; Kounin, 1967), based on their research on the classroom management of deviant behavior, represents what I consider to be a productive and relevant approach to a theory of instruction, more so than the efforts of Bruner and Jones. Kounin (1967) has put it well: ". . . the management of behavior in classrooms is not a function of the techniques of directly controlling behavior as such—that is, discipline or desist style. Rather, it is a function of the techniques of creating an effective classroom ecology. Nor is it a simple issue of admonishing teachers that 'prevention is better than cure,' or 'create rapport,' or 'make it interesting.' Nor is it an ebasive preoccupation with 'personality' or the listing of boy scout type characteristics. Nor is it a simple extrapolation from other adult-child relationships—whether these be parents or professional psychotherapists. Nor is it solely a matter of understanding and knowing how to handle an individual child to the exclusion of the group. Rather, the business of running a classroom is a complicated technology having to do with developing a nonsatiating learning program, initiating and maintaining group and individual movement, aiming teacher actions at appropriate targets, and still others yet to be determined. And may I add my belief in the potential value of receptive, naturalistic, ecological researches in arriving at a knowledge of what these dimensions are or might be."

Let me now turn to two related questions I have asked teachers: Is there something about children that makes them *completely* unable to participate in discussion and formulation of crime and punishment in the classroom? Please note that I italicized "completely" because I have never seen a classroom (although I am sure they exist) in which children participated in such discussion and formulation—and we are back, of course, to the constitutional issue. The second question: Assuming that they are incapable, is it also true that they do not think about or are not concerned about crime and punishment in the classroom? To say they are completely unable is at least unjustified and at worst sheer ignorance of what children do outside of school in their spontaneous play groups. One does not need the support of formal research to assert that children in their relationships to each other have some concept of fairness—one needs only good eyes and ears.

The fact of the matter is that the great bulk of teachers assert: (1) that children are not completely unable, and (2) that children do think about crime and punishment in the classroom. *Whatever thinking allows teachers to make these positive assertions is not reflected in what they do, or, more specifically, in the justification of the prepotent response.*

There is another way of looking at the prepotent response, and the thinking surrounding it, and that is that it reflects an individual psychology. That is to say, when a teacher thinks about misbehavior, one thinks primarily in terms of individual children. When the teacher thinks about action, one also tends to think about action in relation to individual children. Although the teacher is quite aware that there is a group of children, this plays far less of a role in thinking and action than one might think. When we discussed Schwebel's study of seating, we saw that teachers arrange seating patterns primarily for purposes of "control," patterns based explicitly on the assumption that one kind of child can influence another kind of child; that is, interrelationships within the group are presumed to be important. By and large, however, teachers do not think in terms of how a group can be organized and utilized so that as a group it plays a role in relation to the issues and problems that confront the group. Since this statement may be misinterpreted, I should be blatantly clear that I am not suggesting that children should run a classroom. All that I intend by that statement is what teachers themselves have asserted to the two questions I put to them. If these assertions were to be taken seriously, it would mean that one would have to think in terms of theories of groups, group processes, the relation of the leader (teacher) to the group, and the role of, as well as the phenomenology of, leadership. This is not to say that one scraps one type of psychology for another. They both have their places. It is the case, however, that in their training teachers have been exposed, almost exclusively, to a psychology of learning that has one past and one present characteristic: the latter is its emphasis on how an individual organism learns, and the former is that the major learning theories were based on studies of the individual Norway rat. *If instead of putting one rat in the maze they had put two or more in the maze, the history of American psychology would have been quite different. Conceivably, the social nature of learning might not need to be rediscovered.*

To illustrate further what I mean let us take the following problem which a number of first and second grade teachers have presented to me. The problem involves what to do about the dependent, crying, anxious, clinging child.[8] In a number of instances and on the basis of my observations in the classroom, I suggested to the teacher that when the child acts in this way she pick him up, cuddle and soothe, reassure him that she would do whatever she could to help, and try to find out about what he was afraid or thinking. A number of teachers responded by saying that they had thought of doing that, but *if they did it with one child other children would want similar treatment.* ■

SBS: It is my impression that the rest of the class recognizes that Jimmy is different than they are. They seem fully to recognize that he is the only one who behaves in this way. What is your impression?

TEACHER: I am sure that's true. In fact some of them have asked why Jimmy cries. And some of them try to soothe him.

SBS: But what if you were to do as I suggest and other children then ask for the same treatment—and I have no doubt that many of them would like the same treatment from you. How might you handle it?

TEACHER: That's what I am afraid of—I don't know.

SBS: Well, one thing you could do is to tell the class that when anybody feels and acts like Jimmy, and that means they are unhappy and need help, you would do for them what you do for Jimmy. Do you think that if you took this up with the class, they would not understand what you were saying or how you expect them to cooperate? You seem to feel that they would take—they want to take—advantage of you.

TEACHER: That's not true. I am sure they would understand. Maybe there's one who would put on an act!

SBS: You mean that you think the children are perceptive, that they would understand, and they would abide by the responsibility you are implicitly placing on them?

TEACHER: I guess so.

SBS: But that means, doesn't it, that you have to present the problem to them, your way of thinking about it, your questions and hesitations,

8. This problem rarely was presented to me in suburban schools. It was a very frequent problem in inner-city schools.

and solicit their thoughts both about what ought to be and what their responsibility should be?

THE POINT IS THAT WHEN ONE BEGINS TO THINK IN THIS WAY, ONE IS INvolved in problems of group process; one is not only involved with a Jimmy, or untested assumptions about what a group of children are and can become, or imagined consequences, but with a process that is deliberately public, involves obligations and responsibilities, and deals with issues of interest and concern to all. It is not a simple process and requires a way of thinking to which teachers are not exposed. It requires one other thing that was well put by one teacher who, with a glint in her eyes, said: "You mean we should treat children the way *we* like to be treated?" ■

A final word about the prepotent responses to misbehavior—I have by now asked hundreds of teachers the following two questions: "How many times in the last month have you, aside from the report card, made it your business to communicate to parents that their child was not doing well, or he was misbehaving, or one or another kind of problem?" I never kept an accurate count, but I would guess that 25 percent of the teachers indicated that they had gone out of their way to contact parents about a child's problem. The second question was: "How many times in the last month have you, aside from the report card, made it your business to communicate to parents that their child was doing well, or very well, or very much better than previously?" At most, 1 percent of the teachers indicated that they had initiated such a contact.

THE GOALS OF CHANGE IN THE CLASSROOM

One does not have to document the statement that there are many people, both from within and without schools, who feel that the quality of life and learning in the classroom needs to be changed. The goals of change vary in their scope and phraseology; for example, the classroom should be more child-centered, it should be more democratically organized and run, it should be more relevant to the world that children do and will live in, teachers should be more creative, and so on. A basic assumption in these statements of virtue is that the teacher will be the agent of change; the teacher will possess that way of thinking, as well as appropriately derived procedures and tactics, that will bring about the desired kind of classroom life. It is rare, indeed, to find in these discussions serious consideration of the consequences of this basic assumption for the change process. That is to say, there is a remarkable blindness to the fact that one is confronted with the extremely difficult problem of how one changes how people think.

This is all the more strange when one recognizes that underlying the different criticisms of classroom life is the more basic criticism that one does not agree with how the modal teacher thinks.

The more I have read about and personally observed efforts to introduce change in the classroom, the more clear several things have become. First, those who attempt to introduce a change rarely, if ever, begin the process by being clear as to where the teachers *are;* that is, how and why they think as they do. In short, they are guilty of the very criticism they make of teachers: *not being sensitive to what and how and why children think as they do.* As a result, teachers react in much the same way that many children do, and that is with the feeling they are both wrong and stupid (Holt, 1964). Second, those who attempt to introduce a change seem unaware that they are asking teachers to unlearn and learn. Third, if there is any one principle common to efforts at change, it is that one effects change by *telling* people what is the "right" way to act and think. *Here, too, those who want change do exactly that for which they criticize teachers.*

The main purpose of this chapter has been to obtain glimpses of how the modal teacher thinks and how this determines, in large part, life in the classroom. Put in another way: the overt regularities that can be discerned in the classroom reflect covert principles and theories. If we wish to change the overt regularities, we have as our first task to become clear about the covert principles and theories: those assumptions and conceptions that are so overlearned that one no longer questions or thinks about them. They are "second nature," so to speak. If these assumptions and conceptions remain unverbalized and unquestioned, which is to say that thinking does not change, the likelihood that any of the overt regularities one wants to change will in fact change is drastically reduced. It would all be so simple if one could legislate changes in thinking.

It is likely that some readers will use the contents of this chapter as grist for their internal mill of prejudice and snobbery. It is not difficult, if one is so disposed, to feel superior to teachers—and many university critics (and others) are so disposed. This would not be worthy of comment were it not for two facts: many university critics spearhead the change process, and, as anyone familiar with the history of anthropology knows, the feeling of superiority ("bringing culture to the primitives") is lethal for the process of understanding and change.

My former colleague, Dr. Murray Levine, developed a concept on the basis of his intensive work with teachers in inner-city schools.

The Child Comes by His Problem Honestly

FROM THE POINT OF VIEW OF THE TEACHER WHO IS CONCERNED ABOUT teaching a large group of children any child who presents special difficulties is a nuisance. As long as education is defined in terms of the preparation and presentation of material to children, the teacher's first inclination, when faced with a difficult child, is to experience the child as trouble. Finding her own efforts frustrated or finding that she must divide her attention in more ways than she feels capable of doing, the teacher frequently feels angered and resentful of a child who demands something different by virtue of his behavior. She may also feel anxious because her image of herself as a competent professional person is threatened. Although we are taught that human behavior stems from sufficient causes, in the classroom situation the teacher is not always able or prepared to seek causes. Understandably, from her viewpoint, the child is at fault for acting as he does, and it is her feeling that both she and the child would be better off if the child were away from her. Sometimes the consultant can serve an important function by helping the teacher to see that the problem has a background. When the teacher sees that a child does come by his problems honestly, so to speak, her tolerance for the problem and her willingness to make the effort to work with the child are sometimes increased (Sarason et al., 1966). ■

Dr. Levine gives case examples of how the thinking and actions of teachers changed in relation to certain children once they understood that indeed they come by their problems honestly, which is another way of saying that teachers understood the child in *their* terms and life experience. If we believe teachers have problems, and they do, we will not get very far in helping them if we do not understand that they come by their problems quite honestly.

Chapter 12

Education for All Handicapped Children (Public Law 94-142)

Few if any people would disagree with the statement that American education has experienced at least two revolutions. The first stemmed from the adoption of compulsory education and the second from the 1954 desegregation decision. We are currently witnessing the third revolution: the "integration" of handicapped children into the "mainstream" of American education. In 1975, Congress enacted P.L. 94-142. The states had three years to develop plans and programs consistent with the legislation, and federal funding for it began in 1978. Implicitly, the legislation is a moral indictment of public schools because they either had ignored, or rejected, or discriminated against handicapped individuals. Such individuals (e.g., profoundly mentally retarded) may have been refused admittance to schools, or automatically put into a special class, or not given the type of help their handicapping condition made necessary. What the legislation was intended to insure is that for every handicapped child there will be a tailor-made program reflecting the effort to maximize that child's participation in the classroom's and school's "normal" activities. The child's program has to meet the criterion of the "least restrictive alternative." It would no longer be possible for the school to place a child in a program because of his or her diagnostic label; placement would be decided by the needs of the *individual* child as those needs would be studied and formulated by a team of school personnel. The expectation was that many schools would need to expand the quantity and quality of alternatives available for handicapped pupils. After all, the legislation was a commentary on the limited number of alternatives schools had provided handicapped children, and it would be a mockery if the legislation did not result in an increase in the number of alternatives. Finally, the legislation explicitly gives parents of handicapped children a role in any aspect of data collection, program planning, and decision making that will impact on their children.

As little as ten years ago (i.e., 1970) you would have been considered strange and unrealistic if you predicted that five years later legislation like 94-142 would be enacted.[1] How do we account for this legislation? What does it tell us about the culture of schools? From what we know about past efforts to change schools, what kinds of changes should we expect from 94-142? Upon what conception of institutional change was 94-142 based? Let us start with another question: How were handicapped children viewed and educated in our schools before 94-142?

TWO CULTURES

I shall begin with some personal experiences. My first professional job was in 1942 at the Southbury Training School (Connecticut), a new, state residential faculty for mentally retarded individuals. In terms of educational philosophy and architecture, Southbury was unique for its time, and for two decades after it opened it was an international showcase. Southbury, like so many other residential institutions built by the states, was in the middle of nowhere. It had long been the practice to build residential institutions for deviant or handicapped individuals away from population centers. That is to say, segregation (social and geographic) was society's prepotent response. If asked, most people would have said that those individuals who required residential care would be better off "being with their own kind." The fact is that it has always been the case, regardless of condition, that those who were segregated in institutions or in special classes in public schools represented a very small fraction of those for whom such facilities were deemed most appropriate. If most of these individuals were not in such segregated facilities, it said more about economics than it did society's view about where they "really" belonged.

Shortly after Southbury opened its doors some communities closed their special classes and sought to arrange to send their pupils to Southbury; others were more selective in that they tried to send only the "troublemakers." In any event, we became aware that the public schools were "dumping" and that many of the students were not mentally retarded. (It was also true that Southbury could admit epileptics regardless of intellectual level, and in that first year a college student with epilepsy was legally admitted to the institution.) In terms of societal and professional attitudes, what I have just de-

---

1. Zigler and Muenchow (1979) noted "that the treatment of the handicapped has frequently been buffeted between social trends with an apparent life span of about ten years." This statement, which certainly holds for the post-World War II era, should be a reminder that what happens in schools, and how educators think about and define "problems," always reflect developments in the larger society that in one or another way conflict with each other. The paper by Zigler and Muenchow is short, but nevertheless raises some of the most important issues surrounding the purposes and implementation of 94-142.

scribed was not at all unusual, and neither was the way in which behavioral factors interacting with these attitudes operated selectively to determine who was segregated where.

The public schools never took kindly to special classes for the mentally retarded. But it would be a mistake to conclude that these attitudes were specific to the mentally retarded. If we know more about these attitudes toward the mentally retarded, it is largely because such classes had long been a feature of school systems, albeit a very small feature. What needs to be kept in mind is that school personnel negatively viewed any child who interfered with normal routine; i.e., with teachers' time-conscious planning and goal setting. This did not necessarily mean that teachers disliked such a child or were unsympathetic to his or her needs, but simply that such a child was an interference to the progress of the rest of the class. There was a further source of "interference": there was nothing in the training of the "regular" classroom teacher that gave him or her a sense of understanding a child who was labelled "special." The preparation of the teacher was based on the myth of two psychologies: the psychology of the "normal" child and the psychology of the "special" child. I call it a myth because it was as invalid a conception as if one were to assert that you needed one theory for the oxygen atom and one for the hydrogen atom. However invalid the conception of two psychologies, the fact remained that in the phenomenology of the teacher the special child required a special understanding that the teacher did not and should not have been expected to have. Whenever the child belonged, it was not in the regular classroom! In this respect, the thinking of educators was quite similar to that of people generally.

Let me illustrate the "two psychologies" because it is so basic to comprehending how in schools two cultures developed, were sustained, and for several decades began to approximate each other in size, costs, and influence. If a child has an IQ of 180 and is discovered to have strangled to death a neighbor's cat, no one would say that it was done *because* the child had an IQ of 180; i.e., the IQ of 180 is *not* the etiological agent without which the behavior would not have occurred. However, if the child has an IQ of 50, many people would "explain" the behavior in terms of the low IQ. There are, then, two psychologies: one for "us" and one for "them," and, therefore, unless you know "their" psychology, you cannot be helpful to them, *nor should you be expected to deal with such children.*[2] There was (and there still

2. As is so frequently the case, the psychologically and morally adverse consequences of the "two psychologies" have been most compellingly and poignantly conveyed in literature. The two most recent examples are from the theater: Medoff's *Children of a Lesser God* and Pomerance's *The Elephant Man,* both current successes in the Broadway theater. The former is about deaf and the latter about physically handicapped people. Both plays speak volumes about society's prepotent tendency to segregate and about the unwitting but devastating consequences of two psychologies one of which is "superior" to the other. Although both plays provide moving experiences, I found *Children of a Lesser God* more dramatic, perhaps because, unlike the deformed central character in *The Elephant Man,* the deaf central character rebels successfully against the inequities of the two psychologies.

is) little or nothing in the preparation of the regular classroom teacher and "regular" school administrators to make them feel competent to understand and/or to teach children with a label denoting specialness. On the contrary, their training emphasized the need for two cultures in the school: the regular and the special. The two cultures in the school mirrored the same two cultures in schools of education.

The one point of agreement among the educational personnel in the two cultures was that more special classes were needed, an agreement that did not result in any discernible increase until after World War II. There were several points of disagreement. First, the special class teachers resented both their and their children's second-class status in the school; i.e., they were tolerated rather than accepted. Second, the facilities available to the special class teacher (e.g., where the special class was physically situated, teaching materials, and support services) were inadequate. Third, the special class teacher was seen much more in a baby-sitting, behavior managing role than in an "educator" one. Fourth, the special class was frequently and unfairly used as a way of segregating children who were behavior problems in the regular classroom. Fifth, it was far easier (although never easy because there were few such classrooms) to get a child into rather than out of a special class. The special class teacher was essentially powerless and alone in the school culture. There were two cultures, but there was no doubt which was the dominant and controlling one.

How the schools determine the worth of its pupils and personnel reflect criteria employed by the society at large. So, in those days if one asked: What are schools for and for whom do they exist?, the answers were that they primarily existed for the intellectual-educational development of "normal" children. Put another way: whoever and whatever interfered with the education of normal children could not be justified or had to be contained with as few resources as possible. What one has to understand is that this basically moral stance was considered right, natural, and proper. Indeed, this stance was so unquestioned, the school's position so supported, that for all practical purposes parents of children had nothing to say about the placement of their child in a special class. Parents were informed about such placements, they did not have a role in decisions about such matters.

MINORITY REPRESENTATION IN SPECIAL CLASSES

The dispute in the first decades of this century was whether segregation in special classes in the regular school was sufficient to protect the child's self-esteem or whether such a child (relatively few shes) should in fact be segregated into special schools for his or her own protection.

Beginning in the 1960s, research findings (Meyerwitz, 1965, 1967; Jones, 1972) opened up the issue to debate (Dunn, 1968; Kolstoe, 1972). Researchers began fumbling for appropriate measurements, designs, and analyses, as all the while it became more apparent that clear-cut answers to the question of lowered self-esteem would not be easy to establish. Nevertheless, summing up the state of the field, one might, as Dunn did in his seminal article in 1968, raise the ultimate question: "Special Education for the Mildly Retarded—Is Much of It Justifiable?" The article set off quite a furor, but for many reasons Dunn had sensed the changing wind and his article pointed in the direction of that change.

In reviewing some of the controversy stirred up by Dunn's article, Hammons (1972) correctly indicated that the article was "only symptomatic of a growing disenchantment with emerging practices of special education" (p. 565). Concerns had begun to appear at least as early as the 1930s; the issue of the deleterious effects of labeling a child mentally retarded had often been raised and the question of the appropriateness of classifying handicapped children by medical criteria instead of social and educational needs was not new to the literature. Nevertheless, Dunn's article articulated the disenchantment at a time when that disenchantment was combining with other social discontents to provoke a fundamental challenge to the system of special education which had gradually been built up over three-quarters of a century.

What we would like to focus on at this point is one of the aspects of special education for the mildly retarded that caused Dunn to question its validity. This aspect concerns the overrepresentation of impoverished minority group children in special education classes, and the appropriateness of such educational placement for these children. Dunn had opened his argument by stating that:

A BETTER EDUCATION THAN SPECIAL CLASS PLACEMENT IS NEEDED FOR socioculturally deprived children with mild learning problems who have been labeled educable mentally retarded. Over the years, the status of these pupils who come from poverty, broken and inadequate homes, and low status ethnic groups has been a checkered one. In the early days, these children were simply excluded from school. Then, as Hollingworth pointed out, with the advent of compulsory attendance laws, the schools and these children "were forced into a reluctant mutual recognition of each other." This resulted in the establishment of self contained special schools and classes as a method of transferring these "misfits" out of the regular grades. This practice continues to this day and, unless counterforces are set in motion now, it will probably become even more prevalent in the immediate future due in large measure to increased racial integration and militant teacher organizations. For example, a local affiliate of the National Education Association demanded of a local school board recently that more special classes be provided for disruptive and slow learning children (Dunn, 1968, p. 5). ∎

In Dunn's estimation, 60 to 80 percent of the pupils taught by special education teachers "are children from low status backgrounds—including Afro-Americans, American Indians, Mexicans, and Puerto Rican Americans; those from nonstandard English speaking, broken, disorganized, and inadequate homes; and children from nonmiddle class environments" (p. 6). It was Dunn's thesis that such deprived children should not be labeled mentally retarded.

Independently of Dunn, others were concerned about the disproportionate representation of minority group children in special education classes. For example, a number of surveys and research studies undertaken in California in the 1960s clearly demonstrated the overrepresentation of Spanish-surname and black children in the special education classes of that state. In 1966, a survey of enrollment in special classes by ethnic group membership revealed that for every county having 5 percent or more black or Spanish-surname children enrolled in school, the percentage of such children in special class placement exceeded the percentage of such children in the total school population for that county. In the thirty-five counties involved, the percentage of these minority children in the special classes was often two to three times what it was in the total school population (Mercer, 1970). Again, in 1969-1970, 15.2 percent of the total school population of California's public day schools were of Spanish surname, while 28.3 percent of all pupils classified as educable mentally retarded were of Spanish surname. Blacks constituted 8.9 percent of the total school enrollment by 25.5 percent of the educable pupils. In contrast, white, non-Spanish-surnamed children were underrepresented in the classes for educable children. While such white children constituted 72.4 percent of the total school population, they represented only 44.3 percent of those classified as educable (Dunn, 1973). It is hardly surprising that Mexican-American and black parents brought court challenge to the diagnostic and classificatory system utilized by the public schools in setting up their special education classes.

A series of articles written by Jane Mercer in the early 1970s, based upon her years of research on the special education programs of California, gives some excellent insights into the workings of that diagnostic and classificatory system. Mercer's approach to the understanding of educable retardation rejects the medical or "disease" model, however appropriate that might be for moderate or severe forms of retardation, and utilizes instead a social systems approach:

FROM A SOCIAL SYSTEM PERSPECTIVE, MENTAL RETARDATION IS NOT VIEWED as individual pathology but as a status which an individual holds in a particular social system and a role which he plays as an occupant of that status. In this context, mental retardation is not a characteristic of the individual, but rather, a description of an individual's location in a social system, the role he is expected to play in the system, and the expectations which others in the system will have for his behavior. Mental retardation is an achieved status. It is a position in the group that is contingent upon the performance or, in this case, the lack of performance, of the individual. Thus mental retardation is specific to a particular social system. A person may hold the status of a mental retardate in one social system and may play the role of a mental retardate in that system, yet may also participate in other social systems in which he is not regarded as mentally retarded and does not hold that status. If a social system does not place a person in the status or role of mental retardate then he is not retarded in that system, although he might qualify for the status of mental retardate if he were participating in some other system. Consequently, the "prevalence" rate for mental retardation is relative to the level of the norms of specific social systems and will vary with the expectations of the definer (Mercer 1970, pp. 383–384). ■

Using a social system analysis, Mercer then identified a number of clearly differentiated stages through which a child may move in progressing from the status of a normal student to that of an educable mentally retarded child (EMR). The first step toward acquiring EMR status is enrolling in the public schools. Mercer makes it clear that this is not a trivial statement. In the community she was studying there were 2,500 elementary school students in Catholic parochial schools. These schools had no special classes for mentally retarded children, and although there were several dozen children in these parochial schools who by intelligence test scores would have been eligible for EMR status in the public schools, they could not achieve that status in the parochial school because the status of mental retardate did not exist within that system. The best that could be achieved was to be classified as a "slow learner."

In a public school, children are assumed "normal" students if not visibly defective. Normal students remain as such until they fail to meet the role expectations of the teacher. They may then be required to repeat a grade and achieve the status of "retained" students. Some 72 percent of the EMR students in the study had repeated one or more grades in the course of their educational careers. As retained students, the children may meet expectations and again move ahead as "normal" students. Failing expectations, the teacher exercises one or two options: "an unearned social promotion" which sidesteps EMR status, or a referral to the principal as an "academic problem." At this point each child is evaluated by teacher and principal and may be assigned some label such as "reading problem," "speech problem," or "underachiever," which keeps one's status in the regular class but may make special educational resources available.

Alternatively the child may be sent to the psychologist for evaluation. The psychologist then exercises one of several options. The decision may be made that the child is "emotionally disturbed" or "situationally distressed" and the child might return to regular class status. On the other hand, it may be decided to give the child an individual intelligence test. If the child scores too high for EMR class placement, he or she returns to the regular grade. If, however, the child scores below the accepted standard, he or she is a possible candidate for EMR status. A parental conference and a staff planning session now determine whether or not the child will be assigned to a special class. Adamant parents and a borderline IQ may cause the staff to decide the child is emotionally disturbed and one's IQ not really representative of potential. The child returns to the regular class. Otherwise, and barring the parents removing the child from the school, the child has achieved the status of a mental retardate. Very few are reassigned to regular classes once such status is achieved. As Mercer notes, "The limited nature of the special education curriculum makes reassignment to the regular class curriculum virtually impossible after a period of time" (p. 388).

It is important to note that in this detailed analysis there are many decision-making points where subjective judgments of teacher, principal, and psychologist can affect the labeling of the child.

WE HAVE FOUND THAT, AT EVERY STAGE IN THE LABELING PROCESS, A child of Spanish surname is exposed to a higher probability of going on to the next stage in the process than is an English-speaking Caucasian child or a Negro child. Those children most likely to complete the sequence are those who have many academic problems, who come from homes where little English is spoken, and who have difficulty communicating in English. The English-speaking Caucasian children who are most likely to escape the label after initial referral are those with mental health problems, with many interpersonal problems, and with poor social adjustments. Those with physical handicaps, neurological involvements, and poor speech facility complete the course. These factors did not differentiate labeled from nonlabeled children of Spanish surname. Negro children who were eventually placed in EMR classes tended to have significantly more interpersonal problems than did English-speaking Caucasian children who were placed (Mercer, 1970, p. 388). ■

The subjective element in EMR placement is further indicated by data from a desegregation study that Mercer reports in the same article. The Wechsler Intelligence Scale was administered to all Spanish-surname and black children in three segregated elementary schools, and to a random sample of English-speaking Caucasian children in the predominantly Caucasian schools in the same district. While 1.2 percent ($N = 6$) of the Caucasian children tested had IQs below 80, 15.3 percent ($N = 78$) Spanish-surname, and 12.4 percent ($N = 36$) black children had similar IQ scores. Nevertheless, all of these children were holding the status of "normal" children in the regular classroom. Furthermore, *there was no significant difference between the average IQ of these children who were holding a "normal" student status and children of the same ethnic group, in the same schools, who were in special education classes.*

What is evident in this account of Mercer and several other reports on her work (Mercer 1971, 1974) is that in California, in the late sixties, an IQ score equal to or less than 79 was a sine qua non for the diagnosis of mental retardation within the public school system. That is, one could not achieve the status of a mental retardate without obtaining such a score on an individually administered intelligence test such as the Wechsler Intelligence Scale for Children. What is equally evident is that such a low IQ score was not in itself indicative of mental retardation.

It is also clear in Mercer's reports that once the status of mental retardate is achieved within the public school system it is rarely lost, and from this Mercer concludes:

THE SOCIAL SYSTEM PERSPECTIVE HIGHLIGHTS THE EXTENT TO WHICH THE medical perspective in mild mental retardation may be implicated in creating and perpetuating the very condition it seeks to prevent. Once assigned the status of a mental retardate, an individual soon becomes socialized to play the role and to meet the lesser expectations of his retarded status. When being mildly retarded is viewed as a social process in which a person moves from one status to another, new approaches to prevention and intervention are revealed. There are many alternative labels and programs available. By what rationale should some children be placed in an EMR status in the public schools when . . . other children of equivalent intellectual attainment remain unstigmatized? (Mercer, 1970, p. 391). ■

One other development in the schools in the post-World War II period has to be recognized because it illustrates how strong the tendency is to segregate problem children, especially if you can label them so that they appear to be different and will require different understanding and treatment. We have been talking largely about mentally retarded pupils. In the pre-World War II period there were a few urban school systems where one could find a special class for behavior problem children or physically handicapped children or hard-of-seeing children. What was a very small trickle became, comparatively speaking, a flood in the post-World War II period. For example, in 1970 there were 728,000 mentally subnormal pupils in public elementary or secondary schools receiving special instruction either in special classes, which numbered 54,300 by ancillary instruction within the regular school program, or by independent instruction (Grant and Lind, 1976). Those figures would have been inconceivable to educators in the pre-World War II period. *But those figures have to be seen in relation to even more astounding figures and projections about all handicapped children regardless of the source of handicap.* Addressing himself to the need for teachers of the handicapped in all areas of exceptionality, Bruce Balow, as director of the division of training programs in the Bureau of Education for the Handicapped, noted:

MANPOWER NEED, BASED ON A RATIO OF APPROXIMATELY 20 HANDICAPPED pupils per teacher, is estimated currently at 370,000 qualified teachers to adequately serve the six million school-aged handicapped in the U.S. With some 125,000 teachers employed, of whom one-half are estimated to be not certified for such teaching, there is a current need for 245,000 teachers of school-age children plus another 60,000 to serve about one million preschool handicapped. Thus about 300,000 additional teachers of the handicapped would be needed immediately if the states were to fulfill the commitment of equal educational opportunity for the handicapped (Balow, 1971, p. 44). ■

What Balow was reflecting, and as director of a federal bureau was encouraging, was the fantastic increase in special classes that was occurring. Classes for the emotionally disturbed, for those with minimal brain damage, for dyslexics, for those with learning disabilities, for the perceptually impaired—the labels were many and varied (and by no means easy to define or to distinguish one from the other), and each label was a rallying cry for a new program and type of segregated class. It was hard to avoid the impression that each school system was dividing into two: the regular and the special, and in terms of size, costs, and influence, they were far more equal than ever before. It was also hard to avoid the impression—indeed, it was an argument advanced explicitly and forcefully—that the emphasis on and segregation of handicapping conditions, requiring as they would better diagnosis and educational treatment, would ultimately and indubitably benefit all children. Not only would the size of regular classes decrease (or at least not increase), but the regular class teacher would now be able to give far more than before to the "normal" pupils. Earlier I pointed out that in the pre-World War II period the regular and special educators agreed on one thing: there should be more special classes. That agreement became, so to speak, contractual, in the two-and-one-half decades after World War II, a period of gradually rising affluence that, together with increased state and federal expenditures, was able to support the variety of special classes the public and the educator were calling for.

How should we characterize the changes I have described in the several decades after World War II? Was minority representation in special classes a new development? Was the increase in the variety of special classes due largely to outside pressures to which school personnel had to accommodate? Was there a fundamental change in the relationship between regular and special class educators in the public schools as well as in schools of education? Did the quantitative changes reflect significant qualitative changes in the culture of the school and in school-community, school-parent relationships? The answer to all of these questions is *no*. All of the changes had long been sought by educators, and if these changes finally began to occur in the post-World War II period, it was due, first, to favorable economic conditions and, second, to the dawn of the Age of Mental Health, i.e., heightened consciousness throughout the society about the problems, fragility, and misery-producing features of modern living. The educators gained strong and prestigious allies in the mental health professions. Whatever changes occurred were congruent with longstanding features of the school culture. There was no "problem of change" in the sense that basic behavioral and programmatic regularities in the school culture had to be altered. There was relatively little conflict between outside and inside forces. And what could have been internal conflicts over resources between special and regular teachers and administrators were discernibly diluted by increased funding from state and federal sources.

How come, then, that within a few years Public Law 94-142 (Education For All Handicapped Childrens' Act) was enacted? Did opposition to "mainstreaming" melt away? Was there an unprecedented attitudinal and moral change in our society? Were welcome signs erected by schools and communities? What was going on in the society that in a short period of time would confront schools with a third revolution, only two decades after the Supreme Court had proclaimed the beginning of the second revolution: Was 94-142, like the 1954 decision, to be beset by a host of obstacles, deliberate and otherwise? Remember, there were some naive people who greeted the 1954 decision with a sigh of relief: thank God the moral cancer was spotted and could now be excised—maybe not tomorrow or next year, but certainly in a decade or so. We have learned otherwise. Deeply rooted attitudes, ingrained and reinforced by tradition and institutional and social structure and practice, are not changed except over a long period of time (Sarason, 1973). Why should the goals of 94-142 have a different fate? Have we learned nothing about *mandated* changes in thinking, attitudes, and institutional structure and practices? But let us examine more closely the factors that contributed to making mainstreaming an issue in public policy in an amazingly short time. I shall do this in terms of the field of mental retardation because it illustrates so well how diverse forces converged to present our schools with the mandate to change.

POLITICAL PRESSURE AND THE COURTS

The first set of facts represented a convergence of events and forces: the quick growth and power of a national parents' group; the Kennedy family's personal and political interest in mental retardation powered by the financial resources of the Kennedy Foundation; and exposés in the national media of degrading conditions in state institutions that made mental retardation a topic of public interest. But this change is not comprehensible unless one sees it in the context of an even more drastic social change accelerated by the Great Depression: the widespread acceptance of the idea of governmental responsibility for citizens rendered dependent or handicapped for reasons beyond their control (Sarason, 1976).

Before the thirties, it was not seen as the federal government's responsibility to intervene in matters of education and health. There were a few handicapping conditions such as blindness for which there were modest programs, but they were the exceptions and not to be considered forerunners of an increased federal role. The philosophy of "that government is best that governs least" made it extremely difficult to sustain national attention on issues in education and health. At best, they could receive attention in the states, but even the states were guided by the prevailing philosophy. It took a national economic calamity to start the process of philosophical change, and today our prepotent response to a social problem is to think in terms of federal policy and programs.

At the time mental retardation started to receive national attention and the pressures for a federal role began to mount, there were social forces, at first unrelated to policy issues about mental retardation, that later had the most influence on how these issues were to be transformed. We refer here to the civil rights movement, which came from the desire to eradicate racial discrimination but which soon spread far beyond these confines to include the rights of women, homosexuals, older people, members of the armed forces, and children. What were their constitutional rights? What constituted their equality before the law, and how had tradition and practice come to rob them of their basic constitutional rights as citizens? On what constitutional grounds can mental patients be confined in a state hospital? What are the legal restrictions to the use of psychological tests as a basis for job promotion? What legal procedures must be observed before a child can be suspended or expelled from school?

One could ask scores of similar questions, all testifying to a resurgence of attention to individual liberties and rights. Put in another way, the law and therefore the courts became agents of social change. The most pervasive changes have been through judicial decisions essentially reinterpreting or enlarging the scope of laws and existing constitutional language. And many of these decisions were not greeted with anything like unanimous approval, involving as they did radical changes in institutional thinking and practice. That is the point; although these court decisions were stimulated by "plaintiffs" seeking change, they were opposed by "defendents" who were by no means few in number if lacking in strength. To interpret a decision in favor of the plaintiff as a "victory" is understandable, but one should never underestimate how long it can take for the spirit of victory to become appropriately manifest in practice.

When mental retardation first became a topic of public discussion, moral-humane rather than legal-constitutional matters were in the forefront. Mentally retarded people "deserved" as much attention and programmatic support as other groups with disabling conditions. In fact, advocates for the mentally retarded wanted no more, and certainly no less, than "separate but equal facilities." No one was calling for elimination of state training schools or special classes. However, it did not take long before the rationale behind the historic 1954 Supreme Court desegregation decision began to influence the thinking of advocates for the mentally retarded.

Central in that rationale was the argument that segregation has pernicious effects both on the segregator and the segregatee. The 1954 decision marked the first time that the Supreme Court had ruled the findings of social science research admissible as evidence, and the weight of that evidence was that segregation had adverse effects on white and black children (Fellman, 1969). Generalizing from that rationale, it is not surprising that its judicial relevance to mentally retarded people began to be examined. As a consequence, the status of mentally retarded people became a focus of legal scholars.

Lawyers did not have to be sophisticated about mental retardation to see, study, and write about legal-constitutional issues long ignored by everyone. And once the forces behind the movement for more and better facilities started to go down the legal-constitutional road, their goals became more encompassing and radical in that they found themselves at a familiar root: segregating mentally retarded people in schools or elsewhere was demeaning to all involved. Blatt and Kaplan's (1966) *Christmas in Purgatory*—a pictorial essay of scandalous institutional conditions that was given such a big play in the mass media and placed in the hands of every United States Congressman—told only what happened to those who were segregated. In his subsequent books (*Exodus from Pandemonium,* 1970; *Souls in Extremis,* 1975; *The Revolt of the Idiots,* 1976), Blatt rounded out the picture by telling us what happens to the segregators.

The literature on the impact of court decisions on mentally retarded people in schools, institutions, the community, and work is vast. It is also staggering in complexity of details and the niceties of legal argument to those unfamiliar with constitutional law and the workings of the judiciary. But to someone interested in history and social change it is a fascinating literature. I recommend *The Mentally Retarded Citizen and the Law* (Kindred et al., 1976), which discusses the major court decisions as well as suggests the major problem areas whose legal-constitutional status has yet to be clarified. Another important and instructive book is *Right to Education* by Lippman and Goldberg (1973), describing the development and consequences of the landmark Pennsylvania court decision affirming the right of all handicapped children to an education. It is interesting that the authors, who participated in the litigation, saw the case as a variation of the 1954 Supreme Court desegregation decision.

I have given this very brief overview in order to make a point too easily overlooked: the change in societal attitude and social policy was spearheaded by a dedicated minority relying on political pressure and the courts. At every step of the way this minority encountered opposition, especially from those in schools, institutions, and state agencies who saw how drastic the proposed changes would be for them.[3] This opposition, of course, is quite understandable. After all, few people look with relish at the necessity of redefining their roles, activities, and values. Those who opposed the proposed changes were not evil or unintelligent people. Far from it. They were people engaged in public service, carrying out their tasks in ways that their professional training as well as longstanding custom said was right and effective. To be told that their values were wrong, that they had been contributing to evil, and that they would have to accommodate to new procedures and practices, it is no wonder that opposition did not dissolve. It may have had an opposite effect.

The pressures for mainstreaming did not come from within educational institutions and that fact alone allows one to predict that these pressures would be resisted. It is not a case of the "good guys and the bad guys." Personalizing the polarities in such ways overlooks how both sides are reflecting tradition, history, *and* a fast-changing society. Institutional custom and practice are effective bulwarks to forces for change, and this, we too easily forget, has both good and bad features. On the one hand, we do not want our institutions to change in response to every new fad or idea; on the other hand, we do not want them blindly to preserve the status quo. In regard to mainstreaming, how one regards the oppositional stance of our schools and university training centers will depend on how one feels about mainstreaming. If one is for mainstreaming, then one will tend to view opposition as another instance of stone-age attitudes. If one is against mainstreaming, one will tend to view it as another misguided effort that will further dilute the quality of education of everyone.

The important point is that opposition to mainstreaming was predictable. To proceed as if that would not be the case is to deny the obvious about institutional custom and practice, especially when they have always been congruent with societal values and attitudes. What happens when societal attitudes begin to change, at least among segments effectively organized to bring about change, and that change, like mainstreaming, is generally seen as related to many other matters involving basic constitutional issues? As we indicated earlier, the legal and human issues emerging from segregation practices in regard to mentally retarded individuals can only be understood in the

---

3. For a more detailed account of the growth and vicissitudes of special education in the public schools, see Sarason and Doris (1979) *Educational Handicap, Public Policy, and Social History. A Broadened Perspective On Mental Retardation.*

context of an upswell of protest against discriminating practices in regard to many other groups.

What frequently happens is that legislation is passed and public sentiments are translated into public policies having the force of law. From that point on, institutional opposition must conform to the law's intent and requirements or suffer sanctions. This, of course, does not mean that by virtue of the law, longstanding attitudes and practices have been dissolved and reconstituted to willingly accept its new thrust. One has to expect that ways will be sought to circumvent the new intent or to implement it minimally. This has been true in the case of discrimination against any minority. Passing laws is far easier than getting them implemented consistent with both their spirit and their letter. This says less about human capacity to be socially perverse than it does about the strength of institutionalized custom and practice. We are not dealing with opposition based on "personality," but on institutional custom, organization, and values.

Before taking up some of the consequences, intended and unintended, of 94-142 for the culture of the school, a summary of the federal law is presented:

State Plan

To be eligible for money under EHA-B, a state must develop policies and procedures in a "state plan" to insure that the requirements of the law are carried out in every school district in the state (whether or not that school district actually receives EHA-B money). State plans must be available to the public for comment and then submitted for approval to the Federal Bureau of Education for the Handicapped (BEH) in the U.S. Office of Education. The state plan must demonstrate that the state has established and will enforce the following:

1. *Full Services Goal*—a goal of providing all handicapped children with "full educational opportunities"; at least 50 percent of the EHA-B funds must be given to children who are receiving *no* education at all (i.e., are not in school) and children who are severely handicapped. The plan must provide a timetable showing how services, personnel, equipment and other resources will be developed and assigned in order to reach "full services."
2. *Due Process Safeguards*—policies and procedures describing due process safeguards which parents/children can use to challenge decisions of state and local officials about how a child has been identified, evaluated or placed in a special education program. These safeguards must include:

   a. prior notice before a child is evaluated or placed in a special program;

   b. access to relevant school records;

   c. an opportunity to obtain an independent evaluation of the child's special needs;

   d. an impartial due process hearing to challenge any of the decisions described above; and

   e. the designation of a "surrogate parent" to use these safeguards for each child who is a ward of the state or whose parent or guardian is unknown or unavailable.

3. *Least Restrictive Alternative—local and state procedures to assure that handicapped children are educated with non-handicapped children to the extent possible. Separate schools, special classes or other removal of any handicapped child from the regular program are only allowed if and when the school district can show that the use of a regular educational environment accompanied by supplementary aids and services is not adequate to give the child what he/she needs* (emphasis in original).

4. *Non-Discriminatory Testing and Evaluation—*procedures showing that tests and other materials or methods used to evaluate a child's special needs are neither racially nor culturally discriminatory. The procedures should also assure that whatever materials or methods are used, they are not administered to a child in a discriminatory manner.

5. *Confidentiality of Information about Handicapped Children—*procedures to guarantee that information gathered about a child in the process of identifying and evaluating children who may have special educational needs, is kept confidential. State procedures must conform to regulations, issued in the February 27, 1976 Federal Register by the Commissioner of Education, which include requirements that parents must be given the opportunity to see relevant school records before any hearing is held on a matter of identification, evaluation or placement of a special needs child. These regulations also apply to the requirements for confidentiality of information under the Education for All Handicapped Children Act.

1. *Full Service Goal—*"free appropriate public education" must be available to all handicapped children ages 3-18 by September 1, 1978 and to all handicapped children 3-21 by September 1, 1980 unless, with regard to 3-5-year-olds and 18-21-year-olds, "inconsistent" with state law. States must place a priority in the use of their funds under this Act on two groups of children: 1) handicapped children who are *not* receiving an education, and 2) han-

dicapped children with the most severe handicaps, within each disability, who are receiving an inadequate education.

2. *Due Process Safeguards*—as of October 1, 1977 the policies and procedures describing due process safeguards available to parents and children in any matter concerning a child's identification, evaluation or placement in an educational program must include:
   a. prior notice to parents of any change in their child's program and written explanation in their primary language, of the procedures to be followed in effecting that change;
   b. access to relevant school records;
   c. an opportunity to obtain an independent evaluation of the child's special needs;
   d. opportunity for an impartial due process hearing which must be conducted by the SEA or local or intermediate school district, but in no case by an employee "involved in the education or care of the child." In any hearing, parents have the right to be accompanied by a lawyer or any individual with special knowledge of the problems of special needs children, the right to present evidence, to confront, compel and cross-examine witnesses, and to obtain a transcript of the hearing and a written decision by the hearing officer. Parents have the right to appeal the hearing decision to the SEA and, if they are still dissatisfied the SEA ruling in federal or state court;
   e. the right of a child to remain in his/her current placement (or, if trying to gain initial admission to school, in the regular school program) until the due process proceedings are completed; and
   f. the designation of a "surrogate parent" to use the procedures outlined above on behalf of children who are wards of the state or whose parents or guardians are unknown or unavailable.
3. *Least Restrictive Alternative*—handicapped children including children in public and private institutions, must be educated as much as possible with children who are not handicapped.
4. *Non-Discriminatory Testing and Evaluation*—the tests and procedures used to evaluate a child's special needs must be racially and culturally non-discriminatory in both the way they are selected and the way they are administered, must be in the primary language or mode of communication of the child, and no one test or procedure can be used as the sole determinant of a child's educational program.
5. *Individualized Educational Plans*—written individualized educational plans for each child evaluated as handicapped must be developed and annually reviewed by a child's parents, teacher, and

a designee of the school district. The plan must include statements of the child's present levels of educational performance, short and long-term goals for the child's performance, the specific criteria to measure the child's progress. Each school district must maintain records of the individualized education plan for each child.

6. *Personnel Development*—comprehensive system to develop and train both general and special education teachers and administrative personnel to carry out requirements of this law must be developed by the state, and each local school district must show how it will use and put into effect the system of personnel development.

7. *Participation of Children in Private Schools*—free special education and related services must be provided for handicapped children in private elementary and secondary schools if the children are placed or referred to private schools by the SEA or local school districts to fulfill the requirements of this law. The SEA must assure that private schools which provide programs for handicapped children meet the standards which apply to state and local public schools, and that handicapped children served by private schools are accorded all the same rights they would have if served in public schools (pp. 363-365).[4] ■

Public Law 94-142, like any major piece of legislation contains ambiguities, compromises, expectations, and history. This federal law is very complex, containing many provisions for priorities, time schedules, funding levels, diagnostic and testing practices, advocacy for children, parental role, etc. In late 1976, the *federal* regulations, spelling out in detail the criteria by which the law would be administered, were published. Those regulations determine the confines and substance of required *state* plans and regulations which, in turn, determine the plans and regulations required of *local* districts. Congress passed a law, the executive interprets and administers it, and so on down the line. At every step of the way one is dealing with interpretations of interpretations.

We are still too close to the implementation of 94-142 to state with assurance what its consequences will be. However, precisely because of the scope of the intended consequences of the legislation, and given our interest in the school culture and the problem of change, we should not avoid attempting to discern the outlines of the changes that seem to be occurring.

---

4. Adapted from "Your Rights under the Education for All Handicapped Children Act" (Washington, D.C.: Children's Defense Fund, 1976).

SOME CONSEQUENCES

Although 94-142 is known as the "mainstreaming law," the word *mainstreaming* never appears in the legislation. That, I am assured by several people who helped write the legislation, was not happenstance. That is to say, the proponents of the legislation understood well that the schools were not prepared for mainstreaming, if by that term was meant the integration of handicapped children into the traditional classroom, thus drastically reducing (if not eliminating) special classes. If one examines the ways in which the concept of "least restrictive alternative" is incorporated in the law, it becomes clear that when a school district can show that the use of a regular educational environment accompanied by supplementary aids and services is not adequate to give the child what he or she needs, educational segregation is permissible. As I said in earlier pages, to the extent that the law recognizes and implicitly criticizes the limited number of alternatives schools have offered handicapped children, to that extent the law should result in significantly more alternatives *and* in a significant decrease in the number of special classes and/or children in these classes. But given the way the concept of least restrictive alternative is described in the legislation, plus the longstanding tradition in schools to segregate handicapped children, one would not expect these predictions to hold up. It would be a rejection of every theory of individual and institutional behavior, if school districts did not seek ways to continue what they regard as right and proper. *What the law intended, and my experience bears out, is that the number of segregated individuals should be reduced somewhat. If anything, however, there has been an increase in the number of special programs housed outside of the regular classroom.* In short, it appears as if the concept of the least restrictive alternative is being interpreted in ways that "protect" the regular classroom from the spirit of mainstreaming; i.e., to maintain as much of the *status quo* as possible.

What I have just described has to be seen in relation to another consequence of the legislation: the requirement that there must be a placement team comprised of different educational specialists whose main functions are to evaluate each handicapped child, to develop an individual educational plan, and to involve the parents in planning and decision making. The idea of an integrated, clinically oriented team has not been part of the school culture. In fact, when I first started to work in schools I was struck by the absence of the case conference. Coming as I did from a background in clinical psychology, it seemed strange that teachers and other school personnel never got together to present problems to each other, to learn from and about other educator's thinking and practices. I am reminded here of Murray Levine's recommendation for any clinical facility: it should have two staffs, one to go to case conferences and the other to do the work.

In schools, each educational specialist, as well as each teacher, worked primarily alone. What 94–142 mandated was that in regard to handicapped children those specialists would function as a team. In some schools the placement team has not only developed smoothly, but has dramatically lowered the feeling of aloneness so many of these people had previously experienced. In most instances, however, the placement team has been riddled by conflicts over status, competition, and power. You can mandate "team work," but unless the culture of the setting contains ingredients favorable to such functioning, it is most unlikely to become manifest. But the most thorny consequence of 94–142 derives from the fact that placement teams have come under increasing pressures to define least restrictive alternative and mainstreaming in terms of the local district's policies, which in practice boils down to the containment of financial expenditures. Some members of placement teams see their primary responsibility to be to the handicapped child, consistent with the law's intent to avoid, whenever possible, segregated experiences. But that view of responsibility, however consistent with the spirit of the legislation, is frequently not appreciated by administrators and boards of education struggling with increasing opposition to escalating budgets.

I know of many instances where professionals participating in the formulation of a child's individual educational program have not made recommendations because they would conflict with district policies. And I know of other instances where the placement team has never been able to function smoothly because of internal disagreements about "who is the client?" Is the placement team to serve handicapped children and their families or the wishes and policies of the local district? At the very least, any attempt to evaluate 94–142 has to confront how the dilemmas of and the pressures on placement teams should temper the seriousness with which one accepts and interprets data on the numbers of handicapped children in segregated and nonsegregated classes. The data may be facts, but like so many facts they can obscure the truth. As best as I can determine, the number of handicapped children in nonsegregated classes is far less than would be the case if placement teams did not feel under pressure to conform to local district policies. P.L. 94–142 was very much influenced by a Massachusetts law (Chapter 766) passed in 1972. Weatherly and Lipsky (1977) evaluated the consequences of Chapter 766 and there are marked similarities between what they found and I have observed in relation to the federal legislation. What deserves special emphasis is their finding that the requirements of Chapter 766 so increased the time pressures on school personnel as to reduce significantly the attention any one child could receive.

The article by Weatherly and Lipsky merits close study for at least several reasons. First, it was a study informed by a sophisticated understanding of schools. Second, the authors obviously sought to be fair; i.e., they were not out to do a hatchet job. Third, although they were partisans for mainstreaming, they make understandable the moral and organizational dilemmas that mainstreaming poses for schools. Fourth, "the case of special education in

Massachusetts provides a sober lesson in how difficult it is to integrate special services for a stigmatized population, particularly when that population is attended by professional specialists, funded through separate channels, championed by people fearful that they will lose hard-won access to decision making, and perceived to cause work-related problems for those responsible for managing the integration. In such a situation the role of law in legitimizing new conceptions of the public order and in mobilizing resources should not be overlooked."

Just as the omission of the word *mainstreaming* from 94–142 was not accidental, the inclusion of sections on the rights of parents and children was not token or casual. Indeed, one of the writers of that legislation said: "the guts of the legislation was in *due process*. We wanted to guarantee that parents would have explicit rights and roles, that they would no longer be pushed around by school personnel who looked on handicapped children as second or third class citizens, that parents would be in on all decisions and could take advantage of an appeal process." In my opinion, the hostility reflected in this remark accurately reflects that of many community groups toward school personnel, a hostility the depths and sources of which school personnel had been insensitive to. In earlier chapters I raised the question "who owns the schools?" and I indicated how, legalisms to the contrary notwithstanding, school personnel acted as if the schools belonged to them. No groups in the community resented this stance more than did those who advocated for handicapped children. Whether it was a refusal to admit a child to school, or grudging provision for a part-time program, or justifying an inferior program on a "take it or leave it basis," the parents of handicapped children were not disposed to appreciate the school's inability or unwillingness to regard their children as no less worthy than nonhandicapped children.

P.L. 94–142 was essentially one way of answering the question: Who owns the schools? It was an answer that said that parents of handicapped children would now have the power to participate in and influence educational policy and resource allocation in regard to their children. I have attempted to obtain data on the frequency with which parents are involved in decision making and with which parents utilize the appeal process when they disagree with a decision about their child. In regard to involvement there is the "fact vs. truth" problem: some informants report that parents are very much involved, most informants report that the letter of involvement is honored far more than the spirit of it, and the great majority of informants agreed that it is extraordinarily difficult for most parents to assert themselves at a meeting with a group of educational specialists who, if they do not intend to be intimidating, nevertheless create such feelings in parents. In regard to the use of the appeal process, the data are hard to come by, but my impression is that in several middle eastern states the frequency is not miniscule.

In the year before 94–142 was to go into effect I had occasion to meet with administrators from various school systems around the country. By and large, these administrators seemed favorable to 94–142. That is to say, morally they realized that handicapped children could and should not be denied whatever education they could absorb. Indeed, a number of these administrators reported with pride about the rapid increase in special programs they had supported. Other administrators were already experiencing the economic pinch as well as the decrease in the school population, and they looked forward to 94–142 as one way of avoiding layoffs and school closings. Every administrator was going on the assumption that 94–142 would bring new monies into his or her system, and would not require any substantial outlays of local funds; i.e., as one administrator said a year later, "I never realized that we would be in a rob Peter to pay Paul situation." Despite the fact that past experience with federal funding had proved otherwise, these administrators truly believed that the level of funding implicit and explicit in the legislation would never be lowered. As the time for actual implementation of 94–142 approached and it became obvious that the requirements of the legislation would cost school systems far more than they would be getting from the federal government, attitudes toward 94–142 began to change. And when it later became clear that the level of federal funding would be less than expected or promised, the moral stance for the legislation began to show cracks. So, for example, the mayor of New York acknowledged the fact that when he was a member of Congress he was a vociferous supporter of 94–142, unaware then, as he was keenly aware now, that the legislation would require outlays of local monies far in excess of federal funding. If he had to do it over again, he said, he would vote against the legislation unless federal funding for all new costs was explicitly guaranteed. (For fiscal year 1981–1982 for the Board of Education in New York, expenditures for the Division of Special Education were projected to be $370 million dollars, $74 million more than in the previous year.) Mayor Koch was saying out loud what many educators, elected officials, and educators were saying privately.

One must keep separate two issues: the economic and the moral. That 94–142 puts an additional financial burden on communities goes without saying, a burden made more onerous by virtue of an economic recession. But what must not be obscured is that the economic issue was not created by 94–142, but by the recognition of a longstanding moral problem; i.e., the failure of schools and the society at large to view handicapped children as no less worthy than other children—more concretely, the practice either of denying some handicapped children access to the schools or segregating them from the "mainstream." To recognize the moral problem but to have its resolution depend solely on economic considerations is tantamount to reinforcing the implicit assumption that schools are primarily for nonhandicapped children. To indict the federal government without at the same time indicting the value and practices that made schools so unhospitable to handicapped children is to reveal two features of the school culture: how it is organized to serve some children far better than others, and how strong are the obstacles to efforts at change.

We are too close to the beginning phases of 94–142 to say with any assurance how it will affect, if it will affect at all, the basic regularities of the school culture. Currently there are scores of studies being done to evaluate the consequences of the legislation.[5] Public Law 94–142 was intended to bring about significant changes, but, as is always the case, legislation always has intended and unintended consequences.

I have already indicated that 94–142 does not contain the word *mainstreaming* and that, unlike the 1954 desegregation decision, it does not "outlaw" segregated programs and sites. In rendering its 1954 decision, the Supreme Court ruled that desegregation should be carried out with "deliberate speed," a phrase that recognized that desegregation would take time but that it would *have* to take place. Public Law 94–142 does not give such legal force to mainstreaming, and yet many people have regarded the legislation as giving mainstreaming the force of law. If such force was not intended, it nevertheless has put mainstreaming on the social agenda. Precisely because among legal scholars (stimulated as they are by groups advocating for handicapped people) the concept of mainstreaming is increasingly seen as a derivative of the 1954 desegregation decision, one should not be surprised if the omission of mainstreaming from 94–142 gets challenged in the courts. That is to say, to the extent that 94–142 increases the number of segregated programs, or does not significantly and meaningfully put handicapped children into the regular classroom, or results in a "backlash" against the spirit of the legislation, or creates new friction between parents and schools, one should expect that the issues will be joined and fought in the courts. And if that happens, as I think is likely, then what we mean by mainstreaming will be decided more in terms of legal theory and precedent and less in terms of educational theory, practice, or economics. If anything has been clear in the post-World War II era it has been the impact on schools of judicial decisions. Someone has said that we have become a litigious society: resorting to the

---

5. I am well acquainted with one ongoing study, that by Professor Robert Bogdan of Syracuse University. I am indebted to him for allowing me to read the comprehensive ethnographic reports about schools considered to be successfully carrying out the intent of 94–142. These reports strongly support several conclusions. First, "mainstreaming" means different things in different schools. Second, and very relevant to discussion in earlier chapters, the most successful schools are those whose principals solidly backed the law's intent. Third, and again relevant to earlier discussion, success is a function of the teachers responsible for overseeing the program for handicapped pupils. Indeed, it is these outstanding teachers who are seen by regular teachers as *the* major factors in the amount and equality of integration that takes place. These teachers seem to possess the characteristics of Jackson's outstanding teachers, but in addition seem to have and act on an acute sense of the culture of their schools. Bogdan's ethnographic reports are most revealing documents about the culture of schools, perhaps because they are written about a part of the school heretofore ignored.

courts as a way of dealing with legislative inaction and insensitive, traditional institutions, in the process burdening the courts with issues that are best handled through other means. Precisely because the courts have tended to support handicapped people in their role as plaintiffs and have ruled against schools in their role as defendants, we should expect that the courts will be asked to play no less a role in the future than they have in the past. And in that future, the meaning and legal status of mainstreaming will get clarified, with consequences that are not foreseeable now.

We come now to a major deficiency of 94–142. We have already said that the law can be construed as criticism of what our schools have been. Handicapped and nonhandicapped students are human beings, not different species, and their basic makeup in no way justifies educational practices that assume that the needs they have for social intercourse, personal growth and expression, and a sense of mastery are so different that one must apply different theories of human behavior to the two groups. If we respond to the handicapped as if basically different, we rob them and us of the experience of similarity and communality. We can no longer allow schools to segregate children and educational personnel, based on conceptions that are invalid and morally flawed. That is the message that Public Law 94–142 implies.

But where did school personnel learn such conceptions? There are two answers, one general and one specific. The general answer is that they learned those conceptions, and justified them morally, by growing up in a society in which these conceptions and moral precepts were seen as valid, right, and proper. In short, they learned them in the same ways everybody else learned them.

The specific answer is that school personnel are graduates of our colleges and universities. It is there that they learn there are at least two types of human beings and if you choose to work with one of them you render yourself *legally* and conceptually incompetent to work with the others. As we pointed out earlier in this chapter, what we see in our public schools is a mirror image of what exists in colleges and universities. *One of the clearest implications of Public Law 94–142 is that the gulf between the special and regular education has to be bridged, and yet the law requires no change in our college and university training centers.* We therefore have the situation in which the law mandates changes in our schools. School personnel must change in attitude, thinking, and practice, at the same time our training centers educate school personnel in the traditions of the "most restrictive alternative."

At its root, mainstreaming is a moral issue. It raises age-old questions: How do we want to live with each other? On what basis should we give priority to one value over another? How far does the majority want to go in accommodating the needs of the minority? The emergence of mainstreaming as an issue raises but does not directly confront these questions. To the extent that we put discussion of mainstreaming in the content of education and schools, we are likely to find ourselves mired in controversies centering around law, procedures, administration, and funding. These are legitimate controversies because they deal with practical, day-to-day matters that affect the lives of everyone. But the level of difficulty we encounter in dealing with these matters will ultimately be determined by the clarity with which the moral issue is formulated. At the very least it should make us more aware of two things: so-called practical matters or problems are always reflections of moral issues, and differences in moral stance have very practical consequences.

Any effort to introduce and sustain an educational change is based on assumptions about what schools are or should be. Public Law 94-142 is as clear an example of this as one will find. In the next chapter I take up the question: What are schools for—in the context of 94-142? Although the next chapter was written for a book on mental retardation, the thrust of the argument and the examples used are no less applicable to handicapped children generally. As we shall see, mainstreaming (whether to the limited extent permitted by 94-142 or to a fantasied "extreme" where all special classes would be eliminated) brings to the surface the extent to which the school culture is based on a "production ethic," a point I stressed in an early chapter when we were discussing the time pressures under which teachers perform.

Chapter 13

What Are Schools For?[1]

Although this chapter was stimulated by a discussion of 94–142, it addresses a question that talks to the entire public education enterprise. It is a question that before 1954 was discussed on the level of rhetoric on those occasions of ritual when people saw fit to extol the existence of public education as the gateway to the good life and good citizenship. If the question "What are schools for?" was answered differently in rhetoric than in practice, it said less about the difficulty of an answer than it did about how well we all have been socialized to accept schools pretty much as they are. One of the major significances of 94–142 is that it forced, as did the 1954 desegregation decision, a question to be asked with a sharpness of focus ordinarily not associated with it, "How shall we live together?" That question, too, of course, had to be asked about where we lived and worked. "What are schools for?" and "How shall we live together?" were obviously related. It says a good deal about the culture of the school and about centers for training educators that these questions are given amazingly little serious thought until developments outside of the school intrude to force the questions to the fore, albeit in a global and temporary way. P.L. 94–142 raised these questions in a very concrete way; i.e., who should be in a regular classroom and what purposes should that classroom serve? If these questions were raised concretely, they were answered concretely but

---

1. This chapter is taken from S. B. Sarason and J. Doris *Educational Handicap, Public Policy, and Social History. A Broadened Perspective on Mental Retardation.* (New York: Free Press, (Macmillan), 1979) and reprinted with their permission. Very minor additions and deletions have been made.

in terms of the way schools are, not in terms of the universe of alternatives
of what they might be. It is my belief that no less illuminating of the school
culture than the way things are is the degree to which people are aware of,
and the rationale they employ to reject, alternatives to the way things are.
What it illuminates, in the present instance, is the myth of "homogeneity,"
the relationship of the school culture and the production ethic, and,
ultimately the most fateful, the self-defeating ways in which resources are
defined.

Few things are as highly valued as "smartness"; to be called a genius is
high praise. As a society, however, we do not value high intelligence as such
unless it leads to socially approved achievement. If we know someone of
high intelligence who contents himself with a lowly job, we consider it a
tragedy because he is not "using" his intellectual gifts. When we say that a
person "should make something of himself," we mean that he should use
his mind to achieve goals on which *we* put our stamp of approval. If a person decides to make something of himself through a life of crime, we consider that a tragedy. What we look for is productive, socially valued
achievements. It is hard to overestimate the importance we place on
achievement, and the psychologically debilitating consequences the lack of
such achievement so frequently has in the lives of people. The sense of un-
worthiness people may have because of their lack of achievement reflects
how well society inculcates in us its importance.

In the abstract, we are sympathetic to people who are unable to
achieve because of conditions beyond their control. They did not ask to be
dependent and nonproductive. But our sympathy has limits and one of
them is reached when caring for the dependent person interferes with the
productive goals of other people. At that point, we tend to segregate the
dependent person. The justification is usually phrased in terms of his best
interests, downplaying the fact that a decision was made on moral grounds:
the productive achievements of the many should not be interfered with
because some people require special attention. That is to say, the interests
of those who lead "productive" lives justify segregating those who are
"unproductive."

Nowhere has this been taken as seriously as in our schools. There have
always been some dissenters who have pointed out that there were other
values no less important than ability that should be heeded in deciding who
shall live in what ways with whom. The longstanding controversy about
homogeneous versus heterogeneous classes in schools is a case in point.
Those who favored homogeneous classes put forth three arguments. First,
heterogeneous classes penalized students who could learn at a faster rate
than less capable students. Second, the less capable students were at an unfair competitive disadvantage and could not get the kind of attention they

needed. Third, heterogeneous classes were a major source of frustration to teachers who were put in the moral dilemma of deciding who should get the inevitably limited time and attention. There was really a fourth argument: the needs of our society required capable citizens, especially highly capable ones, and it would be socially self-defeating to dilute their education in any way. The minority who argued for heterogeneous classes presented these arguments: the importance of pupils to learn to live amicably and democratically with different kinds of people; the dangers of producing an elite group isolated from other people; and the injustice that would be done to pupils who would be misplaced in lower "tracks" but who might have flourished if stimulated by more able students.

The controversy about homogeneous versus heterogeneous classes was about "normal" children. A similar controversy, far less frequent and heated in its eruptions because it took place outside of "regular" education, concerned the efficacy of special classes for "high functioning" mentally retarded children. Did children placed in these classrooms perform better than comparable children in regular classrooms? Although the preponderance of studies failed to establish advantages of the special class, they had no effect on school practice. Neither controversy could change the belief in and practice of tracking and segregation. It would have been strange if they had, because educational beliefs and practices reflect dominant features in the larger society. We like to think that schools are "outside" of society, somehow untouched by the harsh realities of the "real world," a kind of protected retreat in which the child can learn and grow so that when leaving school, his or her individuality will not be overwhelmed by the harsh realities of living and working. However, many people who hold such beliefs do not find it inconsistent to act on another belief: it is a major function of the schools to determine the capabilities of students and to so organize the schools that children of different capabilities do not interfere with each other's educational growth. In other words, *the perceived limits of capabilities are the major criterion for determining with whom they live in schools. At its root, this rests on production-achievement as the major criterion for judging people.* This went virtually unchallenged until the 1954 desegregation decision; and the passage of Public Law 94–142 joins the issue even more clearly because it has to be confronted independent of race. Mainstreaming puts back on the discussion table the question of how we want to live together. What are schools for? How shall we judge them? If we want to judge them differently than in the past, if we want them to change, where are the major obstacles and what constitutes a realistic time perspective for overcoming them? In the remainder of this chapter we will examine some of these obstacles.

If one examines the products coming off the assembly line, it is virtually impossible to discern differences among them. By definition and intent an assembly line produces products that are homogeneous in appearance, content, and function. Obviously, when we talk of homogeneous classrooms we do not mean homogeneous in the assembly line sense. Take the situation where a sixth grade classroom consists of children all of whom have an IQ of 160. One does not have to see the children, only the tests, to know that it is most unlikely that any two of the children got their scores by passing or failing exactly the same test items. The fact that they have identical test scores says more about the test than it does about the children. Indeed, if one gave them a different intelligence test, it would be most unlikely that they would end up with similar test scores.

Now, if we were to sit for a few days in the classroom, the word *homogeneous* in anything like its literal sense would not easily come to mind. In fact, in regard to some of these children we might find ourselves wondering where their "IQ of 160" was because they would not match our picture of brightness in action. But we really do not have to sit in the classroom; we only have to interview the teacher. In what ways, we would ask her, are the children homogeneous? We would likely be greeted with staring disbelief. John is lazy, Andy is imaginative, Harold is hostile, Robert does not do his homework, Ruth is manipulative, Richard is really not bright at all, Susan is bright but doesn't believe it, Allan is a predelinquent, Cathy and Herbert are delightful, and so on. From the standpoint of the teacher, the students may be homogeneous according to a psychological test but in the classroom she sees a bewildering array of educational, intellectual, intrapersonal, and interpersonal styles.

It is a cliche to say that each human being is unique. No proponent of homogeneous classrooms would argue that individual differences do not exist. What they do argue is that these classrooms reduce the range of these differences. To our knowledge no one had demonstrated that the *range* is discernibly lessened. That is to say, from the standpoint of the teacher, the range of differences is always great and troublesome. What the teacher has to deal with is not IQs but "whole" people, the "parts" of whom are embedded in that whole in dramatically different ways. So in the case of two students with IQs of 160, the teacher may have no doubt that one is "dumb" and the other is "smart." The writers of this book have decades of experience working with graduate students: high test-scoring people with superb undergraduate records, and with glowing letters of recommendation from their undergraduate teachers, so that they are "homogeneous" on more than test scores. Given the competition to get into graduate school, those who are finally accepted have as good paper credentials as one could desire. And yet, within weeks after beginning graduate school, the faculty is reminded that despite its screening procedures the entering class is fantastically varied in personal style, creativity, curiosity, work efficiency, and any other characteristic the faculty considers predictive of future achievement.

If homogeneity in the classroom is a myth at variance with the realities of these classrooms, what sustains the myth? The answer is in the belief that intellectual excellence, predictive of future socially valued productivity, should be accorded top priority by society. Society needs many kinds of individuals and among them it needs the intellectually superior individual the most—this is the value on which the argument rests. What is wrong with such a view? There is nothing wrong with such a view as long as one recognizes and articulates that some people will be more valued by society than others, that the farther away an individual is from the top of the intelligence scale the less society needs him or her. There is nothing inherently wrong in stating that our society should treasure one value more than others and, therefore, that it needs some people more than others. Does society need a seriously retarded child as much as it needs a budding "genius"? How can you justify putting them into the same classroom? How can society justify penalizing the more intelligent person by robbing him of the kinds of stimulation and ambience appropriate to his potential? How can society justify any waste of talent? It is, the argument continues, a sad fact of life that individuals differ in how much they have to contribute to society and to deny that fact, to organize our schools as if that were not true, is a form of societal suicide. It is not an argument for the survival of the "fittest"; it is not intended to deny the needs and rights of others, but rather a clear assertion that some people are valued more than others.

For some, the argument presents no problem; it has a self-evident plausibility. For others, the argument creates unease because it smacks of an elitism to which they are opposed. To handle this dilemma they would say: Schools have two major functions: one is to foster the academic-intellectual growth of children, and the other is to inculcate in them those values appropriate to life in a democracy. If the inculcation of these values is done well, we have nothing to fear from homogeneous classrooms. There is no conflict between ability groupings and learning the values of a democratic society. This argument, however, leads to an issue that far transcends ability groupings in importance. What are schools for? How should we evaluate how they meet their purposes?

THE GOALS OF EDUCATION

The dilemma of homogeneous classes is resolved by saying that schools have two major purposes. In effect, what is said is that values underlying the argument for homogeneous classrooms should not be given priority over the values of democratic living. The values are coequal. However, there is every reason to conclude that coequality has been taken seriously only on the level of rhetoric. For example, although schools have been criticized over the decades for many things, no criticism comes close in frequency or heat to that about the schools' failure to educate students properly in academic skills and content.

When Russia was the first country to orbit a satellite in 1956, there was an uproar in the United States as a reaction to this wound to national pride. A ready explanation was at hand: our tradition-bound schools were doing a poor job, and a thoroughgoing revamping of the academic curriculum was in order. The criticism directed at the schools also spoke to the stifling atmosphere in schools, but the importance of that lay primarily in its consequences for academic learning.

A more current example concerns why so many children cannot learn to read. There is no point in multiplying examples. From society's standpoint, schools are expected to give top priority to the educational-intellectual development of children in order for them to "take their places" in society. That value has no coequal. We are reminded of a story, related by Dr. Edward Zigler, one of the early formulators of the Head Start program and the first director of the Office of Child Development. One of the items in his budget was for meals for Head Start children. Early on, he learned that when he went before a congressional committee to justify his program and budget, he could not say that Head Start children should be fed because they may be hungry. He had to say that if these children were fed they would be better learners! It is not very much of an exaggeration to say that any proposal about formal schooling has to be justified in terms of its contribution to the intellectual-academic development of children.

One can look at the issue from the standpoint of educational research. A modest sampling of books, journals, and technical reports would quickly show that the bulk of educational researchers devote themselves to evaluating the effects of all sorts of things on cognitive skills and academic performance, or the relationship of personality and social class with academic progress. Relatively speaking, there has been very little research on the effects of formal schooling on children's absorption of democratic values and modes of adapting to group living. The studies spearheaded by Lewin and his colleagues (Lewin, 1948; Lewin, Lippitt, and White, 1939; Lippitt, 1939; Lippitt, 1940) almost forty years ago in experimentally created social climates (democratic, autocratic, laissez-faire) had little impact on the direction and methodology of educational research. There is no evidence at all that it had any impact on school personnel.

During the turmoil of the turbulent sixties, when the controversies in the larger society were also manifest in our schools, the whole issue of the quality of group-classroom living came to the fore, and the group dynamics movement, growing in splinter-fashion and holding out promise of being a panacea for the problems of individual and group living, had several origins and one of the most important was the early work by Lewin and his colleagues on social climates in schools. It is both ironic and saddening that the frantic and unsuccessful attempts in the sixties to change the quality of group living in schools were a consequence of massive social unrest, not a reflection of values and traditions indigenous to schools.

Similarly, it should be noted that this work by Lewin and his colleagues was in the most direct way a reaction to the world-wide forces of fascism and the approaching Second World War. It was not by chance, of course, that Lewin, a refugee from Nazi Germany, riveted on the responsibility of schools for inculcation in children of the values of group living in a democratic society. As Gordon Allport (1948) noted:

THERE IS A STRIKING KINSHIP BETWEEN THE WORK OF KURT LEWIN AND the work of John Dewey. Both agree that democracy must be learned anew in each generation, and that it is a far more difficult form of social structure to obtain and to maintain than is autocracy. Both see the intimate dependence of democracy upon social science. Without knowledge of, and obedience to the laws of human nature in group settings, democracy cannot succeed. And without freedom for research and theory as provided only in a democratic environment social science will surely fail. Dewey, we might say, is the outstanding philosophical exponent. More clearly than anyone else has he shown us in concrete, operational terms what it means to be a democratic leader, and to create a democratic group structure (p. xi). ■

Unfortunately, neither Dewey nor Lewin have had an influence on the quality of formal schooling. Each is a highly respected and quoted person but that should not be confused with having an impact on classroom organization and practice. We would not agree with Allport that Dewey was only the chief philosophical exponent of democracy; he was also an educator who took his philosophy seriously and put it into practice. Like Lewin later, Dewey understood that theory without practice could be an arid and dangerous affair. In 1896, at the University of Chicago, Dewey put his ideas to the test by starting his own school. How little we have traveled since that time can be seen by comparing the detailed description of his school (Mayhew and Edwards, 1966) with that of a school today.

Jencks's book *Inequality: A Reassessment of the Effect of Family and Schooling in America* (1972) is relevant here and not because of his conclusion, based on a literature review, that far more important in its effects than formal schooling on inequalities in cognitive-academic development of children are their families: the influence of family on what a child is like when he or she begins schools, what the child brings, so to speak, to school. Even if one believes that Jencks and his colleagues are not fully justified in such a conclusion, there is no room at all for complacency about how well schooling has intended cognitive benefits for children.

More directly relevant for our purposes is Jencks's assessment of the effects of schooling on noncognitive traits.

COGNITIVE SKILLS ARE NOT THE ONLY OUTCOME OF SCHOOLING. EDUCATORS claim schools teach virtues ranging from patriotism and punctuality to curiosity and creativity. Critics claim that schools teach an equally wide range of vices, ranging from competition and conformity to passivity and authoritarianism. None of these traits is well measured by cognitive tests.

We would like to be able to give the factors influencing each of these traits as much attention as we give cognitive skills, but we do not know enough to do this. We do not even have generally agreed upon names for these traits, much less a system for measuring them. Our discussion of them must therefore be largely conjectural (p. 131).

The evidence of our senses tells us that non-cognitive traits also contribute far more than cognitive skills to the quality of human life and the extent of human happiness. We, therefore, believe that the non-cognitive effects of schooling are likely to be more important than the cognitive effects. But we do not know what these non-cognitive effects are likely to be (p. 134). ■

Jencks finds himself able to devote only one chapter to noncognitive traits. A chapter of four pages! There is no better evidence that the preponderance of educational researchers implicitly consider cognitive-academic achievement of children to be the most important criterion by which to judge schools. So, let us listen to one of Jencks's final recommendations:

THESE ARGUMENTS SUGGEST THAT THE "FACTORY" MODEL WHICH PERvades both lay and professional thinking about schools probably ought to be abandoned. It is true that schools have "inputs" and "outputs," and that one of their nominal purposes is to take human "raw material" (i.e., children) and convert it into something more "valuable" (i.e., employable adults). Our research suggests, however, that the character of a school's output depends largely on a single input, namely the characteristics of the entering children. Everything else—the school budget, its policies, the characteristics of the teachers—is either secondary or completely irrelevant.

Instead of evaluating schools in terms of long-term effects on their alumni, which appear to be relatively uniform, we think it wiser to evaluate schools in terms of their immediate effects on teachers and students, which appear much more variable. Some schools are dull, depressing, even terrifying places, while others are lively, comfortable, and reassuring. If we think of school life as an end in itself rather than a means in some other end, such differences are enormously important.

Eliminating these differences would not do much to make adults more equal, but it would do a great deal to make the quality of children's (and teachers') lives more equal. Since children are in school for a fifth of their lives, this would be a significant accomplishment (p. 256). ■

And so Jencks brings us back to the concerns of Lewin in the thirties and John Dewey at the turn of the century. How shall we live with each other? This question is given further force by Rosenbaum's (1976) detailed study of the effects of tracking on ability groupings in a high school very homogeneous in terms of the social class background of students. We shall only concern ourselves here with the effects of tracking on students' perception of themselves and others.

THE INTERVIEWS ASKED RESPONDENTS TO DESCRIBE THE STUDENTS IN EACH track . . . because all students come from the same social background, we might expect that most respondents would say that students are all pretty similar. Furthermore we might expect that if they offered distinctions, their distinctions would be related to the official definition of tracking. Thus they might say that college-track students are "academically oriented," "interested in college," or "want a job that requires college." But if administrators have succeeded in imparting the official definition of tracking as an open contest, then we would not expect students to say that students in different tracks differ in personal capacities.

My interviews reveal results quite discrepant from the expectations. More than three-quarters of the Grayton respondents provide stereotypes of the students in each track, and the stereotypes refer to personal capacities of the students. College-track students are characterized as smart or "brains" by more than a third, these descriptions being offered by a substantial number of respondents from each track. College-track students are also characterized as "snobs" and as "conformists" ("momma's kids," "brown nose") by one-sixth of the students.

The most common descriptions for non-college students are the opposites of the preceding. They are described as unmotivated (or "lazy," "goof-offs," or "don't care about school") by more than half of the respondents, as negativistic (trouble-making or tough) by more than one-third, and as not very smart (or stupid) by more than one quarter (Rosenbaum, 1976, p. 163). ■

As for students' perceptions of themselves, Rosenbaum presents data and observations indicating the negative effects of tracking. When one puts together the findings of Coleman (1966), Jencks (1972), and Rosenbaum (1976), one comes to the unpleasant conclusion that our schools leave much to be desired in terms of meeting their two major goals: to nurture the cognitive-academic development of pupils; and to provide them with experiences in classrooms informed by the values of a democratic ethos. Since the values behind mainstreaming, as those behind the efforts at racial integration, are identical to those of a democratic ethos, it is obvious that mainstreaming would confront serious obstacles. This is not because schools are evil places, or school personnel insensitive people, but rather because schools are instruments of the larger society in which these same obstacles have long been a feature. Let us try to get a glimpse of how this may work in regard to mainstreaming.

AN IMAGINARY MAINSTREAMED CLASSROOM

Let us imagine the situation in which all special classes are abolished, and in any one classroom there would now be, in addition to the "regular" children, one child labeled mildly mentally retarded, one emotionally disturbed, and one learning disabled. To make the situation even more difficult, if not seemingly outrageous, let us add a fourth child who in addition to being *profoundly* retarded also has defects in motor coordination. The class size may be between twenty-two to twenty-seven pupils. How should the teacher be thinking about his or her tasks and goals? What new elements, principles, and problems have to be confronted? If one takes seriously that learning to live with others is no less a goal of schooling than acquiring academic knowledge and skills, how does this determine the teacher's thinking and actions? This question does not arise because of the heterogeneous composition of the class; that factor only complicates the answer. It is a question that should always be center stage.

To illustrate what we are getting at, let us turn to a study on how a teacher and students forged the "constitution" on the basis of which they were going to live together. More specifically, we were interested in the process by which classroom "laws" were discussed and implemented, and how in the process predictable issues in group living were anticipated. When we say that a classroom is organized, we mean that there are explicit rules by which members are expected to govern themselves in interaction with others. It will not surprise very many readers to learn that the constitution was never forged by teachers *and* students; the constitution was, so to speak, written and promulgated by the teachers. Students "received" the constitution; they had no part in its development. Invariably, the constitution was clear about what the teacher expected of students. There was little or no clarity about what students could expect of teachers. For example, the one thing that both teachers and students could count on—the one thing the teacher knows will be the greatest single source of problem and challenge—is that the students will differ in all kinds of ways. How does one deal with these differences? How does one get students to recognize these differences and how can they be helpful in regard to them? How does one create a sense of mutuality among students and between students and teachers?

It is obvious that our observations and questions reflect several assumptions. First, students are desirous of being treated as if their opinions were worthy of attention and respect. Second, students are capable of learning about and adapting to the dilemmas and complexities of group living. Third, students can be counted on to be curious about themselves and others, and to be willing to try to be helpful to others. Most students love to be helpful to the teacher, if only because the reward system encourages it, but that also provides the basis for assuming that students can be helpful to each other. Fourth, the process of being helpful is one of the most potent ways of feeling respect for oneself and those one helps. Fifth, the recognition, understanding, and acceptance of diversity are among the most important experiences any person can have.

When applied to the classroom, these assumptions in no way imply a philosophy of permissiveness, and they are not intended to conjure up images of the teacher as a passive leader of student opinion. On the contrary, to act consistently on these assumptions requires the teacher to be a leader sensitive to and respectful of students' needs and opinions, at the same time enlarging their experience with the opportunities of being part of a group with a purpose. Such a leader does not abdicate responsibility or mindlessly do what others want. But neither does such a leader deny others a role in matters affecting their lives or shield them from problems in group living that they will confront throughout their lives. If school is not a preparation for life but life itself, then the teacher together with the students must cope with the obvious: Classroom living contains almost all of the problems and opportunities of group living.

These observations were made in regular elementary school classrooms, and they talk directly to the question of the purposes of formal schooling. The thrust of our answer is no different than the one to the question we asked earlier: How should a teacher think and act when her classroom will contain some handicapped children? *Mainstreaming raises no new questions. It brings to the fore old and poorly answered questions.* But let us listen to one of the teachers to whom Milofsky (1977) spoke about mainstreaming.

"I DON'T HAVE ANY REAL PROBLEMS, I THINK SOME OF THESE TEACHERS make too much of all this." He is impressed with the way the children take care of each other. "I have one kid who has C.P. (cerebral palsy)," he says, "and he comes down here with the rest of the class. He has some trouble cutting paper, and whenever we have a project that requires cutting I go to help him. But before I can get there some kid is already helping. The other thing is that he drools. At first, you know, it was kind of revolting to me. The first half-hour or so, maybe more, it bothered me to see it. It's not nice to say, but it's the truth, and I think it bothered the kids, too. But now if he drools the kid sitting next to him cleans it up. It's amazing.'' ■

It is "amazing" only if one operates on assumptions about children different from those we stated earlier. In the case of the teacher Milofsky quotes, one would predict that if we could observe him and his students we would conclude that he does operate on these assumptions, however implicit and unverbalized they may be.

The introduction of four handicapped children into our imaginary regular classroom has to be viewed not as a problem but as an opportunity that allows one to put to the test a basic value and goal of the classroom. If most teachers do not see it in this way, it says less about teachers and more about how the emphasis on cognitive-academic goals in teacher training accurately reflects what the larger society considers primary. To see our imaginary classroom as a problem and burden is the clearest testimony that schooling is viewed as having one superordinate value and goal. If teachers generally feel this way, how should we expect the parents of the children in our imaginary classroom to feel and to react?

Before addressing this question, however, two aspects of teachers' reality have to be noted. The first of these aspects is that mainstreaming is being mandated at a time when school personnel, particularly those in urban settings, perceive cutbacks in school budgets as making a bad situation worse. The second aspect is that school personnel feel under attack because articulate members of their communities are dissatisfied with the education their children are receiving, and the criticism has to do with academic skills and achievement. In short, it is hard to overestimate the strength of the pressures coming from the community for improving children's academic achievement; and the effects of these pressures tend to make teachers focus even more of their efforts in these directions.

One must expect, therefore, that our imaginary mainstream classroom may even heighten tensions and pressures in that parents of "regular" children may protest against what they would see as a further dilution in academic standards and goals. Nor should we overlook the fact that some parents of handicapped children would fear the consequences for their children being in a classroom where academic goals are of primary importance. Mainstreaming not only raises the "internal" question of how children should live together in our schools but, no less important, the question of how differences among parents can be confronted and reconciled.

In 1946, Taylor wrote a book *Experiments with a Backward Class.* This class in a British elementary school consisted of thirty-two boys, some of whom we would call mentally retarded, some we would call emotionally disturbed, and others we would call learning disabled. As Taylor states: "as miscellaneous an assemblage of boys as one might hope to find, but a group bound together by the one characteristic of its prevailing mental dullness" (p. 14). Taylor justifies the book in these words (the italics are hers):

THE PRIMARY AIM OF THIS ACCOUNT IS TO DEMONSTRATE HOW, IN AN actual case, the activities described came into being, to show how they sprang *from the suggestions and ideas of the boys themselves,* and to record the manner in which, by the combined energies of teacher and class, it was possible to translate them into useful and acceptable vehicles of education, revealing the potentialities inherent in even dull children if given the opportunity to display and to pursue their natural bent, and to follow a curriculum which takes into consideration their particular needs and adapts itself to their ascertained interests (p. xii, italics in original). ∎

Taylor's is a remarkable account, starting with her descriptions of each boy, describing the usual class day, then zeroing on one event that opened Taylor's eyes to the necessity of radically changing her conceptions of learning and the nature of classroom living. She devotes the remainder of the book to the transformation of classroom life and its relation to cognitive achievement.

Taylor's accomplishments, as she well recognized, could only be understood as a consequence of the insight that if she changed the constitution governing classroom living (if its goals of classroom living were granted the same importance as those of academic achievement), she and the student might be saved from boredom, frustration, and hopelessness. But why did Taylor have to be hit over the head to gain this insight? One part of the answer is that she, like many others, was teaching labels not children. Indeed, even at the end of the book she expressed surprise that "dull" children could have done what they did, rather than asking what "dullness" means, if it serves any other purpose than as an administrative basis for segregating students? But the other part of the answer is that Taylor had been trained to give priority to academic achievement. That she managed to escape from the baleful consequences of such training is a tribute to her. Some people do overcome their training. But in overcoming it Taylor opened herself to another source of sadness. At the end of the book she says: "The story of IIIB was now ended, and the boys passed on to the next standard. They returned once more to the old regime—to the collective class-instruction, the dictated syllabus, the formal timetable, and the classroom restrictions of former times" (p. 98).

THE DEFINITION OF RESOURCES

A major objection to our imaginary classroom and the elimination of special classes could be put in this way: your imaginary classroom reflects the spirit of fairness in that it does not deny a child the opportunity to live with his peers; by not segregating one type of child from another you minimize the chances that educational resources will be distributed unequally. Your utopian example breathes fairness but it creates injustice in that it would be impossible for the teacher to respond to the needs of the children. Granted that how children live together is as important as the academic knowledge and skills they acquire, in practice your classroom will end up giving far more attention to living together than to the acquisition of formal knowledge and skills. You are asking the teacher to do the impossible.

There are several ways of replying to this objection. It is an objection that can be raised in relation to any classroom. It is the rare teacher who will not say that in order to do justice to the individual differences of pupils, additional resources should be available. As long as we view mainstreaming as raising a resource problem, we miss the obvious point. From the standpoint of teachers, there has always been a resource problem in that they have never felt that students received what they needed.

The guilt that many teachers have felt has two sources. First, like the rest of humanity they have been aware that they have limitations in knowledge, understanding, and skills, an obvious enough point to anyone who has had to deal with groups of children. For a long time the community expected teachers to be equally effective with all children; and if teachers knew otherwise, self-serving professionalism or misguided pride prevented them from saying so. The second source of guilt was less personal but no less significant. It had to do with the frequent clash between the needs of children and the structure and organization of schools and, in the case of the latter, teachers resented having no voice.

One cannot understand the meteoric rise of teacher militancy unless one recognizes the strong feeling of teachers that the community and school administrators did not comprehend the plight of the classroom teacher in dealing with diverse children with diverse problems. If teachers were criticized for the authoritarian way they ran their classrooms, it was the same criticism that teachers directed at administrators and boards of education. The turmoil of the post-World War II period, the population explosion, and the increasing role of the federal government in public education combined to dramatically increase new resources available to schools.

There were two characteristics of these developments that are central to our present purposes. The first was that needed resources were defined as they always were: specially trained, highly educated professionals who had to be paid. Put more generally, a resource was that for which one paid and therefore controlled. And if one had no money, one could not obtain the resource. The second characteristic was the belief that the money necessary to purchase these resources, indeed to obtain even more, would always be forthcoming. The myth of unlimited resources was not exposed for what it was until the seventies.

The events of the past few years not only exposed the fact that resources are always limited but also emphasized the need to reconceptualize what we mean by resources. More specifically, as long as schools define resources as those for which they can pay, the discrepancy between what schools can and should do will always be large. This is not only a problem for schools but for almost every type of human service that by tradition and public sanction is dominated by professionalism. The disease of professionalism is in the tendency to define human problems in ways that require highly educated professionals for their solution, thus rendering the problem unsolvable. This statement should not be construed as antiprofessionalism. The antidote to the disease is to see its limitation. There are two circumstances when the limitations of professionalism are recognized and willingly circumvented. One is war time, the requirements of which make strict adherence to professionalism dangerous. One cannot accept the criteria of professionalism if they do not produce the necessary human resources. Therefore, the question becomes not "who has the qualifications?" but rather "who can quickly learn to be helpful?" The other circumstance is in those rare times when there is a dramatic shortage of professional personnel to perform a function deemed vital by society. This happened during the sixties when the demand for teachers far exceeded the supply. As a result, there was a willing relaxation of the formal requirements for becoming a classroom teacher. There is no evidence whatsoever that in either of these circumstances the redefinition of resources had adverse effects. But as soon as the "crises" are over, there is a reversion to professionalism.

We will pose a question in terms of our imaginary mainstreamed classroom: How can additional resources be made freely available to that classroom in ways that are not only helpful to teacher and pupils but at the same time contribute to the education, growth, and worth of those who will become part of the classroom scene?

Fortunately, it is a question for which a rather large body of experience and research is relevant. Whether it is older pupils helping younger ones, or using college students, or community people, the evidence is rather clear that resources can play a very valuable role in the classroom. We are not discussing "volunteerism" which in practice usually means that the giving is in one direction. What experience and research demonstrate is that there has to be an exchange of resources so that all parties feel that they are learning and changing, not only "doing good" for others but expanding knowledge of self and the world. This cannot be accomplished unless several conditions are met:

1. One has to accept the fact that professional resources will never be made available to the degree required by the traditional definition of resources. The problems of schools have not been and will not be resolved by reliance solely on professionals.
2. One has to believe that there are diverse types of people who can be helpful in the classroom even though they have no professional credentials. This in no way means that those who lack these credentials have, as a group, a kind of folk wisdom absent in professionals. Wisdom and imaginativeness are distributed in the same way among professional and nonprofessional groups.
3. The crucial task is how to locate, select, and train these new resources so that their needs for new and productive experiences are met at the same time they are helping to meet those needs in others.
4. School personnel have to see themselves as resource locators and coordinators, constantly scanning school and community in order to match needs in a mutually productive manner.

These are not pious statements of virtue but directions substantiated by research and experiences.[2] They permit us to look at our mainstream classroom not as a creature of well-intentioned but unbridled imagination, but rather as a real possibility, the obstacles to which are in our ways of thinking. The teacher in that classroom need not be "alone" in the struggle to meet the needs of children to learn more about the world of ideas, skills, and social living.

It has been pointed out that although a school is one of the most densely populated settings on earth, "teaching is a lonely profession" (Sarason et al., 1966; Sarason, 1971). It is not the loneliness of solitude but a feeling compounded of isolation, frustration, and the pressure to appear competent to handle any and all problems. It is a sense of loneliness that

---

2. Without question, Cowen et al.'s (1975) project in the Rochester schools is the most systematic, longitudinal effort to detect and prevent school problems. It is a project that developed over a period of nineteen years. Cowen and his colleagues describe a series of studies on the selection, use, and contributions of nonprofessionals in classrooms and in their contacts with children. Books by Rappaport (1977), Zax and Specter (1974), and Zax and Cowen (1972) contain sections reviewing the research on the use of nonprofessionals with diverse clinical populations. The reviews leave little doubt that carefully selected and trained nonprofessionals can be of great value. In an article, "Keeping Exceptional Children in Regular Classes," Christoplos (1973) asserts that "the first critical condition for successful integration of exceptional children into regular classes is the use of interstudent tutoring so that (a) teachers will not be overwhelmed by the variety of children, curricula, and materials; (b) children will have one to one relationships in learning relationships . . .; and (c) fostering cooperative attitudes and mutual self respect. . . ."

gnaws, debilitates, feeds on itself, and frequently leads to a sense of stagnation. The reasons for this are many but chief among them is the traditional way of defining roles and resources. This is not to suggest that by redefining roles and resources problems will disappear and the educational millennium will be in sight.

What we suggest is a redefinition that takes several things seriously: diversity, even extreme diversity, in the classroom is as much an opportunity as it may be a problem. Schooling has two coequal goals: productive learning and mutuality in living. The classroom teacher should not be expected to meet these goals alone; additional resources in the classroom are required. These resources as traditionally defined have never been available in anything resembling adequate numbers. The needs of children and teachers can be met in part by matching these needs with those of other people in or out of school. Classrooms are not only for children but can serve as a resource for others who also strive for productive learning and social mutuality.

Public Law 94–142 recognizes the need for additional resources at the same time that it meets those needs in the most traditional way. What is ironic in all this is the implicit assumption that the need for new resources arises because of mainstreaming. The fact is that one of the major factors maximizing the gulf between educational goals and accomplishment has been the way resources have been defined. This was the case long before mainstreaming was even an idea. Mainstreaming does not create a resource problem; it exacerbates a problem stemming from a self-defeating definition of resources. The funding provisions of 94–142 in no way challenge or seek to alter the traditional conceptions of resources, and, therefore, one has to predict that the law will fall far short of its intended goals. Further, despite its funding provisions, the other provisions of the law will have the effect of forcing increases in the budgets of local school districts, thus aggravating further what is already tense school-community relationships.

That resources are always limited is axiomatic in economics. If other fields did not recognize this, they have in recent years been rudely awakened to the significance of that axiom in all major spheres of public policy. During much of the post-World War II era, most people accepted the myth of unlimited resources; as a society we could do whatever we decided to do and whatever limitations existed were a function of a lack of national resolve. We are now faced with the issues and dilemmas of choice. This has been dubbed by some people as the "dialysis problem": How do you justify spending several millions of dollars to keep alive a very small number of people with kidney disease, and proportionately spend far less money for much larger groups with serious problems in living?

As Fuchs (1975), a medical economist, points out in his book *Who Shall Live?* we can no longer answer this question as if we could do everything for everybody. This is not the conclusion of a political conservative or a reactionary insensitive to the real needs of real people but rather a description of the realities of the formulation and implementation of public policy in any country, however different its political structure may be from our own.

There are two major implications of limited resources that will have to be faced. The first is that any agency, like a school or school system, can no longer define resources only in terms of purchase by money. On the contrary, agencies like schools will have to become resource locaters and developers but on a basis that meets mutual needs so that there is resource exchange without money exchange. A somewhat similar position in relation to communities has been described and implemented by Schindler-Rainman and Lippett in their book *The Volunteer Community: Creative Use of Human Resources* (1975). Although they do not directly confront the fact of limited resources, they make a very persuasive case for viewing the volunteer not only for what he or she can contribute but for what the experience can mean for the personal growth of the volunteer. Where most volunteer programs are inadequate and inefficient is in their "one way street" stance. They put far more emphasis on what they can get than what they can give to the volunteer. Their chapter "The Motivational Dynamics of Voluntarism" should be required reading for professionals and agency personnel.

In a recent book, Sarason et al. (1977) described the development over three years of a "barter economy" network of individuals that vastly increased resources available to any network member.[3] If that description is not persuasive, we urge the reader to consult the monograph size testimony of Daphne Krause (1975) before a congressional committee. Taking the fact of limited resources seriously, she describes how she was able to get individuals and agencies to exchange resources without exchanging money, with everyone being benefited.

The concept of the barter economy is obviously not new and, equally obviously, it conflicts with professionalism. More correctly, the traditions of professionalism rather effectively obscure how they inevitably create a gulf between those who need a service and the numbers available to render that service.

THE STANCE OF THE SCHOOLS IS TYPICAL OF ALL AGENCIES: ADDITIONAL resources are needed, but it requires money to obtain them or to be the basis for an exchange of resources. As a consequence, agencies spend a good deal of time trying to get more money, in effect competing with each other for these additional financial resources. And that stance

---

3. In a second book, *The Challenge of the Resource Exchange Network* (Sarason and Lorentz, 1979), the rationale for resource exchange, and descriptions of how it has been applied in educational and other settings, are presented in detail.

makes it inordinately difficult, and in practice almost impossible, to do three related things: to confront (if only as a possibility) that resources are and will be limited; to examine critically the accepted relationship between problems and solutions; and *to figure out possible ways in which agencies can learn to exchange resources in mutually beneficial ways and without finances being a prerequisite for discussion or the basis for exchange.* We have italicized the last point to emphasize the contrast between a typically "market" and "barter" way of viewing and exchanging resources. In the former, money is absolutely essential; in the latter, it is primarily a matter of determining whether there exists different needs that can be satisfied in mutually satisfying ways: "What do I have that somebody else can use in exchange for something of his that I need?" To be able to put the question in this way already suggests that vehicles need to be developed that not only maximize knowledge about available resources but also facilitate the processes of exchange. (As we shall see, networks can be such a vehicle.) The question is based on a way of thinking that is drastically different than that ordinarily governing relationships among agencies. In everyday practice, agencies do not seek each other out for the purposes of resource exchange; each agency sees itself as independent of all others, dependent only on its own subsidized resources to meet its goals, and energetically seeking new monies to purchase more resources. Each agency is an island, seeking ways to expand its land areas, fearing erosion from uncontrollable and unpredictable sources; and nurturing the fantasy that there must or there should exist the quantity and quality of resources that could ensure a safe and goal-fulfilling life.

Our experience led us to see how the usual way of thinking maintains or increases the gulf between what needs to be done and the resources available to do it. In suggesting that there may be other ways of thinking about the issue, we in no way are suggesting that the gulf can be eliminated, but rather that it can be reduced (Sarason et al. 1977, p. 21, italics in original). ■

Let us take a concrete example:

How MANY MORE PHYSICIANS WOULD BE NEEDED TO GIVE ADEQUATE MEDical care to all in our society? We can safely assume that there would be controversy about defining adequate care, but it is also safe to assume there would be general (but no unanimous) agreement that many more physicians would be required. Whether the increase would be of the order of 25, or 50, or 100 percent, the absolute number of new physicians would run into the thousands. These numbers could not be trained without creating a few score of new medical schools, the cost of which would run into billions of dollars. If our society were to go that route, several problems would have to be confronted. Where would one get the personnel to man these new facilities? It could be argued that existing medical schools vary tremendously in quality, in part because the number of truly first-rate physicians is small and in part because only a few medical schools have the traditions, atmosphere, and resources to attract and keep first-rate faculty. As a consequence, it would be argued, there is a concentration of such faculty in relatively few centers, and the bulk of medical schools must settle for less able people and, therefore, their students are less well prepared to give adequate care. So, if you create twenty new medical schools, the competition for scarce quality personnel could intensify with at least two possible results: The quality of the best medical schools would be diluted (they are brought closer to the mean), or the new medical schools will be unable to compete "in the market" and they will settle for second best. This line of argument could be much more developed and it is one guaranteed to arouse violent differences of opinion. But everyone would agree that quality of medical personnel was not uniform and, indeed, there is no evidence to suggest that the distribution of quality is other than a normal one; that is, a small percentage would be excellent, an equal percentage would be poor, and the bulk of personnel would be bunched somewhat above *and* below the group mean. Quality is a limited resource, and to plan as if it were in large supply is to deny reality.

One could counter this argument by saying that training physicians to give adequate care does not require a largely first-rate faculty, who for the most part are more interested in research than they are in teaching for practice. What is required are good teachers, and although they are not an unlimited resource, there are more of them than there are first-rate medical faculty and researchers. Furthermore, this argument could continue, even if the first argument had some validity, there are so many people receiving no or scandalously poor medical care that they would benefit immensely from the increase in the number of physicians who, although not receiving the highest quality of medical training, would nevertheless be far better than no service at all. The major task is to increase the number of good teachers. This argument, like the opposing one, assumes that the quality necessary for a desirable outcome is limited. Unfortunately, in the heat of controversy in which the proponents of one position try to demolish the proponents of the other position, both manage to overlook their area of agreement: The quality of human resource considered by each to be desirable and necessary is in short supply. And by overlooking this agreement, they no longer are in a position to confront the implications of a major obstacle to a desirable outcome.

But let us assume there is no controversy and everyone agrees that we need more physicians, more medical schools, and the only obstacle to overcome is finding the additional billions per year such an expansion would cost. Can we afford to do it? There are those who would say that the more appropriate question is: How can we justify not doing it? That is to say, the problem is at root a moral one and, when seen in that way, what is required is an act of national will and the problem will be solved. Some who take this stance would maintain that, given our riches as a country, we could mount such a program without taking away resources from other programs. (This is like the sixties, when some people said we could afford to go to the moon and conduct the war on poverty at the same time we were conducting a foreign war.) By formulating the solution in moral terms, the assumption about adequacy of resources goes unexamined. Furthermore, this moral stance about a particular program glosses over the fact that other people take a similar stance about other programs. Moral stances are not in short supply and when one arrays the programs to which such stances give rise, the assumption of unlimited resources is seen for what it is: an uncritically accepted assumption.

When proponents of a new program confront the reality of limited resources, they accept (or are forced to accept) a scaling down of their plans. So, instead of twenty new medical schools, they may be willing to settle for five, hoping that in the future they will gain new resources. After all, five does represent an incremental gain, even though the discrepancy between what needs to be done and will be done is still large. Morality has, so to speak, won a battle in a long war. But this sense of satisfaction is based on the assumption that available resources will either remain constant or increase. What if available resources decline or the competition for existing resources becomes more fierce because new needs arise from within or without our society? Anyone familiar with our history knows that our economy has long had the characteristics of a yo-yo. And anyone familiar with recent international history knows the degree to which the definition of the scope of our society's resources has become dependent on what happens elsewhere in the world. Therefore, to assume that resources available to us will be constant or increase is, to say the least, dangerous. Yet that assumption has been given a wide degree of acceptance. The exposure in practice of its invalidity has caused widespread disappointment and even cynicism, but, unfortunately, there continues to be a resistance to the idea that among the reasons for program failure or inadequacy, the assumption of unlimited or increasing resources occupies an important place.

The size of available resources to deal with any social problem is a function of many factors, but certainly one of the most important is how the problem is defined. For example, in presenting the problem of providing adequate medical care, the problem was defined in a way so that its solution *required* training many more physicians. *Such a defini-*

tion contains the "solution," but, as we tried to demonstrate, it is a
solution that renders the problem unsolvable. Put in another way,
resources are always limited, but the discrepancy between what needs to
be done and resources available to do it is frequently widened by our
definition of what needs to be done (Sarason et al., 1977, p. 16). ■

For the spirit of mainstreaming to be appropriately reflected in
schools, the dilemmas of limited resources cannot be ignored. And this
leads us to the second major implication of limited resources and that is the
importance of a community approach by which we mean scanning,
understanding, and relating to the community so that the possibilities of
resource exchange are considerably enlarged. To rely only on those
resources within one's setting is to doom one self to never ending disappointment. As a society, we are beginning to face, albeit reluctantly, the
fact of limited resources. It should in no way be surprising that in analyzing
recent public policies affecting mentally retarded people the centrality of
that fact should emerge. And, we must conclude, if that fact is not faced
squarely, we are likely to find that the more things change the more they remain the same.

Chapter 14

The Ends and Means of Change

In this chapter I shall endeavor to make explicit a way of conceptualizing the change process that, hopefully, may make disillusioning failure less likely to occur. What I now make explicit was in earlier pages either implicit, or not given the emphasis it merited, or not put into relationship with other important features of the change process. In doing this I am not suggesting that what I present is comprehensive, or even valid in the sense that available evidence or experience supports my conceptualization and no other one. What I shall have to say is, first, a reaction to the rationales behind past failures, and, second, an effort to present an alternative rationale that justifies hope but not great expectations. I thoroughly understand why so many people who are sensitive to and concerned with the deficiencies and inadequacies of our schools set goals for their change efforts that are the opposite of modest. Few of us are comfortable setting goals that are a good deal below what our vision and passion tells us needs to be done. Similarly, few of us are comfortable with the knowledge that in setting our sights high we set ourselves up for disappointment. I am not advocating modesty or timidity, let alone passivity. What I am advocating brings us immediately to the first aspect of my conceptualization of the change process.

RESOURCES: QUALITY AND QUANTITY

As the end of World War II approached, Stalin, Roosevelt, and Churchill met at Yalta to plan a strategy for hastening the day of victory. During the discussion President Roosevelt brought up the concerns of the Pope about the conduct of the war and the goals of a peace settlement, to which Stalin replied with a question: "And how many troops does the Pope have?" The fact that Stalin was one of history's all time barbaric dictators should not obscure the significance of the principles from which his question derived. One principle is that achieving goals is integrally related to the quantity and quality of resources you can muster. A second and related principle is that the fewer resources one can muster, *relative to those required by the formulation of goals,* the less chance there is to realize any goals and the more one has reason to reformulate goals. A third and related principle is that in order to have an impact the quantity and quality of resources have to be perceived by others as having strength or power; i.e., they are perceived by others as forces they cannot or should not ignore.

How one formulates goals implicitly or explicitly determines the quantity (number and type) and quality of resources one will need. Readers will recall that in an earlier chapter I imagined the situation where Congress passed a law mandating that class size be cut in half and appropriating the funds to do so. I pointed out that although we have the material resources to build the additional schools we would need, we could not train twice the number of teachers, especially if the criteria for selecting teachers emphasized quality. Contained in the formulation of the goals of the legislation is a statement of the human resources that would be required; i.e., each classroom would have a teacher who would have had a number of years of higher education and training. In formulating the goal in such a way, the problem is rendered unsolvable. The formulation is also based on the assumption that training centers have the capability to train twice the number of teachers—an assumption that never had and does not now have a basis in reality. It is not necessary to agree with my conclusions to recognize that the way in which goals are formulated dictate the resources that will be necessary. But for those who do agree with my conclusions, in whole or in part, then they have to reformulate the goals so that they become more realistically related to available or potentially available resources. One could, for example, ask that if the one-teacher/one-classroom goal is unattainable, what are the alternative ways one could bring to the classroom resources that would increase the time available to the individual student? There is always a universe of alternatives one can consider and if we do not confront that universe it is largely because we are committed to *a* way of defining who should be in a classroom. *That* commitment is based on a set of values and beliefs that are effective barriers to seeing and accepting alternatives. There is a big difference between stating goals that have a single "solution" and those that recognize and permit a variety of alternatives. The difference resides in large measure in the degree to which the relation between formulated goals and the resources dictated by those goals have been thought through. Unfortunately, many of the efforts to change and improve schools have been based on well intentioned goals for which available resources were simply inadequate.

Another aspect of the resource problem comes to the fore in the question: *Who* has formulated the goals of change? In many efforts at change the formulator has been an individual or a small group of individuals. Let us assume that the individual or small group has gained clarity about the relationship between goals and human resources. There is another type of resource: time. Assuming there is clarity about the relationship between goals and human resources, a question arises: Does the individual or small group have the time to locate and develop those resources consistent with goals? If anything is clear from my observations of the change process, it is the frequency with which the formulators of goals become aware early in the process that they have not (and will not have) the time to implement or oversee the process in ways that maximize the chances for success. The reasons for this are not hard to identify. There is, at the outset, the understandable but mistaken overestimation of how smoothly the process will go. That is to say, how you would like it to go, or how some theory says it should go, leads you vastly to underestimate the degree of unpredictability and unmanageability of the change process. I am not suggesting that the change process is inherently chaotic or unpredictable, but rather that the effort to initiate a change in a complicated social-institutional setting in which there are different groups with different interests—all in a world not under one's control—has to assume that things will happen that will make additional demands on one's time. To proceed as if that assumption is invalid is to court failure.

Another reason, illustrated most clearly in efforts that are externally funded, is the totally unwarranted assumption that one can program the change effort by the calendar, e.g., the project will start on September 7, by mid-October we will be at this point, by February we will be at that point, and by the end of the school year the change will be in place and we can begin to write how successful we have been! I have seen an uncomfortably large number of efforts proceed in just that kind of unrealistic way, with the results one would predict. Having started that way, the overseers of the effort rapidly start seeing reality, enter a stage of frenetic activity, begin to see that they simply do not have the time to deal with the realities, and cannot wait for the project and school year to end.[1]

I have been talking about time as a resource for the initiators and overseers of the change effort. In an earlier chapter I discussed how insen-

---

[1] Most people have heard about Murphy's Law: if anything can go wrong, it will. A student of mine has come up with Sullivan's Law: Murphy's Law is a gross underestimation. Murphy's Law is well known to graduate students in connection with doctoral dissertations. Among them, as among proponents of educational change, there is a small group who understand Murphy's Law *before* they begin the dissertation, and it influences their time perspective. Most understand the law *after* the dissertation has been finished (if it is).

sitive the proponents of change tend to be to the time demands their efforts require of teachers. The proponents seem to assume that because they are convinced about the value of the change, teachers should be willing (even enthusiastic!) to accept more demands on their time. Any attempt to change regularities in the classroom places the teacher in an unlearning and learning process, a fact that has obvious implications for the time perspective of those seeking the change.

THE REDEFINITION OF RESOURCES

Resources are always limited, and if that fact is taken seriously by proponents for change, it requires that they redefine what they mean by relevant (actual or potential) resources. But why is the redefinition of resources so difficult in practice? The answer to that question is extraordinarily complex because the obstacles to the process of the redefinition process is rooted in our society's social history.

Of all the obstacles to the recognition of limited resources, none is more powerful than "great expectations." In countless ways, both in the past and present, we have been taught that our society can do anything it decides to do. This has been a land of opportunity. Our streets may not have been paved with gold, but we had all the resources for which one could wish or need. We were a divinely favored land not encumbered by the stifling, oppressive traditions of the rest of the world. And we had boundless resources that only required ingenuity and hard work to develop and to be made available to everyone. From the standpoint of individuals, the only restriction on their partaking of the good life was the strength of their motivation to better themselves. There was enough of everything to go around, and there always would be. And, if some people got less than others, it said more about their lack of ambition, or the impersonal workings of Lady Luck, than it did about how much there was to go around. There could be doubt about the fate of individuals to get what they wanted, but not about the fate of the larger society. It was onward and upward, because there were no limits to what we possessed. We were a nation of individuals, and the more rugged we were, the better. Individuals should look to their resources and not depend on those of others. Individualism was so important that the most healthy thing a government could do was to stay out of the lives of people. We had a supply and demand market economy—the most thriving the world had seen—and only cynics or fools could doubt that supply could keep up with demand. "A chicken in every pot and a car in every garage"—that was only a small sample of all that people could expect. To expect less was simply to misunderstand what had made the country great and would make it even greater.

Rhetoric alone cannot explain the hold of great expectations on the minds of people, nor can any concept of indoctrination. The fact is that there were kernels of truth in the rhetoric. Comparatively speaking, this country did seem to have boundless resources as well as opportunities "to better oneself." Individual freedoms existed (not for blacks, of course), and it did not take long before education was available to all. The standard of living rose steadily, and scientific and technological advances provided a basis for the belief that our society could (and would) make a heaven on earth, or a reasonable facsimile thereof. The inevitability of progress and the belief in endless growth were regarded as facts and not the stuff of fantasy. The inscription on the Statue of Liberty was both fact and rhetoric. If the rhetoric was a kind of hard sell, there was, nevertheless, something of value to sell. Not everyone bought the rhetoric, least of all Henry Adams (1974) who questioned the belief in progress as well as the identity between quantity and quality, and who was prescient about the consequences of the twin evils of rootlessness and materialism. One of those rare books that is as illuminating of a society as it is of the writer is *The Education of Henry Adams.* It is history, autobiography, social commentary, and foreboding prediction. What comes through in that book is the inexorable hold that the ideas of growth, expansionism, and progress had on nineteenth-century America. Limitless growth could be counted on as a fact. Even Henry Adams—pessimistic, dysphoric, questioning, and questing soul that he was, gripped and disheartened by his view of a future soulless society—had no doubt about limitless resources. One might say that it was the boundless riches of the country that Adams saw as a contributing factor in leading the society down wrong paths.

We live each day as if we are immortal. The way we structure our days, the phenomenological substance of our experience, are based on the unverbalized assumption that there will be a tomorrow, an infinite number of tomorrows, and no death. The fact of our mortality holds too much terror to permit us to confront its implications for today and the finite tomorrows (Becker, 1973). Consequently, when circumstances remind us that what we believe is a fact is instead a fiction, the forces of denial and avoidance assert themselves, and everything in us wants to be allied with these forces. The strength of these internal obstacles to perceiving reality has to be seen in relation to the countless external reminders that we are mortal. Analogously, when a society has been reared, so to speak, to believe in the existence of limitless resources and growth, it will experience powerful obstacles to altering its treasured assumptions. The power of these assumptions is not understandable only in terms of an individual psychology (just as the denial of death is not comprehensible only in terms of the individual psyche). The belief in limitless resources has been institutionalized in the nature, structure, and future thrust of our economy and political institutions. It is part of an outlook that has suffused almost every aspect of our society's functioning. It is not hyperbole to say that the possibility that limitless resources is a fiction strikes terror in the minds of individuals and those responsible for institutional policy and continuity. After all, if it is a fiction, it will require a radical redefinition of purpose and direction.

In addition to outright denial rooted in our social history, there is the reaction that accepts the possibility of limited resources but considers it dramatically overdrawn. With some people who hold this view, it turns out that they strongly believe that science and technology will somehow manage to come up with discoveries that will obviate any need for radical redefinition of resources and social outlook, much as in the song from World War II: "We did it before, and we can do it again." But when these people talk about resources they obviously mean material resources. It does not occur to them that human resources may be no less limited than material ones—that for the major social problems with which our society is wrestling, defined as they are and dictating the human resources they would require, there are qualitative and quantitative resource limitations. In fact, in today's discussions about resources, the emphasis is almost exclusively on natural or material resources. We hear a great deal about preserving the environment, learning how to use natural resources more efficiently, and giving up our habits of wasting these resources. So we are (rightly) bombarded with pleas and plans for the efficient use of energy. In regard to the efficient uses of human resources, discussion tends to be scanty and hortatory. There is recognition that whatever we do or should do in regard to natural resources has obvious implications for the quantity and quality of human resources: availability, shifts from one work sector to another, and, fatefully, the degree to which funding of social programs is effected. But that recognition has not led, as it has in the case of material resources, to creative, bold thinking, let alone to any change in public polity.

We have long prided ourselves on being a highly sophisticated, technological society capable of producing products efficiently and in great quantities. When Henry Ford set up his assembly line, it was regarded as quintessentially American in its level of efficiency. Today we know that the assembly line was not all that efficient in terms of its effect on the physical and human environment and in its bedrock belief that the future was a carbon copy of a present in which the supply of oil was limitless and cheap. If that lesson has been learned, it is one that needs to be learned again and again, and applied no less to human as well as to material resources.

It is by no means easy to explain why it has been so difficult to confront the possibility that human resources are limited in the ways natural resources are. Put in another way, faced with mammoth social problems, why are we unable to entertain the possibility that one of the many sources of difficulty in coping with these problems is in restrictions in the quantity and quality of available human resources? When we talk about natural resources, we are referring to concrete, measurable things, the characteristics of which we can study, manipulate, and even drastically transform. More than that, we can combine resources. We can transform and combine them in ways nature cannot. We can, for example, by a process of either splitting or imploding atoms, create vast amounts of energy. All of this is obvious enough, but it is not explainable by technology. If one had to pinpoint the decisive factor, it would be that part of the traditions of science that says, "Seek knowledge, never let your imagination rest, try anything that gives promise of illuminating the nature of our world, do not take anything for granted, especially those cautions that say that something cannot be done or will not work." Among scientists, as among other groups, there are great differences in imagination, the capacity to combine ideas and things and to come up with something new.

If you show a random sample of the population a pencil and ask these people what it is, we would have no doubt how many "right" answers there would be. If now you were to show them a pencil and ask about all the different uses to which it could be put, we would find a small number of people who could come up with scores of ways for which the thing we call a *pencil* could be utilized. Most people are so tied to the familiar and concrete that when they are asked to perceive the familiar differently, to redefine it, they are unable to do so. It is our impression that people have less difficulty in altering their thinking in regard to things as resources than to people as resources. Whether or not this is the case is not decisive. The fact is that when it comes to thinking about people as resources in regard to major social problems, "imagination" seems remarkably absent, with two results: not only is the possibility of limited resources diverted from recognition but also, and of more immediate import, the extent of the limitation is enormously increased. Here too we run the risk of trivializing the issue by explaining it in terms of variations among human psyches.

The influence of culture, social structure, and social history are always omnipresent. For example, we applaud scientists who can "dream up" new combinations of things and forces, especially if these combinations will provide society with what it wants. We have always been ambivalent about people who are "playing around" with problems of no immediate practical import. We have never been ambivalent about the "practical" scientist and inventor. We respect imagination in the service of coping with "real" problems. But when it comes to dreaming up new ways of defining people as resources, new ways by which heretofore unused human resources can be applied to major social problems, our track record is poor. More correctly, our record is poor when attempts to implement these new ways are made. The obstacles reside not only in the difficulty of redefining human resources and dreaming up new combinations among people that will dilute the consequences of limited resources, but also in the threat that poses to the established order (as in our example of nurses and physicians). Oil is more than oil, in the sense that the human mind was given free play by society to figure out the different uses to which it could be put and the different ways it could be transformed. And so we have a mammoth petrochemical industry that transforms oil into myriad products. But that kind of "figuring out" runs a mined obstacle course when the issue is how to define and transform human resources. Transforming oil gores the oxen of few people; transforming human resources gores the oxen of many people. The differences between the two types of transformation are noticeably decreased during periods of crisis.

There is another obstacle, no less powerful for its subtleness, that also has its roots in our culture. Up to this point, we have been talking about people whose roles make them influential in the definition of social problems and, therefore, in defining the nature of available resources. But what about people generally? Let us put the question more concretely: Why did it take so long for nurses to see themselves as more capable and differentiated than society generally saw them? Why did it take so long to redefine themselves as resources now and in the future? For that matter, why did it take so long for women generally to liberate themselves from the narrow confines assigned to them by society? We ask these questions not because we are prepared to answer them (that would take at least one good-sized volume), but because they are suggestive of the rigid way in which people are "slotted"; *more important for our present purposes, they suggest that people come to accept society's narrow definitions of them as resources.* It is understandable that if one enters a role in which functions are clearly defined by tradition and training (and often these definitions have a legislative and judicial basis), the tendency is to believe that one is not capable of going beyond the stated boundaries. (Of all the horrors accompanying the institution of slavery, none rivals the acceptance of inferiority, the sense that one is unworthy or incapable.) Indeed, when training programs of all sorts are studied, one is struck by the effort to define rigidly what students can do and, by implication, what they are incapable of doing. And when one adds to this the obvious fact that as a society we are in our working and social lives very sensitive to the implications of differences in status, and the consequences of going beyond one's assigned role, it should occasion no surprise if most people accept society's view of them. This is not to say that most people passively accept society's view, because fantasy and reality so often stimulate us to think of ourselves as more capable and differentiated than our existence suggests. But between these thoughts and actions is a chasm too intimidating for most people, and they retreat. It is safer to believe that one is incapable of managing the feat. The obstacles to acting on these thoughts are both external and internal. The obstacles are real.

As long as we continue unreflectively to define educational resources in the customary way, the goals of change cannot be met. That is to say, as long as we define resources in terms of people with credentials that can only be attained through years of education and training, we automatically create an unbridgeable gulf between means and ends. This is not a criticism of professionals, let alone formal education and training. Rather it is to state what I consider to be a brute fact that should lead us to and not away from the need to redefine people as resources. As I pointed out in an earlier chapter, there are times when as a society we willingly and quickly engage in the redefinition process. World War II is an especially clear example because it required radical redefinition and use of human and material resources, not only in regard to the needs of the armed services but in civilian life as well. Criteria for selection for different roles, how people would be trained, and the length of training changed quickly. Older people, physically handicapped people, mentally subnormal people, and women suddenly were seen as important "resources." As important as what people had (or had not) done was what they could quickly learn to do. Necessity required that individuals be viewed not as *a* resource, not perceived in terms of the narrow confines of work labels (such as lawyer, medical internist, accountant, businessman, farmer), but potentially capable of being and doing many different things. Over the course of the war years, literally millions of people were doing things that they never had expected to do and, in many instances, with little or no "training." The lives of many of these people were positively affected as they discovered in themselves new interests and capabilities. It is perversely strange that it takes a total war for a society to recognize how narrowly people are defined and utilized as a resource.

Once the war was over, our society reverted to its accustomed narrow ways of locating and training people as resources. But World War II planted seeds of rebellion against the "old ways" that have flowered in the last decade or so. Women, handicapped people, and older citizens are no longer content to be "slotted"—that is, to accept the implications of labels that constrict what these people are supposed to be capable of, at the same time distorting what they would like to experience.

The concept of human resources has two aspects: (1) society's impersonal and conventional definition, and (2) people's subjective perceptions. It used to be that these aspects were not dramatically in conflict with each other, but that is far less the case today. They were less in conflict during World War II because of the dictates of necessity. Today they are in conflict because the rigidities of conventional definitions, formalized in institutional concrete, seem to be becoming stronger as people's needs and perceptions of themselves are increasingly incongruent with these conventional definitions. The reduction of conflict between these two aspects is as much a necessity today as it was during World War II, but, unfortunately, necessity is not always the mother of invention.

Any effort to change behavioral and programmatic regularities in schools will first require a change in the proponents' ways of defining resources. The seriousness with which that process of redefinition will be undertaken will in large part be a function of how serious the fact of limited resources will be confronted.

CONSTITUENCIES

Schools are political institutions in that their organization reflects conceptions of power: how it can be attained, who should have it, what can be done with it, and what one should do when the possession of power is challenged. I am *not* using the words power and political in any pejorative sense but simply as concepts that describe characteristics of roles and their interrelationships in the culture of the school. The student in the classroom, the teacher, the departmental chairperson, the curriculum supervisor, the director of pupil personnel services, the associate superintendent of schools, the superintendent—the people in each of these roles is exquisitely aware that he or she has assigned, circumscribed power. The boundaries of power may, in writing, be clear, but be very fuzzy in practice. More frequently, both in writing and practice, the degree and direction of power are unclear and that leads to the jockeying, infighting, and support seeking that is no less political for taking place in schools. At any one time in any school system there are ongoing power struggles that impel the combatants to develop and enlarge their constituency; i.e., those from whom they seek support, to whom they feel some obligation, and with whom they share certain concerns. That way of describing the culture of school may be distasteful to those who like to think of schools as oases of peace in which rational minds in selfless personalities seek only to stimulate the intellectual development of pupils. Those who think in this way invariably have been surprised when what they considered a reasonable and needed change in the schools either never received a favorable reception from school personnel or in the process of being implemented was transformed beyond recognition. Over the years I have come to know scores of new superintendents and new school principals and new members of boards of education who were initially impressed with their "power," but who came to see that power in the abstract and power in practice were very different things. What they learned was that power unrelated to dependable and variegated constituencies was empty power. Put another way, the power of office is an opportunity to develop and enlarge constituencies in the service of certain goals. Here again what I am saying may sound unseemly, crass, and too much like the seamy side of "politics." The fact is that I have never met anyone who has been part of the culture of the school who has ever contradicted my description. Many of these people wish it were otherwise, and nurture the belief that some day somewhere it will be shown that power and the political process need not characterize something as socially complex as a school or school system. But in the here and the now they have no doubt that power and the political process are part of the school culture.

If what I am saying is obvious, and I do consider it a glimpse of the obvious, why have so many proponents of change ignored the obvious? Why have they paid so little heed to the need to develop constituencies? Why have they proceeded as if the power to propose and even to legislate change obviates the need to develop constituencies; i.e., to seek and to obtain the support of individuals and groups without whom the proposed change will not occur? As was made clear in an earlier chapter, the high frequency of failure in efforts at change can in part be attributed to the failure to see teachers as a constituency that, therefore, needed to be informed and involved at all stages of the change process. That is to say, the task was to get teachers to feel committed to the process and goals of change. But that task cannot be accomplished by acts of or the display of power or by ignoring the power that teachers have in deciding the fate of the change effort. In the past, as well as in the present, most efforts at change should never have been attempted because there was no evidence that constituency building had been accomplished. As Berman and MacLaughlin (Chapter 5) noted, in the small number of instances where change seemed to have been successful, teachers had become a constituency *for* change.

The recognition of the importance of constituencies returns us to resource issues: time and the redefinition process. The development of constituencies for the purposes of educational change is a time-consuming affair. It cannot be done by letters, memoranda, or speeches. It requires face-to-face discussions only through which competing self-interests stand a chance of being reconciled. To get an individual or group to see the change process as *theirs* (or *ours*)—not as *yours* requiring sacrifices by *them*—is not a task that can be described in some "how to do it" book. The important point is that it is in the self-interests of the proponents of change, first, to recognize the importance of constituencies, second, to view power as an opportunity to develop constituencies, and, third, to realistically confront the time demands of constituency building. There is a fourth factor: *constituency building in the way I have discussed it implies that redefinition of resources has taken place in that the constituents are now viewed as possessing power and resources heretofore unrecognized or unused; i.e., their roles have been redefined as has their relationship to educational change—they become as much the implementers as the objects of change.*

Constituency building is not a token gesture or a consequence of *noblesse oblige*. It is a willing alteration of power relationships through which the self-interests of participants stand a chance of being satisfied. This is a point that John Dewey understood very well (Sarason, 1981, Chapter 6). He not only illustrated the point in the way he created and conducted the lab school at the University of Chicago in 1896, but also in the corpus of his writings on theory and practice, the theorist and the practitioner. In invoking the name and work of John Dewey, we come to the status of parents and other community groups as constituents in the change process. Almost a century ago he understood in an amazingly clear way that all those who would be affected by the educational enterprise should in some way be part of it, not out of considerations of courtesy or as token gestures to the implications of the legal status of schools, but because the goals of education would not be met unless they had the support of diverse constituencies. In almost all of the research and evaluation literature on educational change there has been surprisingly little discussion about the parochial conception of constituency that the proponents of change have had. That teachers have to be part of the change process has gained some acceptance, but it still amazes me in 1981 how frequently that acceptance is rhetorical and not actual.

AND WHO OWNS THE SCHOOL?

The very fact that this question has come forcefully to the fore in the last two decades is glaring evidence of the consequences of ignoring the constituency issue. The polarizations within the schools and between schools and the community speak volumes about power and conflict in the service of narrow, and ultimately self-defeating, conceptions of self-interest. This is not to say that these polarizations do not revolve around important issues, but rather to emphasize the simple fact that these polarizations have been unproductive. They have been productive only in the dysphoric sense that everyone involved feels less hopeful, more angry, and more dispairing. Indeed, anyone knowledgeable about the current scene is aware of how many people influential on the policy level seriously seek alternatives to the public schools as we have known them.

   The rationale that justifies involving teachers in the change process, beginning with planning, is precisely the rationale that justifies the involvement of parents and other community groups. This is not, I must emphasize, a matter of courtesy or the recognition of legal rights. It is a matter that derives from the principle that those who are or may be affected by the change should have some part in the change process because only through such involvement can they become committed to the change. They, like the teachers, come to see the change as *theirs*. What I am suggesting can be summarized in the following ways:

1. The more committed more groups are to a proposed change, the more likely the goals of change will be approximated. (Commitment is no guarantee of success. Commitment is a necessary but not sufficient condition for success.)
2. The recognition that parents and other community groups should be involved in the change process is tantamount to redefining them as resources; i.e., to see them as possessing power and knowledge essential to the change process, and capable of understanding and contributing to the substance and process of change.
3. The more differentiated the constituencies related to the change the greater the likelihood that the adverse consequences of limited resources will be diluted.

When constituencies are viewed in this way, an answer is provided to the question: Who bears responsibility for schools? That answer is: those groups who are or may be significantly affected by any proposed change. As soon as the question about "ownership" arises, it signals conflict in what is almost always a win-lose situation. From the standpoint of changing schools, issues around responsibility are far more productive than those of ownership. From the vantage point of hindsight, one could argue that the single most significant mistake made by educational personnel was to accept responsibility for schools; i.e., willingly (even eagerly) to permit parents and others to give them responsibility. It was shortsighted then, as it is shortsighted today, because there has *never* been a time when educators had the resources to deal with problems as they and the community defined those problems. That resources were being defined in ways that made problems utterly unsolvable was one thing. But the consequences of that mistake were enormously compounded by the willingness of school personnel to accept responsibility because in doing so they effectively kept parents and others in ignorance about the unbridgeable gulf between problem definition and resources. It was inevitable that whenever conditions in schools became a matter of public outcry and concern, criticism would be directed at those who had taken responsibility for schools. And why not? Had not educators taken responsibility for what went on in schools? Had not educators divided the world into the "inside and outside," the "we and they," and "professionals and lay people"? Were not parents (like teachers) unwelcome in the arena of policy and the halls of power? There is no point in multiplying questions in order to emphasize how insensitive school personnel have been to the issues of responsibility and constituency. They have paid a very high price and nowhere more than in their efforts to change schools.

The available literature on educational change efforts points to the principal's crucial role, especially in regard to the seriousness with which he or she redefines the role of teachers in planning and implementation. The implications of that finding for the redefinition of parents and other community groups in matters of policy and change should be obvious. What is at stake is not only the principle that those who are or may be affected by proposed changes should be in some meaningful relationship to planning and change. What is also at stake is a political-tactical principle: How do you develop constituencies that maximize the chances that the goals of change will be approximated? If I draw any conclusion from the literature it is that educators (like professionals generally) are politically naive and parochial in blatantly self-defeating ways.

There are two major obstacles to actions based on this way of thinking. The first is the difficulty professionals have in sharing responsibility with nonprofessionals, because what I have been suggesting gives rise to a process in which the goals of the professionals may (more likely will) require change and compromise. The second obstacle is the familiar one of time: the development of constituencies in regard to policy or change takes time. It not only takes time, but it almost always is a frustrating experience precisely because there are many constituencies differing in outlook and self-interest. On the surface, it is a process that may appear to be "inefficient"—far more apparently inefficient than the traditional mode of developing, proclaiming, legislating, and implementing a policy or change. But, as the literature compellingly indicates, the apparent inefficiency (as seen by the professionals) has to be judged in comparison to the disillusioning failures of the traditional mode that I and scores of others have described. That failure is disillusioning is bad enough, but the perceived degree of failure has dramatically sharpened and increased the tensions between school and community. And where tensions are absent, it is frequently because an atmosphere of hopelessness exists.

It is not in contradiction to what I have just said to note that there are many instances where the issues of power, responsibility, and constituencies have been redefined and implemented in realistic, creative, and productive ways. What these instances tend to have in common is that they are isolated instances; i.e., each is a demonstration in a school, or a part of a school, that what I have been suggesting is practical and productive. It would be more correct to say that what I have been suggesting derives from my observations, frequently sustained ones, of these isolated instances. The rationale I have briefly outlined is certainly not original with me. The significance of these many isolated instances is in the demonstration of the rationale's fruitfulness.

We are used to hearing that predicting the future is to indulge presumption. There is a prior difficulty: reading the current scene and assigning weights of significance to this instance or that development is inevitably problematic. On the one hand, I am impressed by the number of people in and out of schools who continue to strive for educational change.

I am also impressed by the people and organizations devoted to the principle of self-help and, therefore, the need for redefining people as resources. And one cannot lightly dismiss the degree to which there is a general awareness of the fact and implications of limited resources. On the other hand, one's optimism must be restrained in the face of the fact that for all practical purposes, and despite the demonstrations I and others have observed, the substance of educational policy (federal, state, local) hardly differs from the past. That is to say, the incentives for change in the direction I outlined are notable by their absence. Indeed, there is a way of looking at the current scene that leads one to say that little will happen to contradict the maxim that the more things change the more they remain the same.

CHANGE AND THE FEDERAL ROLE

I have said nothing in this chapter about the role of federal initiatives in the change process. The reason, from my standpoint, is a simple one. What I have outlined is a way of thinking and proceeding that is essentially local in scope. If that way of thinking and proceeding does not exist, then whatever the federal government does will be largely unproductive. The fact is that in the overwhelming bulk of our communities that way of thinking and proceeding is absent. To act as if that were not the case, to proceed as if federal dollars will facilitate on the local level the giving up of conceptions that have led to failure, is to play the game of acting for the sake of acting. The rationale I have outlined does not, *initially at least,* require money. I have read hundreds of grant requests in which some, if not all, of the aspects of the rationale I outlined and *future* actions consistent with it are described (e.g., Sarason and Lorentz, 1979, Chapter 7). *In almost every instance many parts of the plans required no money at all, forcing one to ask why they had not already been implemented, and forcing one to conclude that the written statement of the rationale was more rhetoric than conviction, more token gestures to presumed virtue than a reflection of hard-won conviction.* The clearest example is the Experimental Schools Program discussed in Chapter 5.

We are living at a time when there is generally the sentiment that many of federal initiatives should be assumed by the states. Insofar as educational change is concerned, that transfer does not lessen the thorniness of the question. Assuming (a very large assumption!) that the rationale gets embodied in formal policy, what role can government adopt that makes it more likely that the goals of the rationale will be approximated? The most hopeful answer is that whatever the sequence of events that lead to the rationale's clear embodiment in formal policy, that sequence will already testify to a general change in public thinking conducive to partial success, at least. More often than not, public policy, far from being a stimulus to change, is a recognition of a change that has already taken place. What that sequence of events may be, I cannot say. But I can say that the sequence of events will first show up outside of our schools. And precisely because the rationale will have gained such general societal acceptance, it will signify that many people within our schools will be prepared to accept and implement the rationale. The present is not pregnant with one future, but with many possible futures. That fact alone requires us to avoid despair and nihilism and to pursue the goals of change.

Bibliography

ADAMS, H. *The Education of Henry Adams.* Boston: Houghton Mifflin, 1974.

ALLPORT, G. Foreword to *Resolving Social Conflicts,* by K. Lewin. New York: Harper & Row, 1948.

AMERICAN ARBITRATION ASSOCIATION. Arbitration in the Schools, 1978, supplement to report Nos. 104 and 105. New York: American Arbitration Association (140 W. 51st St., New York, N.Y., 10020).

AUSUBEL, D. P. "Crucial Psychological Issues in the Objectives, Organization, and Evaluation of Curriculum Reform Movements." *Psychology in the Schools* IV (1967): 111-120.

BALOW B. "Teachers for the Handicapped." *Compact* 5, no. 4 (1971): 43-46.

BARKER, R. G. *Ecological Psychology.* Stanford: Stanford University Press, 1968.

BARKER, R. G., AND GUMP, P. V. *Big School, Small School.* Stanford: Stanford University Press, 1964.

BEACH, F. A. "The Snark Was a Boojum." *American Psychologist* V (1950): 115-124.

BECKER, E. *The Denial of Death.* New York: Free Press, 1973.

BENTZEN, M.M., GOODLAD, J. I., LAHADERNE, H. M., MYERS, D. A., NOVOTNEY, J. M., SINCLAIR, R. L., SPITZER, L. K., AND TYE, K. A. *The Principal and the Challenge of Change.* Los Angeles: Institute for Development of Educational Activities, 1100 South Glendon Avenue, 1968.

BERMAN. P., AND MCLAUGHLIN, M. W. *Federal Programs Supporting Educational Change, Vol. VIII: Implementing and Sustaining Innovations.* Santa Monica, Calif: Rand Corporation, 1978.

BILLINGTON, R. A. *The Protestant Crusade 1800-1860.* New York: Macmillan, 1938.

BLATT, B. *Exodus from Pandemonium.* Boston: Allyn & Bacon, 1970.

BLATT, B. *Souls in Extremis.* Boston: Allyn & Bacon, 1975.

BLATT, B. *The Revolt of Idiots.* Glen Ridge, N. J.: Exceptional Press, 1976.

BLATT, B., AND KAPLAN, F. *Christmas in Purgatory.* Boston: Allyn & Bacon, 1966.

BOOTH, P. New York Times Book Review Section (June 22, 1969).

BOURNE, R. S. *The Gary Schools.* Cambridge, Mass.: MIT Press, 1970. (Introduced and annotated by Adeline and Murray Levine.)

BOYKIN, J. C. "Class Intervals in City Public Schools." *Report of the Commissioner of Education for the Year 1890–91, Vol. 2.* Washington, D.C.: Government Printing Office, 1894.

BRUNER, J. S. *Toward a Theory of Instruction.* Cambridge, Mass.: Harvard University Press, 1966.

CHERNISS, C. *Professional Burnout in Human Service Organizations.* New York: Praeger, 1980.

CHRISTOPLOS, F. "Keeping Exceptional Children in Regular Classes." *Exceptional Children* 39 (1973): 569–572.

COHEN, D., AND FARRAR, E. "Power to Parents? The Story of Education Vouchers." *The Public Interest* 48 (1977): 72–97.

COLEMAN, J. *Equality of Educational Opportunity.* Washington, D.C.: U.S. Government Printing Office, 1966.

COLEMAN, J. S. (Chairman). *Youth: Transition to Adulthood.* Chicago: University of Chicago Press, 1974.

CONANT, J. B. *The Education of Teachers.* New York: McGraw-Hill, Inc., 1963.

COWDEN, P., AND COHEN, D. "Divergent Worlds of Practice. The Federal Reform of Local Schools in the Experimental Schools Program." Unpublished manuscript, Huron Institute, Cambridge, Mass.

COWEN, E., TROST, M. A., LORION, R. P., DORR, D., IZZO, L. D., AND ISAACSON, R. J. *New Ways in School Mental Health: Early Detection and Preventions of School Maladaptation.* New York: Human Sciences Press, 1975.

CREMIN, L. A. *The Transformation of the School.* New York: Alfred A. Knopf, Inc., 1961.

CROWSON, R. L., AND PORTER-GEHRIE, C. "The Discretionary Behavior of Principals in Large-City Schools." *Educational Administration Quarterly* 16, no. 1 (1980): 45–69.

DE TOCQUEVILLE, A. *Democracy in America.* New York: New American Library (Mentor Books), 1956.

DUNN, L. M. (Ed.). *Exceptional Children in the Schools: Special Education in Transition.* 2d Ed. New York: Holt, Rinehart & Winston, 1973.

DUNN, L. M. "Special Education for the Mildly Retarded—Is Much of It Justifiable?" *Exceptional Children* 35 (1968-1969): 5–22.

EPSTEIN, J. Book Review: New York Review of Books (December, 1964) Vol. 3.

FEHR, H. F. "Sense and Nonsense in a Modern School Mathematics Program." *The Arithmetic Teacher* XIII (1966): 83–91.

FELLMAN, D. (Ed.). *The Supreme Court and Education.* New York: Columbia University Press, 1969.

FLEXNER, A., AND BACHMAN, T. *The Gary Schools: A General Account.* New York: General Education Board, 1918.

FOUNTAIN, P. "What Teaching Does to Teachers. The Teachers as Workers." Doctoral Dissertation, Yale University, 1975.

FUCHS, E. *Teachers Talk.* Garden City, N.Y.: Anchor Books, 1969.

FUCHS, V. R. *Who Shall Live? Health, Economics, and Social Choice.* New York: Basic Books, 1975.

GARNER, W. R. "The Acquisition and Application of Knowledge: A Symbiotic Relation." *American Psychologist* 27, no. 10 (1972): 941–946.

GARNER, W. R. *Uncertainty and Structure as Psychological Concepts.* New York: John Wiley, 1966.

GOLDHAMMER, R. *Clinical Supervision.* New York: Holt, Rinehart & Winston, 1969.

GOLDHAMMER, K., SUTTLE, J. E., BECKER, G. L., AND ALDRIDGE, W. D. *Issues and Problems in Contemporary Educational Administration.* Eugene, Oregon: Center for Advanced Study of Educational Administration, University of Oregon Press, 1967.

GOODLAD, J. I. "The Schools and Education." *Saturday Review* (April 19, 1969).

GRANT, W. V., AND LIND, G. C. *Digest of Education Statistics, 1975 Edition.* Washington, D.C.: U.S. Government Printing Office, 1976.

GREEN, T. F. *Work, Leisure, and the American Schools.* New York: Random House, Inc., 1968.

GREEN T. F. *Predicting the Behavior of the Educational System.* Syracuse, N.Y.: Syracuse University Press, 1980.

GREENBERG, D. S. *The Politics of Pure Science.* New York: New American Library, 1967.

GROSS, N. "Sociology of Education, 1944–45." In *Sociology in the United States of America: A Trend Report,* ed. H. L. Zetterberg. Paris: UNESCO, 1956.

GROSS, N., AND HERRIOTT, R. E. *Staff Leadership in Public Schools.* New York: John Wiley & Sons, Inc., 1965.

GUMP, P. V., AND KOUNIN, J. S. "Issues Raised by Ecological and 'Classical' Research Efforts." Paper read at 1959 meeting of the Society for Research in Child Development.

HAMMONS, G. W. "Educating the Mildly Retarded: A Review." *Exceptional Children* 38 (1971–1972): 565–570.

HARRIS, W. T. *Report of the Commissioner of Education for the Year 1898–99, 1.* Washington, D.C.: Government Printing Office, 1900.

HENRY, J. *Culture Against Man.* New York: Random House, Inc., 1963.

HILGARD, D. M. "Historical Development of Grades and Departments in the Public Schools of Memphis, Tennessee." *The Elementary School Journal* 47, no. 3 (1946): 157–160.

HILL, K., AND SARASON, S. B. "A Further Longitudinal Study of the Relation of Test Anxiety and Defensiveness Test and School Performance over the Elementary School Years." *Monographs of the Society for Research in Child Development* XXXI, no. 2 (1966).

HILLYARD, M. "Differences in Kindergarten and Primary Teachers' Conceptions of Classroom Behavior." Doctoral Dissertation, Yale University, 1971.

HOLSINGER, M. P. "The Oregon School Bill Controversy, 1922–1925." *Pacific Historical Review* 37 (1968): 327–341.

HOOK, S. *Reason, Social Myths and Democracy.* New York: Harper Torchbooks, 1966.

HOLT, J. *How Children Fail.* New York: Pitman Publishing Corporation, 1964.

JACKSON, P. W. *Life in Classrooms.* New York: Holt, Rinehart & Winston, Inc., 1968.

JENCKS, C. *Inequality: A Reassessment of the Effect of Family and Schooling in America.* New York: Basic Books, 1972.

JONES, R. L. "Labels and Stigma in Special Education." *Journal of Exceptional Children* 38 (1971–1972): 553–564.

JONES, R. M. *Fantasy and Feeling in Education.* New York: New York University Press, 1968.

JORGENSON, L. P. "The Oregon School Law of 1922: Passage and Sequel." *Catholic Historical Review* LIV (1968): 455–466.

KELLEY, E. C. *Education for What Is Real.* New York: Harper, 1947, 114 pp.

KINDRED, M., COHEN, J., PENROD, D., AND SHAFFER, T. (Eds.). *The Mentally Retarded Citizen and the Law.* New York: Free Press. Macmillan, 1976.

KOERNER, J. D. Basic Education. *Education* 79 (1959): 372–374.

KOHL, H. *36 Children.* New York: New American Library, 1967.

KOLSTOE, O. P. "Programs for the Mildly Retarded: A Reply to the Critics." *Exceptional Children* 39 (1972–1973): 51–55.

KOUNIN, J. S. "Observation and Analysis of Classroom Management." Paper read at 1967 meeting of the American Educational Research Association.

KOUNIN, J. S., FRIESEN, W. V., AND NORTON, A. E. "Managing Emotionally Disturbed Children in Regular Classrooms." *Journal of Educational Psychology* LVII (1966): 1–13.

KOUNIN, J. S., GUMP, P. V., AND RYAN, J. J. "Explorations in Classroom Management." *Journal of Teacher Education* XII (1961): 235–246.

KOZOL, J. *Death at an Early Age.* Boston: Houghton Mifflin Company, 1967.

KRAMER, H. Book review of *The Humanities in American Life.* Report of the Commission on the Humanities. *Book Review* section, *New York Times,* Dec. 28, 1980, p. 1.

KRAUSE, D. U.S. Congress. House Select Committee on Aging. Hearing before the Subcommittee on Health and Long-Term Care, 94th Cong., 1st sess., July 8, 1975. (Available from Superintendent of Documents, U.S. Government Printing Office, Washington, D.C. 20402. Stock number 050–070–02903–0.)

LAUTER, P. "The Short, Happy Life of the Adams-Morgan Community School Project." *Harvard Educational Review* XXXVIII (1968): 235–262.

LEVINE, A. G. "Marital and Occupational Plans of Women in Professional Schools: Law, Medicine, Nursing, Teaching." Doctoral Dissertation, Yale University, 1968.

LEVINE, A., AND LEVINE, M. Introduction and annotation to *The Gary Schools* by R. S. Bourne. Cambridge, Mass.: The MIT Press, 1970a.

LEVINE, M., AND LEVINE A. *A Social History of Helping Services: Clinic, Court, School and Community.* New York: Appleton-Century-Crofts, 1970b.

LEWIN, K. *Resolving Social Conflicts.* New York: Harper & Row, 1948.

LEWIN, K., LIPPITT, R., AND WHITE, R. "Patterns of Aggressive Behavior in Experimentally Created 'Social Climates.'" *Journal of Social Psychology* X (1939): 271–291.

LIPPITT, R. "Field Theory and Experiment in Social Psychology: Autocratic and Democratic and Democratic Group Atmospheres." *American Journal of Sociology* 45 (1939): 26–49.

LIPPITT, R. "Studies on Experimentally Created Autocratic and Democratic Groups." *University of Iowa Studies: Studies in Child Welfare* XVI, no. 3 (1940): 45–198.

LIPPMAN, L., AND GOLDBERG, I. I. *Right to Education: Anatomy of the Pennsylvania Case and Its Implications for Exceptional Children.* New York: Teachers College Press, 1973.

LORTIE, D. C. *School Teacher.* Chicago: University of Chicago Press, 1975.

MACNEILL-LEHRER REPORT. "Teacher Burnout." Transcript of TV program, June 13, 1980 (WNET/Thirteen), New York City, N.Y.

MARRIS, P., AND REIN, M. *Dilemmas of Social Reform.* New York: Atherton Press, 1969.

MAYHEW, K. C., AND EDWARDS, A. C. *The Dewey School.* New York: Atherton Press, 1966.

MERCER, J. R. "Sociological Perspectives on Mild Mental Retardation." In *Social-Cultural Aspects of Mental Retardation,* ed. H. C. Haywood. New York: Appleton-Century-Crofts, 1970.

MERCER, J. R. "The Meaning of Mental Retardation." In *The Mentally Retarded Child and His Family,* ed. R. Koch and J. C. Dobson. New York: Brunner/Mazel, 1971.

MERCER, J. R. "A Policy Statement on Assessment Procedures and the Rights of Children." *Harvard Educational Review* 44, no. 1 (1974): 125–141.

MEYEROWITZ, J. H. "Family Background of Educable Mentally Retarded Children." In *The Efficacy of Special Education Training on the Development of Mentally Retarded Children,* ed. H. Goldstein, J. W. Moss, and L. J. Jordan. Urbana: University of Illinois Institute for Research of Exceptional Children, 1965, pp. 152–182.

MEYEROWITZ, J. H. "Peer Groups and Special Classes." *Mental Retardation* 5 (1967): 23 26.

MILLS, C. W. *The Sociological Imagination.* New York: Grove Press, 1959.

MILOFSKY, D. "Schooling for Kids No One Wants." *New York Times,* January 2, 1977, magazine section.

MURNANE, R. *Review of Organizing an Anarchy* (by Sproull, L., Weiner, S., and Wolf, D.). Economics of Education Review, 1981, in press.

PORTER-GEHRIE, C. (Book review article) "Ethnographic Data and Educational Policy Analysis: Recent Qualitative Research." *Educational Theory* 29, no. 3 (1979): 255–262.

RAPPAPORT, J. *Community Psychology.* New York: Holt, Rinehart & Winston, 1977.

RAVITCH, D. *The Great School Wars.* New York: Basic Books, 1974.

RICKOVER, H. G. *Education and Freedom.* New York: Dutton, 1959, 256 pp.

RICKOVER, H. G. "Education in the U.S.S.R. and the U.S.A." *Graduate Comment, Wayne State University* III, no. 3 (1960): 2–6.

ROGERS, D. *110 Livingston Street: Politics and Bureaucracy in the New York City School System.* New York: Random House, Inc., 1968.

ROSENBAUM, J. *Making Inequality.* New York: Wiley, 1976.

SARASON, E. K., AND SARASON, S. B. "Some Observations on the Teaching of the New Math." In *The Yale Psycho-Educational Clinic: Collected Papers and Studies,* ed. S. B. Sarason and F. Kaplan. Boston: Massachusetts State Department of Mental Health (Monograph Series), 1969.

SARASON, S. B. "Towards a Psychology of Change and Innovation." *American Psychologist* XXII (1967): 227–233.

SARASON, S. B. "The Creation of Settings." In *The Yale Psycho-Educational Clinic:*

Collected Papers and Studies, ed. S. B. Sarason and F. Kaplan. Boston: Massachusetts State Department of Mental Health (Monograph Series), 1969a.

SARASON, S. B. The School Culture and Processes of Change. In *The Yale Psycho-Educational Clinic: Collected Papers and Studies,* ed. S. B. Sarason and F. Kaplan. Boston: Massachusetts Department of Mental Health (Monograph Series), 1969b.

SARASON, S. B. *The Creation of Settings and the Future Societies.* San Francisco: Jossey-Bass, 1972.

SARASON, S. B. "Jewishness, Blackishness and the Nature-Nurture Controversy." *American Psychologist* 28 (1973): 962–971.

SARASON, S. B. "Community Psychology and the Anarchist Insight." *American Journal of Community Psychology* 4 (1976): 243–261.

SARASON, S. B. *Work, Aging, and Social Change. Professionals and the One Life—One Career Imperative.* New York: The Free Press (Macmillan), 1977.

SARASON, S. B. "An Unsuccessful War on Poverty?" *American Psychologist* 33 (1978): 831–839.

SARASON, S. B. *Psychology Misdirected. The Social Scientist in the Social Order.* New York: Free Press, 1981.

SARASON, S. B., CARROLL, C. F., MATON, K., COHEN, S., AND LORENTZ, E. *Human Services and Resource Networks.* San Francisco: Jossey-Bass, 1977.

SARASON, S. B., DAVIDSON, K., AND BLATT, B. *The Preparation of Teachers. An Unstudied Problem in Education.* New York: John Wiley, 1962.

SARASON, S. B., DAVIDSON, K., LIGHTHALL, F., WAITE, R., AND RUEBUSH, B. *Anxiety in Elementary School Children.* New York: John Wiley & Sons, Inc., 1960.

SARASON, S. B., AND DORIS, J. *Educational Handicap, Public Policy, and Social History. A Broadened Perspective on Mental Retardation.* New York: The Free Press. Macmillan. 1979.

SARASON, S. B., HILL, K., AND ZIMBARDO, P. "A Longitudinal Study of the Relation of Test Anxiety to Performance on Intelligence and Achievement Tests." *Monographs of the Society for Research in Child Development,* 1964, No. 98.

SARASON, S. B., AND LORENTZ, E. *The Challenge of the Resource Exchange Network.* San Francisco: Jossey-Bass, 1979.

SARASON, S. B., LEVINE, M., GOLDENBERG, I. I., CHERLIN, D. L., AND BENNETT, E. *Psychology in Community Settings.* New York: John Wiley & Sons, Inc., 1966.

SCHINDLER-RAINMAN, E., AND LIPPITT, R. *The Volunteer Community: Creative Use of Human Resources.* Fairfax, Va.: NTL Learning Resource Corporation 1975.

SCHWEBEL, A. "Physical and Social Distancing in Teacher-Pupil Relationships," Doctoral Dissertation, Yale University, 1969.

SKAIFE, R. A. "Conflicts Can Be Solved." *Education* 78 (1958): 387–391.

SMITH, L. M., AND KEITH, P. *Anatomy of Educational Innovation.* New York: John Wiley, 1971.

SPINDLER, G. D. (Ed.). *Education and Culture.* New York: Holt, Rinehart and Winston, Inc., 1963.

SPROULL, L., WEINER, S., AND WOLF, D. *Organizing an Anarchy.* Chicago: University of Chicago Press, 1978.

STEPHENS, J. M. *The Process of Schooling. A Psychological Examination.* New York: Holt, Rinehart and Winston, Inc., 1967.

STOKES, A. P. *Church and State in the United States: Historical Development and Contemporary Problems of Religious Freedom under the Constitution.* 3 vols. New York: Harper & Bros., 1950.

SUSSKIND, E. "Encouraging Teachers to Encourage Children's Curiosity: A Parietal Competence." *Journal of Clinical Child Psychology* (Summer 1979): 101.

SUSSKIND, E. C. "Questioning and Curiosity in the Elementary School Classroom." Doctoral Dissertation, Yale University, 1969.

TAYLOR, D. W. (Chairman). "Education for Research in Psychology." *American Psychologist* XIV (1959): 167–179.

TAYLOR, E. A. *Experiments with a Backward Class.* London: Methuen, 1946.

The Humanities in American Life. Report of the Commission on the Humanities. Berkeley: University of California Press, 1980.

TROEN, S. K. *The Public and the Schools: Shaping the St. Louis System, 1838–1920.* Columbia: University of Missouri Press, 1975.

TYACK, D. B. "The Perils of Pluralism: The Background of the Pierce Case." *American Historical Review* LXXIV (1968): 74–98.

USDAN, M. D. "The School Administrator: Modern Renaissance Man." *The Record* (Teachers College, Columbia) LXIX (1968): 641–648.

WALLER, W. *The Sociology of Teaching.* New York: John Wiley & Sons, 1932.

WATSON, J. D. *The Double Helix.* New York: Atheneum Publishers, 1968.

WEATHERLY, R., AND LIPSKY, M. "Street-Level Bureaucrats and Institutional Innovation: Implementing Special-Education Reform." *Harvard Educational Review* 47 (1977): 171–197.

WEINBERG, A. M. "But is the Teacher also a Citizen?" *Science* (August 6, 1965): 601–606.

WERTHEIMER, M. *Productive Thinking.* New York: Harper & Row Publishers, 1945.

WHITEHEAD, A. N. *The Aims of Education.* New York: Mentor, 1929 (paperback).

WICKER, A. W. "Undermanning Theory and Research: Implications for the Study of Psychological and Behavioral Effects of Excess Populations." *Representative Research in Social Psychology* 4 (1973): 185–206.

WICKER, A. W., AND KIRMEYER, S. "From Church to Laboratory to National Park." In *Experiencing the Environment,* ed. S. Wapner, S. B. Cohen, and B. Kaplan. New York: Plenum Press, 1976.

WOLCOTT, H. F. *The Man in the Principal's Office.* New York: Holt, Rinehart and Winston, 1973.

WOLCOTT, H. F. *Teachers vs. Technocrats.* Eugene: Center for Educational Policy and Management, University of Oregon, 1977.

ZAX, M., AND COWEN, E. *Abnormal Psychology: Changing Conceptions.* New York: Holt, Rinehart and Winston, 1972.

ZAX, M., AND COWEN, E. L. "Early Identification and Prevention of Emotional Disturbance in a Public School." In *Emergent Approaches to Mental Health Problems,* ed. E. L. Cowen, E. A. Gardner, and M. Zax. New York: Appleton-Century-Crofts, 1967.

ZAX, M., AND SPECTER, G. A. *An Introduction to Community Psychology.* New York: Wiley, 1974.

ZIGLER, E., AND MUENCHOW, S. "Mainstreaming. The Proof Is in the Implementation." *American Psychologist* 34, no. 10 (1979): 993–996.

PART II

REVISITING:
25 YEARS LATER

Chapter 15
Why Revisit?

It may be hard for the reader to believe, but the fact is that I have never reread the book being revisited. One reason is temperamental or personal. It is very difficult for me to read *anything* I have thought through, written, and published, even though upon completion I am always plagued by the feeling that I could have done better. That is not to say that I am not satisfied with what I have written but rather that I know that the problems I have discussed are more complicated and ramified than I know—i.e., nothing is as encapsulated as I have put it; everything is related to everything else; the more you think you know the more you need to know; I do not (cannot) have a monopoly on truth; the marketplace of ideas will inform you about the limitations of what you have thought and written.

Writing, *like teaching,* requires chutzpah: You not only have something to say, something you deem important that others should know, but, fatefully, you think you know how to get it across, how to help others assimilate what you have to say. But if writing, like teaching, requires chutzpah, it also obliges you to acknowledge that you will very likely fall short of the mark. It is that acknowledgment that many writers and teachers have difficulty confronting, a difficulty that makes them very unreceptive to change. So, when the fruits of their efforts are criticized, it is regarded not as a spur to a possible change but as an uninformed attack that must be resisted.

Not many of us possess the combination of chutzpah and humbleness. That combination makes life difficult. We would rather appear as confident and certain rather than as confident and tentative. When I finished the school culture book I was certain (not too strong a word) that I had said what I wanted to say. I was far from certain that I had said it well or that I had put it in an appropriately large social-historical context. The evidence that I had no cause for unalloyed satisfaction and certainty is demonstrated by the fact that everything I have written after that book represented a way of rounding out the picture, i.e., variations on themes that early book contained. Indeed, nothing I have written after that book is truly comprehensible without reading that book. At least that is the way I see it. More correctly, that is the way I saw it until I finally reread the book. More about that later.

Temperamental and personal reasons aside, there was one factor that, so to speak, played into my resistance to rereading the book. (Needless to say, I always thought I knew precisely what I had written; resistance to rereading was not a form of amnesia.) The book was very positively received. No one pointed out a major flaw. Even today the book is very frequently cited. I began to receive (and still do) scores of letters from people telling me how helpful the book was in making sense of their experience. I had no reason to reread the book.

However, there was one nagging thought that bothered me when I wrote the book. From the time I left graduate school in 1942, and up until very recently, I have always been in and around the field of special education. So why is there next to nothing in the book about a very important feature of our schools, a feature of great interest to me, witness the several books I have written about mental retardation? That omission was the result of a very conscious decision based on the belief that to include it would muddy the conceptual waters, besides which the great bulk of educators have no interest in special education except to support the segregation of children with special problems in special classes. As soon as the book was published I felt increasingly guilty about that omission, as if I had not been true to myself or to the field. I had made, I had to admit, an inexcusable, egregious mistake, if not a failure of nerve. No one, orally or in print, noted or criticized that omission.

I was right, of course, that educators in general were not interested in special education, and that if I included what I should have said, they would have skipped those pages or perused them superficially. My mistake inhered in two things. The first is that precisely because the educational community viewed special education as "special" was reason enough to ask what that view said about the culture of schools. Imagine the situation where schools have decided that children markedly below or above the average height for their age, or weight, should be in special classes. We would be aghast. How do you justify such obvious discrimination? On what evidence is such a practice based? Is it a practice to make life easier for teachers in "regular" classrooms? Are these children so aesthetically displeasing as to make them objects of derision from other students? What does such a practice say about the school's conception of its obligation to further the intellectual–educational–social development of students, and why is that practice the best or only means to discharge that obligation?

There are other questions, but the point is that segregation is always based on, among other things, values about how people *should* live together or not live together, and alternatives to "should" are wrong! If I had done what I should have done in 1970, I would have discussed all those questions for the light that conventional answers would have provided for how an institutional culture defines educational policy and practice, i.e., what it judges to be right, natural, and proper both for children who are segregated and children who are not segregated. At the very least, I would have been able to raise and make the point that educational institutions are not only "educational" institutions but moral ones. However you define culture, morality is always in the picture. What we expect of ourselves and others in our interactions has an ethical and moral basis. And too frequently we forget that basis until our ox is gored, at which time we become acutely aware that fairness is a sometime thing. That is as true in our individual lives as it is for us in our institutional roles.

The second aspect of my mistake was less a mistake than it was a misweighing of the strength of the public dissatisfaction with schools, and the anger, force, and organizational savvy of parents of handicapped children. Neither of these two factors was recognized in the educational community. I knew about both factors, but within the school culture there was, for all practical purposes, no consideration of their possible future significances. Within the confines of schools there were two worlds: here in the school and the "outside" world. And in the daily concerns of educators the outside world was just that: outside where it belonged. If I knew both factors well, I was not the only one who, when I wrote the book (in 1970), could not have predicted the passage of the 1975 Public Law 94-142, which was intended to and did affect every school in the country. That law was a reflection of the social change brought about by World War II and nothing illustrates that change better than the Supreme Court's 1954 desegregation decision from which 94-142 is a direct descendant. If I did not predict the passage of that law, I was not surprised by its passage. In the educational community, surprise and bewilderment were the dominant reactions. The point is that in the encapsulated school culture there was (and still is) a conception of the outside world that was insensitive, unsophisticated, and maladaptive. That was a lesson that should have been learned in the sixties when schools were almost totally unprepared for the consequences of the social change that made the decade legendary. It was a lesson that could not be learned in a school culture riveted on its internal workings. So, when a second edition of the book was published in 1982, it differed only from the first edition by a new chapter on 94-142.

Another change to the second edition of the book was the elimination of the chapter on the Dewey school. This was done at the urging of the publisher, based on the fact that I was adding the chapter on PL94-142. I agreed to cut the Dewey chapter; however, this was in no way an acknowledgment that Dewey's great contribution to the field was obsolete—quite the contrary. I had written that chapter to make the point that in order to understand schools today—as they modally are— you have to contrast them to schools based on a very different theoretical and organizational rationale. How and why are they different and with what consequences for their common purposes? When I wrote the book, calls for school change were loud and clear. By describing Dewey's school I was asking: Did not his school speak to many of the criticisms directed at schools? Is there not much to be learned from what he created? Should we not take him seriously? The answers to the questions were yes. However, my summary was minuscule compared to the large volume (Mayhew and Edwards, 1966) from which it was taken. Therefore, as in the second edition, in this current work I have left the chapter out. I will take up the significance of Dewey's contribution in much greater detail in Chapter 16 and I refer the reader to *The Dewey School,* by Mayhew and Edwards, for a full description of the school itself.

There have been changes in the culture of the school, although one has to be on guard to avoid confusing change with improvement. Would those changes require me to change what I had written? Wherein had I been incomplete or wrong? Was it possible that I had not taken seriously enough the practical implications of what I had written? That I had underestimated the force of the school culture in regard to change? That by focusing on *the* school I was not giving sufficient attention to the larger culture? That what I had written was on target but it was a target embedded in a larger relevant context? That what was at stake for the society was far more serious than I had indicated?

Should I revisit the culture of the school and the problem of change? I could not let go of that question even though in other books (Sarason, 1983, 1990, 1993a, 1993b, 1995) I was doing just that based on the assumption that what I had written in the school culture book needed no revision. Could I do such a revisiting keeping in check the tendency to be soft on one's self, to own up to the possibility that I had not had a corner on the truth? So, I read, reread the book, and talked with informed friends who had used or had been influenced by the book, none of whom was a shrinking violet. None of them even hinted that there was reason to change anything, but in light of what had been happening, they said I should feel obliged to talk about changes that have occurred and how, if at all, those changes should be assessed. One colleague put it this way. "There are people today who feel that a book on the school culture written 25 years ago cannot speak to what they perceive as a changed scene. By revisiting you have an opportunity to demonstrate, if you can, that the basic argument is sound, and would be even sounder if you elaborated on what the book either contains or implies."

An anthropologist friend said, "Cultures do change, slowly or quickly, and some of the most important stimuli to changes in theory and method in my field have been the result of revisiting cultures initially studied and written up years or decades earlier." That had particular significance for me because early in my career I had a very close collaboration with an anthropologist, Thomas Gladwin, from whom I learned a great deal, not the least of which was that discerning cultural change required more than an initial visit. He later went back to the South Pacific culture we in our different ways had studied and it was a very illuminating revisit in terms of the appearance and reality of changes. Indeed, that collaboration was the background from which emerged a feature of my book that practically every reader (if I can believe what people told me) found intriguing, fascinating, and instructive. I refer to my man from Mars parked on a space platform above a school, possessed of the most avant-garde computers enabling him to correlate every observation with every other observation of *overt* behavior, thus enabling him to discern the most frequent *regularities.* His problem was that he did not know our language and he did not know what was in the heads of those he was observing. And, the fantasy continues, he learns our language and then asks us what is the rationale for the regularities his computers discerned. For example, why is a school one of the most densely populated places on earth for five consecutive days and then is devoid of people for two consecutive days? That must, he assumes, have an educational rationale; otherwise why not a 4–3 regularity, or 6–1, or any other combination? He is dumbfounded to learn that the observed regularity, let alone its assumed superiority, has no basis in comparative experience. If it says nothing about educational rationale, it speaks volumes about the nature and history of our larger culture. My man from Mars was a deliberate means for discerning aspects of the school culture independent of my subjectivity. As I shall endeavor to show in later chapters, putting the man from Mars to work today is no less instructive than it was a quarter of a century ago. I would go so far as to say that if the man from Mars gimmick had been employed in the years since the book was written, we would have a far more secure basis than we have for determining how changes in the school culture have had their intended impact.

There are other *impersonal* reasons for revisiting. Let us say you have been a classroom teacher or school principal (or in any other school system role) for 5 or 10 or more years. And let us assume that it was the practice in your system to videotape such personnel during the first month of each year to allow you (not anyone else) to determine if and how you have changed in the discharge of your obligations. Presumably, one would hope, you have changed in small and large ways. What would you think of an educator who after viewing his or her tapes says that no change was discernible and is pleased to say so? What would you think of an educator who says that he or she cringes when viewing the early tapes because of the inadequacies they reveal, and how much he or she has changed? Are we not likely to look dramatically more favorably on the second educator than on the first? Yes and maybe. Yes because we expect that a person should learn from experience. Maybe because we, who have not seen the tapes, cannot conclude that the changes the second educator saw were, from our standpoint, educationally productive for students. *That* we can only determine by independent observation allowing us to pass judgment on whether the educator is achieving his or her *stated goals,* and whether that achievement runs counter to our values, conceptions, and goals. In and of itself change can be desirable or undesirable, productive or unproductive, depending on why you think the person should, so to speak, be in the business. Revisiting is not an empty, routine endeavor. It is not for the sole purpose of noting change. It is also for the purpose of noting whether the thinking that informs those changes is consistent with stated educational purposes and goals. And it is also for the purpose of putting those changes out on the table so that they can be contrasted to other ways of thinking and acting. Revisiting is a necessity, but it is not a panacea.

Let me get at the issue with a very different kind of example. During the 1960s, I met, on an individual or group basis, with hundreds (perhaps thousands) of educators about the obstacles to school improvement. The list of obstacles they gave was quite long but, with rare exceptions, at or near the top of the list was inadequate financing of schools. All other obstacles did not come near that of inadequate budgets. Although the number of such meetings noticeably declined after that decade, the number was still on the high side. Why did it take me at least 15 years (1970–1985) to become aware of the fact that relatively few educators any longer believed that money was a crucial obstacle? This is not to say that they regarded financing of schools to be unimportant (far from it) but rather that they no longer believed it was the root problem, which if overcome, would bring about improvement. It took me as long as it did because I was not sensitive to the difference between what people say in public and what they will say in private or off the record. In the sixties, educators said right out loud to the general public that schools would never improve apart from an influx of increased funding.

But by 1985 I became aware that although some educators still believed it, a number of them would say only in private that they had changed their minds. Money was important but it did not speak to more serious problems. *That* was a change! But it was not a change you could have noted if you had no experiential baseline from the sixties. I had that baseline but, even so, it took a while until I could become aware of the change. But the significance of that change was by no means immediately apparent. What caused these educators to change their minds? Was that change correlated with other changes in attitude, values, and experience? Was it an encapsulated reflection of a more general change, the substance and direction of which were unclear? I changed. I began to talk with educators about the sources of the change in regard to the power of money to improve educational outcomes. But I could not have done so unless I had the sixties as a baseline. As a result, I learned a great deal about how the school culture was changing, but I also had to conclude that I had not taken seriously enough what I had written earlier. I will go into greater detail about this in later chapters.

Why revisit the school culture after 25 years? The briefest of answers is to provide a baseline in the present that can be compared to the past and serve as a baseline for future revisits (which, of course, I will not be around to do or read). The other part of the answer is, obviously, that I regard the early book as in need of elaboration, not revision. It may be self-serving or narcissistic blindness, but I could see no virtue whatever in summarizing that book. It states and justifies my basic position. Without it, a discussion of the changes that have taken place would lack context. The more I thought about it, the more I realized that if the present volume did not contain that book and was restricted to the current scene, *I would end up having to rewrite it anyway in order for the reader to comprehend where I was coming from.* The reader could not truly understand what I would say unless that reader understood what I *had* said. I gave much thought to summarizing what I had said. I had to conclude that if I resorted to summary it would be another example of what we too often experience in restaurants: the descriptions on the menu are far more enticing than the dishes served.

Two years ago Dr. Emory Cowen of the University of Rochester found the following in his mailbox. The author is unknown.

HORSE STORY

COMMON ADVICE FROM KNOWLEDGEABLE HORSE TRAINERS INCLUDES THE ADAGE, *"If the horse you're riding dies, get off."* Seems simple enough, yet, in the education business we don't always follow that advice. Instead, we often choose from an array of alternatives which include:

1. Buying a stronger whip.
2. Trying a new bit or bridle.
3. Switching riders.
4. Moving the horse to a new location.
5. Riding the horse for longer periods of time.
6. Saying things like, "This is the way we've always ridden this horse."
7. Appointing a committee to study the horse.
8. Arranging to visit other sites where they ride dead horses efficiently.
9. Increasing the standards for riding dead horses.
10. Creating a test for measuring our riding ability.
11. Comparing how we're riding now with how we did 10 or 20 years ago.
12. Complaining about the state of horses these days.
13. Coming up with new styles of riding.
14. Blaming the horse's parents. The problem is often in the breeding.
15. Tightening the cinch. ■

The significance of *Horse Story,* to me at least, is less in its satire and more in the fact that its author is expressing what the bulk of people today are thinking and feeling about the reform effort of the past 25 years. If I had had *Horse Story* when I first wrote the book, and included it because it did express things I was trying to say, I would have been regarded as a sourpuss, or a wet blanket, or a nihilist, or all of these and more. I used the story in a recent book (Sarason, 1995) and I was not surprised that many people wrote or said to me that the story encapsulated their thinking, feelings, and attitudes. There have been changes in the past quarter of a century. We have learned a good deal from our mistakes. We have learned far more about what to do and far less about what to do. As the following pages will indicate, there are too many people in the educational community who are insensitive to what I regard as the most significant change since I wrote the book: For the first time in our history, increasing numbers of people find themselves concluding that our schools, generally speaking, are inadequate and obsolete. From my perspective that is good news. The bad news is that there is reason to believe that their disillusionment will cause them to support nostrums of the type indicted by the unknown author of *Horse Story.*

Chapter 16

Are Schools Unique Organizations?

If you spend your adult years in a particular type of organization, the chances are that you will regard that organization as having special characteristics no other one has. That is the case for a cleric in the church, a professor in the university, a hospital employee, an educator in our schools. The perception of specialness in these instances is reinforced by a general culture that regards these organizations as not only special but unique. It seems so obvious that we overlook or fail to see the myriad similarities among these organizations. Indeed, we are likely to resist a point of view that holds that these organizations are different; they are not unique. And the *practical* consequences that follow seeing them as different but not unique are enormous.

Imagine it is 1971 (when the book was published) and we asked educators if schools were like General Motors, or IBM, or Coca Cola. They would have looked at us with staring disbelief, at best, and given us a hostile response, at worst. Schools are schools, IBM is IBM, and why ask a nonsensical question suggesting that apples are oranges? Now let us imagine that we asked the same question of IBM or Coca Cola employees. And the near universal answer would have been similar to that the educators gave: "Schools are very special places, requiring very special personnel, serving a very special preadult population, and with unique purposes. You are confusing apples and oranges. We are very vitally interested in our schools because the students they educate are ones we need and employ. If they are sending us inadequately prepared students, we insist they do a better job. We cannot tell them how to do a better job just as they cannot tell us how to do our job. What we can and have to say is that schools are not doing a good job. Schools are not business organizations. They are unique organizations doing a unique job, but that does not mean that we should not tell them when they are doing a lousy job. And they are."

In 1970, those answers had a surface plausibility, the "of course" kind of answers that are the hallmark of a culturally determined belief or attitude which, I should hasten to add, does not mean it is invalid or misleading. In this case, however, they are both on at least two grounds. I draw upon personal experience to illustrate the first of them.

I WAS ASKED IN THE MID-1970S TO SERVE ON THE GOVERNING BOARD TO CREATE Yale's School of Organization and Management (SOM). I knew that business schools historically had no interest whatsoever in education generally and public schools in particular. But the new school was intended to include the public as well as the private sector. How, I argued, could such a school not include *something* about public schools? They were more respectful of me than they were of my opinions. That made it hard for them to say no to my offer to conduct an elective seminar for students, the lengthy title of which was "Policy and Management Issues in Human Services Institutions (Including Education)." In at least two of the years I conducted that seminar I had the students read the school culture book with this question in mind: Are schools unique organizations?

It is worthy of emphasis that the students in this elective seminar had come to SOM precisely because of its public-sector emphasis. All had previously worked in private-sector organizations, and their average age was between 30 and 35 years. None had ever worked in a school. What was common to all of their written answers could be put this way: "Your description of life in a school and school system is no different than life in any hierarchically, bureaucratic private-sector company. The same top-down style of management, the conflicts about status, role, and power, the hostility surrounding change—so what else is new? Schools have the unique *purpose* of educationally rearing students; they have their special jargon, methods, and internal structure. But despite their unique purpose, and because of the way schools are structured and organized, the way this part is supposed to be related to that part, they differ not at all from life in private-sector companies. The problems are amazingly similar. Their so-called bottom lines are uniquely different, but little if anything else is. Companies have to make a profit and they will not if they do not satisfy their customers in a competitive market. Schools are also in a competitive marketplace, but a dramatically less competitive one, e.g., parochial and private schools. For all practical purposes they have a monopoly but, even so, they have to satisfy parents and others. Your book says they are not satisfying them and they are not. If this situation continues or gets worse, everything we have learned about the private sector says that the day will come, has to come, when the dissatisfied customers will say, 'No more.'" ∎

Schools are not unique as organizations. They are different. In a footnote on page 216 of the first edition I said:

IN RECENT YEARS THERE HAS BEEN AN INCREASING AWARENESS OF THE NEED TO study and conceptualize the change process in relation to the schools, e.g., Miles, 1964; Watson, 1967; Bentzen and Goodlad et al., 1968. The interested readers should consult these publications, although they involve for the most part new projects, the results of which will not be known for some time. There are, of course, similarities between some of the points I have made in this book and these publications. There are important differences. Whereas I have strongly emphasized the need for descriptions of the modal process of change (and its variations) as a basis for conceptualization, as well as a control against premature theorizing, these writers (for the most part) seem to assume that we know the modal process. It is also quite clear that their way of thinking about change has been very heavily influenced by those who have studied the industrial setting, an influence that can only be justified by demonstrating that the culture of the school and industry have all that much in common so as to transfer change strategies from one setting to the other. This degree of genotypic similarity has not been demonstrated, and I do not think it can be. Related to this reservation is another one and that is that techniques that seem to have been helpful in the industrial setting—and I refer specifically to various group dynamics procedures—are not only applied in the school setting, but have come to be viewed by many people (not the authors cited above) as panaceas. This is regrettable on three counts: the techniques have come to be viewed as ends in themselves (nowadays everyone, it seems, is in or is urged to participate in some kind of sensitivity training group), they place such an emphasis on "communication" and "interpersonal relations" as to convey the impression that they are the most important source (etiologically speaking) of problems in the school culture, whereas they are, in my opinion, far more symptoms than cause (in contrast, for example, to dilemmas of role, the effects of routine and tradition, life in the classroom, irrelevant preparation, and the usual ways in which teaching and learning are conceptualized); finally, overselling these techniques does a disservice to that which is valid and helpful in their limited use. ■

I was wrong in underemphasizing the genotypic similarities. I was right in saying that methods for change that appeared to be fruitful in industry would not be fruitful for school change. I discuss this topic at length in Chapter 19 when I take up the practical implications of the school's unique purpose.

The answers I got to the imaginary questions in the imaginary interviews of educators and private-sector people were representative of what the bulk of the population would have said. The second reason the answers are both invalid and misleading is no less understandable but far more inexcusable. I was writing a book to describe the culture of the school at a particular era in this society. But cultures, be they of societies or any of their major institutions, are not comprehensible in a comprehensive way apart from their histories. Can you understand the United States apart from its origins, vicissitudes, development? Of course, comparing the country today to what it was in 1776 or 1787 is on a purely descriptive basis the difference between day and night. And, yet, today the country possesses political institutions (the presidency, Congress, Supreme Court) based on a philosophy, set of values, and procedures remarkably similar to what they were when they were created. And those who are in government make sure that the citizenry knows that what they stand for is consistent with what the founding fathers intended. The frequency with which we hear the words *founding fathers* is a way of telling us that the past is still in the present, i.e., the past is not in a museum of dead relics.

Most people may not carry an awareness of that past in their heads, but that does not mean that the past-in-the-present is not shaping their thinking and behavior. That is one reason I initially included the chapter on Dewey and his school. I was indicating, too briefly, that there was an educational past that for some people today (e.g., I and not a few others) was very much alive and, in fact, in the late 19th century and the first three decades of the 20th, Dewey's ideas, theory, and criticisms were greeted warmly by many people. Why do so many educators today not know that? How do they explain why his ideas lost influence? Were his criticisms wrong then and wrong now? On the contrary—today, it is fair to say, Dewey's major criticisms of schools, embodied in the features of his school, are receiving a hearing I did not anticipate, although practically no one recognizes that they are reinventing the wheel. Independently to reinvent the wheel is no small feat. To reinvent the flat tire is no feat whatsoever, and that is precisely what has characterized reform efforts in the post–World War II era.

In all candor I am compelled to say that when I wrote the book in 1970 I was both aghast and discouraged by how many educators did not, for all practical purposes, know Dewey's work. If they had read and digested Dewey, they would have known that his ideas and criticisms were as relevant to *their* problems *today* as they were to their counterparts' problems long ago. *Educators, I had to conclude, were ahistorical, and that had enormous consequences—negative ones—for their efforts to reform schools.* It was Dewey who said that knowledge is external; knowing is internal. History in a book is external and remains aridly so unless you forge, or are helped to forge, its content into your lived experience, i.e., it takes on personal meaning in your lived present; you *possess* that knowledge as *yours*; you "own it."

Including the Dewey chapter was my way of making these points. Although I believed that history is always a variable, I consciously made the decision not to include history because it might divert attention away from my most important goal: to demonstrate to readers, most of whom I assumed would be educators, that their working in schools did not mean that they recognized and took seriously the fact that schools have a culture. The word *culture* does not have a concrete, visible referent such as words like *rock, stove,* or *hat.* We have to conceptualize culture so that we become sensitive to its meanings, interconnections, and directions. In the ordinary course of our days we are not aware of culture. Indeed, we take it for granted without examining it. Some people—probably most—never articulate a conception of culture. It takes special circumstances derived from two factors.

The fact is that in my adult years I came to public schools as an outsider, primarily as a researcher and then as a helper to teachers in their classrooms. Nothing in my professional education as a psychologist in any way prepared me to understand schools. I saw myself as an outsider and I was made quite aware that I was seen by school personnel as an outsider, i.e., I lived in one world, they lived in another. You have to be unusually dense and uncurious not to ask yourself why you are seen not only as an outsider but as a somewhat unwelcome one. I saw myself as a sympathetic, harmless character; they tended to see me as kin to the visitor from Mars. How to explain that? That brings me to the second factor.

I was in the role of a helper and, being a somewhat friendly person, over time I established friendly relationships with school personnel. We did not have to be on guard with each other. As a result—and it took time—I became aware that I was being told things that made it obvious that life in a school was very complex, far more complex than those with whom I talked realized, and dramatically more complex than I had imagined. It was an example of a maxim that we know to be true but we do not take seriously: "Part the curtain, go behind a person's words, style, and appearances and you find another world you did not suspect." And what I found required me to begin to conceptualize the culture of the school. One of the most fruitful ways of gaining insight into the culture of schools (or any other organization) is to determine how its members respond to alternative ways of thinking about and organizing a school because their responses tell you, directly or indirectly, what they regard as right, natural, and proper: the underlying rationale and the practices and structure they require and justify. I included the chapter on the Dewey school not only to indicate that there had been such a school, but also to tell the reader how the culture of today's schools is a mammoth obstacle to anything resembling a dispassionate and serious effort to assess the possible virtues of the alternatives, i.e., it is "impractical" or "utopian," or the stuff of fantasy. Those are the kinds of responses that define that which *is* right, natural, and proper—what is the "right" rationale, structure, and practice—and what is "off limits."

Precisely because I am talking about 1970, I must relate one of my "discoveries" about the school culture because of what it says about changes that have occurred since then in the school culture and about which I will say more later.

I CAME FROM THE FIELD OF CLINICAL PSYCHOLOGY. IT IS A FEATURE OF THE CLINICAL professions that in their training and practice individuals spend a lot of time in case conferences. As a friend and colleague, Dr. Murray Levine once quipped, "Every clinic needs two staffs: one to go to case meetings and another to do the work." I was not long in schools before I realized that the tradition of frequent and regular meetings to discuss individual cases—for that matter, to discuss any meaningful issue—did not exist. That floored me. Each teacher dealt alone with his or her problems; there was no give-and-take forum where one could learn anything from anyone else. That is what Murray Levine meant by "teaching is a lonely profession." ■

How to explain this? Why did teachers say nothing about the absence of such a tradition? Teachers, no less than those in the clinical professions, always have to deal with difficult or hard-to-understand individuals. Why is it expected that a teacher will *always* deal *alone* with those kinds of problems? How was the absence of the collegial case conference reflective of the school culture? What would have to happen for that absence to be recognized and its self-defeating consequences confronted? The questions multiplied. I was not dealing with a personality problem. I was faced with the problem of the culture of the school. Again, one of the reasons I initially included the Dewey chapter was to contrast collegiality in Dewey's school and the public schools of 1970. In that respect, as in many others, the contrast is stark. On theoretical, practical, social-philosophical grounds, Dewey's school *required* a high degree of collegiality.

But the major reason the answers we would have gotten from educators and corporate people in 1970 were historically, inexcusably wrong is far more serious than ignoring Dewey and his school. Briefly put, it goes this way:

1. With the advent of universal, compulsory education, in large part a consequence of waves of immigration, the main purpose of schooling was to tame and socialize the children of immigrants, to make them respectful of American values, beliefs, work ethic, and political institutions. "Tame and socialize" may seem harsh, but only if you read the present into the past. Given the times, schooling was seen as the major means of divorcing children from the "foreign" speech, thoughts, and ways of their parents. Education was indoctrination. The concept of individuality of students was never in the picture.
2. Especially in the growing metropolitan areas, schools became very large; classes of 50, 60, or more students were not unusual. The administrative structure of schools became more differentiated, complex, bureaucratic. The main purpose of schooling did not change.
3. Schools resembled factories. That was not fortuitous. Educators were very much taken with the concept of the efficiency of the assembly line, of a rigid organizational structure, of everyone having his place in the scheme of things. Henry Ford was a revered icon because of his organizational genius, i.e., things went according to a clear, predetermined plan that left no room for individual initiative. Educators sought to emulate Ford who, it should be remembered, said that a customer could have any color car he desired as long as it was black. *Not only were educators influenced by the industrial model but industrial leaders made clear that schools should take that model seriously if they were to "produce" the kinds of workers industry needed.* (That influence, please note, was precisely what Dewey explicitly criticized.)

In short, in our imaginary 1970 interviews with educators and corporate types, there would have been no recognition of the historical fact that schools as organizations were incomprehensible apart from the ways they had been influenced by the private sector. Therefore, they could not see that even 1970 schools, organizationally speaking, were obvious lineal descendants of schools as they were a century ago. And, as I shall discuss in later chapters, for all practical purposes the overarching aim of schooling had changed little. The situation is somewhat different today.

What if we asked today, 25 years later, the same question of educators and private-sector people? I shall give the "average" response of each group even though it masks somewhat the range of answers. And that average response is based on what educational and corporate leaders have said orally or in print. I did not dream up the answers.

THE PRIVATE-SECTOR RESPONSE

THERE HAS BEEN A NOTICEABLE CHANGE IN EMPHASIS ON HOW WE IN THE PRIVATE sector look upon the nature of productive organizations. And that emphasis did not come about by sitting in a chair and thinking. It came about because we were hit over the head by foreign competitors who were making better-quality products and getting a larger share of markets we once dominated. We were in trouble and we knew it. We tried to understand what was so different about these foreign organizations. We did several things. One was that we began to listen to organizational theorists and consultants whom we never had taken seriously. And we began to read about these foreign organizations. The best way to put it is that we began to unimprison ourselves from a self-defeating parochialism. We had our comeuppance.

We learned many things, but two stand out. The first is that you can never take your eyes off the *quality* of what you are producing. At every step of the process you judge quality and that is the only way you can make the necessary changes quickly. You don't wait for the end of the process to judge quality. You are always judging it from step one. That is the preventive orientation in contrast to the old days when we knew what was wrong only at the end of the process when there was little we could do except to repair this or fix that, and that was very expensive and not all that helpful for our ability to compete. We had to change the way we were organized. Those who have changed found it a wrenching experience; so did our stockholders, but they not only survived, they prospered. They satisfied their customers; they listened to them; they even sought their help—quite a contrast to the Henry Ford mentality. Indeed, Ford today is an outstanding example of organizational change in the service of quality and it is not fortuitous that the Ford company began to take seriously the ideas of the person (Edward Deming) who after World War II put Japanese industry on the right road, as a result of which he became one of their secular saints.

The other thing we learned, and this represents a real change (if not a revolutionary one), is that you cannot achieve your goals unless all members at all levels of the organization meaningfully participate in some important way in the organization's affairs. The top-down type of organizational structure made that impossible. Unless everyone has reason to feel respected, listened to, involved, and committed, you may be able to change structure but not the ineffective use of the human resources that make up the organization.

Are schools like private-sector organizations, at least the growing number who are really changing? The answer, unfortunately, is no. Organizationally speaking, they remain what they always were, despite the fact that the world has changed and the educational outcomes of school are near totally lousy. The leadership of our schools is unimaginative or worse in the sense that they seem incapable of self-scrutiny, bold actions, and a willingness to admit that they are part of the problem and not of the solution. Unlike some of us, they have not gotten their comeuppance. They roll with the punch, hoping that their critics will go away. They will not go away. If schools remain what they are, the puzzlement of the general public, especially its tax-paying segment, will turn to anger and you will begin to see the demise of our school systems. And why not? If you are not accomplishing your goals—if your "customers" are dissatisfied—why should you be supported? That is what happened to a lot of companies and it is and will be happening to others. Schools, like some of us, will have to change, and the change cannot be cosmetic. Schools have a lot to learn from us in regard to how we had to change, the turmoil of change, and why in the long run it is worth it. ■

THE EDUCATOR'S RESPONSE

What have we got to learn from private organizations? They have their problems and we have ours and the differences are enormous. What can they tell us about how children learn? They have "customers" and so do we. Our customers are children, parents, and the rest of the community and we have absolutely no control over who our customers are or will be. We have to take all comers regardless of ability, of parental support and interest, disability, and a host of other factors with which the private sector does not have to deal. That variation is dumped on us and we are supposed to perform miracles at the same time as our budgets are static or decreasing. We are not only a teaching institution but a social service one, and sometimes we are an arm of the police. We keep many of our older students in school even though they are not interested, motivated, or even appropriately behaved. As soon as society becomes aware of a social problem, they ask us to do something about it, e.g., drugs, guns, teenage pregnancy, AIDS, delinquency, smoking, racial conflicts, and more. Does a private company have to deal with those problems at the same time it produces what it does? Does the productivity of a company worker suffer because he or she watches TV at night? What our students are supposed to learn and do does suffer from the hours in front of the TV set. We can suggest, implore, and plead with parents to cut back on TV watching, to be more attentive to whether a child is doing assigned homework but, at best, we only get to first base.

That does not mean that we have done as well as we should have. We are not saying that we have not made mistakes. But when critics from the private sector take pot shots at us, it is for several reasons. They don't understand the nature of the learning process, they don't understand schools, and they ignore the things we have tried and are trying, the changes that are taking hold, and they don't understand why schools are organized the way they are, and why, unlike a private company, we cannot snap our fingers saying, "There shall be change," and the change begins. We know our private-sector critics are well intentioned but that does not mean we should refrain from saying that they are basically ignorant of what we are up against. For example, take the case of a large company that has a board of directors. Ninety-nine times out of a hundred, if the CEO of the company makes a recommendation for a change, it will be approved and supported. When the CEO of a school system, the superintendent of schools, makes a recommendation for change, she is far from certain that the board of education will approve. Remember that board members are chosen via the political system and each member has his or her own loyalties and constituencies. We will never know how many times a superintendent refrains from making a recommendation for change because he or she knows that it will be turned down or create a community controversy. The number of those times is very large. And also remember that school systems are creations of the state and that the local system is legally responsible to the state board of education. Can you imagine a private company having so many "owners"? Could they change quickly under such a system?

Private-sector critics are fond of saying that schools are monopolies, they have no competition, no incentive to change, the private-sector marketplace is thoroughly competitive and only those companies survive that have changed in order to compete. So introduce competition into the educational marketplace! So they and other critics are gung ho for vouchers, charter schools, "break-the-mold schools." We have been accused of two things. First, we are too smugly conservative. Second, we uncritically take on new fads and fashions. One says we are stick-in-the-muds; the other says we are always trying this or that. The fact is that we are and should be conservative in the sense that we should hold on to what is best in our traditions and what is best is our unique concern with the learning process in children. But because we are conservative and resist anything that diverts us from the learning process does not mean that we have not made changes that will influence that process in positive ways. We are constantly requiring our teachers to take advanced courses, attend workshops that will inform them about what researchers are reporting, about new techniques of stimulating the minds of children, about new curricula, and, very important, about how to deepen their grasp of subject matter. We have been in the forefront of the fight to reduce class size. We support the utilization of cooperative learning approaches because they supplant the traditional model of one teacher pouring information into the minds of children, which does not permit children learning with and from each other. We have encouraged parents as never before to participate in the formulation of educational policy and practice. And we are supportive of the movement to give teachers a greater role in policy matters, and the number of schools that are dedicated to site-based management by teachers and parents—giving them more opportunity to be responsible and accountable— is certainly increasing. We are moving forward in new directions, but it takes time. There are no quick fixes when it comes to improving the learning process for all children in a classroom, if only because of the variations among them on the factors significant for learning. ■

There are similarities and differences between the responses of each group in 1970 and 1995. In 1970, the private-sector position was that schools were unique organizations but inadequate ones. Being unique was no excuse for doing a poor job. In 1995, their position is the same, but with the difference in saying or implying that if schools go on as they have, they deserve extinction. Whatever the reasons, they say, schools are failing and educators are unwilling or unable to confront the need for radical change the way some companies in the private sector found themselves forced to do. However, although the private-sector critic seems not to deny that schools are unique organizations, he or she is very clear that as organizations they have a lot in common with the private sector in regard to change. Both require bold, visionary leadership capable not only of critical self-scrutiny but of instilling such a stance in everyone in the organization. Also, and again in regard to change, everyone in the organization has to understand what is at stake, they have to be provided with forums where they can be heard, and in their working roles they must participate meaningfully in decision making. Put in another way, the effective leader is one capable of reexamining past ways of regarding and using the human resources in the organization. So, if an organization considered unique is failing of its purposes, it says a lot about leadership and a faulty rationale for its organization. In that respect, schools are in no way different than failing companies.

Neither in 1970 nor in 1995 do the educational spokespersons come to grips with these criticisms. They do not indict inadequate leadership and they avoid saying anything about redefining and utilizing existing resources in more productive ways. What they do say is that by involving more people (teachers, parents) in school affairs, improvements will follow, although they say nothing about why increasing the number of participants should or could affect organizational structure and functioning that for so long regarded that involvement as inimical to its purposes. The private sector was quite clear that desired change required not only a new ethos but a thoroughly transformed organizational rationale adapted to new values, attitudes, and responsibilities. Yes, the private-sector spokespersons are likely in favor of charter schools, break-the-mold schools, and vouchers, but that is primarily because they hold out the promise of increasing competition, and by holding out the promise of demonstrating that these bold ventures will be successful, schools will be forced to consider the kinds of transforming changes of which they have been incapable. Educational spokespersons look with disfavor on these developments and they do not expect them to be successful and they expect that these developments will only make more severe the problems of schools. The spokespersons may or may not be right, but they seem to miss the point that these ventures are getting increasing support not because the private sector is intent on dismantling the public schools (there are critics who have such intent, but I have heard no one in the private sector say that) but because they will consider anything that seems truly bold, i.e., an obvious departure from an obviously unacceptable state of affairs. In 1970, the educational spokespersons were resentful of criticism. In 1995, they not only are resentful, they seem embattled.

The strength and scope of the criticisms have increased over 25 years and there is no reason to believe that these criticisms will not gain added force. Why is that a likely scenario? The answer to this question derives in part from a feature of the school culture that I discussed in 1970 and that has become more obvious and glaring as the years have passed. In a literal sense it is not a "feature" you can observe, record, and chart. It would be more correct to say that it is a feature one should *expect* to observe but does not, i.e., it is nonobservable, an absence, a silence.

IMAGINE THAT FOR A PERIOD OF MONTHS YOU ARE ABLE TO SIT IN ON *ALL* MEETINGS, formal and informal, that take place in a sample of randomly selected schools. You are an observer, not a participant. Your sole task is to note those occasions when discussion centers around the criticisms leveled against schools by external critics. What is the frequency of such occasions, their average duration, the seriousness with which those criticisms are discussed, the willingness to entertain the possibility that at least some of the criticisms have merit, and what courses of action, if any, should be considered and pursued? When you have completed your observations, you should have a good deal to say about how knowledgeable school people are about the substance of the criticisms and about the conceptual-philosophical basis for their positions.

What I am asking the reader to do is in principle analogous to the study I describe in the school culture book about how the "constitution" of the classroom was forged, by whom, and why. For the first month of school, observers sat in classrooms recording those occasions relevant to the "laws" governing behaviors between students and between students and teacher. All classrooms have a constitution; their structure and ambiance are not random affairs—they are reflections of conceptions, almost always unverbalized about what is right, natural, and proper. Challenges to those conceptions are literally regarded by the teacher as countercultural and, therefore, to be resisted, and that resistance is spontaneous and automatic, not reflective, not a spur to self-scrutiny. ■

Our study of the classroom turned out to be an uncomplicated one in that the constitution was *always* "written" by the teacher and written means that there was never *discussion* about what was right, natural, and proper. The rules were articulated by the teacher without any attempt to engage students in a discussion about the whys and wherefores.

Now to our imaginary study of meetings. For all practical purposes, we would not have observed any meetings or series of meetings in which (a) the criticisms of schools were clearly articulated in a semiobjective way; (b) that articulation was based on participants having read and digested those criticisms; and (c) the participants had or developed a reasoned, thought-through response, i.e., they offered more than unreflective, knee-jerk opinion that had no conceptual, philosophical, historical foundation. In short, the discussions could not be dignified by such adjectives as serious, sustained, probing, reflective, and self-scrutinizing. Keep in mind that the issues surrounding school reform are not simple. We should never ignore Mencken's caveat that for every complex problem there is a simple answer that is wrong, nor should we forget another caveat: it is hard to be completely wrong, and that is as true for you as it is for your critics.

SCHOOLS DO NOT CONTAIN THE FORUMS IN WHICH SERIOUS DISCUSSIONS OF EDUCAtional issues—serious discussions that are going on outside of schools—can and are expected to take place. Schools are not places for surfacing and debating the issues that have and will continue to impact on schools. The culture of the school is one which makes it unsafe to bring up controversial issues that implicitly or explicitly are critical of existing practice and call for change. The point here is not why this is so but that it is so. That accounts for the perception on the part of external critics that schools are unresponsive to the call and need for change, that they are so inwardly oriented that they are unaware of how they remain the same in a world that has dramatically changed, and that one should no longer expect that schools as they are can be changed from within the school or school system. ■

Over the past 25 years I have visited several scores of schools. For no more than a handful of schools could I say that they tried to have regular discussions, the main purpose of which was to become sophisticated or knowledgeable about controversial issues the educational community can no longer ignore. I have *never* known of a *school system* that as a matter of policy encouraged and supported systemwide forums for discussion. I have known of instances where a school sought to change itself by setting up such forums and met subtle and not-so-subtle criticisms and obstacles from the larger system.

My experience in schools, since the school culture book was published, forced on me a conclusion that I should or could have reached earlier but did not. With the usual few exceptions, school personnel hardly read books, journals, and similar periodicals that could make them knowledgeable about the most important criticisms and controversies surrounding school reform. For example, I would ask a school person (teacher, principal, superintendent, board of education member) what were the rationales for the different voucher proposals being discussed by political figures and others external to schools. I was not asking if they agreed or disagreed with any voucher proposal. What I was after was how well they understood what these proposals contained and why they were seriously being proposed. Again leaving the usual exceptions aside, the word *voucher* was pounced upon as if it represented evil incarnate, and that those proposing vouchers were intent on dismantling the public school system. No one was able to give a sustained, coherent analysis of the different voucher proposals, although such analyses were plentiful in the educational literature. From their standpoint there was nothing to discuss!

Occasionally I would point out that some proponents of vouchers wanted to maintain the public school system and argued that vouchers might be one way to introduce competition and incentives to change. That possibility was inconceivable to these school personnel. And, sometimes, I would ask if vouchers ought not to be put to the test of implementation. How else can we determine whether they will have their intended positive effects? That suggestion received short shrift. The point here is that these school personnel seemed unaware of two things. First, that within the past several years a relatively large number of state legislatures had begun seriously to consider vouchers; in some states some form of voucher system had become law; and there was good reason to believe that the "voucher movement" would gain, not lose, force. Indeed, a fair number of those with whom I spoke were totally ignorant of the seriousness with which legislatures were considering a voucher system, a degree of ignorance I still find mystifying in light of all that has been written about vouchers.

The second point is that the bulk of my interviewees were unaware that the passion with which they denounced vouchers, and their inability to come to grips with the problems of school inadequacies that so troubled some voucher proponents, would be interpreted as an argument for the status quo, i.e., educators were "stonewalling," they were opposed to any basic changes, they were incapable of self-scrutiny.

Another example. In recent years we have heard much about site-based management, which its proponents endorse as a way of bringing about fundamental changes in our schools. A good deal has been written about site-based management, much of which is more intended as promotion and not as description or as conceptual rationale. However, in the past several years there has been a growing literature on site-based management and, as one could have predicted, it is no simple affair: It involves a departure from tradition, a reallocation of power, the assumption of responsibilities for which teachers have not been prepared, and the brute fact is that it requires a degree of time for meetings that simply does not exist in the usually structured school day. That should not be surprising or disheartening because any meaningful alteration of the school culture should be expected to be beset with problems. What is dismaying is that when I ask teachers what they mean by site-based management, they truly cannot give an informed reply. To say that "site-based management means that teachers will run the school" is not an informed response; it is an oversimplification bordering on the tragic. And it is further dismaying because most teachers have not felt compelled to find out, by reading and other means, what site-based management entails: the predictable problems, the minimal conditions below which one should not attempt such a change. In addition, many teachers are not interested in being part of such a venture. It is as if they are only interested in what they do and are confronted with in their encapsulated classrooms in their encapsulated schools—an outlook that reinforces the view of external critics that schools are not capable of change from within.

I said earlier that there is reason to predict that the gulf between schools and the general public will widen. I have endeavored in this chapter to indicate two reasons for that dysphoric prediction. The first is that there is validity to the criticism by private-sector individuals and theorists that schools, unlike segments of the private sector, seem incapable of organizational change because they are mired in tradition, or they lack the bold and visionary leadership that could gain the energy and commitment of their people to changes that will allow them to better achieve the unique purpose of schools: to create and sustain productive contexts of learning for students that will prevent disinterest, lack of motivation, dropouts, etc. The private-sector critic is on target when he or she says that when an organization—any organization—is not achieving its purposes, one *has* to assume that the structure and culture of that organization is part of the problem and not the solution. The second reason, not unrelated to the first, is that schools almost totally lack forums both for self-examination and for becoming and remaining sensitive to how and why other organizations (e.g., religious, private sector) found themselves forced to change in truly significant ways.

Chapter 17

Changes in Power Relationships

No one would deny that one of the most obvious features of private-sector organizations is the way power is allocated and used. Novels, plays, films, and other mass media have long "entertained" us with power and its consequences in business and industry as well as in nonprofit organizations of which hospitals are clear examples. Politics, we are taught, is about the seeking, allocation, and use of power. Machiavelli is considered the founding father of political science because of the compelling way he described and conceptualized the gaining and uses of power in the public arena. He lived and wrote centuries ago and the world has still not forgiven him for what he said about the uses of power even though the centrality and cogency of the issues he posed are as relevant today as they were in his times. Although we know that power is a fact of social life—one of its inescapable features—we do not like to be reminded of its presence. If we are forced to acknowledge the presence of power we are quick to justify its particular organizational manifestations as necessary and productive, as if reallocating the distribution of power would be destabilizing and injurious to achieving stated purposes, as if the way things are is the *only* way they should be.

Historically, and deliberately, it was considered crucial that public schools be protected against power struggles in the political arenas of local communities. Schools were to be overseen by a locally chosen or elected board of education, but in a legal sense schools were the creation and responsibility of the states who were the "protectors" of schools: their standards, practices, purposes. Boards of education had power, of course, but it was circumscribed power, delegated power. Schools were regarded as places where youth would be educated by personnel whose sole concern was what was best for students and, in discharging their responsibilities, were insulated from the more seamy aspects of partisan politics. Schools were to be oases of peace and learning.

This view of power and schools was as unrealistic as it was well intentioned. Let me briefly note just a few reasons for saying unrealistic:

1. State governments are no less political—no less marked by power conflicts and struggles—than local governments. The politics of state governments are a continuation of local politics.
2. Members of boards of education, elected or appointed, are rarely in agreement about educational policy, practice, and finance. They differ among themselves on a variety of factors for a variety of reasons. Each tends to have a different constituency and debts of loyalty; some will be perceived as having more power than others.
3. The superintendent is chosen by the board. He or she is the agent of the board and is accountable to it. It is precisely because the board has ultimate power that the superintendent must develop his or her own sources of power *within* the board, the school system, *and* relevant segments in the community. The persuasiveness of the superintendent depends on his or her sources of influence and power.
4. Both the individual school and school system are hierarchically organized, an obvious fact that has obvious implications for the exercise and consequences of power.

These and other features of schools and systems can be fleshed out to make the point that they, like private-sector organizations, are literally political institutions because their structure, decision-making processes, and the basis upon which social-professional relationships are largely determined are shaped by the fact that power is unequally distributed.

Up until World War II the obvious presence and dynamics of power in schools were muted, overlooked, covered up, or simply ignored. The rhetoric described an institution in which all adults shared a common purpose that united them in ways that avoided the less pleasant aspects of organizational life. It was an institution literally regarded as an oasis to be protected from, to be different from, the real world. It was a myth then as it is now.

By the time I wrote the book in 1970, the nature of the myth had been exposed. My interest and concern were that in giving up the myth and advocating for this and that school change—replacing outmoded curricula, community control and participation, improving teachers' grasp of subject matter, and a lot more—*people were unaware of some of the fundamental ways that existing power relationships in schools and systems would defeat the goals of change. These were relationships involving power but not power that was ordinarily recognized, and, if it was recognized, it was not subjected to the scrutiny it deserved. There were power relationships so long a feature of schools, so basic to the traditional concept of a school, so "right, natural, and proper," as to make it virtually impossible for all but a few people to recognize how the culture of schools was not only determined by those relationships but also how they were the most potent barriers to change.*

That explains why in *The Culture of the School* I initially concentrated on the "constitution of the classroom." My purpose was not merely to point out that in forging the constitution students had no power; that was a glimpse of the obvious. *The cultural significance of that obvious fact inhered in what it implied about children's capacity and interest in engaging in the formulation of the whys and wherefores of rules and regulations governing classroom life.* And what it implied was that students could not be trusted to discuss the issues, that students needed to be tamed and socialized, that they had no interest in these matters, and that as students went through the grades their sense of powerlessness would not affect their educational performance and/or their interest in learning. Schools were places where the students did what they were told to do. They answered questions—they did not ask them; their special (or not so special) interests and curiosities were to be kept private; they were not to take time away from the predetermined curriculum. *In short, the culture of the classroom lacked almost all of the hallmarks of productive learning. And each level of the educational hierarchy viewed the level below it as teachers viewed students.*

In 1970, I did not have to tell the reader that issues of power dominated the school scene. Those issues were daily fare in the mass media. Militant unions, busing, and racial conflicts were only some of the issues contributing to power conflicts within school systems and between school systems and diverse community groups and external critics. Whoever the participants in these struggles, and whatever the particular facet of power at issue, the goal was to improve educational outcomes, i.e., no one claimed that schools did not need to be changed in order to improve educational outcomes. That is why I titled the book *The Culture of the School and the Problem of Change.* That title was intended to raise three questions: How would the culture of the school be a barrier to change? Why had efforts for change failed? Were there some aspects of the school culture which, if not altered, ensured that all other changes would fail?

What has changed since 1970? There has been an attitudinal change as obvious as it has been sobering. *Changing any important feature of the school culture is no easy affair, a conclusion that may well be the understatement of the century.* My book was an attempt to explain why this *had* to be so, why changing the culture of any complicated, traditional institution required a time perspective that the advocates of change seemed unable to confront. I was gratified, of course, by the warm reception the book received. I began to get scores of letters from people who said that now they understood why their efforts at change had failed. I also began to receive invitations to serve as a consultant to school change projects. I accepted a number of these invitations. Several conclusions were forced on me. The first was that the decision to seek a change rarely (if ever) took into account the ideas, opinions, and feelings of those who would be impacted by the change. And by "taking into account" I mean serious, sustained discussion of what would be required of participants in terms of time, energy, commitment, and motivation. What would be the predictable problems any change process stirs up? How should these problems be handled? What self-correcting mechanisms or forums should be created to deal with these problems? How can we withstand the pressures to demonstrate change quickly enough in order to continue to receive support from funding sources internal and external to the school? What do we do when the principal or this or that teacher leaves the school to go elsewhere? How can we maximize continuity of personnel? How much support can we count on to deal not only with the predictable problems but the unpredictable ones as well? In other words, if what I had written was taken seriously, the process of laying the groundwork for the change effort—determining or establishing the *minimal* conditions justifying going ahead—is a complicated, time-consuming, frustrating one, which if handled in anything resembling a routine fashion means trouble ahead.

The second conclusion forced on me was in two parts, both of which confirmed what I had written. If the leadership for change came from those within the system, they were remarkably insensitive to or ignorant of the culture of the school. And that was no less the case if the leader was someone external to the school, someone with whom the school or school system had agreed to collaborate. I know that sounds both strange and harsh. But that is what I was forced to conclude. Why this is so should not be surprising. When you have spent months and years in a particular setting, it is extraordinarily difficult to take distance from it, to see it from another perspective, to ask the question: If I change A, what does that mean for B, C, or D? Why do I assume that the way things are is the way they should be? If I feel they should be otherwise, on what basis do I assume that others feel as I do?

If your life's work is in schools, you have been socialized to see them in certain ways and to become insensitive to many things you take for granted and, therefore, never examine. For example, I remember well a principal who was relating to me the resistance he was getting from teachers about a pedagogical change he had proposed to them and they had accepted. What the conversation revealed was that indeed he had proposed the change and indeed the teachers had accepted it. I already knew that from previous visits to the school, as a result of which several teachers had told me that they did not see sense in the proposal, they did not want to be seen as oppositional, they were not about to change what they did in the classroom, and they did not expect the principal to "monitor" what they did. The point is that the principal was totally insensitive to how teachers *might* internally react to a call for change, that teachers seek to avoid open conflict with a principal, that any proposal requiring teachers to change classroom practice is likely to be resisted. The principal had been a teacher for many years but he had "forgotten" what enters into a teacher's phenomenology, and in forgetting that he had unreflectively assumed that when the teachers "agreed" with him they were really in agreement. In presenting his proposal to the teachers he had done nothing to make it possible and safe for teachers to voice their true feelings.

Although I raised and discussed the significance of power in the culture of the school, I have to say that I underemphasized how power suffused *all* relationships in that culture: students vs. teachers, teachers vs. principals, principals vs. higher levels of administration, superintendent vs. board, the board vs. the political establishment, and that establishment vs. centers of power in the state capital. Power is not inherently evil. Power is a built-in feature of our personal, professional, and social relationships. If we ordinarily are not aware of that fact it is because its recognition is only forced on us when for one or another reason a relationship becomes problematic, i.e., when we become aware that what was implicit is now explicit, when we are forced to recognize that someone is using power in ways inimical to our well-being or that this use of power is a departure from previous practice or quality of relationship.

By underemphasizing how power suffuses all relationships in the culture of the school I was at the same time underemphasizing the complexity of the change process. Any nontrivial attempt to change a feature of the school culture immediately brings to the fore the power basis of relationships, i.e., "someone" decides that something will be changed and "others" are then *required* appropriately to implement that change. If others have had no say in the decision, if there was no forum or allotted time for others to express their ideas or feelings, if others come to feel they are not respected, if they feel their professionalism has been demeaned, the stage is set for the change to fail. *The problem of change is the problem of power, and the problem of power is how to wield it in ways that allow others to identify with, to gain a sense of ownership of, the process and goals of change. That is no easy task; it is a frustrating, patience-demanding, time-consuming process. Change cannot be carried out by the calendar, a brute fact that those with power often cannot confront.* The change process is not an engineering one. You cannot engineer school change the way engineers build bridges, roads, dams, and much more.

What has happened since the book was written 25 years ago? What recognition has been accorded the issues surrounding power in the school culture? At the time I wrote the book the power issue was manifested in several ways: the increasing militancy and strength of teacher unions; conflicts about racial discrimination and community control; challenges to existing curricula and to teacher effectiveness and competency; the increase in federal and judicial power to influence school practices and programs; and an increase in the power and influence of academics critical of a variety of school practices. Let me briefly describe what I consider to be the most important and revealing developments about power issues since the book was written. Each of these had roots that antedate 1970, but each took on significances, singly and in combination, that they previously did not have.

1. State legislatures began to mandate school councils on which parents and the community were given status and power. Such legislation was explicitly justified on the grounds that decision-making power should no longer rest solely in the hands of educators. Parent involvement had *legal* sanction, the force of law. The state was exercising its power to bring about a school change that was not, of course, warmly greeted by school personnel who saw such a change as a criticism of their handling of parent–school relationships.

2. To an unprecedented degree, foundations began to support the implementation of the ideas of "outsiders" (e.g., Ted Sizer, James Comer, Henry Levin) who gave promise of changing school practices, organization, and ambiance in ways that would improve educational outcomes. Although these new approaches were far from identical in conception and process, they had two assumptions in common: schools could not remain as they were, and the

changes that were necessary could not originate in schools or school systems. There had to be an external force or agent to stimulate, prod, and oversee such changes. There was another assumption that was more implicit than explicit: school personnel would respond warmly to these external initiatives because so many of them had given up hoping that schools could be changed from within. As one teacher said, "Schools are allergic to truly new ideas, especially if they imply that we will be given a status, independence, and influence we never had or could have before. You know the saying that no good deed goes unpunished. Well, in schools no good idea ever goes anywhere; it gets buried in endless discussion and power plays that make you sorry you ever got involved in the first place. So, when we heard Ted Sizer talk about what schools can and should be, we heard him give expression to what we had been missing as teachers."

3. No concept became more popular than site-based management. It was also the case that no concept lent itself to a greater variety of meanings. *What made site-based management a kind of rallying cry was that it stood for a dramatic alteration in the allocation of power in school management. Specifically, if teachers really had the power, authority, and responsibility to organize and administer the school, their creativity would get expressed, their departure from stultifying routine would become possible, their use of existing resources would become more efficient and productive, and classroom life would be more stimulating for students.* If site-based management meant different things to different people, if it has by no means been frequently and seriously implemented, the fact is that its emergence on the educational scene reflected a widespread belief that improvement in educational outcomes was not possible unless power relationships in the school culture changed, i.e., power relationships hinder improvement in educational outcomes.

4. Cooperative learning began to receive increased recognition. More than that, it has—unlike site-based management—received a noticeable degree of acceptance and implementation, although—like site-based management—cooperative learning approaches vary in their conceptual-theoretical underpinnings and mode of implementation.[1] But all the approaches explicitly challenge the "whole-class" pedagogy, the central feature of which is that the teacher is always in control of what and how children will learn. The teacher is the sole source of direction and knowledge; students are considered unable to learn with and from each other. The power to stimulate, direct, and monitor the learning process has to be exercised by the teacher. Cooperative learning was more than a rallying cry; it was a reasoned critique of a longstanding tradition of power relationships in the classroom. In the years since I wrote *The Culture of*

---

1. Sharan (1994) has edited a *Handbook of Cooperative Learning Methods* that is very informative and instructive. In another publication (Sharan and Sharan, 1992) he describes in refreshing detail the time, energy, and demonstrations required to help teachers in a school comprehend the rationale for cooperative learning *before* formal implementation starts. His emphasis on the "before-the-beginning" phase is as unusual as it is productive.

the School, there developed a respectable research literature, and by respectable I mean that the benefits of cooperative learning cannot be argued away. It is no panacea; it has not taken the educational community by storm (far from it) for a variety of reasons, the most important being that it requires teachers to change their conceptions of their role in the learning process.

5. Without question the most clear attempt to change power relationships in schools was the passage in 1975 of federal legislation (Public Law 94-142) specifying and mandating the rights of handicapped children and their parents, as well as making clear what the obligations of schools were for the education of such students. In remarkably detailed language, 94-142 gave a degree of *formal* power to parents in regard to *any* decision affecting their handicapped children. As one of the people who drafted that legislation said to me, "We wanted to make it clear that no longer could schools unilaterally decide what was best for a handicapped child. We wanted the rights of parents spelled out in detail, which is another way of saying that we wanted schools to know that they could no longer do things in their accustomed way. That law was as much a civil rights legislation as it was an educational one."

6. Within the past decade, vouchers, privatization, and charter schools not only have become topics for public discussion but for action as well by several states. The stimulus for these developments is no mystery. "Our schools are not working. Whatever we have tried, the billions spent to improve our schools have not paid off. There are features about schools and school systems the way they are organized and administered—that make them intractable to change. They are mired in attitudes and traditions that stifle creativity and are obstacles to innovation. Schools as they are, are part of the problem, not the solution. What we are trying to do is to free people to go in new directions to insulate them from a system that forces them to conform to the *status quo.*" That is a succinct paraphrase justifying vouchers, privatization, and charter schools. In 1994, the city of Hartford turned over the running of its schools to a private company. That action by the board of education was an open admission that its many past efforts to improve Hartford's schools—for which per pupil expenditure was among the highest in the state—had failed, i.e., whatever the reasons, the school system was, as one person said, a "lost cause." The board had been exercising its power in fruitless ways. Why not transfer power to an external agent who might do better?

Were these developments predictable, at least in broad outline, when I wrote the book? My answer is both no and yes. I say no because my emphasis in the book was on explaining why reform efforts had failed and would continue to fail. I was assuming that if what I said about the school culture was valid, and if school reformers took what I said seriously, the outcomes would be more favorable. And that assumption rested on the belief that the obstacles to change, especially those involving issues of power, could be overcome by forces *within* the school culture. *More correctly, I wanted to believe it was possible even though my pessimism about that belief and hope permeates the book.* (Indeed, 5 years before I wrote the book

I wrote a paper in which that pessimism is clearly stated.) Why did I cling to that belief? For one thing, I did not want to appear nihilistic, despairing, or a wet blanket. But, more important, I truly resisted examining the sources of my pessimism because, I know now, I did not want to face the conclusion to which I would be forced to come: *No complicated, traditional social institution can be changed only from within. There has to be some support for change from within, but there also has to be strong external, powerful pressures for change, powerful in terms of numbers, influence, and legislative legal policymaking responsibilities. Absent those external pressures, the institution will continue to confirm the adage I stated repetitively in the book: the more things change, the more they remain the same.*

I am *not* saying that schools are incapable on their own of changing their practices in any way. That is demonstrably false. What I am saying is that in regard to those features that those in the school culture regard as right, natural, and proper—and directly or indirectly bulwark longstanding power relationships—change is not possible or sustainable within and by the system. That does not mean that school personnel are in principle opposed to change or that they are not critical of many features of the school culture. What it does mean is that when alternatives to the status quo are presented to them, and those changes are seen, as they should be, as noncosmetic, it is completely predictable that different types of personnel will oppose these alternatives for different reasons depending on their perception of who "loses" and who "gains" power. Changing power relationships is always unsettling, stormy, and even destabilizing (for a time at least). If we have learned anything about human behavior it is that we resist change even though we proclaim its necessity. So, for example, when a person who is miserable, unhappy, and despairing makes the decision to seek help from a psychotherapist, he or she seeks not only compassionate understanding but also help to change an unwanted state of affairs. That person knows that things cannot go on as before, that a change is necessary. But, as any experienced therapist knows, when that person is made aware that he or she must confront and take responsibility for change, the person will experience a good deal of resistance to and fear of changing because the person would rather that things stay as they are, however unpleasant, and not have to deal with a new way of thinking and acting. It is the difficult task of the psychotherapist to help the person understand that his or her resistance is not pathological but rather a manifestation of the predictable response to the need for change. As in the case of individual change, the resistance of school personnel to institutional change has a similar dynamic, i.e., they know things have to change at the same time they seek to avoid the perceived consequences of a proposed (noncosmetic) change.

We are used to hearing that in life we can count only on two things: death and taxes. We can also count on our resistance to change. If we can count on it, the fact is that school reformers pay only lip service to that fact, witness the unrealistic time perspective informing such efforts. Somewhere in their thinking they know the road ahead is rocky and they know why. But when I have examined, as I have countless times, programs for change, several things become obvious. There is little or no thinking through, *in the planning process,* the extent, sources, and strength of predictable resistance. There is no serious or systematic effort to identify those personnel who will feel their ox is being gored. Little consideration is given as to the different ways those personnel can be given incentives to change. A time perspective or schedule is adapted that vastly underestimates the complexities of what is being attempted, as if the guiding assumption is that God is on their side, reason will curb or dilute the passions of resistance, and that there is a high correlation between what people say they do (or will do) and what they actually do (or will do). The usual result is that when the reformers begin to face the realities of the change process, their frustration, anger, and impatience mount; subsequently, either they employ what power they have (or seek to increase) in authoritarian ways, or they psychologically begin to disengage from their commitment to the effort.

The reader is probably familiar with Murphy's Law: If anything can go wrong, it will. In light of what I have said in the book and more explicitly in this chapter, the reader will not be surprised by Sarason's Law: Murphy's Law is a gross underestimation. Changing the school culture is conceptually and practically a bewildering, complex affair, unless, of course, the object of change does not address the important features of the school culture, e.g., changing curricula, restructuring the school day, lengthening or shortening the school day or year, altering the time allotted to this or that subject matter, introducing new technologies for classroom teaching, employing new achievement tests, making public the test performance of each school, and more. I do not denigrate any of these changes out of hand. I am asserting that none of these kinds of changes deal with or alter any of those features of the school culture that are distinctive and that set drastic limits to the creation and sustaining of productive contexts for learning. One of my favorite jokes expresses my position. It is midwinter and this man feels ill. He goes to his physician who after examining him very carefully says, "I want you to go home, take off all of your clothes, open all windows, stand in front of one of them, and breathe deeply." The man is aghast. "But if I do that," he says, "I'll get pneumonia." To which the physician replies, *"That* I know what to do about." There is a difference between doing what you know you can do and doing what needs to be done, between shadow boxing and coming to grips with the realities of combat. I use the word *combat* advisedly because coming to grips with the realities of the school culture requires alterations in longstanding power relationships that will engender conflict and controversy. That kind of institutional change is rough stuff.

I said earlier that to the question "Were these developments predictable when I wrote the book?" my answer was no and yes. Let me now give the yes answer.

When I finished the book I was more pessimistic than when I started. I could not avoid the conclusion that if what I said about the school culture was in large measure correct, the reform efforts that were being mounted were doomed to fail. More than that, I truly believed that the situation would worsen, especially in our cities. The more I reviewed my experience in schools, the more I saw that the reformers and school personnel could not take seriously what I had written. After all, not only was I saying, somewhat monotonously, that the more things change the more they will remain the same, but I was explicitly and implicitly saying that reformers and school personnel were part of the problem rather than the solution.

By the time I had finished the book I had, on scores of occasions, presented and discussed my ideas with reformers, school personnel, and policymakers. It took me a while to realize that although they agreed with what I was saying—indeed their very favorable and encouraging responses stimulated me to write the book— their actions and planning said otherwise. If they agreed with me before I wrote the book and continued to do so after publication, it was no less clear that on the level of action they had trouble comprehending the implications of what I had said. Let me be clear on one point. What I had said was not in the form of a blueprint for action, a manual, a how-to-do-it scheme, a "solution" in part or in whole. What I was saying, to put it as succinctly as possible, was that if you want to change and improve the climate and outcomes of schooling both for students and teachers, there are features of the school culture that have to be changed, and if they are not changed your well-intentioned efforts will be defeated.

It is one thing to recognize these features; it is quite another thing to take them seriously. Indeed, for 15 years after the book was published I kept a file of letters sent to me by people who had mounted a reform effort that failed. There were two themes most frequently expressed in these letters. The first was that what I had written about the school culture was what they had long known. Put in another way: What I had written was *obvious* to anyone in the school culture. That was not communicated as criticism. The fact is that what I had said *was* obvious, i.e., I put into words what school personnel had experienced. The second theme was that when push came to shove their efforts revealed they had vastly underestimated the force of existing power relationships and had vastly overestimated the willingness of school personnel to confront the implications of those relationships on the level of action. As one person wrote to me, "No one denied that things had to change, should change, but once we got started and conflicts began to erupt, they lost both interest and courage. I have to admit that I, like many others, expected that we could achieve our goals without serious conflicts. I allowed my hopes to obscure the facts of life in schools." Reading these letters made it difficult to avoid the impression that most of the writers had concluded that changing the most important features of the school culture could not be accomplished by those within the school culture. *That conclusion was one I had come to when I finished the book, a conclusion I did not want to come to and never had expected to come to. It was not easy to live with the conclusion that schools as they were would not change and that by conventional performance criteria they probably would get worse.*

There was a question I could have, should have, asked but I did not. *If my prediction was largely correct, what would happen as year by year the general public came to the same conclusion I held?* If I had pursued that question, the answer, in broad outline, was in four parts. Criticism of our public schools would escalate. Actions consistent with that criticism would become more radical in the sense that reform efforts would seek to pressure and change what was perceived as a resistant, insulated, self-preserving, feckless, unimaginative, change-subverting professional-educational community. The reform efforts would be initiated by forces external to the schools. And, finally, those efforts would seek to alter or bypass power relationships seen as major obstacles to long overdue change. In short, the developments of the past 25 years were predictable, at least in broad outline. And, today, for the first time since compulsory education was universally enacted, increasing numbers of people are concluding that the public school system as we have known it is obsolete.

What if in 1970 I had written a book with the title *The Culture of the Health System and the Problem of Change?* The story I would have told then, and what I would say "revisiting" that arena today, would be amazingly similar to what I am now saying about our schools. Very briefly, here is what I mean.

1. By 1965, it was apparent that the availability and cost of health services were morally and fiscally inequitable. It was a health system that "worked" for those who could afford it. That was glaringly not the case for many older people and for their families.

2. When the Medicare legislation was proposed in 1965, the medical community fought it tooth and nail on two grounds. First, as soon as a powerful external agent (like the federal government) enters the scene the quality of health care and the patient–doctor relationship will deteriorate. If there was a role for government, it should not be one that in any way would alter existing power relationships in the health system. Second, the major role of government should be to allocate funds to older people so as to permit them to obtain services in the traditional fee-for-service mode, i.e., in ways that did not alter that tradition, that did not mean government intrusion. They were arguments that essentially claimed that the problem was one that could be solved by money, not new actors on the stage, not by changing the forces of power.

3. Compromises were reached between political figures and spokespeople for organized medicine, the major consequence of which was that Medicare was a financial bonanza to the medical, hospital, and nursing home segments of the health system, i.e., if they were not given blank checks to write, it came close to that situation. In terms of changing the forces of power—who could do what to whom and for how much—little was changed.

4. Leaving older people aside, with each passing year criticism began to mount about a health system that was not working in the sense that many people had no health insurance, many had inadequate insurance, costs and fees were rising, and it appeared that the health professions were insensitive to the plight of people at the same time their incomes steadily increased. Anger and resentment toward those in these professions became frequent, although there were always a few in these professions who said the anger and resentment were justified.

5. When in his address to Congress, President Clinton said that the health system was inadequate, morally indefensible, and in need of a major overhaul, his words were greeted with relief and praise. There was going to be no tinkering, no caving in to special interests. A new distribution and allocation of power would be required.

The story is far more complicated than I have indicated. The sole purpose of the above five points was to indicate similarities between the histories of health and educational reform. In both cases the two professional communities had been content to continue as they had in the past. Each initially took the position that whatever the imperfections or inadequacies, they could be remedied by increased spending. To steady and increasing criticisms both viewed their critics as unknowledgeable, misguided, and simply wrong. Both resisted any plan or effort to change their systems in any significant way. Both knew what they were against, not what they were for, even though both recognized that the purposes of their systems were not being achieved.

In the education section of the *New York Times* for August 2, 1995, an entire page is devoted to the "grand opening" of the first Edison school. Three other such schools will be opened in subsequent weeks in Kansas, Michigan, and Massachusetts.

SHERMAN, TEXAS, AUGUST 1   AN APPLE COMPUTER FOR EVERY CHILD TO TAKE home. An E-mail system and a computer "chat room" allowing schoolchildren, their parents and their teachers to communicate at any time of day. A school day that is an hour and a half longer than the national average, and a school year that is 30 days longer. Special classes in everything from dance to personal finance to character and ethics. Spanish for everyone.

These were just a few of the things offered when pupils arrived at George Washington Elementary School today for the first day of classes. George Washington is the first school in the nation to open in partnership with the Edison Project, an ambitious venture whose mission is to provide a superior education at prevailing public-school costs and make money for its investors at the same time.

... The opening of the partnership school was preceded by a deluge of applications from outside the immediate neighborhood; 140 children transferred in and swelled George Washington's enrollment to about 500. Only 15 or so pupils asked to be transferred out, Dr. Denton said.

For the standard per-pupil cost of a given school district—around $4,500 annually at the elementary school here—Edison pledges to dramatically improve education and test scores, in part by providing a computer in every home, lengthening the school day (to 8 hours for elementary students), extending the school year (to 205 school days) and giving teachers month-long training sessions, or "institutes," in the summer.

... At the ribbon cutting today, in front of a huge sign that read, "Welcome to an Awesome Learning Adventure," Mr. Whittle and Mr. Schmidt were given a hero's welcome, and Sherman's mayor, Julie Ellis Starr, gave them keys to the city. Rick Tichenor, the vice president of the school board, said, "In Texas, I think we hit the Lotto jackpot winner."

While the computers generated by far the most attention, Mr. Whittle urged teachers, parents, and schoolchildren to focus on other aspects of the curriculum as well. He cited the longer day and year, the immersion in foreign languages, and the character-and-ethics component, in which, among other things, students are urged to make their own trading cards depicting their personal heroes and including vital statistics and history. ■

In its news section, beginning on the first page, for August 15 and 16, 1995, the *New York Times* reports the latest developments in the political power war between New York's mayor and the overseers of the city's public school system. From the standpoint of the mayor the school system is bordering on collapse, incapable of change, fiscally wasteful, and the victim of a bloated, unimaginative bureaucracy. Preceding the latest blast were others by the mayor, only somewhat less polemical. Mayor Guiliani has said that unless he is given more power in matters of educational policy, no improvement of the schools can be expected.[2]

I did not cite these two reports for the purposes of judgment or prediction but rather to emphasize two points. The first, and the more obvious one, is that they are symptomatic of a more general dissatisfaction with our public schools, *a degree of dissatisfaction that is and will continue to be a stimulus to the acceptance by people of proposed changes the public has previously never taken seriously or even considered.* The second point is that these changes at their core will call for changes in existing power relationships.

In the case of New York City we are witnessing a naked political struggle in regard to the formulation of educational and fiscal policy. I say naked because a similar struggle is occurring elsewhere but in a more muted way. (As has long been the case, what happens in New York usually happens elsewhere in a less theatrical way.) What if the mayor is given the power he seeks? Why should such a break with tradition improve our schools? To that question the mayor provides no answer or even an inkling of one. It is as if the mayor assumes that *any* change will be better than what now is the case, an assumption with which more than a few are in agreement. And that is my point. Just as in 1970 I underestimated the growing public dissatisfaction with our schools, it would be a mistake today to underestimate the readiness of people to look with approval on proposals that are clear breaks with customary practice.

The Edison schools are a quite different cup of tea in that there is some specificity about the changes that will be made. If it is clear that a private company will have the power to initiate, administer, and monitor these changes, it is not clear what other changes in power relationships are contemplated, e.g., within the classroom, between school personnel and parents, between those personnel and the representatives of the private company. In what ways is it envisioned that classrooms will be different, i.e., student–student, student–teacher relationships? What differences should we expect in teacher–teacher, teacher–administrator, teacher–parent relationships? There is no doubt that the Edison proponents seek to create the conditions that make for productive learning. And, as we quoted from the article,

---

2. In the past 5 years, more school systems have been taken over by the state than ever before. Although the number of takeovers is by no means large, they not only reflect the power of the state but also, more importantly, the public pressures on state departments of education to do *something* to rectify scandalous educational conditions. It is also noteworthy that state department officials take such actions very reluctantly and will say privately that there are more than a few city systems that should be taken over but are not because the pressures to do so are not yet organized and persistent.

there is no doubt that creating those conditions only in part depends on the use of computers. "Mr. Whittle urged teachers, parents, and schoolchildren to focus on other aspects of the curriculum as well." But those other aspects of the curriculum engender a very traditional picture of curriculum and classroom.

THERE ARE FIVE KEY COMPONENTS TO THE CURRICULUM: HUMANITIES AND ARTS, mathematics and science, character and ethics, practical arts and health and physical fitness. The curriculum is tailored to meet the state and local standards set in each state and school district, said Deborah M. McGriff, Edison's senior vice president and the former Detroit school superintendent.

The character and ethics curriculum is an expanded version of one developed by the Heartwood Institute, a nonprofit center in Wexford, Pennsylvania, that advocates the formal teaching of values, like honesty, fairness, integrity, justice and kindness.

Edison students will spend more class time than students in traditional public schools on academic subjects like reading, math, science and social studies and a minimum of 30 minutes a day in art or music classes and in physical fitness classes. ■

I do not think I am being a carping critic when I say that the Edison classroom will probably be a very traditional one in which teachers will actively instruct and children will passively absorb. Having said that, let me hasten to add that the Edison project deserves to be tested and should not be cavalierly dismissed as "la-la land," a characterization made by the president of the United Federation of Teachers in New York City. "La-la land" is one in which educators are insensitive to what many people have publicly and privately concluded: Our schools are intractable to change; they are a lost cause.

Why did I emphasize in the book, as I have in this chapter, power relationships in the school culture? The most succinct answer is that the sense of power is the sense that you have been accorded the respect and given practical responsibility to have *some* voice in determining what and how you will learn and act. To feel powerless is to feel that your ideas, opinions, and interests do not deserve a hearing; you are the object of the discharge of the power of others; your role is to do what you are told, like it or not; your role is to conform, to play the game by the rules of others. What I attempted to do when I wrote the book 25 years ago was to indicate how that sense of powerlessness had self-defeating consequences for everyone in the school culture, i.e., students, teachers, principals, parents. And, I emphasized, reform efforts that did not change that sense of pervasive powerlessness would not achieve their goal of improving the quality and outcomes of schooling. Nothing I have observed and read since I wrote the book has caused me to change my views. I have known a classroom here and a classroom there, a school here and a school there, where power relationships have been appropriately changed with encouraging results. That cannot be said for any *school system* I know or about which I have read.

Chapter 18

What Constitutes a Change?

It would take a fair-size book to describe changes sought in our schools since I wrote *The Culture of the School* a quarter of a century ago. I have briefly described and discussed those changes that in one way or another require a change in power relationships, be they in student–teacher, teacher–administrator, administrator–board, parent–school relationships. These are what may be termed Type A changes: they are explicitly intended to alter what people say, do, think, and feel not only as individual actions but in combination. More concretely, imagine that these changes have truly taken hold—they have not, but let us imagine that they have—and let us also imagine that our 1970 Martian has returned when they have taken hold. How different would the scene *look* to him? And I emphasize *look* because the major changes that have occurred in the past 25 years are far less in what people do than in what they think and feel. That is to say, increasingly there is an awareness that schools as we have known them have to be radically transformed. It is not what you would call an acute awareness, or a formulated diagnosis of what is wrong, or what needs to be done. It is more a fleeting thought and feeling that change is what is called for at the same time that the direction and implications of the change are very murky.

What I am saying here is that the major change since I wrote the book—the one that will power future changes, whatever they may be, is the sense of disillusionment with and disappointment in our schools. That inchoate dysphoric sense represents a momentous change, historically speaking. It is not only about schools; it is more general than that. It is a sense that is not unrelated to a dissatisfaction with many of our social institutions, not the least of which is the federal government. In 1992, under the auspices of Vice President Gore, three documents were published on what I would call the "culture of government." To me, at least, many of the major points made by the vice president are similar to those in my book. It is not happenstance that the vice president called for "reinventing government." In the most explicit ways he makes clear that tinkering with what he calls the "culture of futility" will be no more than that: tinkering. Anyone interested in the culture of the school and the problem of change will find those governmental publications revealing and instructive. Let me give an excerpt from one of the volumes (Gore, 1993), a very typical excerpt:

IS GOVERNMENT INHERENTLY INCOMPETENT? ABSOLUTELY NOT. ARE FEDERAL agencies filled with incompetent people? No. The problem is much deeper: Washington is filled with organizations designed for an environment that no longer exists—bureaucracies so big and wasteful they can no longer serve the American people.

From the 1930s through the 1960s, we built large, top-down, centralized bureaucracies to do the public's business. They were patterned after the corporate structures of the age: hierarchical bureaucracies in which tasks were broken into simple parts, each the responsibility of a different layer of employees, each defined by specific rules and regulations. With their rigid preoccupation with standard operating procedure, their vertical chains of command, and their standardized services, these bureaucracies were steady—but slow and cumbersome. And in today's world of rapid change, lightning-quick information technologies, tough global competition, and demanding customers, large, top-down bureaucracies—public or private—don't work very well. Saturn isn't run the way General Motors was. Intel isn't run the way IBM was.

Many federal organizations are also monopolies, with few incentives to innovate or improve. Employees have virtual lifetime tenure, regardless of their performance. Success offers few rewards; failures, few penalties. And customers are captive; they can't walk away from the air traffic control system or the Internal Revenue Service and sign up with a competitor. Worse, most federal monopolies receive their money without any direct input from their customers. Consequently, they try a lot harder to please Congressional appropriations subcommittees than the people they are meant to serve. Taxpayers pay more than they should and get poorer service.

Politics intensifies the problem. In Washington's highly politicized world, the greatest risk is not that a program will perform poorly, but that a scandal will erupt. Scandals are front-page news, while routine failure is ignored. Hence control system after control system is piled up to minimize the risk of scandal. The budget system, the personnel rules, the procurement process, the inspectors general—all are designed to prevent the tiniest misstep. We assume that we can't trust employees to make decisions, so we spell out in precise detail how they must do virtually everything, then audit them to ensure that they have obeyed every rule. The slightest deviation prompts new regulations and even more audits.

Before long, simple procedures are too complex for employees to navigate, so we hire more budget analysts, more personnel experts, and more procurement officers to make things work. By then, the process involves so much red tape that the smallest action takes far longer and costs far more than it should. Simple travel arrangements require endless forms and numerous signatures. Straightforward purchases take months; larger ones take years. Routine printing jobs take a dozen approvals.

This emphasis on process steals resources from the real job: serving the customer. Indeed, the federal government spends billions of dollars paying people who control, check up on, or investigate others—supervisors, headquarters staffs, budget officers, personnel officers, procurement officers, and staffs of the General Accounting Office (GAO) and the inspectors general. Not all this money is wasted, of course. But the real waste is no doubt larger, because the endless regulations and layers of control consume every employee's time. Who pays? The taxpayer.

… federal employees quickly learn that common sense is risky—and creativity is downright dangerous. They learn that the goal is not to produce results, please customers, or save taxpayers' money, but to avoid mistakes. Those who dare to innovate do so quietly.

This is perhaps the saddest lesson learned by those who worked on the National Performance Review: Yes, innovators exist within the federal government, but many work hard to keep their innovations quiet. By its nature, innovation requires a departure from standard operating procedure. In the federal government, such departures invite repercussions.

The result is a culture of fear and resignation. To survive, employees keep a low profile. They decide that the safest answer in any given situation is a firm "maybe." They follow the rules, pass the buck, and keep their heads down. They develop what one employee, speaking with Vice President Gore at a Department of Veterans Affairs meeting, called "a government attitude." (pp. 3–5) ∎

What the vice president has done is to give voice to feelings and attitudes engendered in people in the post–World War II era. It is those kinds of feelings and attitudes the public has come to have about schools. There is another (related) similarity. There have been numerous efforts to change the "culture of government," just as there have been similar efforts to change schools. The results have been minimal, if not nonexistent. The diagnosis the vice president has made (based on scores of concrete examples) is in principle similar, if not identical, to that which I gave in the book about why efforts to change schools are fated to be disappointing.

If readers think that what Vice President Gore describes may be overdrawn or overgeneralized, they should read Diane Ravitch's 1995 article "Adventures in Wonderland: A Scholar in Washington." She describes her experience, beginning in 1991, as assistant secretary in the U.S. Department of Education. Ravitch always has written clearly and dispassionately and this article is no exception. In reading between the lines I found it hard to avoid concluding that she struggled mightily to control expression both of her anger and disappointments. What the vice president describes is similar, if not identical, to what Rogers described in 1968 in his book *110 Livingston Street. Politics and Bureaucracy in the New York City School*

System. When I wrote the book in 1970, I did not, as I should have, emphasized the predictive significance of his conclusions about how issues of power and turfdom suffuse a school system. I relegated my comments on the book to a footnote (see page 163). If someone like Rogers were to write a similar book in 1996, the New York saga would be just as disillusioning or more. The New York story was and is representative of all of our larger cities, which is why I contend that the future of our society will in large measure be determined by what happens (or does not happen) in our city school systems.

In 1994, Walter Annenberg gave, with much fanfare, a gift of half a billion dollars for educational reform of our largest school systems. From what I have been able to gather from my counterintelligence sources, I have to conclude, unfortunately, that the money will be used in ways that will have little impact because the efforts are not *explicitly* informed by what I consider to be the two basic criteria for judging change that I discuss in Chapter 19. At a meeting I attended—a meeting presumably designed to be advisory—the participants were informed at the outset that the major decisions had already been made! I (and others) were flabbergasted. Only one decision was explicit and, therefore, understandable: the money would not go *directly* to schools and school systems. Aside from that, nothing was explicit or understandable. There were no governing psychological or educational or sociological or philosophical conceptual rationales. I am willing to bet and to give attractive odds that in none of these cities is there or will there be an effort to describe what is being done, why, and with what consequences. That is to say, none of them will have a David Rogers whose accounts will allow us to learn what and what not to do. Each will start with a Model A and we will never know what a Model B should be. What the Annenberg gift represented is a classic example of what the philosopher Pogo said: "We are faced with unsurmountable opportunities." Humor, we have been told, is a way of expressing anxiety in a diluted, subliminal way. Pogo had it right.

What are Type B changes? There have been many Type B changes since I wrote the book. The introduction of computers, team teaching, assessment of teacher competency, increasing the length of practice teaching, increasing class time devoted to the "basics," more and careful monitoring of homework, raising standards for and expectations from students, more ethnically, racially, and gender-sensitive curricula—these are examples of what I call Type B changes. Each of these (and more) can have a legitimate justification. What they have in common is their discreteness or, to put it negatively, none addresses the school qua school, i.e., the truly distinctive features of the school culture. Put in another way, Type B changes are not intended to be systemic ones. Each is intended to change and improve something but that something is not the school or the system. That would not be a limitation if there was reason to believe there was agreement that the system was accomplishing its purposes. But that is patently not the case. It would not be a limitation if there was evidence that the school culture did not possess features that could subvert the intended purposes of each of these discrete changes, or, if not subvert, dilute the quantity and quality of outcomes. The evidence is otherwise.

I do not hold the position that if you cannot change the system, do not try to change anything. That would be stupid, ridiculous, and unfair. There are Type B changes that are trivial and some that are not. My point is that precisely when they are not trivial (e.g., computers)—they require changes in attitude and custom— the process of implementation confronts features of the school culture that are obstacles to change. Systems are both conservative and reactionary, conservative in the sense that they seek to conserve that which is perceived to be worthy, a bulwark against uncritical acceptance of the plethora of fads and fashions that come and go. They are reactionary in that they are too often resistant to *anything* that will require meaningful change.

Karen S. Louis's article (1994) is very relevant and clarifying of the differences between what I call Type A and Type B reform efforts. She very deftly and succinctly summarizes and judges those efforts and concludes that without Type A changes little will come from Type B changes. So, for example, she says that "most of the current alternative paradigm models [for school change] are incomplete because they do not address all aspects of the needed changes in schools. For example, neither Sizer nor Comer deal systematically with needed changes in leadership and governance." Her article is very relevant to an assessment of the efforts in the past 25 years to effect and sustain school change. Her emphasis on productive "organizational learning" is similar in principle to that of Kenneth Wilson whose book *Redesigning Education* (1994) I discuss later in this chapter, except that Wilson places the issues in the larger system in which schools as organizations are embedded. You could say that Louis emphasizes the characteristics of a learning *organization* whereas Wilson's emphasis is on learning *systems,* which facilitate and support organizations as self-conscious, self-improving agencies.

What I emphasized in the book, as I am now, is that we do not confuse Type A and Type B changes. If each has its place, it is obvious that Type A changes are in some ultimate sense the more important, if only because that kind of change makes it more likely that the Type B change will stand a better chance of being appropriately implemented and evaluated.

The day after I wrote these words I received an unpublished paper by Wasley, Hampel, and Clark (1995), who had carried out an in-depth evaluation of five of the many schools involved in the Coalition of Essential Schools (CES). The CES was conceived and initiated by Ted Sizer, whose book *Horace's Compromise* (1985) had a marked impact on the educational community and beyond. There are now several hundred of these high schools, each of which committed itself to implementation of the nine principles Sizer has spelled out. It is a commitment to school change, which is to say that it is clearly a Type A effort. In their paper, Wasley, Hampel, and Clark very succinctly present their major conclusions, which in the next year or two will be spelled out in detail in a book.[1] That paper is very

---

1. Earlier, Muncey and McQuillan (1993) reported on a small sample of the earliest CES schools. The Wasley, Hampel, and Clark paper is about schools that had been in the program for at least 4 years. The two papers should be seen in relation to each other, and both in relation to Hampel's paper I discuss later in this chapter.

important for my purposes here for several reasons. It is about the largest Type A project carried out since I wrote the book. It is obviously a critical but very sympathetic report.

The differences in tone and conclusions between Muncey and McQuillan's paper (1993) and the later one by Wasley, Hampel, and Clark are ones of degree. The former is sympathetic but clearly more critical; the latter is sympathetic and somewhat less critical, i.e., it is not until they come to the recommendation section of their paper that it becomes clear that they are not in any basic disagreement with the earlier assessment. Having read both papers—as well as the manuscript of the forthcoming Muncey and McQuillan book (1996)—I cannot deny that *some* desirable changes took place in *some* schools. But I feel justified in saying that the evidence that any school qua school changed in any comprehensive way is indeed scanty. Furthermore, the few schools where CES principles were most in evidence were schools that displayed those principles before they joined CES. The following excerpts are from the Wasley, Hampel, and Clark paper. I am grateful that the authors of the paper gave me permission to give excerpts from their paper, with the proviso that I tell the reader that it is a rough draft. The paper is crucial for my present purposes because it will enable me to say some things I consider a most important part of the answer to the question: What constitutes a change? I could have said these things without the excerpts, but I would have subjected the reader to generalizations and abstractions that I could not assume would be all that meaningful. I needed some concrete basis for what I would say and these excerpts provide it.

FINDINGS

FINDING #1. ALL FIVE OF THE SCHOOLS ENCOUNTERED DIFFICULTY MAKING THE schoolwide changes that many believed would be helpful, because they did not have a shared common image of a different, more rigorous kind of schooling on which to base their actions. While all of them had engaged in the kinds of vision/mission setting activities common in schools sometimes more than once, when it came time to change structures or practices to put new "visions" in place, their individual interpretations of that vision stretched along a continuum from "that's what we already do"—i.e., no change is necessary—to "everything, the schedule, textbooks, departments, my old lessons, must go!" ...

Finding #2. These five schools were either stopped or made progress based on their ability to grapple with highly charged, values laden, controversial issues both as a whole school group and as smaller units like teams or departments within the school. In the schools where faculty were direct with each other, where they developed processes for airing controversy collaboratively, the faculty were able to make changes that endured and grew stronger over time. Where faculty had no capacity to grapple with controversy, they were unable to move beyond maintaining existing practices. In addition, the tone of the school was more hopeless, more bitter because the issues rankled, unresolved....

Finding #3. Building and maintaining processes for obtaining and acting on good critical feedback from external sources contributed to being able to move forward, and separated them from those who could not. This worked on all levels from individual teachers to teams to whole faculties. Those who did not gather external feedback relied largely on self-report that was sometimes very good, but more often focused on teacher comfort rather than on gains for students.

Finding #4. Gaining feedback from others provides staff with an important analytical tool, but it is not enough by itself. Equally important is the ability to engage in tough, direct self-analysis. We mentioned above that we frequently saw self-analysis that was good, but did not push far enough. For instance, staff focused on logistical issues: "Did that lesson work out according to the time we allocated?" Or teachers asked themselves, "Was I able to cover all that I wanted?" Or "Did the kids seem to like that activity?" However, it was in the schools that were in the habit of asking tough questions of themselves by focusing on their students that we saw significant gains.

Finding #5. In the School Change Study schools we were predisposed to look for circumstances where curriculum, instruction, and assessment were attended to simultaneously because of previous work done in CES schools (Wasley, 1994). The five study schools corroborated that all three must be considered simultaneously, but that school culture constituted a fourth dimension that was part of the total equation. We encountered two contrasting approaches to these four dimensions of schoolwork. The first approach, in the majority of our study schools, involved selecting a focus for faculty efforts. For some it was authentic assessment. In other schools, the focus was on active learning or on innovative curriculum.

For instance, in several of the schools, faculty were working on authentic assessments—developing portfolios. Without attention to the other dimensions, portfolios turned out to be collections of student work from traditional classroom practices—lab worksheets or math homework problems and tests. They were passed from one year to the next, but not used by staff as a source of powerful history and information on a given student. Common assertions that authentic assessments drive changes in instruction or in curriculum or in school culture did not always prove to be the case.

Or faculty and parents were very busy changing student council, redoing the schedule, establishing new kinds of faculty meetings or governance structures where little collective or individual attention was paid to daily interactions with students. Where one or even two of these dimensions was considered in isolation from the others, the gains were not as comprehensive as was hoped.

Finding #6. The presence of a coherent sense of the interconnectedness of all efforts underway in one building was a rare but enabling factor in the school's ability to influence student experience. One school faculty mentioned a laundry list of activities that represented their work to change the school: a new schedule, a new grant for dropout prevention, a new parenting program, integrated English and social studies, portfolios in science, and so on. What they didn't have was a consistent view of how these things fit together, which prevented them from pulling disparate ends together, and from viewing their reform efforts as a series of unrelated personally motivated projects.

CRITICAL CONSIDERATIONS

Skills for More Civil Discourse

The study schools found themselves needing far stronger skills of civil discourse—a nebulous term at best that requires some definition. By discourse we mean extended thoughtful conversation between multiple parties on a particular topic. We mean civil in two senses: It maintains the mutual respect of the participants, that is, people are civil to each other, but it also means more than simply adhering to procedural due process—the rules of consensus decision making, for instance—but extends beyond to genuine sensitivity to the rights, feelings, and aspirations of colleagues. Moreover, it seeks the best interests of the group as a whole in order to achieve the civic good. Far too often secondary schools are characterized by territorial, competitive behavior. When faculty and school communities begin taking the improvement of student learning as central to all decisions, they move away from a focus on special-interest groups to a shared focus.

Civil discourse is also about values, not merely techniques. Discussions to develop simple policies to direct attendance, tardiness, attire, or classroom behavior—crucial concerns in all five schools—could rarely be sustained because of underlying views regarding kids' trustworthiness, their basic decency or lack of it that had not yet been directly discussed. Examples of how race and gender expectations varied from teacher to teacher abounded in our classroom observations and in our discussions with students, but these important topics rarely arose in faculty discussions. These issues, steeped in individual values and beliefs, need to be brought to light, raised up for consideration in respectful recognition that we will not all agree but that to ignore it limits the possibilities for our students.

Schools have long had reputations as polite places—places where everyone abides by the rules, and no one confronts too directly. Or, schools have been places where many engage in covert behavior (see Wasley, 1991). Teachers who disagree with decisions complain in private and ignore the decisions in practice. Neither polite places nor covert places ever manage to build the kinds of coherent educational program that truly develop more of their students' potential.

The incentives to engage in this kind of discourse seem shallow to those considering this step. To put difficult issues on the table would appear to foster greater divisiveness. The schools we watched who've pushed themselves to engage in a more rigorous civil discourse have come to understand a whole set of incentives that were not obvious at the outset. The climate of the school becomes more professional, less subversive. Those usually labeled the resistors sometimes gain the grudging respect of their peers because of their ability to ask the most important questions. Staff feel professionally relieved that they won't be stuck in the same tedious arguments for years to come. And, they begin to see that benefits of direct conversation improve their capacity to work with students.

Self-Analysis Focused on Student Gains

Over the 3 years, we saw many an example that these schools were very good at adopting new approaches or practices—like cooperative learning, or authentic assessments, or integrated learning—and terrific at defending the choices they'd made in the ensuing months or in the face of challenges. It was rarer to find a faculty focused on tough, rigorous reflection about whether what they were getting was what they wanted. However, in the schools where faculty examined their efforts in light of their students, the likelihood that faculty achieved their ends increases dramatically.

This kind of self-reflective analysis is different than taking action. It means planning for and taking the time to step back from action to examine it in light of its original intentions. It is also different than the regular checking that teachers do at the end of a class or a faculty meeting: "Did we do everything we said we would? Was it good enough? I ran out of readings so I will have to have more copies made." These questions examine immediate concerns, the mechanics of a given activity. Self-analysis focused on student gains requires that staff examine activities in light of overarching goals and hoped-for outcomes. One school instituted advisory programs in order to make the school a more personal place. One teacher, who'd been doing school business during advisory, asked herself and then her colleagues, "Am I really getting to know kids better when what we are really doing in advisory is running class meetings?" This kind of stepping back to examine action needs to be continuous, a regular part of faculty's work as a whole group, as teams and as individuals, and it must be focused on the effects of action taken on students.

The Need for Regular Feedback

These schools convinced us that regular external feedback is different than, but complementary to, heightened self-reflective analysis. We need both. External feedback refers to that given by people less involved, who are external to the immediate culture. They bring with them clear eyes and less emotional attachment to both actions taken and to existing outcomes.

This kind of feedback is also unfamiliar to many in schools. Since most people who work in school only experience feedback in their yearly evaluations, exploring the distinction between summative evaluation or formative feedback is critical. Formative feedback is given so that mid-course corrections can be made. It is designed to help individuals and groups grow by offering them a perspective they cannot have on their own work.

Many teachers over their careers see few others teach, find few who are willing to come into their classrooms, have limited access to any kind of external information about what and how they are doing. Thus, they rely on their own self-analysis, and we rely on their self-report of how things are going. We know from both interviewing teachers, principals, and kids that self-reports can describe quite a different reality—given a culture that promotes and rewards success stories rather than critical feedback or thoughtful analysis. (Wasley, Hampel, and Clark, 1995) ■

My own experience with three CES schools permits me to express complete agreement with the thrust of the recommendations because in these three schools—which were wildly different in numerous ways—they varied from, at best, a sincere, successful but very partial implementation of the principles to, at worst, a lack of understanding of the principles that ruled out appropriate implementation. When Wasley, Hampel, and Clark recommend "civil discourse," it is not something they have dreamed up. And when they discuss the bedrock importance of self-scrutiny, it is based on their extensive observations.

On this last point I must express my admiration for Ted Sizer for something which comes close to uniqueness in the literature of school change. He sought and obtained support that allowed Muncey and McQuillan, and then, Wasley, Hampel, and Clark to undertake the extensive descriptions and evaluations they did. It takes courage to support *independent* description and evaluation. The school reform literature—when and since I wrote the book—contains (to my knowledge) no instances in which a large (indeed national) effort to effect school change supported a very extensive, independent series of evaluations at the same time that the effort was ongoing. The only semicomparable instance is the *Eight Year Study* (Aiken, 1942) initiated in the 1930s. *That kind and degree of self-scrutiny is what is missing in schools and is what Wasley, Hampel, and Clark rightly emphasize.* And they are also on target in pleading for a professional collegiality that is other than a sometime thing. Collegiality is more than a form of friendly togetherness. It represents a willing desire to learn from each other and to assume the responsibility to be knowledgeable about the ideas, efforts, and writings of people who, like themselves, have devoted their energies to the goals of improving schools as well as the field profession. In these regards the findings from the CES are not what you could call robust; the CES findings point to a critical issue.

On the basis of what I wrote 25 years ago, there is nothing surprising about what Muncey and McQuillan, and now Wasley, Hampel, and Clark report about coalition schools. But since I wrote the book, I see such reports in a different light. Why should any effort at innovation be expected to be other than a first approximation of what needs to be done if one's purposes are to be achieved? What permits an advocate for such an effort to assume that his conceptual rationale and implementation strategy will not be found wanting in some important respects when they run up against institutional realities? Should not such advocates regard their starting points as *only* Model A in a process from which one will learn what Model B should be, a process in which Model B will be superseded by Model C, and so on? The first computer is truly a museum piece compared to the computer of today. The changes took place in a developmental process characterized by feedbacks between developers and users, between what a computer could do and what users wanted it to do, between what a developer considered a satisfactory model and the dissatisfactions of those using the model. It was a self-correcting process in which theory, technology, knowledge, and practice were a seamless web. It was a process in which failure, whole or in part, was productive of new models. It was and is a process whose end is not in sight.

Although I would argue that developing and improving computers is a cup of tea compared to what is involved in changing a nation's schools, the educational reform movement has been almost totally unaware that its initial models *never* should have been regarded as other than just that: first approximations that would be found wanting in very important respects. On the contrary, each discrete effort at change seemed to assume that its rationale was *the* model, not an initial one that would lead to better ones. There were no built-in, self-correcting procedures because they were not required by a stance reflective of the assumptions that you already possessed the best and only way to achieve your purposes. Holding to that assumption, advocates promised far more than they could deliver, with the predictable consequence that the "buyers" and/or fiscal supporters are, to say the least, disappointed and look elsewhere for answers to their problems.

As luck would have it, in today's mail is a letter from a friend, Bruce Thomas, who is very knowledgeable about the history of educational reform. In his letter he is referring to comments contained in my book *The Predictable Failure of Educational Reform* (1990).

JUST CAME ACROSS YOUR COMMENTS ON THE CHICAGO CORPORATE COMMUNITY School which, you wrote, is "unlikely to achieve its goals." Here's the current history. The school ran for 5 years; was never evaluated in any serious way (not evaluated at all, in fact, as far as I know); encountered a steady erosion of corporate support; and was eventually merged into the Chicago public school system (this year). Dubbed as "a catalyst for change," it effected no change whatsoever. And as a part of the public schools, it is rapidly becoming indistinguishable from the public schools. Five million dollars spent for what? And I doubt very much any of the corporate heads who supported the school learned a damn thing for their money and time. ■

His last sentence is what is especially relevant here. It took no special wisdom to predict that the school would fail. It is as if they had read my school culture book and decided to do everything against which I had cautioned. (I could give many other examples.) The point is that never in a million years would the corporate sponsors have supported anyone in their research and development departments who proposed the development of a product lacking all of the features of a self-improving, feedback process. They would never think of putting time and money to develop a product, present and sell it to the public, and not carefully, and at each step of the process, seek to determine whether the product had shortcomings, needed to be altered in some ways, and what the next version of the product should be. Indeed, it is not unusual for a company to seek the advice and reactions of potential users *before* the product is even marketed.

So how should we regard the two reports on the Coalition of Essential Schools? Was CES a failure? A mixed bag? A very worthy attempt that brought about few of its intended purposes? My present answer is in two related parts. The first part is in the form of a criticism: the conception and implementation of the project did not allow for early recognition and response to clear problems and inadequacies that were apparent. (Some of these problems were predictable; others were not.) The second is that CES should be regarded as Model A, equivalent, so to speak, to Henry Ford's Model T car or to the earliest computers. In other words, what should a Model B CES look like? My criticism is that that question should have been asked early on but was not. But it is not too late. What we need to know is how Ted Sizer and his colleagues would answer this question: *On the basis of what you have experienced and learned, and assuming that funding sources would be supportive, and further assuming that you have the time, energy, and desire to develop and implement Model B, what would that model look like and how would it be different from the model with which you began?* There are projects that fail and should not be resurrected. The CES is not one of them. It did bring about some desired change in some schools; a great deal has been learned. How could this learning be incorporated in a Model B?

Wasley, Hampel, and Clark are right in saying that changing schools is a time-consuming and daunting affair. But one (and it is only one) factor that makes it so time consuming is a conception of the change process that has no self-correcting signals or procedures. Changing schools confronts one with problems no less predictable than that the sun will rise tomorrow. If we have learned anything, we have learned *that,* which is why I consider the school culture book to contain glimpses of the obvious. But when we ignore the obvious and in addition proceed as if our Model A will not *have* to be changed, we court disaster.

There are two assumptions in the question I directed to Sizer and his colleagues. One was the assumption that funding sources would be supportive. That is one big assumption because the usual funding sources, public and private, seem to believe that you can bring about school change according to calendar time, that the first year you should be at point X, at the end of the second year you should be at point Y, and so on. That, of course, is patent nonsense, reflective of an engineering mentality. But it is unfair to direct all criticism to funding sources because those who are seeking funding present their plans as if they can achieve their results according to calendar time. But let us assume that you have a good idea for a school change project and you apply for support for, say, 3 years. Let us also assume that in your application you clearly state that it really is impossible to say with confidence that you will not encounter problems (theoretical, methodological, practical) that will require you to make changes, which would mean your time schedule could not be adhered to, i.e., you might not be at point X or Y as you hoped to be at the end of the grant period. Funders have trouble with an application that contains the realistic possibility that the direction of the project may have to undergo a "mid-course correction."[2] In regard to mechanical systems, such corrections are expected. Indeed, the words *mid-career correction* come from experience with mechanical systems. But when it comes to human social systems both the granter and the grantee reinforce each other's belief that school change is an engineering process. It never is; it cannot be.

The second assumption in the question directed to Sizer and his colleagues was that they had time, energy, and desire to develop Model B to remedy the inadequacies of Model A. Let me just say that the list of burned-out school reformers is very long. This is not only because changing schools is a personally demanding and draining task—reason enough to initiate a burning-out process. It is also because when they realize early on the inadequacies of their Model A, and that developing and implementing Model B will not be warmly greeted, especially by funding sources, a kind of professional-moral conflict starts to build, a conflict between what you are doing and promised to do and what you *now* know you should do. That is not a conflict easy to live with; it makes you want to leave the scene. One reformer put it to me this way: "It's like getting married with the rosiest expectations, then finding that it will not be rosy, and then spending days, months, or years in conflict about how to end a marriage that you now know was fated to fail." What he did not say is that many marriages fail because one or both of the spouses have met the equivalent of Model B, someone they believe will help them avoid the pitfalls they encountered in their Model A marriage.

In 1994, Kenneth Wilson and Bennett Daviss wrote *Redesigning Education,* one of the first of several books that will reflect the conceptualizations and recommendations of Wilson. That book is a reasoned, historically based critique of the education reform movement, and in a nonpolemical way it explains why that movement has failed and must continue to do so. The book is worth its price if only because it will be the rare reader who will not grasp the fact that innovations and new ideas in education run a gauntlet of obstacles that are not (and were not) peculiar to schools. In a most clear and stimulating way, Wilson and Daviss illustrate that point with instructive examples from agriculture, the development of aircraft, and much more. They also give us a working picture—not vague generalizations that have the quality of inkblots—that is applicable to educational change. In three paragraphs under the heading "The Key to Reform," the authors state:

---

2. Relevant here is Hampel's article (1995). In a very succinct way he indicates why diffusing a Model A effort before you know what experience has shown you Model B should be is self-defeating. More than that, he identifies the sources of pressure for premature diffusion. I have to assume that Hampel is drawing on his extensive experience with the Coalition of Essential Schools, i.e., it was unfortunate that CES grew so large so fast that breadth swamped, indeed buried, depth. In any event, Hampel's paper should be seen as related to the Muncey–McQuillan and Wasley–Hampel–Clark papers.

OUR DECADE-LONG EFFORT TO REFORM U.S. EDUCATION HAS FAILED. IT HAS FAILED because it has not let go of an educational vision that is neither workable nor appropriate to today's needs. Until traditional assumptions about the nature and meaning of education are upset (and new paradigms replace outworn ones), good ideas will languish regardless of their appropriateness. Reforms that seek to correct symptoms without first addressing causes are doomed. Just as no amount of bailing could have kept the *Titanic* afloat, no amount of improved content can save our crumbling educational structure. To effect fundamental meaningful reforms, *all* educators must first be able to admit and agree that our traditional guiding vision of education is no longer relevant in a postindustrial, knowledge-based society. This admission and agreement are inevitable but, because of the discomforts of change, remain far from universal. Second, educators must accept, then build on, the model that the needs of a new society demand. Finally, when our schools do acknowledge education's new paradigm, they will need an ordered process of change that will enable them to exchange the patterns rooted in an antiquated structure of ideas for those needed to enact a new vision.

Luckily, industrial society has already perfected such a process of continuous, guided innovation. Though children are not products, schools are not factories, and educators are not assembly-line workers, human energies can be organized to produce the consistent improvement and excellence that have been achieved in agriculture and in industry. When our schools embrace the vision and adopt similar strategies of change that other enterprises have pioneered, we will have taken the first step not only toward improving our schools but toward addressing the social dilemmas that effective education alone can correct.

In the following pages we will propose a practical way in which an orderly process of progressive change can be incorporated into our educational infrastructure. Chapter 2 explores this process to understand how and why it is so consistently effective. Chapter 3 details one of today's most effective learning reforms, a program that has made education's most productive use of this process yet. Chapters 4 and 5 investigate the forces that have long rendered education impervious to structural change and also demonstrate how these traditional forces can be overcome. Chapter 6 takes special note of the role that educational measurement must play in effective reform. Finally, in chapters 7 and 8, we outline one method by which an ordered process of change can be made effective and affordable in our schools. (Wilson and Daviss, 1994, pp. 20–21) ■

What that section promises, the book delivers.

I have been fortunate to have gotten to know Dr. Wilson well. In the post–World War II era there have been many well-known people in the science community who saw themselves as types of saviors of failing schools (hardly able to hide their disdain of the educational community), some of whom were wrong for the wrong reasons, but most of whom were right for the wrong reasons. And when I say right it is in the sense that it is hard to be completely wrong, albeit some managed to be just that. All of them confirmed Mencken's caveat that for every important problem there is a simple answer that is wrong. Wilson not only immersed himself in the history of innovations in diverse arenas but he did the same in regard to educational history (going back to Comenius) and educational reform. Like me, Wilson quickly gave up the myth that in regard to the design and redesign process schools are unique social systems. *Indeed, what is ironic is that Wilson is the first scientist to take the concept of system seriously in regard to education.* He does not waste time inveighing against the supposed intellectual and personal frailties of educators because that would be a stance of blaming the victim. And precisely because he thinks in terms of system, he makes it clear why the culture of the school is as I have described it. And by placing that culture in a wider concept of system, he has deepened our understanding of the problem of change. Wilson is not and does not see himself as a savior, as giving us an answer. Consistent with his conception of system, as well as of the process of design and redesign, he knows that his Model A will have to be improved or replaced by Model B, which in turn will be followed by another model. This is in the spirit of the most central characteristic of the scientific enterprise: the more you learn and know, the more you have to learn and know. The history of science, like the history of education, provides ample evidence of the wisdom of that character in the comics who said, "We have met the enemy and it is us." The human animal, as an individual or as a member of a social setting, is a wondrous, frustrating combination of virtues and failings.

What reception and influence Wilson's book and future writings will have I cannot predict. However, I have no doubt that what he has written and will write will not be the whole truth but will contain much wisdom, which is in very short supply. If he is taken seriously, the culture of the school and the problem of change will look very different to my Martian on his next visit.[3] It had better not be a visit in the near future because changing a culture and the system that spawns and reinforces it is as difficult a task (conceptually and practically) as humans can confront. That is implied in Wilson's saying that "children are not products, schools are not factories, and educators are not assembly-line workers." Unfortunately, there are and have been many reform efforts in the past 25 years that did regard children as products, schools as factories, and educators as mentally impoverished assembly-line workers—views that justified approaching school change in the most narrow engineering terms, as if human cultures and systems can be theoretically and practically kept separate. They can and should be kept separate if your intention is to fail. When I wrote the school culture book it was an effort to explain failure and to

---

3. Wilson is doing more than critiquing and conceptualizing. He is engaged in the beginning, *action* phases of systemic reform. John Dewey created the lab school at the University of Chicago to demonstrate and test his ideas. Dr. Wilson has recently started the action process of demonstrating and evaluating his conceptualizations about systemic reform. He has taken on an awesome task. I am not likely to be around when the fruits of his efforts can be judged but, if I had to bet, I predict that his impact will be positive and persuasive.

predict continued failure. Wilson has demonstrated why the culture of schools is a consequence of the wider system in which they are embedded. Wilson did not build on or amplify what I wrote; he provided (or will provide) a more comprehensive explanation for why that culture has to have the features I emphasized and why the redesign process he describes is the most fruitful way of changing that culture.

What constitutes a change? I answered that question by saying that the change required will involve a *combination* of changes in what people say, do, think, and feel. Wilson agrees but rightly goes on to show that the combination will be the result of changes in the system qua system, i.e., a discernible alteration in relationships—I would say power relationships—in the system.

I know that many people will react negatively to my emphasis on power relationships. It engenders imagery of controversy, conflict, unseemly passion, and even destructiveness. The fact is that that kind of imagery is precisely what is engendered in the bulk of school personnel by existing power relationships in our schools, and, of course, in many parents and other community groups, as well as in university faculty who have commerce with schools, and, finally, in many politicians who are bewildered by their ineffectiveness in changing schools.

In 1992, the New American Schools Corporation awarded Bensenville, Illinois, $1.25 million to design and implement a "break-the-mold" educational program. It was a debacle that Mirel (1994) has described and thoughtfully analyzed. His instructive emphasis on factors of power—within the school and between it and diverse community groups—is right on target. That emphasis is also one that Darling-Hammond (1995) writes about in commenting on several "restructuring" efforts. From a historical perspective, Tyack and Tobin (1994) are relevant to read. If my counterintelligence about other sites awarded grants by the New American Schools Corporation is semivalid, the Bensenville fiasco will not be an exception, although no sites yet appear to be the complete failure that Bensenville was. One hopes that each of them has someone like Mirel to serve as documenter or historian.

So, when I emphasize power relationships, it is because existing power relationships are part of the problem and can never be part of the solution. There is a maxim in the political arena that you cannot make an omelet without breaking some eggs, a maxim that means that when you seek to change an existing state of affairs—the equivalent of making a new kind of omelet—you should always expect that some people will prefer that you leave the eggs intact. To expect that there is a universal solvent that will make alterations in existing power relationships a peaceful affair in which no one's feathers will be ruffled is to believe in the tooth fairy. There have been many reformers who believed just that when they initiated their programs; they soon became, or ended up, converts to reality.

Changing schools involves more than changing power relations. What purposes are to be served by those changes? I answered that question in the school culture book, but in subsequent years I came to see that my answer was not as forceful as it should have been. I make another try in the next chapter.

Chapter **19**

Two Basic Criteria for
School Change

There is, as I indicated in the previous chapter, general agreement about the overarching purpose of schooling. But how will we know if that purpose has been achieved in whole or in part? Realistically we can only approximate the achievement of that purpose. Aside from the fact that we are imperfect people in an imperfect world, and taking into account that there are somewhere around 20,000 independent school districts in the United States, among which is a bewildering array of conditions, traditions, and more, we expect there will be discernible variation in accomplishing that purpose. (Even if there was unanimous agreement and commitment to that purpose, the complexity of the implementation process guarantees variation in outcome.) So how will we know to what degree that purpose is being approximated? And by *know* I mean criteria depending little on personal opinion but on findings of a nature that will engender general agreement that changes reflective of that purpose have occurred.

Revisiting the culture of the school and the problem of change has enabled me to state two criteria, which if not convincingly met, means that other important criteria are unlikely to be satisfied. Stated differently, *the thrust of all critiques of our schools, and the aim of every noncosmetic program for change, implicitly and sometimes explicitly lead to the two criteria. The imagery conveyed by these critiques and programs is imagery of social contexts in a school in which the behavioral regularities of children and teachers are obviously different in quality and quantity than they are now. It is imagery capable of being systemically and rigorously evaluated.*

In light of the previous chapter it will come as no surprise that the first criterion concerns *question asking in the classroom*. As I indicated in *The Culture of the School,* the modal classroom is one in which teachers ask questions and students give answers. Students hardly ask questions and certainly that is not because they have no questions. From their earliest days in school they have been socialized to see themselves as passive recipients of facts and knowledge, not as active instigators and participants in the creation of knowledge. Teachers (the usual exceptions aside) do not start with "where children are" but with the requirements of a predetermined, time-allocating curriculum. In 1993, I wrote *Letters to a Serious Education President,* an imaginary correspondence between me and someone elected president in the year 2000. The book is about the "big idea," which is very simple: Productive learning starts with "where children are." One of the letters puts it this way:

DEAR MR. PRESIDENT:

There are many perspectives from which human history has been written. It is not surprising that the one that fascinates me describes how difficult it has been for people to change their conceptions about human capacities. It is not happenstance, of course, that there has been an intimate relationship between the struggle for human freedom and changes in conception about what people are capable of becoming. Over the millennia the most frequent situation was one in which rulers viewed the ruled akin to cattle who needed and wanted to be told what to think and do. To the rulers their people were an undifferentiated mass, each human atom of which had an undifferentiated "mind." I speak as if all that is in the past. As you well know, Mr. President, there are many places in the world today where that situation is all too obvious.

Why do we continue to be astounded by the early Greeks? How do we explain them? Thousands of books have tried to answer that question and thousands more will be written. If our explanations still leave us with mystery, there are things about which we are certain. One is that these early Greeks asked questions—about the world and the human mind—never asked before. It is as if the shackles on the human mind disappeared and the questions poured out, questions for which answers gave rise to new questions in the tradition of science where the more you know the more you need and want to know. No society, *then or now,* had such *respect* for the human mind, all Greeks' minds. Not only the minds of rulers but the ruled as well. The other thing we know is that they took seriously the idea that everyone had the obligation and capability to participate in ruling. For me the Greek "lesson" is that how you regard the human mind is never logically separable from how you nurture that mind. And that, Mr. President, is as true for what happens in a classroom as it is in the society at large.

The history that fascinates me is a history of the struggle against the underestimation of the capabilities of the people. I trust you are aware that in our national history there has never been an immigrant group that was regarded as other than intellectually stupid, culturally barbaric, and a source of pollution in the body politic. And what about the capabilities of women? Of blacks? Of old people? Of handicapped people? We have a national history of which we should be proud, but that pride should not blind us to how we have been victims of underestimating the capabilities of people. We like to believe that we are no longer victims of that tendency. If that is true, how then do you explain why you have been forced to put education at the top of the national agenda? Clearly, I assume, you did not do that because you believe that schoolchildren are incapable of learning and thinking better than they do. You believe that they are more capable than educational outcomes indicate. You *know* that they are not being "reached." You *know* that too many of them have not been turned on but rather turned off by schooling. And there is one other thing a moment's reflection will tell you you know: when you observe these turned-off youngsters—both in our inner cities and suburbia—*outside* of schools, they are active, motivated youngsters seeking to understand themselves, others, and their world. They have curiosity, questions, and creativity in regard to matters or goals you and I may not like. We would want them to be more interested in ideas, history, literature, and science but they are not. Why not?

One reason is that in our well-intentioned but misguided efforts to pour information into the minds of children we are rendered insensitive to what *their* interests, concerns, and questions are. Let me put it this way: Although we know that much is in their heads—they do think, feel, fantasize, and strive—we regard what is in their minds as unimportant, or irrelevant, or (worse yet) as an obstacle to what *we* want *them* to know, feel, and strive for. We do not *respect* what is in their heads, i.e., they are not thinkers, they have unformed minds which it is our job to form. It is as if our job is to clean out their Augean mental stables. How can you take seriously people whose minds you regard as unformed and chaotic? What is there to get out of them? Empty heads need to be filled! The fact is—and it is a fact, Mr. President—that children, even very young children, have minds that are organized, stamped with purpose and curiosity.

There is a second reason that is no less fateful. *In practice* we regard children as incapable of self-regulation, unconcerned about or ignorant of the rules of social behavior, as organisms one step above (if that) animals or cannibals. Give them an inch and they will demand a mile. Trust them to be responsible and you will regret it. Open up the sluice gates of "permissiveness" and you will drown. Give them their "head" and they will take your body. My words may strike you as caricature, but please remember that caricature is a way of emphasizing a truth. In this instance the truth is that we regard children as in need of taming.

When you put the two reasons together we have a situation characteristic of our classrooms: *"where* students are" is ignored and *"what* students are" is something we should fear and, therefore, tame or extinguish. As a result, we have classrooms in which students are passive, uninterested, resigned, or going through the motions, or unruly, or all of the above. It is a classic case of the self-fulfilling prophecy, i.e., we begin with invalid assumptions and then act in a way that "proves" their validity.

I have to ask you this question: Do you react to what I have said as if I was an advocate of a mindless permissiveness which assumes that if you let children be "where and what they are" they will find their own ways to values and goals you and I cherish? That if we get out of their way, they will do the right thing in the right way, as if they possess a kind of wisdom we who teach them do not? If you, like many people, react in these ways, it is because you have not had the opportunity to test your assumptions, thereby confusing assumption with empirical fact. *Sit in classrooms, Mr. President.* Make your own observations. Fairness requires that I tell you that there are classrooms in our public schools where teachers have taken the big idea seriously. Far from being chaotic or devoid of law or order, or a struggle between a well-intentioned teacher and passively aggressive, bored students, they are lively places where learning is pursued, where minds are active, searching, challenged. Please note that I did not say happy minds because true learning is and should be experienced as challenging, at times frustrating, and puzzling but always energizing. Unfortunately, these classrooms are, relatively speaking, minuscule in number. The modal classroom is a boring, uninteresting place unconnected to the interests and questions of students. Forgive me for being repetitive. For these students there are two worlds: the isolated world of school and the "real world" of passions, personal needs, strivings, personal and social identity, and, yes, questions about what is, what should be, and what will be.

Back in the legendary sixties it became fashionable for college students to take a year off and go abroad. A wag quipped about one such student, "He went to Europe to find himself except he wasn't there." Well, Mr. President, young children begin school expecting to find themselves but they end up disappointed.

If you take the big idea seriously, the educational task is quite clear: How do you capitalize on, exploit, direct, and interconnect "where and what children are" to bodies of knowledge and concerns that contribute to an examined life in which horizons broaden and a sense of historical identity is forged? In short, how do you bring the two worlds together? If we do not seek to enter their worlds, they will not seek to enter ours.

One of the books I suggested you read was *Teacher* by Sylvia Ashton-Warner, an account of how she went about teaching the native Maoris of New Zealand to (among other things) read. More correctly, how she *thought* about how to get these children to *want* to read. She did not regard these native children the way too many Americans view the capabilities of our natives, or blacks, or Hispanics, or our poor, rural "hillbillies." Mrs. Warner had no doubt whatsoever that these Maori youngsters had active, curious minds. So what did Mrs. Warner do? She asked each child what words he or she wanted to learn, *not* what a predetermined "curriculum" said children should learn. It made no difference if the words concerned the body, sexual matters, or whatever. If they wanted to learn a word—which was then written on a card for them—that is what she helped them learn. And they learned! And at a pace and with a level of motivation she did not find at all surprising. She did have problems with the educational authorities! The important point, Mr. President, is that Mrs. Warner was a hedgehog whose central, big idea was that if you start with "where and what children are"—if you intellectually engage and hook them—you can then, and only then, help them want to acquire knowledge and skills that expand their horizons and options.

Mrs. Warner's book had, I think, the status of a best-seller. Obviously, it had for many people the ring of personal truth. Unfortunately, for all practical purposes it had no impact on *our* educational practices. The perception of a truth does not necessarily make you "free."

In, I suppose, typical professional academic style I have not given you a direct, persuasive answer to why we have not taken the obvious seriously. That was not evasion on my part because I wished first to persuade you that you have to come to grips with where you stand in regard to "what and where children are." So in my next letter I shall try to be more direct and, I hope, persuasive. If I am persuasive, I predict that there will be a part of you that will regret it.

Respectfully,

Seymour B. Sarason, Ph.D. (pp. 16–21) ■

Nothing is more revealing of the failure to take the big but simple idea seriously than the inability, or reluctance, or fear of students to ask questions in the classroom. Here is another letter, a variation on the theme.

DEAR MR. AND MRS. PRESIDENT:

Esther said something the other day which she has said many times before, with which I agree, but which we have been reluctant to say out loud. On a couple of occasions when we did, we were viewed as flaky. I owe it to you and to me (us) to say it now. Dropping out of high school— I need not give you statistics—has always been considered a "negative symptom," a reflection of maladaptive features of an individual. There is another way of looking at it which leads to the conclusion that dropping out is a *realistic* response to a high school culture which many students experience as deadly boring, unrelated to their non-school contexts, and which will lead nowhere. As I shall expand on in my next letter, I have spent far more time in elementary schools than in middle or high schools. But I have spent enough time in the latter, and I continue to try to read what researchers and observers say about high schools, to allow me to conclude that to regard dropping out as due to personal inadequacies is truly to blame the victim. If that is not always true, it is true far too often.

Think of it in terms of demand and supply. If schools do not supply, in some significant way, what students demand, why should they "buy" schooling? Why buy something which bears no relation to your perceived need to feel worthy, competent, productive, and the sense of belonging? Why buy something that far from giving you "kicks" puts you to sleep? At the very least, should we not say out loud that from the supply–demand criterion high schools in particular have had and will continue to have a shrinking market? Or, as in the case of the Detroit car makers who required decades to confront the fact that they were not competitive, will we continue to tinker, to "strengthen" what we have been doing even though it has not been effective, sedulously to avoid the question: On the basis of past experience, on the basis of scads of research, on the basis of what we know about the ingredients of productive learning and its contexts, *would we, if we had the opportunity to start from scratch, come up with high schools similar to what we have?* I have *never* spoken to a teacher or administrator who replied in the affirmative. They, no less than their students, don't buy high schools as they are. There is nothing inherently wrong with mass production, except when the number of faulty products does not pass muster.

Respectfully,

Seymour B. Sarason
Professor of Psychology Emeritus

P.S. I hope my letters are not depressing you. But I have no alternative to speaking truth to power. If, as I clearly hope, you are developing a realistic picture of what you as president will be up against if you take the big idea seriously, I do not envy you. The punchline of my favorite Jewish joke is: "It could be worse; I could be in your position." But I do envy you the opportunity to initiate policies and actions that ensure that you will be more than a footnote in future history books. (pp. 57–58) ∎

There is question asking and question asking, just as there is question answering and question answering. Obviously I am talking about a relationship between the two that *sustains* a process of willing inquiry because it is literally mind expanding at the same time that it sets the stage for new challenges. For the question asker it is a process combining feeling and intellect, distinguishing between facts and truths, and it has the motivational quality of "pulling" one forward to new questions about unknowns. It is a process that does not absolve the asker of responsibility for seeking an answer; it is not a process in which the answerer provides ready answers, short circuiting further inquiry by the asker. The answerer is a supportive coach who has the admittedly difficult task of deciding when and how to be supportive, to be a suggester, to be a partner in a quest. To say that it is an admittedly difficult task is an understatement. But what conception of productive learning—which is always social in nature—suggests that it is an easy task? And the research literature, as well as more informal observation, is replete with examples of the self-defeating consequences of (a) the lack of spontaneous question asking and (b) the overlearned tendency to absolve the asker of responsibility by unreflectively and quickly providing the asker with answers.

What I am saying here I said in the book but, I have since concluded, I did not sufficiently emphasize how bedrock the asker–answerer relationship is for school change. *Any effort at systemic reform that does not give top priority to altering that relationship will not improve educational outcomes. Since I wrote the book I know of no evidence disconfirming that assertion.* You can seek to change this or that aspect of the existing system, but unless those changes directly or indirectly change the student–teacher relationship, classroom learning will be unproductive, i.e., children will "learn" but it will not be learning that has personal and motivational significances for the learner. There is a world of difference between *wanting* to learn and *having* to learn. The enemy of productive learning is disinterest, boredom, and the feeling that what you think and feel is seen as irrelevant by others; learning is a chore, a chore of routines developed by adults who see the learner as an empty vessel to be filled for reasons the student neither comprehends nor accepts. The difference between productive and unproductive learning is the difference between teaching children and teaching subject matter—differences John Dewey pointed out a century ago.

Let me preface discussion of the second criterion by an assertion: *Teachers cannot create and sustain contexts for productive learning unless those conditions exist for them.* The significance of that assertion hit me with full force decades ago when I began to work in schools and realized that there were absolutely no forums, no traditions that brought teachers together on a scheduled basis seriously (a) to discuss the practical problems and issues of classroom and school living, and (b) to discuss and evaluate articles and books bearing on those issues and problems, i.e., publications about which any educator who purports to be a professional should be knowledgeable. What I found was a culture of *individuals,* not a *group* concerned with pedagogical theory, research, and practice. Each was concerned with himself or herself, not with the profession's status, controversies, or pressures for change.

In 1966, we published our first book describing how the Yale Psycho-Educational Clinic worked in classrooms and schools (Sarason et al., 1966). One of the chapters was titled "Teaching Is a Lonely Profession," written by Professor Murray Levine. That chapter elicited more nonsolicited letters from teachers than any other. The theme in these letters was clear: "You have it right. Teaching is a lonely profession. For all practical purposes teachers spend their time talking to and with children. We are alone with our thoughts, dilemmas, and feelings."

A teacher in one of the schools in which Professor Levine worked told him that she looked forward to his visits to her classroom less because he was helpful and more because he was a sympathetic adult. "For me," she said, "your visits have the relaxing and stimulating features of a cocktail hour."

In 1993 I wrote *You Are Thinking of Teaching?* The title suggests that it is a book for people considering teaching as a profession, and it attempts to convey the realities of the culture of the school and the professional obligation teachers should feel and discharge in dealing with those realities. The fact is that the book was written in the hope that teachers of teachers would read it because it is their obligation to convey to their students a conception of professionalism that involves far more than practicing in isolation, than practicing as if one does not need to know what others are thinking, saying, and doing. Here is a brief excerpt from that book.

ALMOST 20 YEARS AGO, THE FEDERAL GOVERNMENT COMMISSIONED AN EXTENSIVE study to evaluate the outcomes of federal efforts to improve education. It is a landmark study. There are two ways you can respond to the study. One is with discouragement because the outcomes were far from favorable. The other is with encouragement because one of the few clear findings was that favorable outcomes were associated with schools where teachers and administrators (and frequently parents) cooperatively planned and implemented actions for change; that is, the proposals for change were themselves outcomes of intellectual–professional discussions reflective of a collegiality making for commitment on the part of all participants. That was a very important finding, the significance of which cannot be overestimated, flying, as it does, in the face of the "traditional" way proposals for change originate and are implemented in our schools. That is not only my opinion but that of others who read the study. If there were people who read the study, how do I explain the sad fact that among the many scores of teachers I asked, *none* had read the study and only a handful had even "heard" about it? Before you scapegoat teachers, you should know that *none* of them had ever been exposed to that study in their preparatory programs. Having said that, however, I have to point out that the study received a good deal of play in professional journals, weeklies, newspapers, and newsletters. Even if the teachers with whom I spoke had not been told about the study in their preparatory programs, it is not unfair to say that there were numerous opportunities for them to become aware of that study. But only if they felt the obligation to read what was going on in the field. Not to feel such an obligation is, I must in all candor say, inexcusable. A professional person is, among other things, someone whose responsibilities include knowing what others in the field think, do, and have found and reported. *If you knew that your physician, or lawyer, or tax accountant read next to nothing in his or her field, would you not consider finding someone else to whom to bring your problems?* In recent years, there has been a dramatic escalation in the number of malpractice suits against physicians. That escalation has several valid and invalid sources, but let us not forget that one basis for a malpractice suit is that the person did not know something he or she *should* have known; that is, if the person had read what he or she should have been reading in the *normal* course of professional living, that person should have acted otherwise. A professional person is not one who stopped reading after finishing formal training. Reading is more than desirable, it is crucial. If I were czar of education, I would seek to stimulate and support the professionals in each school to devote at least one hour each week to a meeting in which is discussed a published study, report, or book that everyone had read beforehand. Professionals should always be "going to school." (pp. 133–135) ∎

The last two sentences in that excerpt relate to the second criterion. The first criterion emphasized the responsibility students should be helped to accept in furtherance of their learning. The second criterion places similar emphasis on the responsibility of teachers for their learning over the lifetime. *I am in no way suggesting that the criterion would be met by taking courses, workshops, or what passes for staff development days. Those types of experiences occasionally (and only occasionally) are rewarding, and I say that because too frequently they are experiences teachers have less because they* want *to have them and more because local or state rules and regulations say they* have *to have them.*

What the second criterion requires is that schoolteachers accept the obligation *as a group* to develop a forum specifically devoted to their growth and development, a forum that acknowledges that there is a world of ideas, theory, research, and practice about which they should be knowledgeable (which is *not* to say expert) if they are not to wither on the vine, if they like their students are to avoid passive resignation to routine. Since I wrote the book, the necessity and implications of the second criterion have begun to be articulated and recognized. That is a change, albeit the pace of change is slow. As I indicated in a previous chapter, the conception of site-based management and the support given to the creation of charter schools are two instances of recognition of the second criterion. Recognition is one thing; implementation consistent with the spirit of the second criterion is another thing. When my Martian returns in 25 years we may have answers.

In previous pages I indicated that group or cooperative learning requires (indeed demands) a partial transfer of power and responsibility to groups of students. The second criterion requires a similar transfer to teachers.

The reader may be troubled by my argument that however you seek to achieve systemic change, ultimately your effort should be judged by how effectively the two criteria are, so to speak, being met in a self-sustaining way. I say "troubled" because there are proponents for systemic change who seem to assume that the power to make changes in the structure and organization of schools is *the* crucial issue. It is a crucial issue, but changing power relationships is a necessary but *not* sufficient basis for meeting the two criteria. Unless the power to change the system is clearly informed by the requirements of the two criteria, it is unlikely that the goals of the criteria will be met.

But there is another source of "trouble" for the reader who will, I hope, see that in order to get to the point where the criteria are being met, if only in part, changes will be required in agencies beyond, but related to, schools. I refer specifically to legislatures, state departments of education, and colleges and universities. Each in its own ways is part of "the system," i.e., stakeholders who cannot be ignored. That is a point that Kenneth Wilson emphasizes. Yes, a school is a system, and so is what we conventionally call *a* school system. But both are very much related to other systems, the power and support of which are required if Type A changes stand a chance of being implemented and realized. *That* is an awesome, troublesome conception and task for which the saying "easier said than done" is quite appropriate. That conception and task are what Kenneth Wilson is tackling and they are implied in Louis's article I referred to in the previous chapter. We are used to thinking of the imagery of school change, not systems (please note the plural) change. Changing our imagery and thinking is and will be no simple affair, because once that change begins to occupy us, we very understandably feel overwhelmed by its implications for action. Where do you start? Who will or should start it? How do innovative, unsettling ideas percolate and get diffused? What is a realistic time perspective? Those are questions Wilson began to address in *Redesigning Education* and he will continue to do in future publications. What he will seek to make clear in these publications is that the initial requirement involves a dramatic change in the system of relationships between the university and educational practitioners, a change that will be informed by the history and implementation of the Reading Recovery Program in New Zealand, Ohio State University, and other college and university centers in our country. More correctly, perhaps, it will be informed by a distillation of principles derived from a long history of how new ideas, theories, and technologies came to have the pervasive impact they did, an impact that did not occur by chance. It is a history of paradigm shifts in which previously unresolved problems are seen in new ways that are not only productive but which then change the thinking and behavior of a larger community.

Should women be allowed to vote? Are they capable of assuming the responsibility of a major elective office? Can they discharge well, administering large, corporate enterprises? Can they be in leadership positions in the military? Fly military aircraft? Can they make scientific contributions? There was a time when these questions would have been dismissed with derision. Why the change in public attitude and acceptance? The answer, of course, is not a simple one, but one of its essential ingredients is the fact, the demonstration, that women *could* perform these tasks. And that is Wilson's point about Reading Recovery: its relationship between the college or university and the practitioners on the firing line is an example of a circumscribed but very important system change that can serve as Model A for other, more far-reaching systemic changes. Dr. Wilson, let it be said, has no illusion that changing the university will be any easier than changing our public schools. Indeed, he is crystal clear that redesigning education requires redesigning higher education in some important respects. Once that idea gains a currency it does not now have—which is tantamount to saying that a paradigm shift is occurring—systemic change stands a chance of being realized, a change marked by a variety of self-correcting forums and procedures.

As I see and read the current scene, it appears that disappointment with, and even anger about, the inadequacies of our schools—together with the puny results of past reform efforts—is figuratively driving people, within and without the professional educational community, to the realization that systemic reform is necessary. The good news is that the realization, long overdue, is gaining currency. The bad news is that it may lead to actions that may be instances of the cure being worse than the illness, because the cure is not fueled by a conception of the system but by desperation, resentment, and other understandable but self-defeating attitudes. From the time I wrote the book I have never received a negative reaction from anyone to this assertion: *What has happened and is happening in our schools, especially in our cities will, if it continues, have pervasive negative consequences for our society.* Agreement with the assertion came not only from "ordinary" citizens but from every educator to whom I made that assertion. Their agreement, however, is not all that encouraging, for reasons I take up in the next chapter.

Chapter 20

The Culture of the School and the Problem of *Social* Change

No one, to my knowledge, ever said, in print at least, that my book should have said more than it did about schools and *social* change. That would have been a legitimate criticism. The fact is that I was quite aware that I was not placing the issues in a wider context, although that context is taken into account in various parts of the book. If I was aware of that, my reasons for restricting the scope of the book were several. For one thing, I wanted the major focus to be on those features of schools that stamp them as distinctive, features that to me at least had previously not been seen as interconnected, as comprising a pattern of ideas, attitudes, values, behavioral and programmatic regularities that did no less than socialize everyone in the school. It was a pattern that, so to speak, ensured that anyone "living" in a school would in some ways absorb and reflect that pattern.

As a foreign visitor to our schools said to me, "It made little or no difference whether I was visiting a classroom in New York, Sioux Falls, Atlanta, or wherever. They were amazingly similar in organization, the educational rationales people verbalized, their conception of the learning process, the problems they were encountering, and their frustration about the community's ignorance of or misconceptions about what educators were up against." What he said reminded me of John Goodlad's observation based on his truly heroic studies he reported in *A Place Called School* (1984). He noted that it made no difference whether he was in a good, bad, or indifferent school—elementary, middle, or high school—the regularities of the classroom, of teacher–student interactions, of the question asking–question answering transactions, were startlingly similar. Why that was so was what I had tried to explain in the book. A comprehensive explanation would have required going into the history of schooling in America and how that history influenced and still influences schools. I decided against that kind of comprehensiveness for several reasons. For one thing, I felt a sense of urgency to describe the culture of the school as I experienced, observed, and studied it at a time (the 1960s) when schools were objects of strong concern and criticism. And, related to that, it was clear to me that the culture of the school had defeated and would continue to defeat efforts to change it. There was an element of tragedy in the situation because the opponents and proponents, both of whom were well intentioned, were on a collision course that would defeat each of them because neither of them understood the force of the culture of the school. More correctly, neither started with anything resembling a conception of the culture of the school.

It was not unlike what was then happening to American foreign aid programs: underdeveloped countries needed and wanted our aid, we wanted to be helpful, but our conception of aid was insensitive to, and unknowledgeable about, the culture of these countries. And it was also the case that these countries glossed over the kind of aid that could and should be absorbed by *their* culture. The history of our foreign aid programs was not pleasant reading. I mention our foreign aid programs because I was quite aware at the time of the similarities in outcome between our foreign aid and school reform programs.[1]

My sense of urgency had as much to do with the problem and strategies of change as with describing the culture of the school. That sense of urgency was a direct response to what I perceived was a dramatic *social* change that had occurred in the post–World War II era, a change that had major consequences for schools. I have described that social change in my most recent book (Sarason, 1996). When I wrote the school culture book I only vaguely sensed the dimensions of that social change, although its different discrete facets were already apparent. Let me very briefly summarize the major thrust of my recent book, which is most relevant to my present purposes.

1. The origins of the post–World War II social change were during the war years. Racial issues came to the fore (there were riots) in and out of the military contexts. The role of women in the workplace changed. There were mass migrations from rural to urban manufacturing centers where war-related jobs were plentiful, a migration of southern blacks and whites that began to alter the urban scene racially and culturally.
2. A staggering number of males were rejected for military service because of illiteracy, mental retardation (as determined by an IQ test), or personal instability. Illiteracy was by far the most frequent reason. But there were many who were accepted whose educational knowledge and skills made them unfit

---

1. As I explain in my autobiography *The Making of an American Psychologist* (1988), one of the major influences on my intellectual development (and more) was my relationship and collaboration with an anthropologist, Thomas Gladwin, who taught me a great deal about culture and the complexities engendered by trying to change it.

for military service. The reader should consult Ginzberg and Bray's book *The Uneducated* (1953).

3. The baby boom that followed the war overwhelmed the resources of communities, especially in our urban centers. What came to be called the "urban problem" was recognized, especially in regard to youth. Housing was in short supply, the inadequacies of schools were plain to see, juvenile delinquency soared, racial conflict increased, as did teenage pregnancies. This led to federal support for education, and that represented a momentous change in policy because previously education was explicitly viewed as a local and state responsibility. (The constitution says nothing about education.)

4. Precisely because science–technology played such a crucial role in winning the war, anxiety was expressed about whether the country's leadership in science and technology could be sustained given the inadequacies of our schools. That anxiety was transformed into scathing criticism—from the military and the science–technology part of the university—of colleges and departments of education, schools, and educators generally. The era of curriculum reform began: the new math, physics, biology, etc. With each passing year the criticism seemed to increase in intensity and the sources from which it came.

5. The rise and militancy of the women's liberation movement, in addition to even more militant civil rights movements, added fuel to the critical fires directed to schools. Both movements were critical of what they saw as an institution mired in numerous ways in discriminatory practices and attitudes, e.g., the content of textbooks, partiality to male students, employment, and underrepresentation of minorities at higher administrative levels. Racial minorities called for greater community control of school.

6. The postwar social change centered around the expansion and protection of individual and group rights and the obligation people should feel to personal expression. The past had to be overcome, the impersonality of faceless, large bureaucracies had to be pierced, and new traditions begun and fostered. No major institution was exempt from criticism and attack, least of all public schools, which were regarded as in need of radical transformation. That kind of criticism also came from increasingly growing and militant teacher unions, albeit for different reasons. Schools had become, so to speak, sitting ducks at which diverse groups took aim.

7. Beginning in the early 1950s, and in an amazingly few years, parents of handicapped children became a most powerful lobby and force who succeeded in getting legislation passed—initially in state legislatures—that reflected their dissatisfactions, resentments, and anger with the attitudes and practices of schools in regard to handicapped children. The 1975 federal law 94-142, the so-called mainstreaming legislation, was modeled on and drew from experience with legislation in several states, notably Massachusetts. It should be noted and emphasized that the National Association for Retarded Children changed its name to the National Association for Retarded *Citizens,* a change

that very much reflected the emphasis on rights. *Citizens* have rights, far more than children.

We begin to perceive a social change *after* it has begun. Before that perception we see a discrete change here and a discrete change there. It is only when they begin to coalesce, when commonalities among the discrete changes are recognized, that we say a social change has occurred. Put it this way: we become aware of a pervasive social change when it hits us in the face, when it can no longer be ignored. Today, when I review the decades during which I was in and around schools, I realize that long before I and others could recognize that a pervasive social change was occurring, almost every discrete change was in varying degrees manifest in our schools, especially in our cities. Any one discrete aspect tended not to be seen in relation to other discrete aspects. Indeed, it can be said that schools were very sensitive barometers of diverse changes in the larger society, except no one knew how to read or interpret the readings the barometers were signaling. Schools inevitably responded or were forced to respond to this or that discrete aspect, i.e., teenage pregnancy, drugs, violence, high school dropout rate, racial altercations, children in single-parent families, terrorizing youth gangs, and more. In an inchoate way school personnel sensed that these discrete aspects may have been part of a more general change, but the nature of that change was murky.

From one perspective the direction of the change was clear: the different groups criticizing the schools wanted schools to be agents of social change, not to reflect values and traditions that supported the status quo. Schools did try to adapt to that role. They changed curricula, set up special programs and schools, supported workshops, made efforts to increase the presence of minorities in teaching and administrative roles, increased the budget for staff development, and expressed a willingness to include parents in discussion of school policy. With the usual rare exceptions they adapted in ways reflective of the song "I'm True to You Only in My Fashion." That is to say, little or nothing in the behavioral and programmatic regularities that are the hallmarks of the classroom and the school changed. That was not because school personnel were being perversely stubborn, resistant, or devious. It was because they were defining and responding to the problem in ways that assumed that changes could be accommodated within the existing structure and regularities of the classroom and school. *And, most fatefully, that assumption was never challenged, certainly not explicitly by advocates of this or that change who, for example, never said anything about changing life in the classroom.* So, when advocates called for a greater role of parents–community in school affairs, it was unreflectively assumed that classroom life and educational outcomes would change and improve. You cannot answer a question that is not articulated.

Given my longstanding involvement in mental retardation, I was especially interested in how the 1975 federal legislation was being seen and implemented in the schools. In 1985, Dr. Michael Klaber and I (Sarason and Klaber, 1985) reviewed the research literature on the decision-making processes and forums mandated by the legislation. The following excerpts give the tenor of what the studies concluded:

THE FACT IS THAT SYSTEMATIC RESEARCH ON THE DECISION-MAKING PROCESS IN THE modal school received little attention until Public Law 94-142 in 1975 mandated a formal vehicle for making decisions about handicapped children. As we indicated earlier, that legislation was an explicit attempt to remedy what was seen as an informal, discriminatory decision-making process affecting parents, children, teachers, and administrative personnel. The research on team decision making stimulated by Public Law 94-142 employed self-report methodologies, sometimes accompanied by observation (Fenton et al., 1979; Goldstein et al., 1980; Hoff et al., 1978; Holland, 1980; Yoshida et al., 1978a,b). Other investigators employed teams of researchers who used specific observational systems to answer questions about the effectiveness of the team process (Mitchell, 1980), the domains of data discussed (Rostollan, 1980), the assessment data discussed (Shinn, 1980), the extent to which team decisions were based on data (Richey and Graden, 1980), the participation of other than special educators or personnel (Allen, 1980), and the generation of intervention statements (Poland and Mitchell, 1980). There are four conclusions these studies support: individuals rather than the team are influential in determining the outcome of meetings; parents tend to be involved minimally despite the explicit wording of PL 94-142; there do not seem to be criteria to guide decision making; not infrequently, decisions seem to be made before the team meeting, with the meeting serving only to approve them. (Sarason and Klaber, 1985, p. 128) ■

THERE CAN BE NO DOUBT THAT THE MANDATING IN PUBLIC LAW 94-142 OF PLACE-ment teams has altered social-professional relationships within schools. That the studies cited and described above are not heartening in regard to the quality of performance has to be seen in the light of longstanding tradition in which decision making was the province of individuals. On the one hand, one could argue that, given longstanding tradition, the results to date are as good or better than one might have expected; on the other hand, one could argue that the "new tradition" is developing in ways unlikely to meet the purposes for which this new vehicle was established. There is a sizable literature comparing the behavior and performance of children in two types of classrooms: the traditional ones and those in which children are members of small, cooperative, problem-solving groups. Sharan et al. (1982) in particular has described in eloquent detail the obstacle course the researcher has to run, first to reach the point where it is possible to begin to alter the classroom in terms of its social organization and, second, to find the time and energy it takes to help teachers act consistently with the rationale for small-group, cooperative learning, which is so different from customary practice. What Sharan has described is precisely what could have been predicted when school personnel who, daily performing their duties as *individuals,* are catapulted into *teams.* The difference, of course, is that in the formation of these teams there was no external agent to guide or help the participants. As with so many efforts to change schools as a social situation, the introduction of placement teams did not take the culture of schools into account. (Sarason and Klaber, 1985, p. 130) ■

On the basis of my observations there is a distinct difference in attitude and implementation between city and suburban schools. Suburban more than city parents are seen as oppositional, intrusive, demanding, and critical. As one member of a suburban placement team said, "A fair number of these parents want services and placements that in light of our budget and personnel are simply not possible. I sometimes get the feeling that those parents think the school exists for their child alone or that the demand for service by others is small." And suburban school personnel have told me that suburban parents, whose numbers are not minuscule, are likely to appeal decisions to state authorities, a process that is costly in legal fees both for parents and the school system. The conclusion is warranted that, as a group, suburban parents of handicapped children tend to have a conflictful relationship with school personnel. That does not mean that if city parents are more passive, less likely to be part of the process, less likely to take an adversarial stance, they do not harbor resentment and anger toward school personnel. We do not know, but blithely to assume that they do not harbor such feelings is to assume that these parents are indifferent to decisions affecting their children. That is as foolhardy and unjustified an assumption as one could make. And that assertion reflects a conclusion to which I have come since I wrote the book. It is a conclusion that speaks volumes about the culture of the school.

Baldly stated the conclusion goes this way: Generally speaking, school personnel are amazingly insensitive to the anger and resentment that different segments of the public have to schools. They may be sensitive to such feelings in this or that segment, but that is an example of missing the forest for the trees. And if, as one should, you include middle and high school students as a segment, the insensitivity is indeed general. That conclusion is *not* associated in my mind with the imagery of a General Custer encircled by enemies intent on destroying him and his soldiers. General Custer knew what he was up against! The imagery that gets conjured up in my mind is that of school personnel in encapsulated classrooms (or offices) in encapsulated schools who are unaware that in the post–World War II social change different segments for different reasons see schools as in need of racial change. More than that, these segments see a kinship among themselves, i.e., the criticisms of each reinforce those of others. Another way to put it is that school personnel seem to operate on the assumption that they will ride out the storm, i.e., "this too shall pass." That assumption may be true for this or that specific criticism but what confronts the schools is a storm of criticism. When meteorologists tell us that there is a tropical depression in the Caribbean, we note it but are not upset. When they say it has become a tropical storm, our level of concern heightens. When the storm reaches hurricane strength, our concern becomes anxiety. The post–World War II social change initially consisted of several discrete changes. It reached hurricane-like strength in the 1960s when these discrete changes got interconnected. And that decade should have made clear to our schools that the social game had changed and so did the basis for scoring. And since that decade, as I pointed out in previous chapters, it has become plain to see that a large fraction of the public no longer is content to allow schools to remain what they have been and are. Two things are unfortunately the case: The substance of the external criticisms is largely a replay of past ideas that failed; and there is no agreement at all in the educational community about what, if anything, should or needs to be done, and if one goes by what the more articulate leaders of that community say, the changes they advocate vary from the cosmetic to the *relatively* unimportant.

As a nation we were not prepared for the social changes produced by World War II. We lacked the barometers to tell us about truly sea swell changes in people's thoughts, attitudes, feelings, hopes, and expectations. But one thing was knowable: war, especially a world war, changes everything and everyone. If it was knowable, we did not take that knowledge seriously. The present status of our schools is incomprehensible apart from a postwar social change, the consequences of which are ongoing and the dimensions of which are enormous. And, yet, throughout this hurricane-like social scene our schools have changed little. Vouchers, charter schools, and privatization are some of the indicators that the public (including the political establishment) is willing to take new directions as never before, even if it means bypassing schools as we know them. Educators voice their disapproval of these developments, but they do not tell us what they propose and stand for. They are reactors, not proactors.

What I find discouraging and even frightening is that school personnel rarely (if ever) raise and seriously discuss two questions. What is the overarching purpose of schooling, a purpose which if not realized makes the attainment of other purposes unlikely, if not impossible? What are the characteristics of contexts for productive learning? It does not surprise me that those questions are absent in the critiques of those who seek to change schools. I do not expect the public to be knowledgeable about a research and theory literature that has provided some important answers to those questions. But it is both surprising and inexcusable that those questions are not center stage in the education community, which in part explains why the public is unaware of how basic those questions are.

In earlier pages I have emphasized how in the culture of the school there are no forums or tradition where those questions get examined for the purposes of change. In the culture of the school such self-correcting forums and tradition do not exist. As scores of teachers have told me over the years, "Schools are not places for serious intellectual discussion of important educational issues and practices. Freewheeling discussions are dangerous, they are off limits, because they may lead somewhere."

I am being neither snide nor contemptuous, because if I were, I would be blaming the victim. The truth is that the *professional preparation* of educators is a socializing process that virtually ensures that the culture of the school will be as I have described it. I have argued that the plight of our schools cannot be understood apart from the post–World War II social change. I here add to that argument the point that those who have roles in the school culture are reflecting the inadequacies of preparatory programs, a point I discuss at length in *The Case for Change. Rethinking the Preparation of Educators* (1993b). The characteristics and force of the school culture have many sources and chief among them is how edu-cators are prepared to live in that culture. As I point out in that book, at the begin-ning of this century the professional preparation of physicians (and the quality of their practices) was deplorable—to indulge understatement—far more deplorable than the preparation of educators today. What dramatically and quickly changed that situation was a radical transformation of medical school education. And that transformation—due in significant measure to Abraham Flexner, who was not a physician but an eminent educator—centered around the two basic questions I raised earlier: What is the overarching purpose of medical education? What should be the characteristics of the context of productive learning which the medical stu-dent should experience? To Flexner, all else was commentary.

To some readers, I assume, my analogical use of changes in medical educa-tion will not be persuasive or seen as appropriate. That is to say, education is a dif-ferent cup of tea than medicine. To those readers I have to suggest that they read John Dewey, who not only dealt with those questions more than a hundred years ago but had the wisdom and courage to create a school to implement and test his answers. Those answers were highly similar to those of Flexner, and I would argue that in principle they were identical. Dewey knew the history of philosophy (a gross understatement), but he knew equally well the history of science, a history in which choosing between competing ideas or theories, or any single new theory, was based on experimentation, demonstration, and their pragmatic consequences.

Dewey's lab school was a Model A effort. His hope was that that effort would be applicable to the public school. What Dewey did not grasp were the implica-tions of the fact that *he had created his own school. He did not have to change an existing school. He did not have to deal with the nature and force of the culture of schools.* The processes and dynamics of creating a new setting and changing an existing one are related but very different. How could Dewey's Model A become diffused and appropriately employed in existing schools? In more than a few pub-lic schools Dewey's ideas were enthusiastically embraced. Without exception those efforts were in part or whole failures and the reason was that enthusiasm almost totally obscured recognition of the traditions, conservatism, and nature of the culture of the school. His Model A remained just that: a first approximation that was developed in an idiosyncratic context (a university), not in the "real" world of the school culture. What we are eternally indebted to Dewey for is the clarity with which he formulated answers to the two most important questions. If and when those two questions are taken seriously, the trouble will begin, because the answers will require transformations in our schools for which our society is not prepared. The postwar social change has, not surprisingly, focused attention on the need for changing our schools, an attention suffused with disappointment, bewilderment, resentment, resignation, and even fear. One has to hope that these pressures will not lead to actions that at the same time they give expression to feel-ings continue to keep buried the important questions. We are used to hearing that "if it ain't broke, don't fix it." We know our schools are "broke" but we do not know what the "it" is that should be fixed.

Readers expect (I assume) that a book like this will end on an upbeat note. What I have said in these revisiting chapters is that since I wrote the book 25 years ago we have learned several very important things:

- The overall problem is a *systemic* one.
- We understand better the characteristics of contexts for productive learning.
- We have begun to recognize that teachers cannot create and sustain those contexts if those contexts do not exist for them.
- School change requires changes in existing power relationships.
- Desired changes will not occur without significant changes in the professional preparation of educators.
- Money is not the primary problem.

I would say we have learned a great deal, but that what we have learned has not been interconnected in a compelling way either for the community of educators or (certainly not) for the general public. I said that we are beginning to take seriously that the problems are systemic and that is reason enough to avoid those kind of *ad hominems* that indict individuals or groups as if they have willed the present situation. The general public, no less than educators, have been socialized to accept the system as it has been and is. The values and axioms undergirding the culture of our schools are those of the larger society. The post–World War II social change has had the effect of causing many in the larger society to question that undergirding to a greater degree than is the case in the educational community. The subtitle to my 1990 book *The Predictable Failure of Educational Reform* is *Can We Change Course Before It Is Too Late?* The subtitle was suggested by my editor, Gracia Alkema, who did not want the main title to convey a feeling of hopelessness. I agreed, however, not to satisfy her but because that subtitle captured both my hopes and fears.

A final note. I said that money is not the problem *now*. I feel compelled to reiterate that if what we have learned becomes interconnected and gains currency, the transformations that will be required will cost a lot of money because contexts for productive learning demand an attention to individuality not feasible in our classrooms today. To believe otherwise is to support actions that will confirm the adage that the more things change the more they will remain the same—or get worse.

Chapter 21

Postscript

This postscript is about productive learning.[1] After I thought I had finished this book I had occasion to read a chapter in my 1972 book *The Creation of Settings and the Future Societies.* One of the major themes in that book was one I had very briefly stated in the school culture book a couple of years earlier: You cannot create *and* sustain a context of productive learning for others unless that kind of context exists for you. I found myself reading in the 1972 book the chapter devoted to B. F. Skinner. Reading that chapter forced me to admit that I had glossed over a problem in *this* book to which I should have given more attention because it is one for which systematic research has been scanty, although relevant anecdotal material is on the plentiful side. That is to say, we *know* that it is a crucial problem (theoretically and practically) but its dimensions and implications are far from mainstream research. And, I shall argue, that neglect is as true today as when I wrote the school culture book.[2] And one reason is that few researchers have recognized and experienced the problem, or if they once were teachers they have forgotten how the problem was always in their minds.

---

1. I am safe in assuming that few readers know anything about the network of Waldorf Schools in the United States and abroad. That type of school derives from the ideas and philosophy of Rudolf Steiner. I urge the reading of *School as a Journey* by Torin Finser (1994). Without subscribing to Steiner's spiritual-religious views, Steiner's *educational* rationale is identical with mine and that of many who came before me. Finser's account is very detailed, concrete, and instructive. The network that these schools comprise—its self-correcting features, the collegiality that is the hallmark of each school—in microcosm has the characteristics of a self-correcting network.

2. There are the usual few exceptions among which are books by Lieberman and Miller (1992), Wasely (1994), Heckman et al. (1995), and Fried (1995). Their descriptions and discussions certainly are relevant to what I have said because they compellingly describe what teachers encounter in recognizing the problem.

Here is the relevant part of the chapter:

I SHALL ILLUSTRATE THE PROBLEM BY ASKING THE READER TO IMAGINE HE IS INTER-
ested in the behavior of rats (or pigeons), and he contrives a laboratory situation
in which he thinks he can begin to study behavior, its shapers and consequences.
If he does what almost all animal psychologists do, he will study individual rats,
each of which will have an opportunity to be center stage, namely, with no supporting cast and the psychologist as an audience of one. He gets to know each of
these rats extraordinarily well, and he is able to make certain generalizations
about the behavior of rats. But then the idea occurs to him to repeat his observations with rat A, but this time he will also put rat B into the apparatus. He will
observe new behavior, social behavior, and it is likely that he will not find it
easy to use his earlier generalizations to explain the social behavior he has just
observed. But he will try, and perhaps with a little conceptual straining he will
explain what happened. (He could not, of course, have predicted what would
happen.) And then he decides that he should introduce rat C to rats A and B. At
this point the experimenter is probably aware of several things: that he has to
observe quite differently, that what he is observing is quite complex, that his
ability to predict is not very good, and that he may need new concepts about
social behavior. If he continues adding new but well-understood individual rats
into the situation, he will undoubtedly end up overwhelmed not only by the
complexities of dynamic (ever-changing) social behaviors he observes and his
inability to determine how things got related and changed but by the conceptual
task with which he is faced if he is to make sense of it all. And this does not take
place in the "real" world but in a situation in which the experimenter has as
much control as he wants or can imagine over the animals and their physical
environment.
    Skinner's principles of behavior stem almost exclusively from studies of
individual organisms. In fact, he is one in a long line of American psychologists
who have spent much of their lives designing environments in which to study single organisms. Over the years we have been presented with all kinds of learning
principles and theories which were considered basic for understanding human
social behavior. In fact, since almost every schoolteacher has been required in his
training to take a course in learning, he was exposed to ideas based almost exclusively on the learning of individual rats. Nobody has ever demonstrated in anything resembling a compelling manner that these principles and theories were or
are relevant to learning in the social matrix of a classroom. ■

    The problem? What conception of learning is applicable in the classroom in
which individual learning is, both from the standpoint of teacher and student, obviously, glaringly, compellingly social in nature in that it takes place in a group?
How do we or should we take that into account in a way that increases the chances
that the goals of productive learning will be achieved or approximated for everyone? Can we take it into account from the standpoint of how *an* individual learns,

a standpoint that is not even applicable to a one-on-one situation that is basically social-interpersonal in nature?

Let me illustrate the nature of the problem from another arena where "learning" is a central goal. For the past century we have been presented with scads of theories about how productive, *individual psychotherapy* should and can be done, and the theories continue to multiply. (Individual psychotherapy is big business, if only because no one theory and its practitioners can claim results that are robust and indisputably better than those of its competitors.) What they all have in common is a riveting on an individual patient. In recent decades *family therapy* has come into the picture, and what that has brought to the fore is conceptions of how you treat individuals are minimally applicable to how you treat a family. How you treat a family requires a markedly different conception that determines how you observe and react to the "here-and-now" interactions of the members of the family. I have had the opportunity to observe clinicians in family therapy training programs after they have been in the practice of individual psychotherapy. What these clinicians experienced—and it was a difficult and frustrating experience—was that observing and reacting to a family required understandings and skills for which their previous work had not prepared them. It is not an exaggeration to say that they had to *unlearn* one way of observing and reacting and *learn* new ways. (In the 1960s the advocates of the new math and other curricula did not realize that in the short workshops in which the new curricula were "taught" to teachers an unlearning-learning process was required, as a consequence of which the bulk of teachers left the workshops dazed, or puzzled, or angry, or having all of these feelings.)

In earlier pages I expressed a favorable opinion of cooperative learning. What I need to say now is that at the same time that its advocates know that organizing a classroom along the lines of their particular type of group or cooperative learning (there are several differing approaches) requires—demands—marked changes in how the teacher thinks, observes, and reacts, they also in their heart of hearts know the changes cannot be assimilated in the usual workshop. That is why what passes for cooperative learning in more than a few classrooms has features of a charade, an unintended but inevitable charade. Too many teachers of teachers do not provide contexts of productive learning for *their* students.

For at least 20 years after World War II, every would-be teacher took a course in the psychology of learning. When you peruse the texts students read, you find two things: (a) they are about how individuals learn; (b) the research literature these texts contained largely referred to animal (most frequently the Norway rat) learning: the single rat in the maze. Since then the texts have changed but their basic thrusts have not. The beginning teacher comes to his or her classroom prepared to teach a *whole* class. In the abstract the teacher pays respect to the fact that each child in that classroom is a unique individual. And if the teacher does not know that, he or she very quickly learns it. The problem I am emphasizing has less to do with recognition of individuality, a recognition I take for granted, and more to do with the question: In what ways should I think and act so that at the same time that I recognize individuality I also recognize how, given the social nature of

the classroom, those individualities can be interconnected or organized to contribute to the productive learning of others? That is to say, a classroom is more
than a collection of unique individuals; it can also be an interconnected collection,
a mutually reinforcing, stimulating one. In any classroom, students impact on each
other; that is a given in group living. The task is to recognize and direct that impact
in ways that further learning, let alone the quality of personal relationships.

We are used to hearing that the goal of the teacher is to help each child "realize his or her full potential." If by help is meant what *a* teacher can do for *each*
child, then that help will always fall far short of the mark. In the usual classroom,
time is the teacher's enemy. I am asking the question how students can be allies
to each other, each preserving his or her individuality, but by virtue of being allies
their individuality is broadened and deepened.

How does one do this? Initially that is the wrong question. The first question
is how should I think about it? What changes in my thinking will be required? So
I entertain those changes—I want to act—what universe of alternatives for action
is available to me from which to choose? However I choose, I must never forget
that I am starting with Model A, which experience will show has inadequacies. Why
do I start with "how to think about it"? The first reason is that it is an extraordinarily difficult task (personally and intellectually) to change your accustomed ways
of thinking. That is why in my book *The Case for Change: Rethinking the Preparation of Educators* (1993b) I plead (truly plead) that we give far more attention
than we do in preparatory programs to how we want teachers to think, to prevent
or at least markedly reduce the travails that accompany the process of changing
highly overlearned conceptions. The second reason is that for a person to change
his or her ways of thinking is made somewhat easier if that person is in a supportive, collegial context, and there is the rub. Such a context is the exception, not the
rule, in the culture of schools. That is why I have to repeat: If a context for productive learning does not exist for the teacher, that teacher cannot create *and sustain* a context of productive learning for students. The teacher is regarded by others,
and so regards himself or herself, as an individual—a bounded, isolated one—
whose thinking, problems, and actions are private affairs. Intellectual-professional
collegiality hardly exists. In the culture of the schoolteacher, individuality is not a
resource for other teachers, just as the individuality of students in a classroom is
not a resource to other students. More teachers are beginning to understand this
than ever before, but they feel impotent to do anything about it. That teachers are
recognizing this is a change from when I wrote the book, but going from recognition to action has been for most of them intimidating.

But let us assume that you have undertaken the task of changing the way you
look at the individual–group relationship—how the resources of individuals can
become resources to others—what might actions consistent with that change look
like? The virtue of the process and context of productive learning is that you
become aware that for any problem there is more than one way to approach it.
There is no single answer, certainly no ready-made ones. It is in seeking *the*
answers that a grievous mistake is frequently made: the teacher unreflectively

assumes that it is *only* his or her responsibility to provide *the* answer; what students think, feel, and suggest is not part of the starting point for action; they are given no responsibility in that respect. Fried's (1995) book is especially revealing and helpful in this matter.

I said that time is a teacher's enemy and that is because the culture of the school and its organizational features are not powered by a developed conception of the process and context of productive learning. Quite the contrary, they have been informed by a unidirectional concept of learning (teacher → student) that requires a predetermined, segmented curriculum, each segment of which has a specified time allotment and places complete responsibility on the teacher to show that students have learned what they were supposed to learn. This time-driven conception of learning is exacerbated by the fact that teachers are also responsible for meeting other kinds of goals deemed necessary by the system and the society. As I said in earlier pages, the passage of laws in the late 19th century mandating compulsory education produced schools that were like factories of the time (a development against which John Dewey fought). Schools are not the factories they once were but the conceptions, culture, and organizational features of schools today (the usual exceptions aside) continue as a form of social inheritance. But there is one very big difference. The factory owner is never in doubt about what his or her bottom line is: to show as much profit as possible, to avoid extinction.

Creating and sustaining contexts of productive learning for students never has been the school's bottom line. Passing tests and being awarded a diploma should never be regarded as adequate criteria of productive learning. As I said earlier, a century ago John Dewey said that knowledge is external; knowing is internal. Knowledge for which you feel no sense of ownership, which does not become part of your psychological bloodstream, which has no self-reinforcing, motivational consequences, may be valuable in a game of Trivial Pursuit but not in the game of meaningful living. In an inchoate way educators are beginning to understand, and that represents a change from when I wrote the school culture. But unless that inchoateness becomes clearer, little or nothing will change. If it becomes clearer and appropriate actions begin to be taken, very little of what schools are today will remain the same.

References

AIKEN, W. A. (1942). *The Story of the Eight-Year Study with Conclusions and Recommendations.* New York: Harper Collins.

ALLEN, D. (1980). Participation of regular education teachers in special education team decision making. Research Report No. 40. Minneapolis: University of Minnesota Institute for Research on Learning Disabilities.

ASHTON-WARNER, S. (1980). *Teacher.* London: Village.

BENTZEN, M. M., GOODLAD, J. I., LAHADERNE, H. M., MYERS, D. A., NOVOTNEY, J. M., SINCLAIR, R. L., SPITZER, L. K., & TYE, K. A. (1968). *The Principal and the Challenge of Change.* Los Angeles, CA: Institute for Development of Educational Activities.

DARLING-HAMMOND, L. (1995). Policy for restructuring. In A. Lieberman (ed.), *The Work of Restructuring Schools. Building from the Ground Up.* New York: Teachers College Press.

FENTON, K. S., YOSHIDA, R. K., MAXWELL, J. P., & KAUFMAN, M. J. (1979). Recognition of team goals: An essential step toward rational decision making. *Exceptional Children, 45,* 538–544.

FINSER, T. M. (1994). *School as a Journey. The 8-Year Odyssey of a Waldorf Teacher and His Class.* Ghent, NY: Anthroposophic Press.

FRIED, R. L. (1995). *The Passionate Teacher.* Boston: Beacon Press.

GINZBERG, E., & BRAY, D. W. (1953). *The Uneducated.* New York: Columbia University Press.

GOLDSTEIN, S., STRICKLAND, B., TURNBULL, A. P., & CURRY, L. (1980). An observational analysis of the IEP conference. *Exceptional Children, 46,* 278–286.

GOODLAD, J. (1984). *A Place Called School.* New York: McGraw-Hill.

GORE, A. (1993). Creating a government that works better and costs less. Report of the National Performance Review. Washington, DC: U.S. Government Printing Office, Superintendent of Documents.

HAMPEL, R. W. (1995, February 8). Breadth versus depth. How do we avoid reform "a mile high and an inch deep?" *Education Week,* p. 48.

HECKMAN, P., ET AL. (1995). *The Courage to Change: Stories from Successful School Reform.* Newbury Park, CA: Corwin Press.

HOFF, M. K., FENTON, K. S., YOSHIDA, R. K., & KAUFMAN, M. J. (1978). Notice and consent: The school's responsibility to inform parents. *Journal of School Psychology, 16,* 265–278.

HOLLAND, R. P. (1980). An analysis of the decision-making processes in special education. *Exceptional Children, 46,* 551–554.

LIEBERMAN, A. (ed.) (1995). *The Work of Restructuring Schools. Building from the Ground Up.* New York: Teachers College Press.

LIEBERMAN, A., & MILLER, L. (1992). *Teachers: Their World and Their Work.* New York: Teachers College Press.

LOUIS, K. S. (1994). Beyond "managed change": Rethinking how schools improve. *School Effectiveness and School Improvement, 5* (1), 2–24.

MAYHEW, K. C., & EDWARDS, A. C. (1966). *The Dewey School.* New York: Atherton Press.

MILES, M. B. (ed.) (1964). *Innovation in Education.* New York: Bureau of Publications, Teachers College, Columbia University.

MIREL, J. (1994). School reform unplugged: The Bensenville New American School Project, 1991–1993. *American Educational Research Journal, 3,* 451–518.

MITCHELL, J. (1980). *The Special Education Team Process: To What Extent Is It Effective?* Minneapolis: University of Minnesota Institute for Research on Learning Disabilities.

MUNCEY, D., & McQUILLAN, P. (1993). Preliminary findings from a five-year study of the coalition of essential schools. *Phi Delta Kappan, 74,* 486–489.

POLAND, S., & MITCHELL, J. (1980). *Generation of Intervention Statements by Decision-Making Teams in School Settings.* Minneapolis: University of Minnesota Institute for Research on Learning Disabilities.

RAVITCH, D. (1995). Adventures in wonderland. A scholar in Washington. *American Scholar,* Autumn, 497–516.

RICHEY, L., & GRADEN, J. (1980). *The Special Education Team Process: To What Extent Is It Data Based?* Minneapolis: University of Minnesota Institute for Research on Learning Disabilities.

ROGERS, D. (1968). *110 Livingston Street: Politics and Bureaucracy in the New York City School System.* New York: Random House.

ROSTOLLAN, D. (1980). *Domains of Data Discussed at Special Education Team Meetings.* Minneapolis: University of Minnesota Institute for Research on Learning Disabilities.

SARASON, S. B. (1972). *The Creation of Settings and the Future Societies.* San Francisco, CA: Jossey-Bass.

SARASON, S. B. (1982). *The Culture of the School and the Problem of Change* (2nd ed.). Boston: Allyn & Bacon.

SARASON, S. B. (1983). *Schooling in America: Scapegoat and Salvation.* New York: Free Press.

SARASON, S. B. (1988). *The Making of an American Psychologist.* San Francisco, CA: Jossey-Bass.

SARASON, S. B. (1990). *The Predictable Failure of Educational Reform.* San Francisco, CA: Jossey-Bass.

SARASON, S. B. (1993a). *Letters to a Serious Education President.* Newbury Park, CA: Corwin Press.

SARASON, S. B. (1993b). *The Case for Change. Rethinking the Preparation of Educators.* San Francisco, CA: Jossey-Bass.

SARASON, S. B. (1993c). *You Are Thinking of Teaching?* San Francisco, CA: Jossey-Bass.

SARASON, S. B. (1995). *Parental Involvement and the Political Principle.* San Francisco, CA: Jossey-Bass.

SARASON, S. B. (1996). *Barometers of Social Change.* San Francisco, CA: Jossey-Bass.

SARASON, S. B., & KLABER, M. (1985). The school as a social situation. In M. R. Rosenzweig & L. W. Porter (eds.), *Annual Review of Psychology,* vol. 36 (pp. 115–140). Palo Alto, CA: Annual Reviews, Inc.

SARASON, S. B., LEVINE, M., GOLDENBERG, I., CHERLIN, D., & BENNETT, E. (1966). *Psychology in Community Settings.* New York: John Wiley.

SHARAN, S. (ed.) (1994). *Handbook of Cooperative Learning Methods.* Westport, CT: Greenwood Press.

SHARAN, Y., & SHARAN S. (1992). *Expanding Cooperative Learning Through Group Investigation.* New York: Teachers College Press.

SHARAN, S., KUSSELL, P., BERJERANO, Y., HERTZ-LAZAROWITZ, R., & BROSH, T. (1982). Cooperative learning, whole-class instruction, and the academic achievement and social relations of pupils in ethnically mixed junior high schools in Israel. Final report to Ford Foundation and Israel Ministry of Education and Culture.

SHINN, M. (1980). *Domains of Assessment Data Discussed During Placement Team Decision Making.* Minneapolis: University of Minnesota Institute for Research on Learning Disabilities.

SIZER, T. (1985). *Horace's Compromise. The Dilemma of the American High School.* Boston: Houghton Mifflin.

TYACK, D., & TOBIN, W. (1994). The "grammar" of schooling: Why has it been so hard to change? *American Education Research Journal, 31* (5), 453–479.

WASLEY, P. A. (1991). *Teachers Who Lead: The Rhetoric of Reform and The Realities of Practice.* New York: Teachers College Press.

WASLEY, P. A. (1994). *Stirring the Chalkdust.* New York: Teachers College Press.

WASLEY, P. A., HAMPEL, R. L., & CLARK, R. W. (1995, unpublished manuscript). When school change influences students' accomplishment. Initial findings from the school change study.

WATSON, G. (ed.) (1967). *Change in School Systems.* Washington, DC: National Training Laboratories.

WILSON, K., & DAVISS, B. (1994). *Redesigning Education.* New York: Henry Holt.

YOSHIDA, R. K., FENTON, K. S., MAXWELL, J. P., & KAUFMAN, M. J. (1978a). Group decision making in the planning team process: Myth or reality? *Journal of School Psychology, 16,* 237–244.

YOSHIDA, R. K., FENTON, K. S., MAXWELL, J. P., & KAUFMAN, M. J. (1978b). Ripple effect: Communication of planning team decisions to program implementers. *Journal of School Psychology, 16,* 177–183.

Index

About the Author

SEYMOUR B. SARASON is professor of psychology emeritus in the Department of Psychology and at the Institution for Social and Policy Studies of Yale University. In 1962 he founded and directed the Yale Psycho-Educational Clinic, one of the first research and training sites in community psychology. Fields in which he has made special contributions include mental retardation, culture and personality, projective techniques, teacher training, anxiety in children, and school reform. His numerous books and articles reflect his broad interests. Dr. Sarason received his Ph.D. degree from Clark University in 1942 and holds honorary doctorates from Syracuse University, Queens College, Rhode Island College, and Lewis and Clark College. He has received awards from the American Psychological Association and the American Association on Mental Deficiency.